T3-BHM-354

After the Berlin Wall

After the Berlin Wall

Germany and Beyond

Edited by Katharina Gerstenberger and Jana Evans Braziel

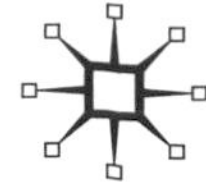

First published in 2011 by
PALGRAVE MACMILLAN® in the United States – a division of
St. Martin's Press LLC, 175 Fifth Avenue, New York, N.Y. 10010.

Where this book is distributed in the UK, Europe and the rest of the world, this is by Palgrave Macmillan, a division of Macmillan Publishers Limited, registered in England, company number 785998, of Houndmills, Basingstoke, Hampshire RG21 6XS.

Palgrave Macmillan is the global academic imprint of the above companies and has companies and representatives throughout the world.

ISBN 978–0–230–11192–9

Library of Congress Cataloging-in-Publication Data

After the Berlin Wall: Germany and beyond / edited by Katharina Gerstenberger and Jana Evans Braziel.
p. cm.
ISBN 978–0–230–11192–9 (hardback)
1. Germany—History—Unification, 1990. 2. Berlin Wall, Berlin, Germany, 1961–1989. 3. Germany—Foreign relations—1990– 4. Germany—Cultural policy—21st century. 5. National characteristics, German. 6. Cold War—Political aspects. 7. Cold war—Social aspects. 8. World politics—1945–1989. I. Gerstenberger, Katharina, 1961– II. Braziel, Jana Evans, 1967–
DD290.29.A35 2011
943.088—dc23 2011019710

A catalogue record of the book is available from the British Library.

Design by MPS Limited, A Macmillan Company

First edition: November 2011

10 9 8 7 6 5 4 3 2 1

Printed in the United States of America.

Contents

Figures and Tables

Figures

Tables

Acknowledgments

Every book has a history and many people who contribute to its success. This project started in the spring of 2008, when the two coeditors began to think about a conference on the occasion of the twentieth anniversary of the fall of the Berlin Wall and its aftermath. Generous funding for this event, which took place at the University of Cincinnati on November 8 and 9, 2009, was provided by the Charles Phelps Taft Memorial Fund, the Faculty Development Council, the University Research Council at the University of Cincinnati, and the German Consulate. Our special thanks go to Wayne E. Hall, Vice Provost for Faculty Development, and Sandra Degen, Vice President for Research, at the University of Cincinnati, for their good advice and their sponsorship. We would also like to express our appreciation to the graduate students who provided support: Sarah Domet and Suzanne Warren were competent and cheerful helpers during the early stages of this book, willing and able to take matters into their own hands when they saw the need for it. Julianne Lynch, our meticulous and perceptive copy editor, kept us on track and helped us see this volume through to completion. Most of all, we are grateful to our contributors. Without their extensive range of expertise and their willingness to abide by our deadlines and endure our criticisms and suggestions, this volume would not exist. For the two of us, this project has strengthened our belief in collaborative work and our friendship.

Katharina Gerstenberger
Jana Evans Braziel

Introduction

After the Berlin Wall: Realigned Worlds, Invisible Lines, and Incalculable Remnants

Katharina Gerstenberger and Jana Evans Braziel

Most of us will readily agree that the fall of the Berlin Wall on November 9, 1989, resulted in dramatic changes in the international scene, yet we are only just beginning to inquire about the long-term consequences of the event that occurred more than 20 years ago. How has it changed German culture and how do Germans respond to it today? How has it been received in other parts of the world? What are some of the comparisons we might draw? What can we see now that was not visible 20 years ago? *After the Berlin Wall: Germany and Beyond* attempts to delineate the realigned worlds, invisible lines, and incalculable remnants that have come to define the post-Wall world in which we have dwelled since that historical event, or perhaps "non-event," as contributor Benjamin Robinson provocatively suggests. Since no one field of academic inquiry can assess adequately these developments, the chapters assembled in this volume—deploying interdisciplinary methods and engaging a spectrum of intellectual debates—explore multiple dimensions and a variety of historical, political, sociological, literary, artistic, architectural, and popular cultural aspects of the Berlin Wall's afterlife in Germany and in the international arena. The chapters argue that 20 years after its fall, the Wall that divided Berlin and Germany presents a conceptual paradox: on the one hand Germans have sought to erase it completely; on the other it haunts the imagination in complex and often surprising ways. Similarly, Cold War divisions resonate in the global image of the "New Germany." Several overlapping themes run through the essays: the exportation of German post-Wall debates into other cultural contexts and representations of the Wall within non-German settings; the emergence of visual, literary, and psychological imagery derived from the Berlin Wall well beyond its existence; the importance of space—geographical, political, as well as imagined—in the aftermath of the Wall; and the continued engagement with East Germany as a state that no longer exists but whose memory reverberates in sometimes unexpected ways, not only today but as a projection into the future. As time passes, the Wall's legacies and memories become perhaps more distant, but also, as the chapters in this volume show, richer and more complex.

Realigned Worlds

The world has indeed changed dramatically since that presumed moment of triumph in November of 1989. We have moved from Cold War into New World Order through neoliberalization and neoconservatism, passing through the ongoing global terror war, and now find ourselves in global economic crisis and drawn into liberation movements in places where we did not expect to see them. Before projecting into a *future past*, or a forward glance into the 1990s from the vantage point of 1989, we must also reconsider the decade of the booming 1980s. Although theorists and ideologues like Francis Fukuyama triumphantly lauded the transcendence of capital and "The End of History,"[1] this "new" moment of global capital was not, for all its basking in the aura of the "new," new at all, nor did it persist without its residual socialist specters (as literary and cultural theorists Benjamin Robinson and Hunter Bivens both compellingly, if differently, assert in Chapters 8 and 9, respectively).[2] The 1980s, we suggest, merit reexamination in continuity with decades-long developments globally, just as the decades since 1989 also form a continuous, if at points disconnected, arc with discordant points and cacophonic tonalities pouring into the present. The commonly accepted notion that the November 9, 1989, fall of the Berlin Wall constitutes *the* victory moment of the Regan-Thatcher-Kohl decade must be rethought in light of recent and ongoing scholarship on the 1980s. Political scientists and international relations theorists Robert Snyder and Timothy White, in Chapter 6 of this volume, meditate on the decade-long geopolitical lead-up to the Wall's fall in 1989 and the end of the Soviet system in 1991. Arguing that Gorbachev needs to be revalued and revalorized for his intellectual and political contributions to the dissolution of the Soviet Union, Snyder and White contend that the leader should be seen—in constructivist, not positivist terms—as a key architect in the demise of the Cold War. Research like this challenges the assumption of a victorious Western socioeconomical system and complicates the idea of a "collapse" of the Soviet Union.

For flag-waving and capital-carrying conservatives, however, the 1980s (which seemed to ceremoniously conclude with the Wall's fall in 1989) created, at least momentarily, the illusion of a world a-spark with electric possibility. Seemingly no longer bound by landmass and open sea, the world witnessed celestial constellations defined by defense and star wars missiles. The decade also marked other significant geopolitical Cold War and post–Cold War world realignments: a transatlantic geopolitical alliance between British Prime Minister Margaret Thatcher and U.S. President Ronald Reagan that began in 1981 and continued until the end of 1989 and was supported by Chancellor Helmut Kohl and President François Mitterand;[3] the fall of the Wall itself on November 9, 1989; the consequent dissolution of the Soviet Union in 1991; and the subsequent splintering off and concomitant creations of newly independent states (NISs) in the former Eastern Bloc. Historically, it also inaugurated the consolidation of a presumed "New World Order" orchestrated by Mikhail Gorbachev and then appropriated by George H. W. Bush in the waning days of the decade from December 1988 until spring 1989, as well as the world championing of Mitterand and Kohl, coarchitects of European integration and German reunification, and later signatories to the Maastricht Treaty (1992), which created the European Union from what began as the European Economic Community in 1957.

From the vantage point of the *future past*, that forward glance into the 1990s from the perspective of 1989, a less optimistic picture emerges. Capitalists the world over celebrated the fall of the Berlin Wall as the belated, if also unexpected, end of the Cold War, which resulted in the soon-to-follow demise of state communism, the triumph of capital in the "New World Order," as Bush Senior heralded (stealing the words right out of the mouth of Gorbachev himself),[4] and the subsequent rapid "exportation" of democracy into formerly despotic regimes the world over through free-trade agreements or military demonstrations of power, whichever proved more expedient. Similarly, the 1990s also witnessed the foreign policy move from "containment to enlargement," as Anthony Lake, then U.S. Assistant to the President for National Security Affairs under President Clinton, articulated in a speech delivered at the Johns Hopkins University in September 1993, all the while that Secretary of State Warren Christopher confidently referred to "a world transformed" and his successor, Madeleine Albright, declared the United States the "one indispensable nation-state."[5] The 1990s was indeed a decade of free-trade agreements and military interventions. In addition to the creation of the European Union in 1992, the North American Free Trade Agreement (NAFTA) was signed in 1992 and ratified in 1994. The period also witnessed, however, air strikes in Iraq in 1991, a U.S.-led military intervention in Somalia in 1993, the U.S.-UN "inter-vasion" of Haiti in 1994, and a NATO-led military bombing campaign in Bosnia in 1995, and, completing this militarized decade of "hot" battles for a post–Cold War world, the NATO military bombing campaign, known as Operation Allied Force, in Kosovo in 1999. If the euphoria of 1989 led us to believe, even momentarily, that we were entering into a "New World Order" defined by peace and prosperity, history should have disabused us of this idea throughout the conflict-rife 1990s.

Similar contradictions arose regarding the Wall itself. Almost as soon as the Berlin Wall fell and people all over the world celebrated its demise, other barriers, borders, boundaries, and even new physical "walls" were speedily constructed in this peremptorily declared "post-Wall" era. According to contributor Christine Leuenberger, over 24 separation barriers have been proposed or constructed since 1989, most notably along the U.S.-Mexico border beginning in 1993[6] and in the West Bank starting in 2002. Leuenberger, thus, takes the notion of a wall in the mind one step further in her exploration of the psychological meanings and interpretations of separation walls, not only in Germany but also in other parts of the world, in particular in the West Bank. In Chapter 3 of this volume she shows that the cultural and psychological importance attributed to walls is at least as divisive, if not more so, than the actual concrete barriers. Adopting the concept of "evocative object," Leuenberger probes the psychological and intellectual dimensions of material barriers—i.e., those deeply interpellated mental frameworks that further rigidify and socially solidify the bricks-and-mortar, or concrete-and-barbed-wire, structures of physical walls. The so-called post-Wall world, as Leuenberger persuasively demonstrates, had become even more fiercely wed to borders, walls, barriers, and geopolitical and ethnic divides.

Still, the post-Wall celebration seemed big and boundless as one gigantic transnational party swept the world (skipping over, of course, the "inconvenient continent"[7] and other stripped-bare, "underdeveloped" places[8]) with its multinational free-trade agreements, running rampant dot.com money, speculation in currencies, free-flowing profits of financial capital, and the international trade in "goods" and "services." In September 2008, however, the world woke up to one massive global hangover as it became indisputably clear that the inebriate 1990s had resurfaced as twenty-first-century crises—those of laissez-faire, unregulated, hypervirtual capital, proliferative deficit spending, speculative and derivative-based financial investments, megacorporate bailouts, rapidly escalating unemployment, increasingly expendable labor, and the radically widening gaps between rich and poor the world over. Following a trajectory from celebration to crisis, the history of the past two decades thus demands we reexamine the fall of the Berlin Wall and its myriad and complex registers of polysemic meanings within the German context as well as in other spatiotemporal sites across the globe.

For example, Jonathan Murphy in Chapter 5 attends to the political and territorial tensions marking German-Polish relations since 1945 over the disputed Oder-Neisse border and the ways this geographical border continued to have politicized ramifications throughout the Cold War and especially up to and after the fall of the Berlin Wall in 1989. Coming from a historical perspective, Murphy argues that the borders between Germany and Poland, imposed by the allies after 1945 but never entirely finalized, had to be settled upon and ratified in complex diplomatic negotiations after 1989 before they could be opened for the significant cultural and economic exchange we have today between the two neighbors. In this case, a border needed to be affirmed and made "real" in order to overcome some of the historical divisions between Germans and Poles. We have thus passed, though obviously not seamlessly, from postwar to Cold War to "New World Order" through neoliberal structural adjustment and neoconservative terror wars to a global capitalist economy in crisis.

Novelist Douglas Cowie, in Chapter 7 of this volume titled "The Seventh of November," an excerpt from his forthcoming novel *Berliner Ensemble*, projects further into a post-Wall future: set circa 2019, when the postapocalyptic global capitalist economy remains in ruin, the protagonist Peter Kokemus, an American, joins a group of terrorist insurgents who bomb the Reichstag and other historical monuments in the capital of Berlin. Imagining a post-Wall world in ruins, Cowie's fiction poignantly and presciently alerts twenty-first century readers to the fine lyrical line between triumph and demise, celebration and disaster. Cowie thus compels readers to envision, in imaginative if dark scenarios of catastrophe, the post-Wall remnants that still resurface in the "age of terror" and in the midst of the ongoing global terror war. Retrospectively painted canvases of the post-Wall world like Cowie's fictionalized dystopia markedly diverge as *future past* from the celebratory ode to capitalist joy that captivated the 1990s. The triumphalism of global capital inaugurated with the "death of communism," the "end of the Cold War," and celebrated as the "end of History," was also marked by what Samuel P. Huntington calls the "clash of civilizations"[9] and the incantatory requiem that Chalmers Johnson defined as the "sorrows of empire,"[10] or the rise of global cultural divisions that many believed culminated in the 9/11 terrorist attacks and the global terror war. While some of these newly emerging divisions in the post-Wall world are highly visible, other remnants of the Wall are less tangible and harder to fathom.

Invisible Lines

According to an oft-repeated conviction, it is virtually impossible in present-day Berlin to see or even remember where the Berlin Wall once was. In reality, some sections of the original wall have been preserved and transformed into memorial sites; its footprint is marked by cobblestones in the area around the Brandenburg Gate; and elongated stretches of green between blocks of houses and roads in some sections of town are evidence of the bare strips between the Wall's Eastern and Western sections. While the inability to recognize where the Wall once stood is to some degree owed to the desire to see unification succeed, it is perhaps correct to say that the Wall's absence determines the city today as much as its presence did from 1961 to 1989.[11]

The perception that the Berlin Wall has become invisible yet maintains a lingering presence has been expressed in a number of contexts, ranging from literary explorations of the topic to the perhaps not altogether serious wish for its reconstruction.[12] The most famous assertion of the Wall's reverberating presence is certainly Peter Schneider's often quoted observation from his 1982 novel *The Wall Jumper*: "It will take us longer to tear down the Wall in our heads than any wrecking company will need for the Wall we can see."[13] Schneider's early insight that the Berlin Wall would continue to linger in people's minds and shape their perceptions beyond its fall, an occurrence which in 1982 by all accounts was unthinkable, resonates in a range of contexts well beyond Berlin and Germany, and, as several of the chapters in this volume show, it has assumed symbolic significance in a variety of frameworks. But even in the German context, the idea of an invisible wall no longer simply refers to enduring differences between East and West Germans and instead stands for more complex reflections about our ability (or inability) to imagine something that once was but no longer physically exists.

So what do we "see" when we contemplate the Wall today? Several chapters in this volume ask this question, often invoking Schneider's ingenious phrase. Paul Kubicek in Chapter 4, for example, approaches the notion of the persisting "wall in the mind" with the lens of political science using quantitative and qualitative sociological methods. Tracing the importance of *Ostalgie*, the longing for certain features of GDR culture that was widely expressed in the 1990s, he shows that the attitude became somewhat more prevalent as time passed, in particular among older people, but that it had little real political impact. Coming from different disciplines and national contexts, these examples reveal some of the complexities of walls and borders in their concrete manifestation and, perhaps even more so, their function as mental, and thus invisible, demarcations.

The rebuilding of Berlin, addressed in Chapters 11 and 12 by Carol Anne Costabile-Heming and Daniel Purdy, was itself the result of a complex negotiation process between the imperative to acknowledge the city's history through architecture and urban design and the concomitant desire to erase the traces of its division except for those remaining sections of the former wall specifically preserved or represented for remembrance. Focusing on the built environment, Purdy analyzes how debates about urban planning and design in China, an emergent economic powerhouse of twenty-first-century production, not only reiterated debates about post-Wall architecture in Berlin and anxieties about size, scope, and high rises, but also revealed anxieties about erecting hypercapitalist monuments and becoming a virtual megacity. Analyzing the German reception of China's current building boom, Purdy's chapter draws attention to yet another incarnation of the Berlin Wall and its aftermath in a different national context. The German criticism of Chinese decisions in favor of postmodern skyscrapers, rather than the preservation of traditional structures, is therefore, partially, a repetition of the debates that accompanied the rebuilding of Berlin in the 1990s, transferring the German desire for an untainted past into the—misunderstood—Chinese context. The chapter by Costabile-Heming on two important government sites in Berlin—one entirely new, one utilizing an existing building—dovetails nicely with Purdy's insights into the complex issues involved in rendering German history through physical construction. Considering the architectural legacies of the Nazi period as well as the GDR, Costabile-Heming refers to the trajectory of the former Wall, as well as the realignment of Berlin envisioned by Hitler's architect Alfred Speer, in her discussion of official building projects and the controversies that accompanied their construction. At least those willing to look and to see, her chapter suggests, can decipher the layers of history inscribed not only on Berlin's structures and streets, but also in its empty spaces and the sites that remain unbuilt.

The Berlin Wall and its fall, as noted historian James Sheehan pointed out in an interview, can be "easily translated into other [historical] narratives."[14] Its power as a symbol of the Cold War carries over into other contexts as well, where it tends to acquire new meanings and implications. Installations of original sections of the Berlin Wall in the United

States, for instance, are intended to signal freedom and demonstrate the victory of one political system over another, whereas those in Berlin serve as reminders of a dark history that should not be forgotten.[15] And the Wall's immaterial presences persist as well. Shannon Granville, exploring the political symmetries and parallels between postwar Germany and postwar Japan in the *Master Keaton manga* series in Chapter 2 of this volume, not only probes the parallels between the two countries during postwar reconstruction, post-Marshall Plan economic redevelopment, and Cold War military occupation, but also the ways in which those historical congruencies continue to inform the post-Wall cultural politics of both countries. In the chapter's focus on the Japanese *Master Keaton* cartoon series, a sequence of stories centered on a Japanese detective in post-Wall Germany, Granville argues that the German example is intended as an appeal to a Japanese audience to reflect on its own history, with the redrawn national boundaries after the Wall's fall raising relevant but as yet unexplored questions concerning the legacies of the past for contemporary Japanese identity.

Incalculable Remnants

What remains? Christa Wolf, one of the most influential writers of the GDR, asked this question in the title of her highly controversial novel *Was bleibt* (*What Remains*). Written in the late 1970s and first published in 1990, with presumably minor but unmarked revisions, Wolf's text has become symptomatic of the difficulties and the ideological forces at work in the assessment of a text once the surrounding political context has changed.[16] The novel, a rather bleak story about an East Berlin writer—not unlike Wolf—who finds herself under observation by the Stasi, asks how to cope with oppression and speculates about what persists in spite of it.[17] Wolf, who has remained a supporter of a socialist economy beyond the end of the GDR, casts her concerns in terms of social values such as the ability to trust someone or to speak the truth. Others have posed the problem of what remains of the socialist legacy after the presumed victory of capitalism by referencing the global repercussions of 9/11 and the international economic crises of the first decade of the twenty-first century. A radical example is *The Coming Insurrection*, a book-length manifesto written by an anonymous group of French activist intellectuals in the aftermath of the 2005 riots in Paris, whose criticism ranges from the creation of artificial and lifeless city centers in Europe to the flawed responses of the U.S. government after Hurricane Katrina.[18] Predicting the complete collapse of Western political and economic institutions, the manifesto, which suggests communal living as an alternative outside of market mechanisms, calls for a return of sorts to communism as "presupposition *and* as experiment."[19] No less far-reaching in its scope and conceived in similar metaphors is the philosopher Slavoj Žižek's *Living in the End Times* (2010), whose response to Fukuyama's proclamation of the end of history is that the capitalist system is reaching an "apocalyptic zero-point."[20] Drawing on the five stages of grief suggested by the psychoanalyst Elisabeth Kübler-Ross, Žižek, whose analysis ranges from Kant to contemporary film, proposes to lead his reader from denial of a crisis to acceptance, at which point the "germs of a communist culture in all its diverse forms" can begin to emerge.[21] While such positions are well to the left of the mainstream, the current international economic crises, dwindling budgets for social services and education, as well as growing inequality within Western societies have assured the continuing appeal of socialist theory and ideals. Less extreme in its conclusions, yet highly perceptive of the entanglements between social consciousness and economic pressures within a global economy, is Jonathan Franzen's latest novel *Freedom* (2010), whose protagonist Walter Berglund—a supporter of the Club of Rome and its anticapitalist demand for zero growth during his youth in the 1970s—in the early 2000s ends up in a highly compromised situation as he tries to save an endangered bird at the price of handing over a region in West Virginia for mountaintop removal mining to an international corporation.[22] More than two decades after the Wall's fall, the tensions between the desire for social justice and the mechanisms of a capitalist economy are far from being reconciled.

The ambiguous outcomes of the fall of the Wall are reflected in a number of chapters in this collection. Chapters 8 and 9 deal with the legacy of Marxism after 1989, using the East German context for reflections about the status of labor and workers today. Hunter Bivens, in his reading of a post-1989 novel by the East German writer Volker Braun, addresses the demise of the socialist project not only as a mass utopia, but also as a way of life built upon and around the experience of work. Without nostalgia for the GDR, Bivens shows, Braun's novel connects specifically East German realities after 1989 with international developments, concluding that the demise of labor as society's foundation leads to a profound crisis of individual and social identity. Benjamin Robinson's chapter, also about texts by East German writers, polemically suggests that the fall of the Wall signifies the end of an event, namely, the termination of the attempt to put into practice the socialist project. Contrasting Uwe Johnson's 1959 *Speculations about Jacob* with Uwe Tellkamp's 2008 *Der Turm* (*The Tower*), Robinson privileges Johnson's high modernist appeal to the reader to think through the challenges of socialism over the aesthetic closure offered by Tellkamp's novel about the end of the GDR.

Sander Gilman's piece and Anna Dempsey's chapter further consider recent German cultural productions and their often ambivalent representations of post-Wall Germany. Gilman, in Chapter 1 of this book offers a critical assessment of internationally successful German literature, such as Bernhard Schlink's Holocaust-related novel *The Reader*, a work which was subsequently turned into a Hollywood movie, or Charlotte Roche's sexually explicit and taboo-breaking *Wetlands*, warning that German culture, in an effort to lay claim to "normalcy," loses sight of its more significant traditions as it sells out to the global market. Focusing on the body as a site of cultural transformation, Gilman draws our attention to the contrast between the high cultural experimentation with physicality that runs from Georg Büchner to Durs Grünbein, on the one hand, and the contemporary exploitation of bodies for purposes of marketability under the guise of Bildung, on the other. Dempsey's analysis of recent paintings by artists from the former GDR in Chapter 10, in particular the works of Neo Rauch, thinks through similar concerns when she reflects on the enlightenment tradition and its reception by German academics as a rich, if conflicted, source of images that comes to bear on Rauch's ambiguous and highly unsettling pictures. With Rauch we have an internationally successful German artist who draws on a range of German traditions for his thoroughly contemporary images that spell both anxiety, and, as Dempsey suggests, redemption.

Over two decades after its fall, the Berlin Wall has taken on a rich and diverse afterlife as a site of commemoration, a point of reference in current political debates, and a cultural icon in Germany and in places across the globe. The chapters assembled in this book hint at some of the ways in which these motifs work. While the fact that there is no one interpretation but many is perhaps an expected outcome, the Wall's ubiquity across geographical areas, fields of study, and ideological stances is important to note. From that perspective, the Berlin Wall is truly a global phenomenon well beyond its fall. Much research remains to be done as archives become available and allow us to explore new and different questions about the Wall as an international symbol and political reality. More than 20 years after the Wall's fall, the euphoria of 1989 is certainly gone. Instead, this volume shows, we need compelling and nuanced analyses to understand our past as we begin to address the economic, political, and cultural complexities the future most certainly has in store for us.

Coda

What can be said with certainty is that the Berlin Wall continues to fascinate—not only in the city that it once divided, but across the globe—taking on different meanings for diverse audiences. Consider, for example, Daniel Kehlmann and Matteo Pericoli's collaboratively composed and illustrated essay "An Invisible Wall," published in the *New York Times* on September 5, 2010, as part of a series-in-process titled *Windows on the World*.[23] In their joint contribution, German-Austrian fiction writer Kehlmann[24] and Milano-born, New York-based architect and visual artist Pericoli[25] capture some of this interest in the Wall and its erasure as they synergistically gesture toward the lost imagery of Berlin's once-divided cityscape now invisible behind the new facades and the unobstructed roads of united Berlin. The double piece captures in prose and in illustration the post-*Wende* urban architecture and Berlin's city streets as seen through Kehlmann's apartment window near the Bahnhof Friedrichstraße. The train station—which, after Checkpoint Charlie, was the most important point of East-West interchange in the former divided city—served as a point of entry and exit for West Berliners and West Germans as well as those citizens of the GDR who enjoyed travel privileges. The building, with its maze of corridors, its mirror-lined checkpoints, and its liquor stores offering East German brands to the travelers from the West, was located inside East Berlin, away from the actual Wall, and constituted an eerie world unto itself. Matteo's drawing does not feature the station itself, referencing by omission this historically important site that defines the neighborhood to this day. But his sketch does show the adjacent Weidendammer Brücke with its cast-iron Prussian Eagle, the emblem of German history invoked by the East German singer-songwriter Wolf Biermann in his elegiac "Ballade of the Prussian Ikarus."[26] Performed at his 1976 concert in the West German city of Cologne, two days after which he was stripped of his East German citizenship, Biermann, in his song, bemoans the division of Germany and the paralysis experienced by those living in the GDR. Political reform not being an option in the "island" state surrounded by barbed wire, the song's third stanza predicts that under the Prussian Eagle's hated regime the singer himself will crash like the exuberant young Ikarus of the Greek legend. Pericoli's inclusion of the heraldic animal at the lower right edge of his drawing is more than an attempt at realism, allowing for the layers of history to shine through the modern facades and disrupting the assumption of a seamless new city. The frame of the double-wing window, which delimits the scene and optically cuts the image in half, underscores the importance of perspective and the power of the invisible. As Lutz Koepnick has noted in his study on windows as a site of inquiry into the complexities of how we view the world and the "perceptual transformations in modernity," windows can "intensify what we have fantasized about all along."[27] Pericoli and Kehlmann's window on a once-divided world gives us an impression of what such an intensified fantasy of the wall and its aftermath might look like.

Kehlmann's narrative picks up on the drawing's interplay between the visible and the invisible and the choices one makes to include certain things in the field of vision while omitting others. In spare, evocative language that meditates on the tension between the seen and the unseen, Kehlmann first catalogues all that he does not see outside his window in the Berlin below—because he works at a desk in his attic with "my back to it." Sites he does not see include the Spree River, the three bridges that cross it between Friedrichstraße and Museum Island, the Bode museum in the distance, the cars, the pedestrians, the barges, and the tourists with cameras. "I see only," he notes, "the spines of books along their shelves." In contrast to the author focused on his work and his imaginary

Figure 0.1 Matteo Pericoli, "An Invisible Wall"

world of fiction, the tourists he envisions in the streets below are busy photographing the historical landmarks of the former East Berlin—the Tränenpalast, or Palace of Tears, through which people exiting East Berlin for the city's Western half had to pass; Bertolt Brecht's Berliner Ensemble as icon of GDR culture; and above all, that which cannot be captured through the photographic lens, the "invisible line where the Berlin Wall once stood." Kehlmann muses about this dialectic of the visible and the invisible, the material and the immaterial demarcations of Berlin:

> Absence can't be captured, not even with the best camera, and so the tourists turn their helpless devices to the gray facades of the new buildings, to the rows of identical windows, one of which, high up near the roof, stands open, and behind it a barely visible figure quickly turns away and goes back to work at his desk.

The entire scene takes place in the head of the narrator, who in the end becomes real to himself through the camera of the imagined tourists. This postmodern twist (something Kehlmann is fond of) places the author, and thus the creator of invisible worlds, into the center, suggesting that this is the location where the Wall now can be found, not only as a lingering division between East and West Germans, but as a site of creative speculation.

Notes

1. See Francis Fukuyama's *The End of History and the Last Man* (New York: Free Press, 1992).
2. See also Slavoj Žižek's "Beyond Fukuyama," in his book *In Defense of Lost Causes* (London: Verso, 2008), 420–438.
3. See, especially, Stevan K. Pavlowitch's *Tito, Yugoslavia's Great Dictator: A Reassessment* (Columbus: Ohio SU, 1992); and Sabrina P. Ramet's *Balkan Babel: The Disintegration of Yugoslavia from the Death of Tito to the Fall of Milošević* (Cambridge, MA: Westview Press, 2002).
4. In his December 7, 1988, address to the forty-third United Nations General Assembly session, Gorbachev declared that "[f]urther world progress is now possible only through the search for a consensus of all mankind, in movement toward a new world order." Excerpts from Gorbachev's UN address are available online at the Woodrow Wilson International Center for Scholars: http://www.wilsoncenter.org/coldwarfiles/files/Documents/1988-1107.Gorbachev.pdf.
5. Anthony Lake, "From Containment to Enlargement." Speech delivered at Johns Hopkins University, School of Advanced International Studies

(September 21, 1993) http://www.mtholyoke.edu/acad/intrel/lakedoc.html. Accessed on November 27, 2011.

6. See Braziel, *Diaspora: An Introduction*: "Transborder economic migration thus continued unabated throughout the 1990s, and into the twenty-first century, despite a series of other failed INS programs—both "Operation Blockade" and "Operation Hold-the-Line" (El Paso) implemented in 1993; "Operation Gatekeeper" (San Diego) in 1994; "Operation Safeguard" (Arizona) in 1995; and "Operation Rio Grande" (Brownsville) in 1997—to prevent the "illegal entry" of Mexican migrant workers; however, points of entry moved further eastward away from the metropolitan border zone of Tijuana-San Diego and into small, rural towns and arid, perilous, and literally deserted parts of the desert" (60).
7. See James Ferguson's "Global Africa? Observations from an Inconvenient Continent," in *Global Shadows: Africa in the Neoliberal World Order* (Durham and London: Duke University Press, 2006), 25–49.
8. See Walter Rodney's illustrative *How Europe Underdeveloped Africa* (Washington, D.C.: Howard University Press, 1981).
9. See both Samuel P. Huntington's "The Clash of Civilizations," first published in *Foreign Affairs* 72, no. 3 (Summer 1993) and his book-length elaboration of the thesis in *The Clash of Civilization and the Remaking of World Order* (New York: Simon and Schuster, 1993, 1996).
10. See Chalmers Johnson, *The Sorrows of Empire: Militarism, Secrecy, and the End of the Republic* (New York: Metropolitan Books, 2004).
11. Adrian Parr's notion of Berlin's urban geographical landscapes as future-driven reckonings of the past, or what we have above referred to as *future past*, rather than memorialization is illustrative. See "Berlin and the Holocaust," in *Deleuze and Memorial Culture: Desire, Singular Memory and the Politics of Trauma* (Edinburgh: Edinburgh University Press, 2008), 143–165.
12. Literary explorations of the topic include Inka Parei's *Die Schattenboxerin* (Frankfurt am Main: Schöffling, 1999), a novel that links the story of Berlin's division and unification to the experience of rape, or Tim Staffel's *Terrordrom* (Zürich: Ammann, 1998), which envisions the reconstruction of the Wall in an apocalyptic future. Paul Kubicek's contribution notes that identification with the GDR among an older East German population has grown stronger with time.
13. "Die Mauer im Kopf einzureißen, wird länger dauern, als irgendein Abrißunternehmer für die sichtbare Mauer braucht." Peter Schneider, *Der Mauerspringer* (Frankfurt am Main: Luchterhand, 1982), 102; in English *The Wall Jumper: A Berlin Story* [1982] (Chicago: University of Chicago Press, 1998), 119.
14. "Remembering 1989: Thoughts on Modern History with Dr. James J. Sheehan." Interview conducted by Nicole Lyon. *Focus on German Studies* 17 (2010), 201–207. Here 205.
15. For instance, a Berlin Wall section installed in Cincinnati, Ohio, is located outside the Freedom Center, a museum dedicated to the history of slavery and the promotion of social justice in general.

16. For a comprehensive overview over the debate, see *"Es geht nicht um Christa Wolf": Der Literaturstreit im vereinten Deutschland*, ed. Thomas Anz (Munich: Spangenberg, 1991).
17. Christa Wolf, *Was bleibt. Erzählung* [1990] (Munich: dtv, 1999).
18. *The Coming Insurrection.* By The Invisible Committee (Los Angeles: Semiotext(e); Cambridge, MA: distributed by the MIT Press, 2009).
19. Ibid., 9.
20. Slavoj Žižek, *Living in the End Times* (London; New York: Verso, 2010), x.
21. Ibid., xxii.
22. Jonathan Franzen, *Freedom* (New York: Farrar, Straus, and Giroux, 2010).
23. *Windows on the World* is a series of illustrations published from August 2010 through July 2011 in the *New York Times* Op ed page.
24. Son of Austrian television director Michael Kehlmann, born in Munich, and alternately residing in Vienna and Berlin, dual citizen and fiction writer Daniel Kehlmann published his first novel *Beerholms Vorstellung* in 1997 and has since published four additional novels and short story collections, including *Der fernste Ort* (2000); *Ich und Kaminski* (2003), translated and published in English as *Me and Kaminiski*(2009); *Mahlers Zeit* (2004); *Wo ist Carlos Montufar?* (2005); *Unter der Sonne* (2005); *Die Vermessung der Welt* (2005), translated and published in English as *Measuring the World* (2007); and *Ruhm* (2009), translated and published in English as *Fame* (2010).
25. Pericoli's published books include *The City Out My Window: 63 Views on New York* (New York: Simon and Schuster, 2009); *World Unfurled* (San Francisco: Chronicle, 2008); *Manhattan Unfurled* (New York: Random House, 2001); *Manhattan Within* (New York: Random House, 2003); and *New York e altri disegni* (Macerata, Italy: Quodlibet, IT, 2005). Pericoli has also published three children's books: *Tommaso and the Missing Line* (New York: Knopf, 2008); *See the City: The Journey of Manhattan Unfurled* (New York: Knopf, 2004); and *The True Story of Stellina* (New York: Knopf, 2006).
26. Wolf Biermann, *Alle Lieder* (Cologne: Kiepenheuer and Witsch, 1991), 284–285.
27. Lutz Koepnick, *Framing Attention: Windows on Modern German Culture* (Baltimore: Johns Hopkins University Press, 2007), 3, 14.

Bibliography

Anz, Thomas. ed. *"Es geht nicht um Christa Wolf": Der Literaturstreit im vereinten Deutschland.* Munich: Spangenberg, 1991.

Biermann, Wolf. *Alle Lieder*. Cologne: Kiepenheuer and Witsch, 1991, 284–85.

Braziel, Jana Evans. *Diaspora: An Introduction*. Malden, MA: Blackwell Publishers, 2008.

Ferguson, James. "Global Africa? Observations from an Inconvenient Continent." *Global Shadows: Africa in the Neoliberal World Order*. Durham and London: Duke University Press, 2006, 25–49.

Franzen, Jonathan. *Freedom*. New York: Farrar, Straus, and Giroux, 2010.

Fukuyama, Francis. *The End of History and the Last Man*. New York: Free Press, 1992.

Huntington, Samuel P. "The Clash of Civilizations," *Foreign Affairs* 72, no.3 (Summer 1993).

———. *The Clash of Civilization and the Remaking of World Order*. New York: Simon and Schuster, 1993, 1996.

Johnson, Chalmers. *The Sorrows of Empire: Militarism, Secrecy, and the End of the Republic*. New York: Metropolitan Books, 2004.

Kehlmann, Daniel. *Beerholms Vorstellung*. Vienna: Deuticke, 1997.

———. *Der fernste Ort*. Frankfurt am Main: Suhrkamp, 2001.

———. *Die Vermessung der Welt*. Reinbek bei Hamburg: Rowohlt, 2005.

———. *Ich und Kaminski*. Frankfurt am Main: Suhrkamp, 2003.

———. *Mahlers Zeit*. Frankfurt am Main: Suhrkamp, 1999.

———. *Ruhm*. Reinbek bei Hamburg: Rowohlt, 2009.

———. *Unter der Sonne*. Vienna, Deuticke, 1998.

———. *Wo ist Carlos Montúfar?* Reinbek bei Hamburg: Rowohlt, 2005.

Koepnick, Lutz P. *Framing Attention: Windows on Modern German Culture*. Baltimore: Johns Hopkins University Press, 2007.

Lake, Anthony. "From Containment to Enlargement." Speech delivered at Johns Hopkins University, School of Advanced International Studies (September 21, 1993), http://www.mtholyoke.edu/acad/intrel/lakedoc.html.

Leonhard, Jörn, and Lothar Funk, eds. *Ten Years of German Unification*. Birmingham, UK: University of Birmingham Press, 2002.

Parei, Inka. *Die Schattenboxerin*. Frankfurt am Main: Schöffling, 1999.

Parr, Adrian. "Berlin and the Holocaust." *Deleuze and Memorial Culture: Desire, Singular Memory and the Politics of Trauma*. Edinburgh: Edinburgh University Press, 2008, 143–65.

Pavlowitch, Stevan K. *Tito, Yugoslavia's Great Dictator: A Reassessment*. Columbus: Ohio SU, 1992.

Pericoli, Matteo, and Daniel Kehlmann. *Windows on the World*. Op ed page, the *New York Times*, September 5, 2010.

Pericoli, Matteo. *The City Out My Window: 63 Views on New York*. New York: Simon and Schuster, 2009.

———. *Manhattan Unfurled*. New York: Random House, 2001.

———. *Manhattan Within*. New York: Random House, 2003.

———. *New York e altri disegni*. Macerata, Italy: Quodlibet, 2005.

———. *See the City: The Journey of Manhattan Unfurled*. New York: Alfred A. Knopf, 2004.

———. *Tommaso and the Missing Line*. New York: Alfred A. Knopf, 2008.

———. *The True Story of Stellina*. New York: Knopf, 2006.

———. *World Unfurled*. San Francisco: Chronicle Books, 2008.

Ramet, Sabrina P. *Balkan Babel: The Disintegration of Yugoslavia from the Death of Tito to the Fall of Milošević*. Cambridge, MA: Westview Press, 2002.

Rodney, Walter. *How Europe Underdeveloped Africa*. Washington D.C.: Howard University Press, 1981.

Schneider, Peter. *Der Mauerspringer*. Frankfurt am Main: Luchterhand: 1982.
———. *The Wall Jumper: A Berlin Story*. Translated by Leigh Hafrey. Chicago: University of Chicago Press, 1998.
Sheehan, James. "Remembering 1989: Thoughts on Modern History with Dr. James J. Sheehan." Interview conducted by Nicole Lyon. *Focus on German Studies* 17 (2010), 201–207.
Staffel, Tim. *Terrordrom*. Zürich: Ammann, 1998.
The Invisible Committee. *The Coming Insurrection*. Los Angeles: Semiotext(e), 2009.
Wolf, Christa. *Was bleibt. Erzählung*. [1990]. Munich: dtv, 1999.
Žižek, Slavoj. "Beyond Fukuyama." *In Defense of Lost Causes*. London: Verso, 2008, 420–438.
———. *Living in the End Times*. New York: Verso, 2010.

1

Sex and the City: Thoughts on Literature, Gender, and Normalization in the New Germany

Sander L. Gilman

In June 2008 the *Bundeskanzlerin* Angela Merkel noted "economic success today means education [*Bildung*] for all."[1] But what does *Bildung* mean 20 years after the establishment of a "normal" state? Goethe's notion of *Bildung* as the secular self-betterment and social self-realization in an imagined Germany is clearly no longer applicable in the newly realized "normal" state of Germany. The great British historian of Germany and Austria Peter Pulzer, as early as 1994, thought about what becoming normal would mean for Germany.[2] He stressed the continuation of the Western ideals and structures inherent in the German Federal Republic but also saw them under strain. But what about the older ideals such as *Bildung* that the Germans, both East and West, had relied on to define themselves as a cultural rather than a political nation? What does *Bildung* mean 20 years after reunification? Merkel sees *Bildung* as a universal goal that is the result of economic success (this before the tottering of the Euro zone) rather than individual achievement. She sees it as part of the commerce of modernity, now a universal goal of all Germans because of the supposed economic advantage of reunification.

Normal Bodies?

The young German poet Durs Grünbein, certainly the most important serious writer in today's Germany, addressed the question of the cultural patrimony of *Bildung* in his speech "Breaking Bodies" ("Den Körper zerbrechen") at his acceptance of the 1995 Büchner Prize. For him it is the body, not in Hobbes's sense of the leviathan state, but in the physicality of experience that underlies *Bildung*:

> What Georg Büchner (1813–37) succeeded in doing was nothing less than a total transformation: physiology that became literature. As it turned out it was not a cultural aside [*Sonderweg*]. It was the beginning of a series of experiments that has been continued until our time.[3]

It is bodies that matter to *Bildung*, and this is not a *Sonderweg*, says Grünbein, evoking that central term that set the path of German history in the twentieth century apart from that of the "normal" state and about which historians still struggle. No, he says, it is the concern with lived experience, with the corporeal, that comes to define high culture. Merkel's notion, shared by too many in Germany and abroad, is that *Bildung* means training for the new economy, something the German system of higher education (in its reaction to the very low rating it receives on almost all international rankings such as the Pisa scale) now wrestles with. High culture, as exemplified by Durs Grünbein, sees not economic advance through training but cultural physicality, an "economy of the body," at the center of post-Wall German culture.

> Without a doubt the body has a significant space in the economy of literature. An entire cohort of writers has recently been concerned in examining the secret of life with a pathological fervor and to tailor anatomical texts with a scalpel. Thus a new literature that one could call the "new interiority" has arisen, which shocks through the opening of the body and believes that a new significance can be found in grubbing about in the guts.[4]

High culture, popular culture, and mass culture in today's "normal" Germany focus on bodies and their representations as the core of the new *Bildung*. Grünbein stresses this as part of a cultural integration into the totality of modern German culture as part of a European and, indeed, world culture. The "new interiority" he evokes is not a literature of self-examination but of a hyperawareness of physicality and its discontents—of bodies in decay, of cultures in transformation.

Culture can be an indicator of cultural change and shifts, but is it also a clue to shifts in national identity? Cultural representations can reflect popular expectations, and this is especially true in the world of the "best seller," whether literature or cinema. If Grünbein is right, then a move to the world of an economy of the body in post-Wall German culture is a move toward the "normal" in contemporary culture rather than an aberration. Yet if such a move is made one can quickly slide into the abyss of commercial exploitation of bodies and their meanings. The self-help health literature that dominates the global market deals with our fantasies about our own failing; the cultural equivalent to this is the fiction of the "new interiority," but its referent is not our own potentially ill bodies but those bodies in the inexorable flow of history and crush of space. The index that the bodies of the German "new interiority" refer us to is within the space of German *Bildung*.

One can speak of the conversion of this "new interiority" into commercial representations as part of the curse of cash for culture or the general curse of capitalism in post-Wall Germany, but this is no different than in any other contemporary national culture. Often it is the villain against which at least some of contemporary German culture and its mavens react. This can be seen with the critical reception of the central texts discussed below that illustrate both the rise of an economy of the body at the center of the novel and the "new interiority" being sold as part of *Bildung* to an international audience.

This creation of a new national idea of culture is even more engaging when popular national reception becomes international resonance, as in the case of the "New German Cinema" ("Junger Deutscher Film") after the promulgation of the Oberhausen Manifesto on February 28, 1962, which dominated German mass and high culture in the 1960s and 1970s. Thus, that which formed or reflected popular images of Germany, the Germans, and their sense of the world and their culture during the height of the popularity of directors such as Rainer Werner Fassbinder, Werner Herzog, Alexander Kluge, Volker Schlöndorff, Margarethe von Trotta, Hans-Jürgen Syberberg, and Wim Wenders came to define what Germany was in world culture, for good or for ill.

Selling the Past as the Present?

The "hottest" topics for cultural objects written in Germany having international resonance since the late 1990s and the first decade of the twenty-first century in Germany *revividus* were, to no one's surprise, the Holocaust and feminism and science. As these topics were dominant in world culture, the German reprise of them had at least the potential of echoing their presence in a new global marketplace of images. Think of the sudden respectability of feminist fiction in the world of literary prizes (The Nobel Prize in Literature for 2009 to Herta Müller; 2007 to Doris

Lessing; 2004 to Elfriede Jelinek; 1996 to Wislawa Szymborska; 1993 to Toni Morrison; 1991 to Nadine Gordimer), and some have said, the obsession with the Holocaust in North American popular and mass culture.[5] Even in France, the rediscovery of the work of Irène Némirovsky, a feminist author and a commentator/victim of the Holocaust, has to date sold over 600,000 copies in French alone. Science remains hot: in the twenty-first century it is not physics that excites the popular imagination but biology. We are, as I have recently written, in the second age of biology, the first had dominated the late nineteenth century. Ours is fascinated with a "new interiority" that of genetics and brain scans, making the interior visible as we imagine it has never been so in the past.[6] What is hot in world culture determines what is hot in German post-Wall culture but with a twist, and that twist is the appeal to *Bildung*.

This was already very much in line with the immediate post-Wall moment when Weimar culture seemed to be the appropriate set of images for the new Germany. In April 1990, Ulrich Eckardt, the long-term director of the Berlin Festival, called a news conference in which he announced that out of the long-existing cultural competition between the island city of "Westberlin" and (East) Berlin, the "Capital of the German Democratic Republic," a new "European cultural metropolis would arise": "We stand at a new moment in Berlin, which, from the standpoint of resources and historical echoes, is very similar to the period before 1933; we stand in close proximity to the cultural palette of the 1920s with its mixing of Western and Eastern influences."[7] The headline above this interview that morning in the *taz*, Berlin's widely read liberal daily, announced: "Berlin Dreams the Dream of the Twenties."

The model for this new dream of Germany was also global, taken straight (or gay) from Anglo-American commercial cinema, specifically the musical *Cabaret* with a book by the American Joe Masteroff, lyrics by Fred Ebb, and music by John Kander. The 1966 Broadway production became a hit and spawned a 1972 film as well as numerous subsequent productions. *Cabaret* was based on the Anglo-American John Van Druten's 1951 play *I Am a Camera*, which was adapted from the novella *Goodbye to Berlin* (1939) by the British novelist Christopher Isherwood. Set in 1931 Berlin as the Nazis are rising to power, it focuses on nightlife at the seedy Kit Kat Klub and revolves around the nineteen-year-old English cabaret performer Sally Bowles and her relationship with young American writer Cliff Bradshaw. No more global image of the new Germany could have been found immediately after the Wall vanished. The fact that Robert Gilbert's German translation first appeared in Vienna on November 14, 1970, in the Theater an der Wien and reappeared as a tourist attraction in Berlin as recently as 2004 at Berlin's Bar jeder Vernunft, which was transformed into the dodgy yet flamboyant Kit Kat Klub of the 1920s. By 2007, 120,000 visitors had attended the musical in German. By 2009, global culture came to define the German historical patrimony. The opening of the 2001 musical version of the satirical film, *The Producers* (1968), adapted by Mel Brooks and Thomas Meehan, in Berlin on May 18, 2009, turned the threatening Nazis of Cabaret into parody. "'Should one be allowed to laugh about Hitler?' asked the daily *Berliner Morgenpost*.[8] And the answer, ringing out from every stall on Friday night, was an affirmative yes. Moreover, Hitler received a standing ovation and some audience members even waved parody Nazi flags bearing wurst instead of swastikas."[9] Here one can truly turn to Marx's admonition that "[Hegel] forgot to add: the first time as tragedy, the second time as farce." Thus, the cultural image of Germany as a productive Weimar comes to haunt post-Wall Berlin as it takes over *Cabaret* and makes it into an "authentic" Berlin experience, analogous to the tourist Zille-Bars that were a landmark of divided "Westberlin." And then turns this cultural image of Germany into parody of the very collapse of Weimar culture, all clothed in global aesthetics, which makes them much more acceptable to a German audience.

A Normal Holocaust Tale?

If there was an answer to American musical kitsch delineating the nature of post-Wall German culture in terms of the Holocaust, it should have been Bernard Schlink's novel *Der Vorleser* (1995). It was sold and is still sold as a serious fiction underlining the moral problems of the perpetrators. And yet, the fascination with the corporeal, with the body that Durs Grünbein signaled, is very much at the center of the reception of this pseudo-detective novel as "cultural pornography." The term is first used by Jeremy Adler, professor of German at King's College, in relationship to Bernard Schlink's *Der Vorleser*, in a serious critique of the novel published as letter in 2002 to the *Times Literary Supplement*.[10] What Adler gestured at was the seemingly grotesque reduction of the murderers to the educationally disabled, of mass horror into individual failing, of a *Vergangenheitsbewältigung* gone horribly bad. But his use of "pornography" also reflected the sexualization of the text, its detailed obsession with bodies.

But it is also a means of imagining German mass culture. Cynthia Ozick soon thereafter called Schlink's novel a "product, conscious or not, of a desire to divert (attention) from the culpability of a normally educated population in a nation famed for *Kultur*."[11] Or perhaps *Bildung*? For at the core of Schlink's novel is the question of German culture and the concomitant inability to read. This is the unspoken cause of criminality and seduction as education, class, and success, that trinity that drives post-Wall Germany, is seen to drive Nazi Germany also. Only the losers, the uneducated, unsuccessful, low classes, were the perpetrators, or so it seemed.

Seduction is the novel's motif, and it is represented in the novel by the older woman's seduction of an ill, young boy: "She put her arms around me, one hand on my chest and the other on my erection."[12] But then "[w]e stood facing each other naked, but she couldn't have seemed more dismissive if she'd had on the uniform."[13] It is the seduction of a people, the Germans, that is at the novel's core. This is the analogy that Schlink seems to want his reader to make. But it was a seduction without a choice. Just say "no," the mantra of the abstinence-only believers in the twenty-first century, seems an impossibility in Schlink's fictive universe.

In the novel, the Nazi camp guard and seductress Hanna Schmitz twice turns the investigation back on the judge questioning her role in the camps: "'What would you have done?'"[14] The judge stammers and cannot answer: "Everyone felt" she "had more or less won the exchange."[15] What would YOU have done is how the reader is confronted with a history deemed real but purely literary in its representation. What would you have done? asks the protagonist, the reader, Michael Berg as an adult:

> What should our second generation have done, what should it do with the knowledge of the horrors of the extermination of the Jews? We should not believe we can comprehend the incomprehensible, we may not compare the incomparable, we may not inquire because to make the horrors an object of inquiry is to make the horrors an object of discussion, even if the horrors themselves are not questioned, instead of accepting them as something in the face of which we can only fall silent in revulsion, shame and guilt. Should we only fall silent in revulsion, shame and guilt? To what purpose?[16]

One must note here that Schlink is questioning the historical moment of the Holocaust, not the narrator's account of his seduction by Hanna Schmitz. The answer to that question (what would you have done being seduced by an older woman?) is implicit in the novel itself and parallels Bertolt Brecht's claim in "The Ballad of Sexual Obsession" ("Die Ballade von der sexuellen Hörigkeit") from the *Three Penny Opera* (1928) that sexual obsession has all *men* in thrall: "Who destroys those who destroy all others? Women."[17] That male sexuality does not allow choice seems a rather archaic notion, one very much at home at least in a fictive Weimar culture evoked so powerfully after the fall of the Wall. Indeed, in an odd way Schlink's novel is a retelling of Brecht's text with Michael as virginal Polly and Hanna as criminal MacHeath. And Schlink serves as the rider who comes in at the last moment to rescue MacHeath from the gallows of history.

But it is not Weimar and not the sexual obsessions of MacHeath and Polly that frame Schlink's historical perspective. The exchanges about "'What would you have done?'" echo (parody?) the sung lyrics "What would you do?" of Fräulein Schneider's aria in the musical *Cabaret* of 1966, in which she bemoans breaking her engagement to her aging, lower middle-class Jewish boyfriend, acknowledging her fear of what the Nazis might do.

The Reader has sold in excess of 500,000 copies in Germany and has become the staple text in high school classes about the Holocaust. In 2004, when the television network ZDF published a list of the one hundred favorite books of German readers, it was fourteenth, the second-highest ranking for any contemporary German novel on the list. (Number one on the list was J. R. Tolkien's *The Lord of the Rings*, and number two was *The Bible*.)

Schlink's novel had worldwide popularity, even becoming an "Oprah Book Club Selection" in 2009 after the film version, written by the British dramatist David Hare and directed by the English theater and film director Stephen Daldry, was released in December 2008. The actors were British and German. Schlink was delighted with the filmic representation as it indicated a worldwide reception of his view of the Holocaust:

> Question by Erin Shea of Oprah's Book Club [March 30, 2009]: Your novel deals with the idea of the legacies we are left and how we grapple with the consequences afterward. You wrote, "The pain I went through because of my love for Hanna was, in a way, the fate of my generation, a German fate." How do you feel about the movie interpretation of this theme?
>
> A: I really like the movie, and I think everyone involved in the movie did a great job [with this theme]. The focus of the movie is more on Hanna than it was in the book, which was on Michael, and certainly there are many good reasons for that. You have this powerful actress, Kate Winslet, while Michael is represented by two different actors, so there is less identification for the viewer as a result. Also, I think they were more interested in talking about her than him. Still, I think the second-generation situation comes out pretty well.[18]

The question, again echoing Grünbein's comment on bodies and their legacies, is whether it is possible to make a self-consciously self-righteous novel into an even worse sex film about the Holocaust? That there had been a global take on sex and the Holocaust before *The Reader* was recognized by critics:

> Sex and Nazis dared previously to be mixed together only in sleazy Hollywood movies such as *Ilsa—She Wolf of the SS* (1975), but *The Reader* is, after four nominations for the Golden Globes, now an Oscar nominee. In films such as the Auschwitz saga *Sophie's Choice* (1982) the love story was still part of a Holocaust drama, in *The Reader* the Holocaust has become part of a love story.[19]

This is slightly too harsh, as the Holocaust film *The Night Porter* (*Il Portiere di notte*), the 1974 film by Italian director Liliana Cavani, starring Dirk Bogarde and Charlotte Rampling, showed how the perversity of fear, horror, and sexual abuse can mimic love. But as another critic noted, "What is missing [in the film] is any sensitivity for [the novel's] complex material. The reader generates pity for the figure of the former KZ guard, so that he can take objection to her murderous deeds. This is above all: global cynicism."[20] Global cynicism becomes a response to German *Bildung*; Hollywood deforms the subtlety of the novel, which was a serious attempt to come to terms with the past as well as an international best seller. (In such arguments the latter is evidence for the validity of the former. The commonplace is that Hollywood transforms great fiction into kitsch. It can also turn kitsch into kitsch, but that is often overlooked.)

The Reader was a blockbuster. It received four Golden Globe nominations: best drama, best director, best supporting actress (won), and best screenplay, and Oscar nominations for: performance by an actress in a leading role (won), achievement in cinematography, achievement in directing, best motion picture of the year, and best adapted screenplay. The British actress Kate Winslet, brought to celebrity by her role in *Titanic*, played the camp guard Hanna Schmitz in the film and was clear about her and its sexual dimension: "I've just been nominated for two Academy Awards, I've played the lead in the highest-grossing film ever. And guess what I'm not skinny. I like having a good pair of tits on me and a good ass."[21] Or as Gemma Wheatley commented: "This year's Baftas [The British Oscars] look sure to be the breast of British as English rose Kate Winslet has been nominated twice. The gorgeous actress, whose natural boobs have taken America by storm, looks set to repeat her Golden Globe triumph. She is nominated for two gongs in the leading actress category for *Revolutionary Road* and *The Reader*."[22]

Indeed, the nude scenes in the film served as one of the most talked about aspects of this film. Bodies do matter now in any worldwide reception of German *Bildung*. And it is not Hollywood that invents them; they are intrinsic to Schlink's garbled message. The seduction here is not of the Nazis seducing the German people, but of global mass culture in the historical dress of the German past seducing the cinema audience.

A Normal Feminist Fiction?

If *Der Vorleser* as novel and then film was a global success as a representation of the Holocaust, the local and then global fame of the television presenter, actress, singer, and author Charlotte Roche's first novel *Feuchtgebiete* (2008) was a surprise to the author as well as to the German reading public. A true product of the post-Wall multicultural world, Charlotte Elisabeth Grace Roche was born in 1978 in High Wycombe, England, and came to Germany as a child. Her novel was an immediate best seller in post-Wall Germany, representing a German version of the global fascination with feminism and the representation of the woman's body in feminist fiction:

> For ten weeks Charlotte Roche's intimate novel *Wetlands* has stood at the top of the *SPIEGEL* best-seller list. More than 650 000 copies have been sold—spurred by massive media coverage and the use of many talk-show appearances. Almost all of her book-tour dates have been sold out. Now the next round of hype is about Roche abroad. Her German publisher, Du Mont from Cologne, has sold *Wetlands* licenses in 16 countries, including South Korea, Taiwan, and Britain. Similarly, an American publishing house has now bought in to the phenomenon: Grove Press in New York.[23]

Roche's *Feuchtgebiete* (published in English as *Wetlands* in 2008) had sold over 1,500,000 copies in Germany by early 2009. It was the eighth most-translated European novel between 2008 and 2009.[24] Its broader, international economic success, as with *The Reader*, was the sole measure of its importance.

Yet its very success was read by some German critics as a continuation of the exploitative best-seller fiction of the day:

> We have in these would-be transgressors all conceivable forms of penetration and bodily excretions! Some in the voice of the Swiss writer Urs Allemann, whose 1991 execrable story "Baby Fuckers" presented his total artistic bankruptcy at the Ingeborg Bachmann Competition in Klagenfurt,

> where he talked about the deflowering of a young child. Or in the form of the French art historian Catherine Millet, an avowed liberal, who tried with the description of her multiple orgasms in swinger clubs and elsewhere (*The Sexual Life of Catherine M.*, 2001) to shock the audience in a similar way as her compatriot Michel Houellebecq had in his tasteless literature of debauchery.[25]

The novel is immediately measured against American (read) global pseudo-feminist popular culture:

> Who would have thought that after *Sex and the City* there would still be taboos? In the U.S. series, the protagonists are portrayed as unscrupulous gossips, who discuss vibrators and threesomes loudly in restaurants. At the very thought of how Roche's protagonist Helen Memel left used tampons in the elevator in order to spread bacteria, even the SATC ladies would blush. A taboo is a taboo is a taboo. And only Charlotte Roche literally craps on it. This *Sex and the City* failed to do, since these American series in their alleged obscenity are really much too prudish.[26]

If we again evoke Marx and the penalty of historical repetition, then *Wetlands* represents a parody of the global comic, or at least critical, feminist novels of the 1970s, such as Erica Jong's *Fear of Flying* (1973) and even Elfriede Jelinek's *Lust* (1989). *Wetlands* is what happens to feminist fiction now become tragedy in its post-Wall seriousness. Indeed, the hallmark of this type of body fixation in Schlink and Roche is their unmediated, excruciating seriousness that shouts *BILDUNG*—pay attention—to the reader. No post-modern playfulness, only the heavy handedness of mass-market serious fiction. (How far from Goethe's own sense of the novel as the vehicle for *Bildung* in *Wilhelm Meister* with its experimental structures and playful awareness of the reader's often misplaced interests and desires.)

Roche frames her family tragedy with Helen Memel's, the novel's protagonist's, fixation on her self-abused body and on her failed suicide. "What would you do? . . ." implicitly asks the narrator, when you are confronted with parents who are divorced. Self-cutting seems to be Roche's answer. This bourgeois tragedy is at the heart of the matter. Given the ubiquity of divorce in contemporary Germany (almost 40 percent of all marriages are dissolved and marriage itself is becoming a rarer choice for all couples), this seems a rather old-fashioned reason for personal trauma within fiction (rather than within life experience). Indeed, it reads like a pastiche of Walt Disney's 1961 film *The Parent Trap*, itself based on Erich Kästner's novel *Das doppelte Lottchen* (1949), where the trauma of divorce is at the core of the actions of children whose sole aim in life is to reconcile their parents:

> "Hello?"
>
> "It's me." Mom.
>
> Mom and Dad want to visit today. They both want to avoid being there at the same time as the other. I want so bad for my parents to be in a room together. I want them to visit me here in the hospital at the same time.
>
> I have a plan.
>
> Mom asks, "When is your father coming?"
>
> "You mean your ex-husband? The one you used to love so much? At four."
>
> "Then I'll come at five. Will you make sure he's gone by then?"
>
> I say yes but think no. As soon as I've hung up with Mom, I call Dad and tell him it would be good for me if he came at five.[27]

Without pushing the analogy too far, one can note that Kästner's reputation, certainly in the twenty-first century, is as one of the quintessential Weimar writers, better known for being the author of the novel on which yet another Disney film was based, *Emil and the Detectives* (novel: 1929; film—not Billy Wilder's 1931 version but Walt Disney's version of 1964) than any other. Weimar returns as the cultural model for post-Wall Germany even if only slightly displaced in to postwar kitsch, but who really knows the difference?

If Kästner's middle-class family norms are at the core of the trauma that is written on the protagonist's body, then it is of little surprise that the conclusion of the novel is an attempt to merge the body politics of the pseudo-feminist text with the middle-class construction of a new family:

> We walk slowly down the hall. We don't hold hands. Suddenly he stops and puts the bag down. He's changed his mind.
>
> No. He steps behind me and ties the gown closed over my bum. He wants to cover me up in public. Good sign. He picks up the bag again, and we walk on.
>
> "If I'm living with you, I guess you'll want to sleep with me."
>
> "Yeah, but I won't do you up the ass for now." He laughs. I laugh.
>
> "I'll only sleep with you if you can suck a pony's insides out through its asshole."

> "Is that even possible—or do you not want to sleep with me?"
>
> "I just always wanted to say that to a guy. Now I have. And I do want to. But not today. I'm too tired." We walk to the glass door.
>
> I smack the button, the door swings open, I throw back my head and scream.[28]

The scream is, of course, Edvard Munch's high-culture image from the 1890s, humanity trapped on the bridge of life, now reduced to being the punch line in a post-Wall best seller. So much for *Bildung* after the Wall.

Now we can think about sex and culture, Durs Grünbein's bodies in culture in a rather different light. The punch line of the Jewish-Russian-German popular performer and novelist Wladimir Kaminer's *Es gab keinen Sex im Sozialismus* (*There Is No Sex in Socialism*) (2009) is that the absence of sex under *Soviet* communism is the punch line to a bad joke! He narrates how a press conference of "America specialists" was held under communism and one of the speakers decried the blatant commercial exploitation of sexuality in the West. Speaking in English one of the panelists stated: "We have no sex in the Soviet Union!"[29] There is indeed, however, much commercial exploitation of sex after the Wall in German culture and in its worldwide marketing. It is, however, *very serious* in its intentions. Even in those objects exported to represent German *Bildung* in the realm of science, this seriousness is to be found.

Science Sex Sells

In what is surely the most important German cultural export after the fall of the Wall, the Heidelberg anatomist Gunther von Hagens' plastination exhibition(s) "Body Worlds/Life Cycle" (in multiple, worldwide exhibitions after 1995 with more than 60 million visitors in 45 cities around the world by 2010, according to von Hagen's website and still circulating), there is a tableau of two people having sex. Here, too, there may be an evocation of *Bildung*, and indeed of Goethe's paragon of *Bildung* Wilhelm Meister. At least one commentator noted that von Hagens exhibits those views "epitomized by Goethe's figures of the prosektor and proplastiker. The former, driven by scientific curiosity, is willing to destroy, even desecrate, the human form to obtain knowledge. The latter demurs at such mutilation of our physical body, wondrous even in death—seeking instead to rejoin what the prosektor has pulled apart, to restore human dignity."[30] Von Hagens clearly agrees with the seriousness of his project, as he "defended the exhibit saying that it combines the two greatest taboos of sex and death and is a lesson in biology, but is 'not meant to be sexually stimulating.'"[31] As with the Sex Films as

Aufklärungsfilme (sex education films) in the Weimar Republic, it is not pornography if the intent seems serious and the work is presented as part of *Bildung*. In Weimar it necessitated a serious "frame" for the film narrated by someone in a lab coat; today, one only needs the title "Professor Dr." appended to the entrepreneur to have the same effect. The critics quickly saw this mock seriousness:

> Following the motto coarse, coarser, and coarsest, the plastinator always has to top himself. His plastized copulating pair is in a full moon position. He lies stiffly on his back, she kneeling with her back toward him. The missionary position would have been too unspectacular. Today, since the *Kama Sutra* cannot shock us, von Hagens' horror and sex show is oh, so educative. It teaches the visitor much more than biology class. This has nothing to do with pornography; it cannot be sexually arousing![32]

The tendency is clear. Dietrich Wildung, the director of Berlin's Egyptian Museum (who should know) called the exhibit "mummy pornography" (not "cultural pornography" but close enough): "If you say that 'sex sells, then you can certainly say that 'mummy sells.' Showing that which should not be shown has a certain prickling sensation.'"[33] Kai Wegner, an MP for the Christian Democratic Union, observed, concerning the effect of von Hagens' work: "I am firmly convinced that he just breaks taboos again and again in order to make money. It is not about medicine or scientific progress. It is marketing and moneymaking pure and simple."[34] It is post-Wall German *Bildung pur*.

This is the normal world of mass-marketed post-Wall German culture on a global scale. Not Durs Grünbein's "new interiority" with its complex physicality and obsessive corporality but rather global, exploitative sex clothed in the discourses of Holocaust memory and feminism and science. In 20 years, Germany has indeed become a "normal" nation, as Peter Pulzer imagined in 1994, and its cultural products, at least in the global marketplace, reveal a normativity that is both global and yet very local. The seriousness of *Bildung* combined with the themes of commercial Western mass and popular culture produced three "blockbusters" for post-Wall German *Bildung*: von Hagens, Schlink, and Roche. To quote Fredrick II of Prussia in a very different context: "denn hier muß ein jeder nach seiner Fasson selig werden," "for here must each in their own way seek the paths of righteousness."

Notes

1. "Wohlstand für alle heißt heute Bildung für alle." *Rede von Bundeskanzlerin Angela Merkel bei der Festveranstaltung „60 Jahre Soziale Marktwirtschaft" am*

12. Juni 2008 in Berlin. http://www.bundesregierung.de/nn_774/Content/DE/Bulletin/2008/06/64-1-bk-soziale-marktwirtschaft.html. Accessed July 12, 2011.

2. Peter Pulzer, "Unified Germany: A Normal State?" *German Politics* 3 (1994): 1–17.
3. "Was (Büchner) gelang, war nichts Geringeres als eine vollständige Transformation: Physiologie aufgegangen in Dichtung. Und es war nicht ein Sonderweg, wie sich herausgestellt hat, es war der Anfang einer Versuchsreihe, die bis zum heutigen Tag fortgeführt wird." http://www.deutscheakademie.de/druckversionen/buechner_1995.html. Accessed July 12, 2011.
4. "Zweifellos hat der Körper in der Literatur Konjunktur. Eine ganze Schar von Autoren ist seit einiger Zeit damit beschäftigt, das Geheimnis des Lebens mit pathologischem Eifer zu erforschen und anatomische Texte mit dem Skalpell zuzuschneiden. So entsteht eine Literatur, die man als neue 'neue Innerlichkeit' bezeichnen konnte, die das Öffnen des Körpers für schockierend und das Wühlen in den Eingeweiden für tiefgründig hält." Ibid.
5. *Pace* Peter Novick, *The Holocaust in American Life* (New York: Houghton Mifflin Co., 1999).
6. See my *Diseases and Diagnoses: The Second Age of Biology* (New Brunswick, NJ: Transaction Books, 2010).
7. *Die Tageszeitung* (Berlin) (April 6, 1990).
8. *Berliner Morgenpost* (May 18, 2009), 30.
9. *The [London] Telegraph* (May 19, 2009).
10. Jeremy Adler, "Bernhard Schlink and 'The Reader,'" *Times Literary Supplement* (March 3, 2002): 17.
11. Cynthia Ozick, "The Rights of History and the Rights of Imagination," *Commentary* (March 1999): 22–27, here 23.
12. "Sie legte die Arme um mich, die eine Hand auf meine Brust und die andere auf mein steifes Geschlecht." Schlink, Bernard. *Der Vorleser*. (Zürich: Diogenes, 1997): 26. In English Bernard Schlink, *The Reader*, trans. Carol Brown Janeway (New York: Pantheon, 1997): 25.
13. "Wir standen uns nackt gegenüber, aber sie hätte mir in ihrer Uniform nicht abweisender vorkommen können." Ibid., 36. In English, 36.
14. "Was hätten Sie denn gemacht?"
15. "Alle empfanden" she "den Wortwechsel gewissermaßen gewonnen hatte." Ibid., 108. In English, 114.
16. "Was sollte und soll meine Generation der Nachlebenden eigentlich mit den Informationen über die Furchtbarkeiten der Vernichtung der Juden anfangen? Wir sollen nicht meinen, begreifen zu können, was unbegreiflich ist, dürfen nicht nachfragen, weil der Nachfragende die Furchtbarkeiten, auch wenn er sie nicht in Frage stellt, doch zum Gegenstand der Kommunikation macht und nicht als etwas nimmt, vor dem er nur in Entsetzen, Scham und Schuld verstummen kann. Sollen wir nur in Entsetzen, Scham und Schuld verstummen? Zu welchem Ende?" Ibid., 99–100. In English, 104.
17. "Wer kocht ihn ab, der alle abkocht? Weiber."

18. www.oprah.com/oprahsbookclub/Bernhard-Schlink-Interview.../5. Accessed July 12, 2011.
19. "Sex und Nazis wagte Hollywood früher nur in Schmuddelfilmen wie *Ilsa—She Wolf of the SS* (1975) zu vermischen, doch *Der Vorleser* gilt nach vier Nominierungen für die Golden Globes nun auch als Oscar-Kandidat. In Filmen wie der Auschwitz-Saga *Sophies Entscheidung* (1982) war die Liebesgeschichte noch Teil eines Holocaustdramas; in *Der Vorleser* ist der Holocaust Teil eines Liebesdramas." Lars-Olav Beier, *Der Spiegel* (December 20, 2008).
20. "Was fehlt, ist jedwede Sensibilität für den vielschichtigen Stoff. *Der Vorleser* drängt zum Mitleid mit der Figur einer ehemaligen KZ-Wärterin, statt dass er an ihren mörderischen Taten Anstoß nähme. Das ist vor allem eines: globalisierter Zynismus." Cristina Nord, *taz* (February 24, 2009).
21. "World According to Kate Winslet," *The Canberra Times* (February 7, 2009).
22. Gemma Wheatley, "Great Winslet; Kate's a Double Hit in Baftas Triumph," *Daily Star* (January 16, 2009).
23. "Seit zehn Wochen steht Charlotte Roches Intim-Roman *Feuchtgebiete* auf Platz eins der SPIEGEL-Bestsellerliste, rund 650 000 Exemplare wurden bisher verkauft - angefeuert durch ein gewaltiges Medienecho und etliche diszipliniert absolvierte Talkshow-Auftritte. Fast alle Termine ihrer Lesereise sind ausverkauft. Jetzt geht der Rummel um Roche in die nächste Runde: im Ausland. Ihr deutscher Verlag, DuMont aus Köln, hat die "Feuchtgebiete"-Lizenzen in bisher 16 Länder verkauft, darunter Südkorea, Taiwan und Großbritannien. Auch ein amerikanischer Verlag hat mittlerweile zugegriffen: Grove Press aus New York." *Der Spiegel* (June 2, 2008).
24. Miha Kovač and Rüdiger Wischenbart, *Diversity Report 2009: Cultural diversity in translations of books: Mapping fiction authors across Europe*. www.wischenbart.com/translation. Accessed July 12, 2011.
25. "Haben uns diese Möchtegern-Grenzgänger nicht bereits mit allen nur vorstellbaren Formen von Penetration und Körperausscheidungen behelligt? Etwa in Person des Schweizers Urs Allemann, der 1991 mit der unsäglichen Erzählung 'Babyficker' beim Klagenfurter Ingeborg-Bachmann-Wettbewerb seinen künstlerischen Offenbarungseid leistete, als er von der Defloration eines Kleinstkindes erzählte. Oder in Gestalt der bekennend freizügigen französischen Kunsthistorikerin Catherine Millet, die mit der Schilderung ihrer multiplen Orgasmen in Swinger-Clubs und anderswo ("Das sexuelle Leben der Catherine M.," 2001) in ähnlicher Weise zu schockieren versuchte wie ihr Landsmann Michel Houellebecq in seiner abgeschmackten Libertinage-Literatur." Hendrik Werner, *Die Welt* (April 11, 2008).
26. "Wer hätte gedacht, dass es nach "Sex and the City" noch Tabus gibt? In der US-Serie werden die Protagonistinnen als hemmungslose Tratschtanten dargestellt, die im Restaurant lautstark über Vibratoren und 'flotte Dreier' diskutieren. Bei der Vorstellung, wie die Roche-Protagonistin Helen Memel gebrauchte Tampons im Aufzug liegen lässt, damit sich ihre Bakterien raumgreifend verbreiten mögen, würden jedoch selbst die SATC-Damen erröten. Ein Tabu ist ein Tabu ist ein Tabu. Und nur Charlotte Roche scheißt drauf,

wörtlich. Das hat *Sex and the City* nicht geschafft, dafür sind amerikanische Serien in ihrer vermeintlichen Obszönität viel zu prüde." Franziska Seyboldt, *taz* (May 17, 2008).
27. Charlotte Roche, *Wetlands*, trans., Tim Mohr (New York: Grove Press, 2009): 95.
28. Ibid., 229.
29. Wladimir Kaminer, *Es gab keinen Sex im Sozialismus: Legenden und Missverständnisse des vorigen Jahrhunderts* (Berlin: Goldmann, 2009): 3.
30. Charleen M. Moore and C. Mackenzie Brown, "Gunther von Hagens and Body Worlds: The Anatomist as Prosektor and Proplastiker," *The Anatomical Record Part B: The New Anatomist* 276B (2004): 8–14, here 8.
31. *The Guardian* (London) (May 7, 2009).
32. "Nach dem Motto krass, krasser, am krassesten muss sich der Plastinator immer wieder selbst toppen. Sein Plastinat Kopulierendes Paar zeigt ein Paar in Vollmondstellung. Er stocksteif auf dem Rücken liegend, sie von ihm abgewandt auf ihm kniend. Die Missionarsstellung wäre wohl zu unspektakulär gewesen. Heute, da uns das Kamasutra nicht mehr schocken kann, ist von Hagens' Grusel- und Sexkabinett ach so lehrreich. Es lehrt die Besucher mehr als jeder Biologieunterricht. Mit Pornografie hat das nichts zu tun, es soll nicht sexuell erregen!" Sofia Shabafrouz, *taz* (May 6, 2009).
33. "'Wenn man sagt: Sex sells, dann kann man sagen: the mummy sells. Die Veröffentlichung dessen, was nicht veröffentlicht gehört, hat einen gewissen prickelnden Reiz.'" *Spiegel Online* (September 28, 2007).
34. http://www.thefrisky.com/post/246-body-politic-sex-statues-cause-controversy-in-berlin/. Accessed July 12, 2011.

Bibliography

Barrett, Bruno. *Responding to Wetlands: Helen Memel's Psychoanalysis*. Translated by Christine Grimm. Norderstedt: Books on demand, 2009.

Donahue, William Collins. *Holocaust as Fiction: Bernhard Schlink's "Nazi" Novels and Their Films*. Semiotics and Popular Culture. New York: Palgrave Macmillan, 2010.

Hall, Katharina. "The Author, the Novel, the Reader and the Perils of 'neue Lesbarkeit': A Comparative Analysis of Bernhard Schlink's *Selbs Justiz* and *Der Vorleser*." *German Life and Letters* 59 (2006): 446–67.

Jespersen, T. Christine, Alicita Rodríguez, and Joseph Starr, eds., *The Anatomy of Body Worlds: Critical Essays on the Plastinated Cadavers of Gunther Von Hagens*. Jefferson, NC: McFarland & Co., Publishers, 2008.

Liu, Sarah. "The Illiterate Reader: Aphasia after Auschwitz." *Partial Answers: Journal of Literature and the History of Ideas* 2 (2009): 319–342.

Sehgal, Parul. "The Feminine Mystique." *Publishers Weekly* 256 (7) (2009): 106.

Schlink, Bernard. *Der Vorleser*. Zürich: Diogenes, 1997.

———. *The Reader*, trans. Carol Brown Janeway. New York: Pantheon, 1997.

Swales, Martin. "Sex, Shame and Guilt: Reflections on Bernhard Schlink's *Der Vorleser* (*The Reader*) and J. M. Coetzee's *Disgrace*." *Journal of European Studies* 33 (2003): 7–22.

Taberner, Stuart, and Paul Cooke, eds., *German Culture, Politics, and Literature into the Twenty-First Century beyond Normalization*. Rochester: Camden House, 2011.

van Dijck, José. *The Transparent Body: A Cultural Analysis of Medical Imaging*. Seattle: University of Washington Press, 2004.

2

Exploring *Master Keaton's* Germany: A Japanese Perspective on the End of the Cold War

Shannon Granville

In the late 1980s and early 1990s, the Japanese manga (serialized comic book) series *Master Keaton* entertained readers with the globe-trotting adventures of its Anglo-Japanese protagonist, Taichi Hiraga-Keaton. Keaton's work as an insurance investigator for Lloyd's of London took him on journeys throughout Europe and Asia, including visits to a newly reunited Germany. When the *Master Keaton* manga was adapted as an anime (animated television series) in the late 1990s, four of the manga's Germany-centric plots were included in the 39 stories selected for animation. The television episodes faithfully reproduced the original illustrations and dialogues created a decade earlier, and were aimed at the same mature audience for which the manga had been written.

The Berlin Wall is a near-constant presence in *Master Keaton*'s Germany. Several of Keaton's adventures involve families divided by the events of the Cold War, and many of the series' plots explore the complex questions laid bare by the fall of the Wall and the subsequent changes in the political and social landscape of Europe. By looking at the four Germany-based stories presented in both the *Master Keaton* manga and anime, it is possible to examine how the *Master Keaton* series provides a uniquely Japanese perspective on the Cold War, one that reflects Japan's singular position as a demilitarized ally of the West during the Cold War era. By focusing on the experiences of ordinary

German people, rather than the grander geopolitical narrative of politicians and international relations, the *Master Keaton* series explains the end of the Cold War in terms of redefining one's individual and national identity—a predicament with which a Japanese audience could sympathize, in light of Japan's own experiences in the half century since the end of World War II.

1989: The Japanese Perspective

By the end of the 1980s, it was clear that Europe's postwar settlement—the boundaries that had shaped nations, identities, and ideologies for more than a generation—would have to be redefined. The destruction of the Berlin Wall precipitated a profound change in the national boundaries of central Europe, directly addressing the division of Germany that had been a product of the outcome of World War II. In light of this change in the status quo, other European countries began to reassess their own internal affairs, a trend that led most notably to the outbreak of civil war in Yugoslavia and the dissolution of the Soviet Union by the end of 1991. Yet these transformations were not confined to Europe; on the other side of the world, Japan was also experiencing monumental changes that would redefine its own post–World War II identity. The death of Emperor Hirohito in January 1989 was a watershed moment for Japan, a break in historical continuity as politically and symbolically charged as the fall of the Wall.[1] By 1989, the emperor had reigned for more than 60 years, longer than the Wall had been in place and longer than most of Japan's population had been alive.[2] In one sense, the emperor's death was a final farewell to World War II, the symbolic passing of the destruction that the war had wrought on Japan—and that Japan had wrought during the war. At the same time, the emperor had been a symbol of national continuity,[3] embodying Japan's ability to survive the hardships of the immediate postwar years under U.S. occupation and to rebuild itself into an economic powerhouse that rivaled (and seemed poised to eclipse)[4] its former occupier. Yet this rebuilding had been possible because much of the political, economic, and social stability of Japan's postwar settlement relied on the nation's ability to avoid openly confronting its past.

In *Embracing Defeat*, the definitive study of U.S.-occupied Japan, John Dower compares the formative desires of defeated Japan and Germany: "More than anything else . . . the losers [of World War II] wished both to forget the past and to transcend it."[5] Japan's postwar perspective rested on the sharp ideological break between the prewar and wartime years and a future that began almost from the moment the Japanese military started to lay down its arms. In the words of historian Carol Gluck, when Emperor Hirohito announced Japan's surrender on August 15, 1945, "It was as if history itself had been severed and could start again from scratch."[6] The occupation forces encouraged this historical division through a textbook reform agenda that was designed to "demilitarize and democratize"[7] Japan by revising the school curriculum to "train students for 'a peaceful state and society.'"[8] Japan's 1951 constitution further encouraged a break with the nation's militaristic past by creating a national identity that purportedly had evolved beyond the use of war. Article 9 of the constitution defined postwar Japan's approach to international relations: "[T]he Japanese people forever renounce war as a sovereign right of the nation and the threat or use of force as a means of settling international disputes."[9] Under the U.S. defense aegis that developed in response to the Korean War and other Cold War military commitments, Japan was freed from the need to confront the national-defense and international-trade concerns that had fueled its prewar expansionist foreign policy. In Japan, as in Germany, the Cold War superpower conflict helped to enable economic recovery from the 1950s onward and provided a broad geopolitical framework in which both countries could work to transcend their tarnished pasts—often by overlooking, ignoring, or neglecting to examine certain unfavorable aspects of those pasts.[10]

The end of the Cold War forced individuals, groups, and entire countries to reassess events, memories, and ideologies that had shaped their ideas of self and nationhood for at least half a century. As literature professor Aleida Assmann commented on the European perspective on this forced confrontation: "After a period of extremely stylized and standardized images of the past, many European nations were finally confronting conflicting, painful, and shameful memories. As the protective shields and myths collapsed, they gave way to controversy and more complex representations."[11] In Japan as well, the standardized and sanitized images of the past were coming under attack from international and domestic critics. On the day of Emperor Hirohito's funeral in February 1989, small but vocal groups of protestors held rallies that denounced their late emperor as a fascist war criminal.[12] In March 1989, in the face of street protests and diplomatic pressure from China, South Korea, and the Soviet Union, prime minister Noboru Takeshita was forced to retract comments he had made at the emperor's funeral that downplayed Japanese aggression in East Asia during World War II.[13] And October 1989 saw the culmination of a five-year-long lawsuit brought against the Japanese government by prominent Japanese historian Saburo Ienaga, one of the original authors of the antimilitaristic Japanese history textbooks of the postwar period.[14]

The court battle was the third anti-textbook-censorship suit that Ienaga had filed in 25 years. In this suit, as in the others, Ienaga claimed that the government's textbook oversight committee had violated his freedom of speech by demanding that he rewrite his proposed history textbooks to omit passages on controversial topics related to Japanese war crimes of the 1930s and 1940s. Although the Tokyo courts ruled that the government had the right to continue to oversee and certify textbooks for use in Japanese schools, the specific instances of committee interference with the content of Ienaga's textbooks were declared unconstitutional. Though the October 1989 settlement awarded Ienaga only nominal damages (¥100,000, about US$700 at 1989 exchange rates),[15] the case marked a crucial moment in one leading Japanese critic's campaign to educate his country's rising generation about some of the less reputable moments of their national history.[16]

Even as Europeans struggled to make sense of the new political and social order after the fall of the Wall, Japan faced an uncertain transition from its postwar period into an era that promised to be less easy to define and describe. One Japanese writer and artist, however, directly confronted the contradictions of the post-Wall, post–Cold War world by illustrating the repercussions of the fall of the Berlin Wall on the lives of ordinary people. In Naoki Urasawa's *Master Keaton*, the Wall within the mind (*die Mauer im Kopf*, to use the German phrase)[17] is not nearly so easy to dismantle or destroy.

Manga: A Brief Overview

Japanese artist Hokusai (1760–1849) was among the first illustrators to use the term "manga" to describe artwork that commented on and caricatured the social order, but some art historians claim that the tradition of Japanese comic art can be traced back more than a thousand years, to illustrations in scrolls of popular Heian-period (794–1185) tales.[18] Modern manga began to appear in the Meiji era (1868–1912), where closer contact with Europe and America allowed Japanese manga artists to draw inspiration from cartoons in the British periodical *Punch* and serial comic strips printed in American newspapers. By the 1930s, newspaper cartoons and manga magazines were widely available to an increasingly literate public.[19] Government-imposed restrictions on subject matter and paper availability curtailed the publication of manga during the war and immediate postwar period, but manga began to assume a more prominent place in Japanese popular culture in the 1950s and 1960s, as manga authors such as Osamu Tezuka (often referred to as the "father of manga") achieved literary fame for their detailed, nuanced stories and artwork.[20] By the late 1980s, serial manga magazines and collected volumes of manga series were ubiquitous in Japan. The popular and fast-selling medium, with stories aimed at all audiences and demographics, built up a devoted readership whose purchasing figures remained steady or increased even as other sections of the Japanese publishing market slumped or were marked by inconstant sales.[21] This trend of growing manga sales in a stagnant or declining general book market was also apparent outside Japan, extending beyond the English-language market often favored for translations. In Germany, for instance, the market for German-language translations of Japanese manga (and its Korean counterpart, known as *manhwa*) grew from around €3 million in 1997 to €66 million nearly a decade later.[22] These sales drew on the growing population of young readers who had been introduced to manga and anime through German-language dubs of several popular children's anime titles, and formed a smaller but no less devoted readership than that found in Japan.

In spite of the medium's increasing domestic and international popularity, academic studies of manga are a relatively new field that is still being developed; institutional legitimacy has been a slow process, even in Japan.[23] English-language studies of manga tend to focus on series currently available in officially licensed English translation and have been restricted by the difficulty (until very recently) of acquiring complete translations of manga series—which depend on the constraints of English-language publishers, preventing translations from being completed for months or even years after a series ends publication in Japan. This scholarly focus on manga in English translation generally does not explore the vast quantity of manga that English-language publishers do not consider commercially viable, and therefore neglects series that may have cultural or historical value but have remained mostly inaccessible to readers with limited knowledge of Japanese. Yet recent research has noted the inherent critical value of manga studies as an approach to Japanese culture: "Manga . . . reflects the reality of Japanese society . . . [and] social phenomenon, such as social order and hierarchy, sexism, racism, ageism, classism, and so on."[24] In the case of *Master Keaton*, the series presents a Japanese perspective on the reality of post-Wall German society, drawing its source material from current headlines to examine the lives of ordinary Germans in extraordinary times.

Master Keaton: An Overview

Master Keaton was created by artist and writer Naoki Urasawa and story artist Hokusei Katsushika (the pen name of another writer whose true identity has been disputed).[25] It was serialized in the men's manga magazine *Big Comic Original*, published by Shogakukan. The series first appeared at the end of 1988 and ran through mid-1994, a total of 144 chapters that later were collected in 18 individual volumes. Shortly thereafter, the animation studio Madhouse acquired the rights to animate the *Master Keaton* series, building on the studio's previous collaboration with Urasawa to animate his popular sports manga *Yawara! A Fashionable Judo Girl* (broadcast from 1988 to 1992). In 1998, Nippon Television aired the first of 24 half-hour *Master Keaton* episodes, which were then bundled with 15 original video animation (OVA) episodes included as bonus materials in the Japanese DVD releases. All 39 TV and OVA anime episodes were adapted straight from their corresponding manga stories with minimal revision of the original illustrations and dialogues.[26]

Within the broad publishing categories used to describe target audiences for manga, *Master Keaton* is a *seinen* (young men's) series, written primarily for young men between 18 and 30 years of age. In keeping with the interests of their readership demographic, typical seinen manga story lines include sports stories about individual athletes or sports teams, slice-of-life drama or comedy series, police procedurals or crime dramas, or tales of corporate or political intrigue. The *Master Keaton* manga story lines often combine these plots, with light-hearted comic tales interwoven among the darker or more action-oriented stories. Above all, seinen series like *Master Keaton* aim to attract readers with sophisticated plot lines, detailed artwork, and careful attention to the details of entertaining storytelling.[27]

Keaton's creator, Naoki Urasawa, was an established manga author whose previous series reflected his interest in contemporary settings and topical story lines, often incorporating real-life events. The title character of *Yawara! A Fashionable Judo Girl* (1986–1993), for instance, is a young judo prodigy training to compete in the 1992 Barcelona Olympics, the debut year of women's judo as an Olympic sport.[28] In addition to Urasawa's interest in using contemporary events as a source of inspiration, his series often feature German characters and settings. His award-winning suspense series *Monster*, published shortly after *Master Keaton* ended, was set predominantly in West and East Germany in the late 1980s and early to mid-1990s and used the complicated post-Wall political situation as a motivating factor in its story.[29] In interviews, Urasawa frequently discusses his interest in contemporary topics, developing characters that are directly involved in the hard-hitting issues of their day.[30] He has also expressed concerns that many young Japanese people are ill-informed about history and politics, especially their own. In a 2009 interview with the *Daily Yomiuri* newspaper about his forthcoming manga *Billy Bat*, set in Japan in the first decade after World War II, Urasawa said, "A lot of young Japanese don't know who Japan fought against in World War II. . . . It's nice to feel that peace is enough, but we need to study the past so we can create our future . . . I don't expect people to use this manga to study history, but I do hope to draw some attention to that period. You know, how did our society become what it is?"[31] The *Master Keaton* series is one of Urasawa's early attempts to illustrate this continuity of past and future.

Master Keaton: The Protagonist

The story of *Master Keaton* revolves around the adventures of its title character, Taichi Hiraga-Keaton, an insurance investigator and part-time archaeology professor. Keaton, the son of a Japanese zoologist and a well-to-do Englishwoman, spent much of his childhood in England. As a young man, he displayed considerable academic and athletic ability—several flashback episodes reflect on his time as an archaeology student at Oxford University and as a soldier (and, later, a survival-training instructor) for the elite British Special Air Service (SAS). Those who meet this ordinary-looking man are often astonished to learn that his SAS combat experience includes on-the-ground service in the Falklands War and in the commando team that ended the May 1980 siege of the Iranian Embassy in London.[32] Keaton's unique skills and talents, particularly his training in various forms of improvised nonlethal weaponry, drive much of the plot and action sequences of the series. Many *Master Keaton* stories require Keaton to negotiate the release of hostages, defuse bombs, thwart terrorist plots, track down missing persons, and uncover complicated cases of insurance fraud or murder. However, many other *Master Keaton* stories—including the four post–Cold War Germany stories adapted for the anime series—seldom focus on Keaton or his work at all. In these stories, Keaton's part in the drama is to be in the right place at the right time, in order to provide assistance to someone in need before continuing on to his next adventure.

In this role, Keaton's character is familiar to both Japanese and Western audiences: the wandering do-gooder, beholden to no one but himself and his sense of justice. In Japan, this character trope drives the plot of numerous popular *jidaigeki*—"period dramas"—that have aired on television since the 1950s, often in near-constant reruns.[33] Jidaigeki, with their basic cast of honorable warriors and dastardly villains and their settings on the lawless fringes of society, are stylistically similar to the Western; one of the best-known associations of these genres is the direct adaptation of Akira Kurosawa's 1954 film *Seven Samurai* to John Sturges' 1960 film *The Magnificent Seven*.[34] Keaton's often peripheral role in his own series places him in the established category of jidaigeki heroes, such as the lone samurai warrior who appears only to right wrongs and solve other characters' problems before continuing his solitary journey. Yet there is a more subtle connection between jidaigeki and post–Cold War Germany. Traditionally, jidaigeki are set in the Sengoku or "Warring States" period of the fifteenth century, or in the Bakumatsu period of the mid-1800s, shortly before the Meiji Restoration. Both eras were times of sociopolitical upheaval, in which old values and traditions were swept away and Japan was forced to redefine itself on a fundamental national level. Furthermore, jidaigeki seldom deal with the politicians, diplomats, or other powerful figures who steer the broader course of history. Instead, they focus on the fates of individuals who have been overtaken by events and must cope with an uncertain future. This format provides a suitable backdrop for *Master Keaton*'s Germany stories, allowing Keaton—a neutral observer with a sympathetic ear and a resourceful mind—to participate in other characters' stories, helping to reconcile the past and the present.

Master Keaton: The Stories

Although few dates are specified within the stories, the *Master Keaton* manga appears to take place in chronological order and in real time, with individual stories set at or around the time of their publication. The four Berlin Wall manga and anime stories take place between mid-1989 and late 1992. The first Germany story, "Journey with a Lady," was published shortly before the fall of the Wall (June/July 1989), but the other three are set in the early 1990s and specifically mention the fall of the Wall and related post–Cold War events, such as the collapse of Yugoslavia in 1991. The anime series is more episodic in its approach—it presents the same four Germany stories, but does not follow the original publication order.[35] As a result, the audience receives the impression that these four stories could have taken place at any time within a few years after the fall of the Wall. However, because the storyboard and dialogue remain relatively unchanged between manga and anime, very little information or context is lost in the adaptation from print to screen.

In "Journey with a Lady," Keaton is traveling south by train through Germany to Basel, Switzerland. The elderly German-speaking woman who shares his train compartment is far from an ideal traveling companion; she is rude and demanding, seems to be paranoid that she is being followed, and even takes advantage of Keaton's generous nature by guilting him into buying a new ticket for her after she insists that her purse, passport, and train tickets have been stolen. As payment for his help, she gives him a ring that she claims is a precious family heirloom and tells him a sad story about her privileged upbringing in Bohemia, the deprivations she suffered after World War II, and the Czechoslovakian government agents who are following her in an effort to acquire the remnants of her family's fortune. Keaton reluctantly agrees to help the woman cross the Swiss border without a passport and successfully tricks the train's passport control officers into letting her pass unchallenged. But once they are safely in Switzerland, Keaton confronts the lady, pointing out the contradictions in her story. Pressed for a real answer, she finally reveals the truth: her name is Helmina Welf, widow of a well-to-do landowner in Saxony, whose world had been torn apart when Germany was divided and the Cold War border cut right through the family's land.[36] She has spent half her life searching for her only son Otto, who, as a young boy, had disappeared (presumably, was abducted) while playing near the border, and finally managed to track him down—only to discover that Otto is now an officer in the East German military.[37] All she has left is her work for the anticommunist resistance, which brought her to Switzerland and into Keaton's life.

"Journey with a Lady" is Keaton's first encounter with the effects of the Berlin Wall and the division of Germany on ordinary individuals. Helmina Welf, an elderly woman making her way across a hostile political landscape without a home, family, country, or real identity, is representative of the Berlin Wall's devastating effect on individuals and families. If the story is intended to take place in real time and correspond with the date of its initial publication, then it would be set in West Germany and Switzerland only months before the fall of the Wall.[38] Helmina Welf's entire identity is caught up in the idea of the Wall, both as the physical barrier that divided her land and family and as an emotional barrier she carries with her, making her a walking symbol of the "Wall in the mind" theme that appears in the other post-Wall Germany stories. Although the Wall's presence and its barriers are still very real in "Journey with a Lady," in the next story, "The Scent Is the Key," Keaton comes face-to-face with the unexpected effects of the end of the Cold War and the actual destruction of the Berlin Wall.

In "The Scent Is the Key," set in 1991, Keaton is contacted by an elderly man named Heinen, a retired official in the West German Social Democratic Party. Heinen asks Keaton to investigate the suspicious death of Heinen's old friend Franz Seidel, whose body had been discovered in the stairwell of his apartment building. Keaton looks into the matter and speaks to one of Seidel's neighbors, a nurse who confirms she had found the body when it was still warm and "had the smell of a person who had just died."[39] Although most of his lines of questioning suggest that the elderly Seidel had died of heart failure, Keaton discovers that another neighbor had seen a strange man with an umbrella standing outside Seidel's apartment building shortly before Seidel's death, and the nurse who found Seidel's body had detected a faint odor of peaches in the stairwell, near the body. When Keaton goes to a nearby park to meet Heinen and share his findings, he arrives just in time to see Heinen being attacked by a man carrying an extraordinary weapon: a gas gun concealed in a furled umbrella. The gas gun contains potassium cyanide, detectable afterward only by its sweet, peach-like odor.[40] Keaton saves Heinen's life, but is unable to prevent the attacker from escaping. Badly shaken by his attempted murder, Heinen informs Keaton of the real reason for his desire to investigate Seidel's death—both he and Seidel had been coerced into working as East German spies while living in West Germany, and the man who had killed Seidel and tried to kill him was their former Stasi case officer. Both Heinen and Seidel had been blackmailed into a life of espionage: Seidel had been an officer in a concentration camp, and Heinen had family in East Germany who would have been sentenced to hard labor if he had not complied with his case officer's demands. Even though the fall of the Wall freed them from their case officer's control, Heinen remarks sadly, "If the Wall was still there, Seidel would still be alive."[41]

"The Scent Is the Key" draws on contemporary revelations of East German espionage in West Germany, including infiltration at senior levels of the West German government and political movements (as demonstrated by Heinen's story).[42] It also contains extensive shots of the Wall, both intact and during its demolition. The anime presents several dramatic background images of German citizens gathered around the Wall and the Brandenburg Gate, with television and flashback scenes of the Wall as a barbed-wire-topped border and as slabs of concrete being disassembled. It even adds a more "concrete" reminder of the Wall's presence by showing that Heinen has kept a small piece of the demolished Wall as an ironic souvenir, displayed on the mantelpiece alongside a photograph of himself as a younger man shaking hands with Social Democratic Party leader and West German chancellor Willy Brandt.[43] The story gives the Wall multiple dimensions, allowing it to act in turns as a barrier and a shield against the painful past—which, in Heinen's own words, is "the smell that never goes away." By the time of the story, the Wall has been reduced to a fragment of concrete, a memento preserved by an elderly man. Nonetheless, the Wall has lost none of its power as a symbol of the past that both Heinen and Seidel hoped to forget—until that past caught up with them, with fatal results.

The 1992 story "Family" sees Keaton traveling to Leipzig in search of Karl Neumann, a former East German Olympic swimmer who had won a gold medal for his record-breaking performance in the 1988 Seoul Olympics. Neumann's reputation had been shattered when the reunification of Germany prompted sports authorities to look into the training regimes of East German athletes, and Neumann became one of several East German world-record holders and medal winners to be stripped of their prizes for taking performance-enhancing drugs. Keaton finds Neumann living like a vagrant in an abandoned Soviet officers' club, along with several families of Yugoslavian refugees. He refuses Keaton's offer to return to the sporting world, claiming that the "vitamin pills" and special injections he had been given to improve his swimming abilities had irreparably damaged his body, leaving him as worthless as his Olympic record. It takes a near-death experience for Neumann to realize that he does have a worth beyond his athletic prowess and that his real purpose in remaining alive is to stay with his new "family": the Yugoslavian refugees who had taken him in when everyone else rejected him.

"Family" addresses two controversial issues of post–Cold War Germany: the doping scandals of East German athletes and the country's treatment of the Yugoslavian refugees. Neumann's story is taken straight from the headlines of the time, as new revelations about the East German sports authorities' involvement in their athletes' use of performance-enhancing drugs rocked the international sporting world in the run-up to the 1992 Barcelona Summer Olympics.[44] Like Neumann, East German athletes who received performance-enhancing drugs often were told that they were receiving injections of medications or vitamin supplements.[45] By the late 1990s, clinical research had documented the drug consumption of hundreds of East German athletes, including Olympic medalists. Werner Franke and Brigitte Berendonk, two authorities on sports doping and its institutionalized use in East Germany, stated that these athletes "included most GDR gold medal winners in the swimming events since the 1976 Olympic Games . . . and all GDR gold medal winners in the throwing events of the 1988 Games."[46] Neumann's shame over his unwilling complicity in the doping scandal leads him to remark despairingly to Keaton that his achievements were "just like this country's socialism. It was all an illusion. The country collapses, and my record and honor fall with it."[47] As in the other Germany stories, the fall of the Wall tore down the wall within Neumann's mind—in this case exposing the deception perpetrated on him and other athletes who were unwitting pawns in Cold War games.

"Family" also brings up another controversial issue of post–Cold War Europe: the chaos caused by the onset of civil war in Yugoslavia in 1991 and the negative reaction of many German people to the influx of refugees. In the story, a gang of Leipzig skinheads attempts to storm the abandoned officers' club and drive out the Yugoslavian families, forcing Keaton and Neumann to help fight off the attackers. After their attackers retreat, one of the Yugoslavian men pragmatically sums up the reasons behind the skinheads' hatred of the refugees: "They thought they'd prosper after unification, but instead they're unemployed. They feel inferior to those who live in the West. They need others to look down on in order to forget that."[48] Urasawa does not intend his audience to feel sympathetic toward the East German skinheads, but by placing their actions in the context of Germany's struggles after reunification he provides them with a motive that resonates with the theme of the greater identity crisis many Germans faced in the immediate post–Cold War period.[49]

The 1993 story "Wall in One's Heart," as its name suggests, makes the most open reference to the effects and lasting repercussions of the Berlin Wall on German families. Keaton has been hired to find Rosa Schreider, the daughter of an East German computer programmer who had to leave his pregnant wife Louisa behind when he escaped to West Germany in the late 1970s. Louisa Schreider had been imprisoned in an East German labor camp after her husband's defection, and gave birth to Rosa in the camp. Keaton's research reveals that Louisa had died in the camp when Rosa was still very young, and the orphaned girl had been adopted by an East German communist party leader not long after her mother's death, but as a teenager Rosa had run away from her adoptive parents and vanished without a trace. Keaton manages to track down some other runaways who had known the missing girl, only to discover that an angry, embittered Rosa is planning to find her father and, in her words, "destroy his life as revenge" for leaving her and her mother to die on the other side of the Wall.[50] Only Keaton's resourcefulness is able to prevent a tragedy, reunite Rosa and her father, and begin the reconciliation process in a family that was poised to become one more casualty of the Cold War.

"Wall in One's Heart" makes the most specific connections between the Wall as a physical symbol of the Cold War and as a psychological barrier between the present and the past. The Japanese word *kokoro* is translated as "heart" in this context, but the word also can be loosely translated as "mind" (in the broader sense of one's thoughts and feelings), echoing the "Wall in the mind" phenomenon. As Schreider's second wife, another East German defector, remarks to Keaton, "Three years ago, the wall separating us came down . . . but the wall within his heart will remain until he sees his daughter again." The story once again brings up the cruel treatments of the East German penal system, but adds an even more sinister dimension by providing information about the fate of the children of East Germany's political prisoners. Like Rosa, these children were taken from their parents, effectively made wards of the state, and placed for adoption with East German families.[51] Through his enquiries, Keaton learns that Rosa's experiences with her adoptive family were far more traumatic than he had first imagined: Rosa had run away after she attacked her East German adoptive father, who had attempted to sexually abuse her and exploit his power over her, the child of political criminals. Although the story leaves the audience with hope that Rosa and her father will be able to overcome the terrors in their past, it stops short of declaring all will be well. The walls within the heart built up by years of separation, as well as Rosa's history of childhood neglect and abuse, have yet to be dismantled. The last page of the original manga version of "Wall in One's Heart" adds a final bleak note:

> [T]he former East German ministry for youth and education, which administered the adoptions, has denied [the forced adoption of the children of East Germany's political prisoners]. In order for the current German government to avoid further confusion, the policy still has not been acknowledged, though the search for East German government orphans has been going on for two years.[52]

Urasawa's conclusion suggests that even though Keaton was able to reunite one family, the Schreider family's troubles are a single instance of a much larger crisis in national identity, which the new German government had not been able to address or even acknowledge.

Conclusion

With the fall of the Berlin Wall, the rapid deconstruction of the Cold War status quo prompted concern from commentators on either side of the crumbling wall—a mindset embodied in international relations theorist John Mearsheimer's 1990 comment, "We may . . . wake up one day lamenting the loss of the order that the Cold War gave to the anarchy of international relations."[53] As another historian noted, for Japan, as for Germany, "[s]uddenly all the givens of this country's postwar attitudes toward the outside world seemed obsolete. It could no longer simply leave its security to the United States while it concentrated on cultivating its economic growth."[54] Nor, for that matter, could either country refuse to confront the uncomfortable questions and unpleasant histories that had been ignored, altered, or erased during the Cold War.

Carol Gluck's study of public memory in postwar Japan provides a thoughtful perspective on the relationship between individual memories and national histories, applicable both in the immediate aftermath of the war and the new historical continuity that characterized the post–Cold War, post-Wall world:

> In postwar Japan . . . the premise of historical discontinuity in 1945 rested somewhat precariously in the individual psyche. For each person had to weave together the past and present out of autobiographical stuff that often displayed no clear inner difference before and after August 1945. . . .[T]hey were the same people, inhabiting the same self, status, and daily life, except that the frame of social meaning had been changed around them. How they remembered—and reconciled—their postwar experience became part of their personal narratives, the stories they told themselves and passed on to their children.[55]

In Naoki Urasawa's *Master Keaton*, the title character acts as an ideal guide through the historical discontinuities of post–Cold War Europe: Japanese and English, scholar and soldier, intimately familiar with the delicate balancing act required to reconcile multiple personal and national identities. Keaton's function in the four post-Wall Germany stories mirrors the function that at least one Japanese scholar of international relations imagined for a post–Cold War Japan—"its longstanding mission of reconciling tensions between East and West in an emerging chaotic and antagonistic world order":

> Japan should not identify itself with either side, West or East, but rather should attempt to play a mediating role between the two in an age of global interconnection which otherwise supposedly engenders a sense of uncertainty and antagonism to cultural difference in the world at large.[56]

Through its hero's mediating role, *Master Keaton* draws attention to the conflicts and contradictions of the post-Wall and post–Cold War world by presenting the stories of those who have suddenly lost the stability provided by the status quo: an elderly woman who had lost her husband and only son behind the Wall, an Olympic hero broken by the system that had once lofted him to the heights of victory, a pair of unwilling spies for whom freedom meant death, a traumatized teenage girl driven to avenge her mother's death at the hands of the communist state. Not all the stories end on a hopeful note; at best, they end with wary optimism about what the future may hold. Yet all four stories of *Master Keaton*'s Germany emphasize that the only effective way to approach an unclear future is to confront and accept the past and work within its continuities, however painful they may be—advice that applied as much to *Master Keaton*'s Japanese audience as it did to the characters on the page.

Notes

1. Carol Gluck, "The Past in the Present," in *Postwar Japan as History*, ed. Andrew Gordon (Berkeley, CA: University of California Press, 1993), 92.
2. In 1989, only 11.6 percent of the Japanese population was 65 years of age or older. The Shōwa era—the designation given to Emperor Hirohito's reign—lasted just over 62 years, from December 1926 to January 1989. Florian Coulmas, *Population Decline and Ageing in Japan: The Social Consequences* (London: Routledge, 2007), 4.
3. Herbert P. Bix, "Emperor Hirohito in 20th Century History: The Debate Rekindles," Japan Policy Research Institute Working Paper 92 (June 2003), accessed July 6, 2010, at http://www.jpri.org/publications/workingpapers/wp92.html. Accessed July 6, 2010.
4. For an example of American concerns about Japanese economic power in the late 1980s, see Clyde V. Prestowitz, *Trading Places: How We Are Giving Our Future to Japan and How to Reclaim It* (New York: Basic Books, 1989).
5. John Dower, *Embracing Defeat: Japan in the Wake of World War II* (New York: W. W. Norton/The New Press, 1999), 24.
6. Carol Gluck, quoted in Stephen Strange, "General Introduction," *Showa Japan: Political, Economic, and Social History, 1926–1989* (Vol. 1) (London: Routledge, 1998), 2.
7. Yoko H. Thakur, "History Textbook Reform in Allied Occupied Japan, 1945–52," *History of Education Quarterly* 35, no. 3 (Autumn 1995), 261.
8. Saburo Ienaga, "The Glorification of War in Japanese Education," *International Security* 18, no. 3 (Winter 1993–94), 116. For a broader discussion of these policies, see Thakur, "History Textbook Reform," 261–278; and Dower, *Embracing Defeat*, 247–251.
9. Cited in Ienaga, "Glorification of War," 116.
10. Roberta N. Haar, *Nation-States as Schizophrenics: Germany and Japan as Post–Cold War Actors* (Westport, CT: Greenwood Publishing, 2001), 3.
11. Aleida Assmann, "Europe: A Community of Memory?" *GHI Bulletin* 40 (Spring 2007), 16.
12. Stephen S. Large, *Emperor Hirohito and Showa Japan: A Political Biography* (London: Routledge, 1992), 201.
13. David E. Sanger, "Takeshita Now Admits World War II Aggression," *New York Times*, March 7, 1989.
14. A more detailed description of the Ienaga lawsuits appears in Thakur, "History Textbook Reform," 275–76.
15. Conversion data from Board of Governors of the Federal Reserve System, "EXJPUS: Japan/U.S. Foreign Exchange Rate," updated July 1, 2010, http://research.stlouisfed.org/fred2/data/EXJPUS.txt. Accessed July 3, 2010.
16. Yoshiko Nozaki and Hiromitsu Inokuchi, "Japanese Education, Nationalism, and Ienaga Saburō's Textbook Lawsuits," in *Censoring History: Citizenship and Memory in Japan, Germany, and the United States*, ed. Laura Hein and Mark Selden (Armonk, NY: M. E. Sharpe, 2000), 117.

17. Hunter Bivens' and Paul Kubicek's contributions to this volume also address this psychological issue.
18. This trend is evident in wide-ranging studies such as Brigitte Koyama-Richard, *One Thousand Years of Manga* (Paris: Flammarion, 2008). However, the legitimacy of this historical tradition of manga has been disputed in the literature; see Nicholas A. Theisen, "The Problem of Manga Theories as Theories of Japanese Identity," conference paper presented at the Graphic Engagement Conference, Purdue University, Indiana (September 2, 2010).
19. Kinko Ito, "A History of Manga in the Context of Japanese Culture and Society," *Journal of Popular Culture* 38, no. 3 (February 2005), 460–464.
20. For an assessment of Tezuka's contribution to the development and cultural legitimacy of postwar manga, see Natsu Onoda Power, *God of Comics: Osamu Tezuka and the Creation of Post–World War II Manga* (Jackson, MI: University Press of Mississippi, 2009).
21. Alison A. Raab. "Manga in Academic Library Collections: Definitions, Strategies, and Bibliography for Collecting Japanese Comics." Master's paper, University of North Carolina (November 2005), http://etd.ils.unc.edu:8080/dspace/bitstream/1901/233/1/alisonaraab.pdf. Accessed July 1, 2010. For more specific publishing figures, see Kinko Ito, "The Manga Culture in Japan," *Japan Studies Review* 4 (2000), 1–16.
22. See, for instance, Bernd Dolle-Weinkauff, "The Attractions of Intercultural Exchange: Manga Market and Manga Reception in Germany" (April 2006), http://www.cct.go.kr/data/acf2006/mobile/mobile_0402_Bernd%20Dolle-Weinkauff.pdf. Accessed April 2, 2011; and "Japanese Manga Made in Germany," Deutsche Welle (November 8, 2006), http://www.dw-world.de/dw/article/0,,2230500,00.html. Accessed April 3, 2011.
23. Mio Bryce, Jason Davis, and Christie Barber, "The Cultural Biographies and Social Lives of Manga: Lessons from the Mangaverse," *SCAN: Journal of Media Arts Culture* 5, no. 2 (September 2008), http://scan.net.au. Accessed July 1, 2010. The article also provides a telling quote: "Not even a decade ago, professors at Japanese universities refused to supervise students who intended to graduate with a thesis on manga . . . some out of disdain for the topic, others out of an awareness of their own ignorance" (Jacqueline Berndt, "Considering Manga Discourses: Location, Ambiguity, Historicity," in *Japanese Visual Culture: Explorations in the World of Manga and Anime,* ed. M. W. Macwilliams (Armonk, NY: M. E. Sharpe, 2008), 300).
24. Ito, "A History of Manga," 456.
25. There has been some controversy over the identity of "Hokusei Katsushika," including speculation that the earliest *Master Keaton* stories were written by more than one author. Additional information on this controversy is available (in Japanese) at "*Katsushika Hokusei to Urasawa Naoki to Nagasaki Takashi*" [Hokusei Katsushika and Naoki Urasawa and Takashi Nagasaki] n.d., http://serifugyakuyunyuu.com/lines/keaton/katsu/. Accessed July 6, 2010.

26. Although the manga series has not been translated into English, English-language production companies Pioneer Entertainment and Geneon USA acquired the license to release an official English-language edition, and English subtitled and dubbed DVDs were released in 2003 and 2004. The English DVDs, unlike the Japanese DVDs, treat the entire set of 39 episodes as if it were a complete broadcast series. At the time of this writing, the license for the English-language DVDs has lapsed.
27. Sharon Kinsella, *Adult Manga: Culture and Power in Contemporary Japanese Society* (Honolulu: University of Hawaii Press, 2000), 44–45.
28. The *Yawara* manga and anime series increased public interest in women's judo, and the Japanese press capitalized on the series' popularity with their own real-life "Yawara"—the nickname they gave to teenage judo athlete Ryoko Tamura, who later won a silver medal in women's judo at Barcelona. The Yawara anime series (1989–1992) even showed a real-time countdown to the Barcelona Olympics at the end of every episode. See "Naoki Urasawa" in *Manga Design,* ed. Masanao Amano and Julius Wiedemann (Cologne, Germany: Taschen, 2004), 118.
29. "Shogakukan Manga Award: Past Winners," Comics.Shogakukan.co.jp, n.d., http://comics.shogakukan.co.jp/mangasho/rist.html. Accessed May 10, 2010.
30. See "An Interview with Naoki Urasawa," in Naoki Urasawa and Hokusei Katsushika, *Keaton's Master Book* (Tokyo: Shogakukan, 2000), 17–21.
31. "On a Wing and a Prayer: Hitmaker Mangaka Urasawa Turns to Period Fiction with His New *Billy Bat,*" *The Daily Yomiuri*, February 13, 2009. http://proquest.umi.com/pqdweb?did=1644461471&Fmt=2&clientId=45714&RQT=309&VName=PQD. Accessed July 25, 2009. For more information about general political engagement in postwar and post–1989 Japan, see Wilhelm Vosse, "The Emergence of a Civil Society in Japan," in *Japanstudien 11. Japan im 21. Jahrhundert—Zivilgesellschaft und Staat in der postindustriellen Moderne* (Munich: Deutsches Institut für Japanstudien, 1999), http://www.dijtokyo.org/doc/dij-jb_11-vosse.pdf. Accessed July 25, 2009.
32. Hokusei Katsushika and Naoki Urasawa, "*Chiisana kyojin* [Little Giant]," *Master Keaton* 3:2 (Tokyo, Shogakukan, 1989), 52.
33. Mark Schreiber, "Jidaigeki: TV Heroes Face a New Century," *Japan Quarterly* 47, no. 4 (October–December 2000), 58.
34. Dolores P. Martinez, *Remaking Kurosawa: Translations and Permutations in Global Cinema* (London: Macmillan, 2009), 117.
35. Three of the four animated stories were aired on television during the series' initial run. The fourth, "The Scent Is the Key," was made as an OVA (see note 24) and included as an extra episode in the DVD release.
36. More in-depth information in the manga places the Welf family squarely in the center of the division between the Germanies: "[The Welfs] had owned land from [Bad] Langensalza to Melsungen for almost eight hundred years. But after the war, when Germany was divided . . . A fence was built in the middle of their garden. The east side of the garden became East German

territory. The west side, where the house was, was in West Germany." Hokusei Katsushika and Naoki Urasawa, "*Kifujin to no tabi* [Journey with a Lady]," *Master Keaton* 2, no. 1 (Tokyo: Shogakukan, 1989), 23. (Translated by S. Granville.)

37. "Journey with a Lady," *Master Keaton: Excavation II*, DVD, Pioneer Entertainment Ltd., 2004.
38. Katsushika and Urasawa, "Journey with a Lady," *Master Keaton* 2, no. 1, 3–28.
39. "The Scent Is the Key," *Master Keaton: Life and Death*, DVD, Pioneer Entertainment Ltd., 2004.
40. The murder method and weapon are similar to those used in the actual KGB-orchestrated assassinations of two Ukrainian émigrés in 1957 and 1958. For more information, see Christopher Andrew and Vasili Mitrokhin, *The Mitrokhin Archive: The KGB in Europe and the West* (London: Penguin, 2000), 470.
41. "The Scent Is the Key," *Master Keaton: Life and Death*, DVD, Pioneer Entertainment Ltd., 2004.
42. See, for instance, "Files Could Shed New Light on East German Spies," Deutsche Welle, July 9, 2003, http://www.dw-world.de/dw/article/0,,915181,00.html. Accessed December 1, 2009.
43. Heinen's work as an East German mole within the upper ranks of the Social Democratic Party echoes the espionage case of Günter Guillaume, an East German spy who worked closely with Brandt in the 1960s and 1970s and whose exposure precipitated Brandt's downfall in 1974.
44. John Tagliabue, "Political Pressure Dismantles East German Sports Machine," *New York Times* (February 12, 1991), B11; Michael Janofsky, "Coaches Concede That Steroids Fueled East Germany's Success in Swimming," *New York Times* (December 3, 1991).
45. Werner W. Franke and Brigitte Berendonk, "Hormonal Doping and Androgenization of Athletes: A Secret Program of the German Democratic Republic," *Clinical Chemistry* 43, no. 7 (1997), 1268.
46. Ibid., 1269.
47. "Family," *Master Keaton: Fakers and Fiends*, DVD, Pioneer Entertainment Ltd., 2004.
48. Ibid.
49. Paul Kubicek's contribution to this volume focuses on the perspectives of former East Germans, primarily on their ambivalent feelings about the outcome of Germany's reunification.
50. "Wall in One's Heart," *Master Keaton: Killer Conscience*, DVD, Pioneer Entertainment Ltd., 2004.
51. "Exhibitions," The Berlin Hohenschönhausen Memorial, n.d., http://en.stiftung-hsh.de/document.php?cat_id=CAT_237&special=0. Accessed October 10, 2009.
52. Naoki Urasawa and Hokusei Katsushika, "*Kokoro no kabe* [Wall in One's Heart]," *Master Keaton* 14, no. 2 (Tokyo: Shogakukan, 1992), 52. (Translated by S. Granville.)

53. John J. Mearsheimer, "Why We Will Soon Miss the Cold War," *Atlantic Monthly* Online (August 1990), http://www.theatlantic.com/politics/foreign/mearsh.htm. Accessed December 1, 2009. Robert Snyder and Timothy White's contribution to this volume addresses in greater depth the broader post–Cold War debate in international relations theory.
54. Alex Macleod, "Japan: A Great Power Despite Itself," in *Role Quests in the Post–Cold War Era: Foreign Policies in Transition*, ed. Philippe G. Le Prestre (Quebec City, Canada: McGill-Queen's University Press, 1997), 88.
55. Gluck, "The Past in the Present," 76.
56. Koichi Iwabuchi, *Recentering Globalization: Popular Culture and Japanese Transnationalism* (Durham, NC: Duke University Press, 2002), 13.

Bibliography

Master Keaton Manga and Anime

Urasawa, Naoki, and Hokusei Katsushika. "*Kifujin to no tabi* [Journey with a Lady]." *Master Keaton* 2:1: 3–28. Tokyo: Shogakukan, 1989.

———. "*Nioi no kagi* [The Scent Is the Key]," *Master Keaton* 7:4: 81–106. Tokyo: Shogakukan, 1991.

———. "*Kazoku* [Family]," *Master Keaton* 11:8: 183–208. Tokyo: Shogakukan, 1992.

———. "*Kokoro no kabe* [Wall in One's Heart]," *Master Keaton* 14:2: 27–52. Tokyo: Shogakukan, 1992.

———. *Keaton's Master Book*. Tokyo: Shogakukan, 2000.

"Family." *Master Keaton: Fakers and Fiends*. DVD: Pioneer Entertainment Ltd., 2004.

"Journey with a Lady." *Master Keaton: Excavation II*. DVD: Pioneer Entertainment Ltd., 2004.

"The Scent Is the Key." *Master Keaton: Life and Death*. DVD: Pioneer Entertainment Ltd., 2004.

"Wall in One's Heart." *Master Keaton: Killer Conscience*. DVD: Pioneer Entertainment Ltd., 2004.

Other Sources

Andrew, Christopher, and Vasili Mitrokhin. *The Mitrokhin Archive: The KGB in Europe and the West*. London: Penguin, 2000.

Assmann, Aleida. "Europe: A Community of Memory?" *GHI Bulletin* 40 (Spring 2007): 11–25.

Bix, Herbert P. "Emperor Hirohito in 20th Century History: The Debate Rekindles." Japan Policy Research Institute Working Paper 92 (June 2003). Accessed July 6, 2010, available at: http://www.jpri.org/publications/workingpapers/wp92.html.

Board of Governors of the Federal Reserve System. "EXJPUS: Japan/U.S. Foreign Exchange Rate," updated July 1, 2010. Accessed August 10, 2010, available at: http://research.stlouisfed.org/fred2/data/EXJPUS.txt.

Bryce, Mio, Jason Davis, and Christie Barber. "The Cultural Biographies and Social Lives of Manga: Lessons from the Mangaverse," *SCAN: Journal of Media Arts Culture* 5, no. 2 (September 2008). Accessed July 1, 2010, available at: http://scan.net.au.

Coulmas, Florian. *Population Decline and Ageing in Japan: The Social Consequences.* London: Routledge, 2007.

Dolle-Weinkauff, Bernd. "The Attractions of Intercultural Exchange: Manga Market and Manga Reception in Germany," April 2006. Accessed April 2, 2011, available at: http://www.cct.go.kr/data/acf2006/mobile/mobile_0402_Bernd%20Dolle-Weinkauff.pdf.

Dower, John. *Embracing Defeat: Japan in the Wake of World War II.* New York: W. W. Norton/The New Press, 1999.

"Exhibitions." The Berlin Hohenschönhausen Memorial. n.d. Accessed October 10, 2009, available at: http://en.stiftung-hsh.de/document.php?cat_id=CAT_237&special=0.

"Files Could Shed New Light on East German Spies." Deutsche Welle, July 9, 2003. Accessed December 1, 2009, available at: http://www.dw-world.de/dw/article/0,,915181,00.html.

Franke, Werner W., and Brigitte Berendonk. "Hormonal Doping and Androgenization of Athletes: A Secret Program of the German Democratic Republic," *Clinical Chemistry* 43 no. 7 (1997): 1262–1279.

Gluck, Carol. "The Past in the Present." In *Postwar Japan as History*, ed. Andrew Gordon, Berkeley, CA: University of California Press, 1993.

Haar, Roberta N. *Nation-States as Schizophrenics: Germany and Japan as Post–Cold War Actors.* Westport, CT: Greenwood Publishing, 2001.

Ienaga, Saburo. "The Glorification of War in Japanese Education," *International Security* 18, no. 3 (Winter 1993–94): 113–133.

"An Interview with Naoki Urasawa." In *Keaton's Master Book*. Tokyo: Shogakukan, 2000.

Ito, Kinko. "A History of Manga in the Context of Japanese Culture and Society." *Journal of Popular Culture* 38, no. 3 (February 2005): 456–475.

———. "The Manga Culture in Japan," *Japan Studies Review 4* (2000): 1–16.

Iwabuchi, Koichi. *Recentering Globalization: Popular Culture and Japanese Transnationalism.* Durham, NC: Duke University Press, 2002.

Janofsky, Michael. "Coaches Concede That Steroids Fueled East Germany's Success in Swimming." The *New York Times,* December 3, 1991.

"Japanese Manga Made in Germany." Deutsche Welle (November 8, 2006). Accessed April 3, 2011, available at: http://www.dw-world.de/dw/article/0,,2230500,00.html.

"*Katsushika Hokusei to Urasawa Naoki to Nagasaki Takashi*" [Hokusei Katsushika and Naoki Urasawa and Takashi Nagasaki]. n.d. Accessed July 6, 2010, available at: http://serifugyakuyunyuu.com/lines/keaton/katsu/.

Katsushika, Hokusei, and Naoki Urasawa. "*Chiisana kyojin* [Little Giant]." *Master Keaton* 3:2. Tokyo: Shogakukan, 1989.

Kinsella, Sharon. *Adult Manga: Culture and Power in Contemporary Japanese Society.* Honolulu: University of Hawaii Press, 2000.

Koyama-Richard, Brigitte. *One Thousand Years of Manga.* Paris: Flammarion, 2008.

Large, Stephen S. *Emperor Hirohito and Showa Japan: A Political Biography.* London: Routledge, 1992.

Macleod, Alex. "Japan: A Great Power Despite Itself." In *Role Quests in the Post–Cold War Era: Foreign Policies in Transition*, ed. Philippe G. Le Prestre. Quebec City, Canada: McGill-Queen's University Press, 1997.

Martinez, Dolores P. *Remaking Kurosawa: Translations and Permutations in Global Cinema.* London: Macmillan, 2009.

Mearsheimer, John J. "Why We Will Soon Miss the Cold War," *Atlantic Monthly* Online (August 1990). Accessed December 1, 2009, available at: http://www.theatlantic.com/politics/foreign/mearsh.htm.

"On a Wing and a Prayer: Hitmaker Mangaka Urasawa Turns to Period Fiction with His New *Billy Bat*," *The Daily Yomiuri* (February 13, 2009). Accessed July 25, 2009, available at: http://proquest.umi.com/pqdweb?did=1644461471&Fmt=2&clientId=45714&RQT=309&VName=PQD.

"Naoki Urasawa." In *Manga Design*, ed. Masanao Amano and Julius Wiedemann. Cologne, Germany: Taschen, 2004.

Nozaki, Yoshiko, and Hiromitsu Inokuchi. "Japanese Education, Nationalism, and Ienaga Saburō's Textbook Lawsuits." In *Censoring History: Citizenship and Memory in Japan, Germany, and the United States*, ed. Laura Hein, and Mark Selden. Armonk, NY: M. E. Sharpe, 2000.

Power, Natsu Onoda. *God of Comics: Osamu Tezuka and the Creation of Post–World War II Manga.* Jackson, MI: University Press of Mississippi, 2009.

Prestowitz, Clyde V. *Trading Places: How We Are Giving Our Future to Japan and How to Reclaim It.* New York: Basic Books, 1989.

Raab, Alison A. "Manga in Academic Library Collections: Definitions, Strategies, and Bibliography for Collecting Japanese Comics." Master's Paper, University of North Carolina (November 2005), Accessed July 25, 2009, available at: http://etd.ils.unc.edu:8080/dspace/bitstream/1901/233/1/alisonaraab.pdf.

Sanger, David E. "Takeshita Now Admits World War II Aggression," *New York Times* (March 7, 1989).

Schreiber, Mark. "Jidaigeki: TV Heroes Face a New Century," *Japan Quarterly* 47, no. 4 (October–December 2000): 57–58.

"Shogakukan Manga Award: Past Winners." Comics.Shogakukan.co.jp (n.d.). Accessed May 10, 2010, available at: http://comics.shogakukan.co.jp/mangasho/rist.html.

Strange, Stephen. *Showa Japan: Political, Economic, and Social History, 1926–1989* (Vol. 1). London: Routledge, 1998.

Tagliabue, John. "Political Pressure Dismantles East German Sports Machine." The *New York Times*, (February 12, 1991): B11.

Thakur, Yoko H. "History Textbook Reform in Allied Occupied Japan, 1945–52," *History of Education Quarterly* 35, no. 3 (Autumn 1995): 261–278.

Theisen, Nicholas A. "The Problem of Manga Theories as Theories of Japanese Identity." Conference paper presented at the Graphic Engagement Conference, Purdue University, Indiana, September 2, 2010.

Vosse, Wilhelm. "The Emergence of a Civil Society in Japan," in *Japanstudien 11. Japan im 21. Jahrhundert—Zivilgesellschaft und Staat in der postindustriellen Moderne* (Munich: Deutsches Institut für Japanstudien, 1999). Accessed July 25, 2009, available at: http://www.dijtokyo.org/doc/dij-jb_11-vosse.pdf.

3

From the Berlin Wall to the West Bank Barrier: How Material Objects and Psychological Theories Can Be Used to Construct Individual and Cultural Traits

Christine Leuenberger

Psychologists Speaking of Borders and Walls[1]

The rise of nation-states in the nineteenth century was based on the assumption that diverse populations aspired to be part of ethnically and culturally homogenous groups; however, instead of national identities preceding state formation, states mostly preceded shared cultural identities. Indeed, the historian Eric Hobsbawm points out that the French state paved the way to the formation of the French people: consequently, only after a state and its borders become established does its population become more homogenous and culturally uniform. At the same time, cultural divergences at the borders increase and notions that surrounding nations are different, including members of the same nation living on the "wrong side" of state lines, become increasingly prevalent.[2] The rise of nation-states thus not only consolidated national identities, but their borders also became powerful dividers between supposedly different cultures.

The psychological effects of the proliferation of borders—whether fortified or open—has not escaped the attention of "the psy sciences."[3] Physical borders can become what Sherry Turkle calls "evocative objects,"[4] which can summon and come to embody various social and cultural meanings. Objects are therefore not inherently meaningful, yet various social groups construct them as being significant in different ways and use them to develop and assimilate ideas and catalyze changes in the way phenomena are perceived. For instance, what for GDR officials was the "anti-fascist protection bulwark" (Antifaschistische Schutzwall) that was to protect East Germany from fascist and capitalist infiltration, was referred to as the "Berlin Wall" by West Germans who perceived it as a tool for oppression and used it as a symbol for political protest. Historically, psychologists have long used material and virtual borders to think about social issues, psychological conditions, and cultural differences. For instance, for Carl Jung, the "Iron Curtain" between the communist East and the capitalist West divided the world like a "dissociated neurotic"; for Donald Winnicott, the Berlin Wall signified a "manic-depressive psychosis," and for East German psychiatrist Dietfried Müller-Hegemann, it coproduced a range of neurotic and psychopathological behaviors in East Germans—a condition he called "wall disorder."[5]

Psychologists also talk about the psychology of "crossing borders." Raymond Babineau coined the diagnosis of the "compulsive border crosser"—people escaping psychological conflicts, while compulsively searching for new identities.[6] Also, Markus Kaplan and Moriah Kaplan argue that nations ostensibly need psychological boundaries, as states with firm borders and strong national identities—such as Egypt and Turkey—were historically more likely to engage in peace processes. Thus, people and nations with strong "ego boundaries" supposedly relate better to others and don't tend to cross borders as a means to deal with psychological conflicts.[7]

The philosopher Ian Hacking points out that particular historical moments provide unique social configurations and conceptual paradigms that create an "ecological niche" for certain psychological conditions and psychiatric diagnoses to flourish. For instance, the rise of popular tourism as a pastime in the nineteenth century provided the niche for the "hysterical fugue," the compulsively pathological traveler, which led to an epidemic of mad travelers. At the same time, the increasing popularity of railway travel enabled the category of "railway neurosis" to become a widespread psychiatric condition.[8] Arguably, the rise of a bordered world also provides an "ecological niche" to think about national psychologies and categorize people into distinct social groups.

In this chapter, I examine how psychological professionals have used both the Berlin Wall and the West Bank Barrier[9] as "evocative objects" to reflect on individual and cultural traits of different communities.[10] Psychological practitioners ascribe various social meanings to these material divides. These meanings are not fixed, but reflect certain cultural circumstances. Dominant bodies of knowledge, political realities, and power inequities impact the social construction of barriers as meaningful objects, the legitimacy of certain psychological narratives, and determine the subject and object of the professional gaze. Moreover, psychologists also use such divides to reflect and implicitly reinforce perceptions of cultural differences and incompatibility across borders. In what follows, I first focus on how the Berlin Wall served as an evocative object to think about psychological issues and cultural divergences across the East-West divide and how it became a dividing line between the "normal" and the "pathological" citizen. Subsequently, I discuss how, despite post-1989 hopes for a borderless world, over 24 separation barriers have been proposed or constructed across the globe. The West Bank Barrier is one of the more controversial barriers being built since 2002 between Israel and the Palestinian Territories. This barrier, much like the Berlin Wall, has become a conceptual tool for "psy" professionals to think about national, ethnic, and individual psychological traits across material divides.

The Berlin Wall as an Evocative Object

Dividing the Normal from the Abnormal

During its existence from 1961 to 1989, the Berlin Wall became the emblem of the Cold War separating socialism to the East from capitalism to the West. Its builders' aim was to stabilize East Germany economically and politically, protect socialist East Germany from fascist and capitalist infiltration, and define the political status of Germany as part of the Soviet alliance.[11] Besides its economic and political significance, the Berlin Wall also acquired various psychological meanings.[12] In 1989, "psy" professionals theorized about the psychological impact of the Wall's fall. According to East German psychologist Hans-Joachim Maaz, the wall symbolized East Germans' "emotional blockage" that had built up over years of a "walled in and restricted existence" marked by "authoritarian" structures in schools, homes, and professions. He argued that "the wall provided the outer framework" for East Germany's "repressive and authoritarian" institutions and practices that had turned its citizens into an alienated, repressed, emotionally split, sterile, inhibited, and compulsive people. The fall of the Wall and the consequent "emotional liberation" provided an opportunity to make visible and treat people's "social pathologies" from which they were thought to suffer.[13]

For Hans-Joachim Maaz, the wall also served as a metaphor to reflect on Germany's psychohistory. He maintained that the division was used to avoid introspection as it served as a tool to suppress, deny, and project undesirable national and individual traits (including the responsibility for the "unresolved legacy" of National Socialism) onto the other German state. The fall of the Wall could thus unite, heal, and make whole all that was split off, dejected, repressed, and projected onto its other side.[14]

The adoption of psychoanalytic accounting practices by East German psychologists, such as Maaz, can be understood as a form of professional identity politics. Post-1989, West Germany's professional stipulations and health-care system were transferred to East Germany. Consequently, only certain treatment modalities, including psychoanalysis, were recognized and reimbursable under Germany's National Health Insurance. As a result, East German "psy" professionals became more inclined to take on psychoanalysis, as its practice retained professional legitimacy and credibility within a changing system of professions.[15]

The fall of the Wall also prompted West German "psy" professionals to apply their professional vision to the East German people.[16] According to psychoanalyst Reimer Hinrichs, East Germans were "unstable" psychotherapeutic patients who "possessed a burdened collective psychological infrastructure."[17] These "GDR patients" needed to mature and adjust to the new political and economic conditions by becoming more autonomous, self-reliant, and independent—skills they had failed to develop in a socialist system. Similarly, other West German commentators also equated socialism with paternalism and a culture of dependency that produced a people who still had to develop the necessary ego strength to endure in a democratic and competitive market economy.[18]

Arguably, for these commentators, the Berlin Wall became a culturally available metaphor for "storying" the psychological properties of selves and societies in transition.[19] The physical wall served as a means to talk about East Germany's cultural idiosyncrasies and how these diverge from West German culture; it also became a symbol for Germans' purported repression of their National Socialist legacy, and it evoked various social ills in East German society that point to what "is" and what "ought to be."[20] Indeed, the Wall represented and made visible East Germans' allegedly dysfunctional psychological makeup that was produced by their previous socialist and "walled-in" existence. The Wall's fall and the adoption of democratic and capitalist institutions into East Germany allegedly provided the conditions to remedy people's psychological deficits while enabling them to develop into independent and self-directed individuals. Thomas Kuhn points out that the outcome of a revolution is always perceived as progress.[21] These sorts of "psy" accounting practices implied that the transition from state socialism was an advancement, as it encouraged and enhanced East Germans' psychological development.

Such "psy" stories not only helped reinforce dominant cultural stereotypes about the dysfunctionality of East German socialism and its subjects but also reified perceptions of social, cultural, and psychological differences across the East-West divide. Indeed, post-1989, the term "mental wall" (*die Mauer im Kopf*), which purportedly signified social divergences and cultural disparities between East and West, became one of the defining metaphors for inter-German relations.

The Berlin Wall's Lasting Legacies

Post-1989, despite its physical demise, the wall reappeared in the heads of the people. "The mental wall" was a "worthwhile invention . . . after the real wall had crumbled."[22] It became an allegory that captured a seemingly insurmountable social divide between East and West Germany that lagged behind their political and economic unification. Even 15 years after its fall, the Wall seemed "firmly lodged in German minds."[23]

Psychological treatises point out that East and West Germans' different economic statuses, cultural traits, and personal idiosyncrasies sustain the mental wall.[24] For Wolf Wagner, East Germans are moralistic, idealistic, and egalitarian, while West Germans are hedonistic, individualistic, and Americanized.[25] For the International Erich-Fromm-Society, a "character wall" between East and West Germans seemed self-evident as, unlike in the West, an "authoritarian character-orientation was structurally predetermined in most people" in the East. However, as the Erich-Fromm-Society's study found no significant difference in authoritarian behavior in East and West, the authors concluded that they could not confirm the existence of a "permanent character wall between East and West."[26]

Despite the Berlin Wall's fall, the Wall-induced split continued to serve as an "evocative object" that could be used to categorize people according to various traits, circumscribe their cultural makeup, and separate them into clearly defined and easily discernible social groups. Walls—real or imagined—can thus become a means to create knowledge and enable the construction of narratives, which, more often than not, speak to the division between cultures and reaffirm the "otherness" of those living on the other side. Historically, borders, walls, and fences have always served as cognitive tools that could unintentionally be used to sediment notions of cultural homogeneity within a border and signify cultural incompatibility across borders. "Psy" narratives that construct people's psychological and cultural makeup in accord with such physical and virtual divides inadvertently help reinforce perceptions of cultural differences. However, the fall of the Berlin Wall in 1989 supposedly ushered in a new historical era. In a promotional campaign, the German Missions in the United States coined this new period: "Freedom without Walls."[27] Ironically, this new age witnessed what seemed to be two contradictory trends: rapid globalization and the proliferation of walls, barriers, and fences.

The Age of Walls

The fall of the Berlin Wall purportedly marked the beginning of a new era of open geographical spaces and unparalleled physical and electronic mobility, replacing a world divided along ideological and political lines. Globalism and internationalism ostensibly superceded nationalism, and bordered spaces seemingly gave way to a borderless and interconnected world. However, since 1989, walls and fences have again been built across the globe, dividing people, cultures, and territories. Indeed, one of the results of global interconnectedness is a proliferation of borders, checkpoints, and physical and virtual frontiers.

Saskia Sassen points out that the post-1989 global dissemination of capitalist forms of governance produced unprecedented wealth, unmatched economic opportunities, and stark inequities.[28] States faced new sets of problems—waves of immigrants, illegal activities along borders, and rising ethnic violence. Politicians, policy makers, and security forces, seeking to curb such social problems, reverted to the historically widespread strategy of constructing strategic defense systems, such as barriers, walls, and fences.[29] The assumption is that such technologies of division can create security, curb terrorism, minimize ethnic violence, and inhibit illegal immigration, smuggling, and drug trafficking. The post-1989 hopes for freedom and mobility have therefore gone hand in hand with a "new age" of walls.[30]

Since 1990, numerous separation barriers have been built or proposed across the globe, including between Mexico and the United States, the United Arab Emirates and Oman, India and Pakistan, and Saudi Arabia and Yemen. Post-1989 Europe is also divided with a new and invisible "Schengen wall." When the European Union (EU) implemented the Schengen agreement, the aim was to create a borderless zone between various European countries, while border controls with non-member states were strengthened.[31]

Barriers are also increasingly being built within different countries: in the Iraqi Green Zone, where fortresses separate the American forces from the local populations; within the Italian city of Padua and in Californian suburbs, where walls and fences guard against "the unwanted other"; in the Brazilian city of Sao Paulo, where the increasing mix of social classes and rising crime rates has led to a proliferation of walled off and secured communities. In Los Angeles "social polarization and spatial apartheid are accelerating,"[32] leading to new strategies of exclusion. Therefore, "the border is everywhere . . . exemplified in today's road-blocks, check-points, fences, walls, CCTV systems, safety zones, mine fields, and killing zones."[33]

Walls, barriers, fences, and checkpoints are ubiquitous in Israel and the Palestinian Territories, enclosing or separating off buildings, neighborhoods, communities, and territories. The West Bank Barrier is the summation of various exclusionary Israeli policies that regulate movement and interchange between Israeli- and Palestinian-controlled areas.[34] While the construction of a barrier has long been part of Israeli debates, it was not until 2002—the height of the second intifada[35]—that the Israeli government started to build a "security fence" that consists partly of concrete walls (along densely populated areas) and a "fence system" in rural areas.[36] Once completed, it is projected to be 721 km long (twice as long as the internationally recognized Green Line, the 1949 armistice line, marking the boundary between Israel and the West Bank).[37] The terms people use to describe the barrier reveal their politics. For Israeli proponents, it is the "security fence" or "anti-terrorist fence," which, according to the Israeli government, was built in "response to suicide bombers who enter into Israel."[38] For its Israeli opponents, it is a demographic separation, colonization, annexation, or apartheid wall that serves to segregate different ethnic groups and to annex land and water resources. For West Bank Palestinians, "the wall" is part of a "wall system" that includes Israeli infrastructure and no-go areas under Israeli control inside the West Bank that dismember the territory into disconnected Palestinian enclaves, and its functions are best encapsulated with terms such as apartheid, segregation, colonization, and annexation.[39]

The barrier affects Israeli and Palestinian communities in very different ways. While Israelis generally feel more secure, Palestinians feel besieged by the wall. Both Israeli and Palestinian psychologists have used their professional gaze to reflect on the barrier's psychological meanings and consequences. Their "psy" interpretations reveal which side of the barrier they are on; mirror a people's experience of its impact (or lack thereof) on daily lives; and echo dominant public, political, and academic discourses about the barriers' construction and effects in Israel and the Palestinian Territories, respectively. In the sections that follow, I will focus on how "psy" experts discuss the psychological meanings of the West Bank barrier for both Israelis and Palestinians and sketch out some of the dominant psychological paradigms and political assumptions that inform their interpretations.

The West Bank Barrier as an Evocative Object

Israeli Psychologists Talking about the "Security Fence"

Many Israeli psychologists maintain that a mental wall has long preceded the physical barrier. This mental wall stems from a long-standing "culture of conflict" that includes a history of violence and territorial and interethnic disputes, which helped consolidate homogenizing stereotypes of the "other."[40] For some psychologists, the wall therefore embodies "the basic notion that [Palestinians] cannot be trusted." This distrust stems from "the ethos, the socialization and the collective memory."[41] Israelis' distrust and fear of the Arab world are also magnified by the long history of Jewish suffering. According to political psychologist Daniel Bar-Tal, historically derived, deep-seated fears of annihilation and fear of attack have produced a "siege mentality" that characterizes Israelis' psychological makeup.[42] Such fears can also serve as interpretative resources to reflect on Israelis' reactions to the West Bank Barrier. One psychotherapist explained:

> We are not a normal society . . . We are surrounded by Arabs . . . The most powerful thing is for a few years buses exploded and people felt like they can't live in Israel—I mean how can I live here and send my children in a bus to school without knowing that they are safe? So . . . everything is coming from this sense . . . that I really want to feel secure . . . I would like to be defended . . . we don't have to go very deep in order to understand Israelis.

According to this interviewee, fear of attack thus explains Israelis' reactions to the "security fence." There is ostensibly no hidden psychological meaning, only people's desire to secure themselves and their children from a threatening outside world. Indeed, "people will say . . . it defends us. Our children are defended."[43] The reactions of many Israelis to the West Bank Barrier therefore seemingly map onto the public and political discourse of the barrier as increasing security in the country. While people living in Israeli border communities have experienced a loss of social networks and economic revenues, psychological studies have not as yet traced the impact of the division on these communities. The lack of academic attention to the concrete effects of the barrier reflects the fact that many Israeli psychologists, like politicians, tend to conceive of the barrier as a project of national enhancement and security.

According to social psychologist Dan Bar-On, Israeli psychologists (unlike some Israeli historians, sociologists, and political geographers who in the late 1990s turned to a more critical post-Zionism[44]) have remained largely committed to Israel's official ideology of Zionism, which presumes that Israel needs to secure itself against continuous threats. Historically, many psychologists have worked with the Israeli military, which tended to reinforce their Zionist vision.[45] Consequently, for many Israeli "psy" experts, Israelis' conception of the barrier as providing security is both reasonable and explicable. Of academic interest, however, are Israeli political groups—such as "Anarchists against the Wall"[46]—that oppose the barrier through weekly demonstrations in West Bank cities. One psychologist expressed his curiosity as follows:

> What is very interesting is . . . that particular groups stick to the issue of the wall (such as Anarchists against the Wall). . . . Why wall? What did happen in their socialization? How did it happen? Who are they? What brings them into activism . . . and why specifically the wall?[47]

As psychologists generally understand the barrier as enhancing security and conceive of Israelis' desire for physical separation as a "normal" psychological need resulting from Jewish history, it is the social groups opposing the wall that are of psychological interest. Consequently, widespread Israeli public concerns for safety and security can became reflected in the sorts of questions Israeli "psy" experts pose.

However, many Israeli psychologists draw on a different set of discourses when reflecting on the psychology of Palestinians and their reaction and opposition to the West Bank Barrier. According to sociologist Nissim Mizrachi, the Israeli psychological sciences have traditionally been informed by a Zionist commitment to ethnicity and biological lineage as an essential explanatory tool, helping to demark ethnic boundaries and conceptualize mental competence along ethnic lines.[48] Indeed, some Israeli psychologists have long assumed that certain ostensibly shared characteristics among "primitives," such as a lack of a sense of self and an inability to understand abstract and causal concepts, were part of their natural makeup. Yet more recent psychological theories have transformed ethnic hierarchies into cultural hierarchies that are not thought to be fixed by nature, but by culture. Not only have such ethnic and cultural typologies traditionally informed the Israeli psychological sciences, but many "psy" professionals have also adopted European and American psychosocial paradigms that decontextualize individual behaviors. For example, "individualizing forms of knowledge," such as psychoanalysis, that equate mental health with autonomy, independence, and individuality have contributed substantially to psychological theories.[49]

The combined commitment to Zionism and Euro-American psychosocial paradigms has given rise to a body of social and psychological studies that takes the distinctiveness of Arab society from Israeli culture as given, treating different civil, religious, social, and ethnic identities as stable and fixed constructs. In studies based on such ethnic and cultural typologies Israel is frequently represented as a "modernizing agent" for the surrounding Arab culture,[50] while "Arab psychology" becomes the negative mirror image of "the healthy modern Zionist mind."[51] As a result, various psychoanalytical studies present Israelis as "Western," democratic, and individualistic, while Arabs are thought to be collectivist, autocratic, and lacking a separate sense of self. According to psychologist Avner Falk, "Among the Arabs . . . separation and individuation are often incomplete; there is no full emotional autonomy and maturity."[52] For some the wall thus "presents a frontier against the Muslim world,"[53] segregates two "clashing civilizations," and divides between the "Arab mind" and the "Israeli mind."[54]

Israeli "psy" experts often draw on these discursive repertoires in order to explain Palestinians' opposition to the West Bank Barrier. For one psychoanalyst, Palestinians' reactions to the barrier are indicative of their collectivist nature and inability to develop independence and autonomy. He maintained: "they can't keep alone for many reasons . . . They are a collective people, for them [the fence] is going against their basic nature. . . . They are not separated . . . and they don't want to be separated from Israel."[55] Hereby the wall becomes an "evocative object" by which to discursively construct two different mind-sets that supposedly map neatly onto Israeli and Arab ethnic identities. It serves as a divide between the "normal" and the "pathological"—"individualized" and "democratic" Israelis and "collectivist" and "autocratic" Arabs. Indeed their very reactions to the barrier supposedly speak to the psychological health of Israelis and the psychopathologies and immaturity of Arabs.

While for German psychologists the fall of the Berlin Wall and the rise of democratic capitalism provided the possibility for remedying East Germans' seemingly stunted psychological development, for Avner Falk it is also only democracy and freedom that may cure the Arab "condition." In the process, Israeli society may serve as a model of modernization, exemplifying democratic governance and psychological health, while the Arab and Muslim world will have to undergo a "very deep and painful psychological change"[56] to bring about democracy, modernity, individualism, and psychological well-being.

However, there are some psychologists and mental health professionals who try to bring politics back into the consulting room.[57] They draw on yet a different set of theories (including relational, intersubjective, and feminist theories) that aim to personalize the political, understand "psy" practices and methods as historical and cultural constructs, and contextualize epidemiology in terms of social and economic disparities, political conflicts, and power inequities. Such politically engaged psychologists frequently attempt to probe the psychological effects of the Israeli occupation[58] of the West Bank and Gaza on Israelis and Palestinians alike, and heed post-Zionist calls to question the official rationale of security for the construction of the "fence." For instance, for them the "wall" is a material manifestation of Israelis' continued attempts to make Palestinians invisible. According to a politically active psychiatrist, "Zionism starts with the notion that Palestinians do not exist. . . . The wall is one of the means to continue this."[59] A psychologist also agreed that the barrier provides a convenient way "to erase the existence of Palestinians."[60]

Some of these psychological professionals work with Palestinian mental health practitioners, conduct joint Israeli-Palestinian projects, and provide health-care services within the Palestinian Territories. As they frequently travel to the territories, they are more likely to experience the West Bank Barrier's social consequences for Palestinians and therefore apprehend Palestinians' reactions to the closures within their social and political context. For example, one psychiatrist emphasized the detrimental effect Israeli checkpoints inside the West Bank have on Palestinian social and family networks: "people are suffering as they are disconnected from parts of their families. In Palestine . . . family is your 'Visitenkarte' (business card). It's everything."[61] While the widespread discursive repertoire about cultural differences between Israeli and Arab cultures may at times still inform the analyses put forth by some of these more socially critical professionals, their understanding of Palestinian circumstances is more aligned with that of Palestinian psychologists.

Consequently, Israeli "psy" experts draw on various psychological theories, and certain cultural and political assumptions, in order to ascribe social and psychological meanings to the barrier. For some, it signifies long-standing interethnic conflict and distrust; for others, it becomes the dividing line between two seemingly incompatible ethnic groups that possess inherently different cultural, social, and psychological constituents. Many perceive Israelis' desire for a wall as a "normal" reaction given the history of Jewish persecution, and a few pathologize Palestinians' opposition to the barrier as indicative of their lack of individualization. However, psychologists who cross boundaries and work with Palestinians tend to understand their reactions as "normal" given the "abnormal" circumstances. Israeli psychologists' political and conceptual commitments thus largely determine how they assess the impact and meaning of the barrier for Israelis and Palestinians respectively. However, Palestinian psychologists maintain that even their more critical Israeli colleagues have little understanding of the psychological consequences of the barrier on Palestinians.

Palestinian Psychologists Talking about the Wall

Palestinian "psy" experts maintain that Israelis cannot understand the psychology of Palestinians and how the barrier affects their everyday lives, as they "do not know *really* what's going on inside."[62] They tend to draw on different academic paradigms in order to assess the barrier's social impact, such as trauma studies, clinical psychology, and community psychology. For community psychologists, the highest potential stress factors include unemployment, poverty, and the breakdown of social networks and support.[63] They argue that the barrier impedes freedom of movement and thereby contributes to the breakdown of social, professional, and family networks, which increases stress levels.

Palestinian psychologists also point out that the wall is not about "security," but about Palestinians' lack of control over their lives and environment. This has led to an increase in various psychological symptoms and social problems.[64] One study showed that the wall can induce feelings of hopelessness, depression, and inferiority, and passing checkpoints can bring on feelings of humiliation, demoralization, denial, anger, or aggression.[65] Exposure to both the barrier and checkpoints produces a sense of "siege"—the feeling of being imprisoned and unable to conduct a normal life. While Israelis suffer from a "siege mentality," a desire to close themselves in so as to protect themselves from a hostile outside world, Palestinian psychologists argue that their patients suffer from a different kind of "siege" induced by Israel's closure policies. Feeling "under siege" has become the breeding ground for a range of psychological conditions including distress, anxiety, dysfunction, depression, disassociation, posttraumatic stress disorder, various psychosomatic conditions as well as personality disorders, including psychosis. The sense of "siege" is also correlated with an increase in domestic and school violence and an upsurge in interpersonal conflicts.[66]

The precariousness of everyday life in the Palestinian Territories is also of concern to humanistically oriented psychologists. According to Rana Nashashibi, people's primary focus on survival negatively impacts their individual development, aspirations, and self-esteem. Accordingly, "this ghetto-like life not only restricts psychological development, but also denies us the chance to reclaim the psychological and social advancements we had once achieved."[67] She blames social conditions for the depletion of people's energy, their lack of attention to psychological matters, and their inability to achieve the top of the Maslow Pyramid—self-actualization.[68] Moreover, Palestinians' structurally predetermined inability to reach their economic, social, and personal goals makes it "easier for both the Israeli military establishment and the Western world to see them as inferior beings."[69] At the same time, Palestinian children also start to feel inferior, lose their self-esteem, and yearn to become powerful Israeli soldiers. Hereby, the consequences of the closures not only affirm for some Israeli and Western observers Palestinians' "otherness" and "backwardness," but also Palestinians themselves, rather than coming together, are drifting apart.[70]

Palestinian psychologists' accounts of the psychological consequences of the "wall system" reflect some of the social and political concerns that are prevalent in public discourse within the West Bank. Politicians point out that the lack of freedom of movement, due to the closures, negatively affects social networks, hampers the exchange of goods and services, and hinders people from reaching work, schools, health-care facilities, and places of worship.[71] Palestinian "psy" experts' assessments of the walls' social impact and meaning are informed by such widely shared concerns. At the same time, conceptual paradigms, such as community and humanistic psychology, help to articulate these sentiments as well as make sense of the walls' impact, which is thought to contribute to various psychological and social problems as well as to stunt individual development. Therefore, just as some Israeli psychologists draw on psychological paradigms that are informed by a political commitment to Zionism or post-Zionism, Palestinian "psy" professionals also tend to frame their analyses in line with wider social and political matters. Dominant psychological theories, political commitments, and public concerns thus frequently form a "seamless web" that can determine the sorts of questions psychological experts ask and the answers they provide.[72]

Conclusion

With a new age of walls upon us, it is paramount to reflect on the social consequences of barriers as "strategic defenses."[73] The Berlin Wall and the West Bank Barrier are just two of many barriers that speak to the cultural consequences of such technologies of division. History teaches us that defense barriers, whether it was Athens' Long Wall, Hadrian's Wall, or even the Great Wall in China, tended to "agitate rather than soothe relations."[74] Mike Davis's analysis of the "ecology of fear" in Los Angeles found that closures and exclusionary mechanisms don't reduce, but create fear and social exclusion, and encourage "mutual suspicion and a profoundly anti-communitarian fortress mentality."[75] Indeed, segregation, enforced by visible security measures, human or nonhuman, ranging from security guards, to watchtowers, to barriers have not deterred, but rather produced aggression and attacks toward the other side.[76] Peter Shirlow also found that in Ireland the walls (known as the Peace Lines) had become "the malevolent face of the people who live on the other side." Social groups who maintained social ties that crossed the divide, however, unlike those who had not, did not display "ethnosectarian" consciousness, fears, or animosities.[77]

Various "psy" experts have used technologies of division, such as the Berlin Wall or the West Bank Barrier, to construct psychological knowledge claims and address various social concerns, psychological problems, and cultural differences. These meanings are not fixed or stable, but are transitory and multiple. They depend on the culturally available discourses that make the barrier matter. Just as the Berlin Wall was commandeered as a model for the "troubled" German psyche, the West Bank Barrier can also be mobilized to induce powerful images of psychological and social ills, help to narratively construct long-standing cultures of conflict, and make discourses, about what Samuel Huntington calls "clashing civilizations," materially visible. Also, as Berlin's "mental" wall continues to serve as a culturally accessible metaphor to think about and enforce the East-West divide, the West Bank Barrier, too, fosters feelings of cultural differences and encourages narratives of "us" versus "them."

Postmodernists point out that dualities are associated with hierarchical arrangements and differentiations. Technologies of divisions may not only help evoke, visualize, and define notions of separateness across the divide, but they also serve as convenient tools to establish the dividing line between the "normal" and the "pathological."[78] Shortly after the transition from state socialism in East Germany, various "psy" experts argued that the Berlin Wall separated Western capitalism, democracy, and individualism from socialism, dictatorship, and collectivism.[79] At the time, some psychoanalysts observed that while socialism had given rise to numerous pathologies such as psychological immaturity, dependencies, and repression, democratic capitalism could provide the conditions for people to progress psychologically toward greater autonomy, independence, and individualization. Thereby such psychological accounts equated the potential for individual psychological advancement with the new political and economic reality of the united Germany. Similarly, for some, the West Bank Barrier has become the dividing line between two separate civilizations: autocracy, collectivism, and the "Arab mind" versus democracy, individualism, and the "Israeli mind." These psychologists also argue that democracy and individualism may cure the "Arab condition."

The use of scientific knowledge to make evaluative judgments is particularly problematic in a colonial context. Christiane Hartnack maintains that, in colonial India, Indian and British psychoanalysts not only asked different questions, but also differed in terms of the behaviors they deemed to be "normal." While British psychoanalysts reflected on the psychological and cultural shortcomings of their protectorate and pathologized Indian anticolonial political activities (associating them with an inability to accept Britain as a father figure and returning to a pre-Oedipal symbiosis with the mother), they did not deem the British colonization of India to be of professional interest. Indian psychoanalysts, on the other hand, argued that colonial repression produced various psychopathologies. They were concerned with the psychological makeup of Indians, but refrained from objectifying their British rulers.[80] Similarly, some Israeli psychologists perceive Israelis' reactions to the barrier as "normal," but judge Palestinians' responses as indicative of the shortcomings of what they deem to be "Arab culture." Conversely, Palestinian psychologists focus on their own plight, rarely reflecting on the psychology of Israelis. Hereby power politics can become reflected in the professional gaze and its objects and dictates the dividing lines between the "normal" and the "pathological."

For Raymond Babineau, the "compulsive border crosser" was a pathological novelty. During the existence of the Berlin Wall and its accompanying wall and fence system across the German hinterland, over 40,000 people tried to cross illegally, and 957 died in the attempt to do so.[81] It wasn't until November 9, 1989, that thousands of East Germans crowded the checkpoints, hoping to take advantage of a newly passed provisional travel regulation, when the overwhelmed guards simply lifted the barriers. Upon the opening of the Iron Curtain in Europe, walls and checkpoints seemed, for a brief historical moment, to become a tale of the past. However, the ever-tightening closures between Israel and the West Bank are just one of many new "strategic defense barriers" that have been built since 1989. The Berlin Wall showed how material divides can turn into "mental walls" and persist in public discourse long after their demise. The Peace Line in Ireland also revealed that it is only border crossers that experience cultural communality where others perceive merely cultural incompatibility. Yet, some Israeli commentators argue for the need of walls and fences in order to "distinguish the two people as a necessary preliminary to eventual cohabitation" and "spatial separation as a precondition to *any* political integration."[82] However, as the physical divide hinders peoples' ability to meet, the "other"—on the other side of the wall—seems ever more remote. Arguably, such material distancing can create "a psychological barrier"[83] that, much like the mental wall between East and West Germans, will persist long after its demise. At the same time, psychological accounts of walls, fences, and barriers may not only reflect power inequities across the divide, but can also become a means to talk about "clashing civilizations" and solidify and enforce cultural differences within communities with walls in the midst.

Notes

1. I am grateful to the Swiss National Science Foundation and the U.S. Fulbright Scholar Program for the Middle East, North Africa, Central and South Asia Regional Research Program for research support (grantee number G48413539). I am also indebted to numerous respondents in Germany, Israel, and the Palestinian Territories for their time and insights.
2. Eric J. Hobsbawm, *Nations and Nationalism since 1780: Programme, Myth, Reality* (Cambridge: Cambridge University Press, 1992).
3. The terms "psy sciences," "psy professionals," and "psychologists" are used as umbrella terms to describe psychiatrists, psychologists, psychoanalysts, and psychotherapists. See Nikolas Rose "Assembling the Modern Self," in *Rewriting the Self*, ed. Roy Porter (London: Routledge, 1997): 224–248.
4. Sherry Turkle, *Life on the Screen: Identity in the Age of the Internet* (New York: Simon and Schuster, 1995).
5. Carl G. Jung, *Man and His Symbols* (London: Aldus Books, 1964); Donald W. Winnicott, *Home Is Where We Start From: Essays by a Psychoanalyst* (New York: W. W. Norton and Company, 1986); Dietfried Müller-Hegemann, *Die Berliner Mauerkrankheit* (Bielefeld: Nicolaische Verlagsbuchhandlung, 1973).
6. Raymond G. Babineau, "The Compulsive Border Crosser," *Psychiatry* 35 (1972): 281–290.
7. Avner Falk, "Border Symbolism," *The Psychoanalytic Quarterly* 4/XLIII (1974): 650–660; Avner Falk, "Border Symbolism Revisited," *Int. Rev. Psycho-Anal* 10 (1983): 215; Markus J. Kaplan and Moriah Kaplan, "Walls and

Boundaries in Arab Relations with Israel: Interpersonal Distancing Model," *Journal of Conflict Resolution* 27/3 (1983): 457–472.

8. Ian Hacking, *Mad Travellers: Reflections on the Reality of Transient Mental Illness* (London: Free Association Books, 1998); Ralph Harrington, "The Neuroses of the Railways," *History Today* 44/7 (1994): 15–21.
9. In this chapter, I will adhere to journalistic conventions in avoiding terms favored by one or the other side in a conflict. The BBC, the United Nations, and Israeli Human Rights Groups use the terms "barrier," "separation barrier," or "West Bank barrier" as acceptable generic descriptions, instead of the politically charged terms of "security fence" (preferred by the Israeli government) or "apartheid wall" (preferred by the Palestinians). However, when describing sections of the barrier that are either concrete or fenced, I will use "wall" or "fence" in order to provide the most exact physical description (see BBC NEWS, "Israel and the Palestinians: Key Terms" (Oct. 12, 2006), accessed June 10, 2010, http://news.bbc.co.uk/newswatch/ukfs/hi/newsid_6040000/newsid_6044000/6044090.stm#barrier.
10. The research reported here is based on (1) a longitudinal sociological study (including 46 in-depth interviews, ethnographic field notes, and archival research) of the East German psychotherapeutic community between 1990 and 2003, and (2) a data set (including 52 qualitative in-depth interviews, archival research, participant observation, and a collection of academic, popular, and media accounts) collected in Israel and the Palestinian territories between 2008 and 2010.
11. Dietrich Staritz, *Geschichte der DDR* (Frankfurt: Suhrkamp, 1996).
12. Christine Leuenberger, "Constructions of the Berlin Wall: How Material Culture Is Used in Psychological Theory," *Social Problems* 53/1 (2006): 18–37.
13. Hans-Joachim Maaz, *Gefühlsstau: Ein Psychogramm der DDR* (Berlin: Argon, 1990), 15:124; Christine Leuenberger, "Socialist Psychotherapy and its Dissidents," *Journal of the History of the Behavioral Sciences* 37/3 (2001): 261-273; Christine Leuenberger, "The End of Socialism and the Reinvention of the Self: A Study of the East German Psychotherapeutic Community in Transition," *Theory and Society* 31/2 (2002): 257–282.
14. Maaz, *Gefühlsstau,* 1990, 152–159.
15. Heike Bernhardt and Regine Lockot (eds.), *Mit Ohne Freud: Zur Geschichte der Psychoanalyse in Ostdeutschland* (Giessen: Psychosozial-Verlag, 2000); Leuenberger 2001; 2002.
16. Michael L. Möller and Hans-Joachim Maaz, *Die Einheit beginnt zu zweit: Ein deutsch-deutsches Zwiegespräch* (Berlin: Rowohlt, 1993); Wolfgang Möller, "Entfremdung. Eine Heilungsgeschichte," *Kursbuch 101: Abriss der DDR* (Berlin: Rowohlt, 1990): 67–73; Harry Schröder, "Identität, Individualität und psychische Befindlichkeit des DDR-Bürgers im Umbruch," *Zeitschrift für Sozialisationsforschung und Erziehungssoziologie* 1 (1990): 163–176; see also Christoph Seidler and Michael Fröse, "Die Utopie von Individuation und Bezogenheit in Deutschland," *Psychologische Beiträge* 35 (1993): 307–314.
17. Reimer Hinrichs, "Patient DDR," *Kursbuch 101* (Berlin: Rowohlt, 1990): 57.

18. Heinz Hennig, "Der Mensch im Spannungsfeld zwischen Mangel und Konsum," *Psychosozial 18*, 1/59 (1995): 59–70; Gerd Meyer, "Zwischen Autoritarismus und Demokratie. Persönlichkeitsstrukturen in postkommunistischen Gesellschaften," *Psychosozial: Geschichte ist ein Teil von uns* 67 (1997): 93–108.
19. James A. Holstein, "Producing People: Descriptive Practice in Human Service Work," *Current Research on Occupations and Professions* 7 (1992): 23–39.
20. Charles Rosenberg, "Framing Disease: Illness, Society and History," in *Framing Disease*, ed. Charles E. Rosenberg and J. Golden (New Brunswick: Rutgers University Press, 1992).
21. Thomas S. Kuhn, *The Structure of Scientific Revolutions* (Chicago: University of Chicago Press, 1962).
22. Monika Maron, "Unüberwindlich? Die Mauer in den Köpfen." *Rede anlässlich der Verleihung des Journalistenpreises der deutschen Zeitungen - Theodor-Wolff-Preis. September 16, 1999, Leipzig*, accessed Jan. 13, 2005, http://www.bdzv.de.
23. Peter Beaumont, "Divided without a Wall, Germans Are Now Split by a Rift of the Mind," *Guardian Unlimited* (April 3, 2005), accessed April 3, 2005, http://www.guardian.co.uk/germany/article/0,2763,1451173,00.html; see also *Deutsch-deutsche Vergleiche: Psychologische Untersuchungen 10 Jahre nach dem Mauerfall*, ed. Hendrik Berth and Elmar Brähler (Berlin: Verlag für Wissenschaft und Forschung, 1999).
24. Berufsverband Deutscher Psychologinnen und Psychologen, *5. Deutscher Psychologentag and 20. Kongress für Angewandte Psychologie an der FU Berlin (Oct. 7–10, 1999)*, accessed April 11, 2003, http://www.bdp-verband.org.
25. Wolf Wagner, "'Deutscher, proletarischer und moralischer'—Unterschiede zwischen Ost-und Westdeutschland und ihre Erklärung," in *Deutsch-deutsche Vergleiche*, ed. Berth and Brähler, 1999: 53–69.
26. Internationale Erich-Fromm Gesellschaft, *Die Charaktermauer: Zur Psychoanalyse der Gesellschafts-Charakters in Ost-und Westdeutschland* (Göttingen: Vandenhöck and Ruprecht, 1995), 250, 270.
27. See "Freedom without Walls," accessed May 13, 2010, http://www.germany.info/Vertretung/usa/en/09__Press__InFocus__Interviews/03__Infocus/04__Without__Walls/__Main__S.html.
28. Saskia Sassen, *Territory, Authority, Rights: From Medieval to Global Assemblages* (Princeton, NJ: Princeton University Press, 2006).
29. Brent L. Sterling, *Do Good Fences Make Good Neighbors? What History Teaches Us about Strategic Barriers and International Security* (Washington, D.C.: Georgetown University Press, 2009).
30. Julian Borges, "Security Fences or Barriers to Peace?" *The Guardian* (April 24, 2007); Stefano Boeri, "Border-Syndrome: Notes for a Research Program," in *Territories*, ed. Anselm Franke, Eyal Weizman, Stefano Boeri, and Rafi Segal, (Berlin: KW and Verlag der Buchhandlung Walter König, 2003).
31. See http://www.rferl.org/content/The_EUs_Invisible_Schengen_Wall/1607507.html, accessed May 13, 2010.

32. Mike Davis, "Beyond Blade Runner: Urban Control. The Ecology of Fear," *Criminal Perspectives: Essential Readings* 23 (Open Magazine Pamphlet Series, 2003): 528.
33. Eyal Weizman, "The Geometry of Occupation," Centre of Contemporary Culture of Barcelona (CCCB), conference lecture at the cycle "Borders" (March 1, 2004): 2, accessed March 1, 2009, www.urban.cccb.org.
34. Valerie Zink, "A Quiet Transfer: The Judaization of Jerusalem," *Contemporary Arab Affairs* 2/1 (2009): 122–133.
35. "Intifada" literally means "shaking." Israelis understand the term as indicative of a Palestinian war against Israel whereas Palestinians understand it as a popular uprising against an occupying regime (see Prime: Peace Research Institute in the Middle East, *Learning Each Other's Historical Narrative: Palestinians and Israelis* (Beit Jallah, PNA: A Prime Publication, 2003).
36. See B'Tselem, "Behind the Barrier: Human Rights Violations as a Result of Israel's Separation Barrier," Position Paper, April (Jerusalem: B'Tselem, 2003); B'Tselem, "The Separation Barrier: Position Paper September 2002," September (Jerusalem: B'Tselem, 2002), accessed Sept. 27, 2010, http://www.btselem.org/english/publications/Index.asp?TF=15&image.x=7&image.y=4. For a detailed barrier route, see http://www.btselem.org/English/Maps/Index.asp.
37. In an advisory opinion, the International Court of Justice (2004) used the term "Separation Wall" as the most accurate term to describe the West Bank Barrier when understood in terms of its material effects. The ruling also declared its construction as illegal under international law (see International Court of Justice (2004) "Legal Consequences of the Construction of a Wall in the Occupied Palestinian Territory: Advisory Opinion" (July 9), http://www.icj-cij.org/docket/index.php?pr=71&p1=3&p2=1&case=131&p3=6 (retrieved June 11 2009).
38. See also Israeli Ministry of Foreign Affairs, www.mfg.gov.il, accessed Oct. 12, 2008. See also UN OCHA, *The Humanitarian Impact on Palestinians of Israeli Settlements and other Infrastructure in the West Bank* (UN OCHA: Jerusalem, 2007): 46, accessed Sept. 27, 2010, http://www.ochaopt.org/generalreports.aspx?id=97&f=2005-01-01&t=2008-04-30. Various NGOs argue that other factors, such as the inclusion of Jewish settlements, demography, and the interests of Israeli real-estate developers also determined the construction and routing of the barrier (see Bimkom and B'Tselem, "Under the Guise of Security: Routing the Separation Barrier to Enable the Expansion of Israeli Settlements in the West Bank" (Jerusalem: Bimkom and B'Tselem, 2005), accessed Sept. 27, 2010, http://www.ochaopt.org/generalreports.aspx?id=97&f=2005-01-01&t=2008-04-30; UN OCHA 2007. For debates on whether it is the barrier and its current route, and not other measures (e.g., checkpoints within the West Bank) that have increased security, see BBC News, "Israel: 'No Need to Finish' West Bank Barrier," May 19, 2009, accessed May 29, 2009; Bimkom and B'Tselem 2005; UN OCHA 2007.
39. UN OCHA 2007; UN OCHA, *West Bank: Access and Closure April 2008* (UN OCHA: Jerusalem, 2008a); UN OCHA, *OCHA Closure Update Occupied*

Palestinian Territory (UN OCHA: Jerusalem, 2008b), accessed Sept. 27, 2010, http://www.ochaopt.org/generalreports.aspx?id=97&f=2005-01-01&t=2008-04-30.

40. Daniel Bar-Tal, "Das Bild der Araber in der israelisch-jüdischen Gesellschaft," in *Zwischen Antisemitismus und Islamophobie: Vorurteile und Projektionen in Europa und Nahost,* ed. John Bunzl and Alexandra Senfft (USA Verlag: Hamburg, 2008): 195–227; George J. Mitchell, "Sharm El-Sheikh Fact-Finding Committee Report—Mitchell Report" (2001), accessed April 24, 2010, http://en.wikipedia.org/wiki/Mitchell Report_%28Arab%E2%80%93Israeli_conflict%29; Jamal El-Deek, "The Image of the Israeli: Its Evolution in the Palestinian Mind," *Palestine-Israel Journal: Psychological Dimensions of the Conflict* 1/4 (1994), accessed May 2, 2010, http://www.pij.org/index.php.
41. Interview B, 2008.
42. Daniel Bar-Tal and Dikia Antebi, "Siege Mentality in Israel," *Ongoing Production on Social Representations* 1/1 (1992): 49–67; see also Avner Falk, *Fratricide in the Holy Land: A Psychoanalytic View of the Arab-Israeli Conflict* (Wisconsin: The University of Wisconsin Press, 2004); Rafael Moses, "Some Sociopsychological and Political Perspectives of the Meaning of the Holocaust: A View from Israel," *Israel Journal of Psychiatry and Related Sciences* 34/1 (1997): 55–68.
43. Interview G, 2008.
44. For a discussion of post-Zionism, see Herbert C. Kelman, "Israel in Transition from Zionism to Post-Zionism," *Annals of the American Academy of Political and Social Sciences* 555 (1998): 46–61.
45. Dan Bar-On, "The Silence of Psychologists," *Political Psychology, Special Issue: Psychology as Politics* 22/2 (2001): 331–345.
46. See "Anarchists against the Wall," accessed May 15, 2010, http://www.awalls.org/about_aatw.
47. Interview B, 2008.
48. Nissim Mizrachi, "'From Badness to Sickness': The Role of Ethnopsychology in Shaping Ethnic Hierarchies in Israel," *Social Identities* 10/2 (2004): 220.
49. Bar-On 2001; Mizrachi, From Badness to Sickness 2004; Nikolas Rose, "Individualizing Psychology," in *Texts of Identity,* ed. John Shotter and Kenneth J. Gergen (London: Sage, 1992): 119–132.
50. Ramzi Suleiman, "On Marginal People: The Case of the Palestinians in Israel," in *Psychoanalysis, Identity, and Ideology: Critical Essays on the Israel/Palestine Case,* ed. John Bunzl and Benjamin Beit-Hallahmi (Boston: Kluwer Academic Publishers, 2002).
51. Mizrachi, "From Badness to Sickness," 2004, 240. Scholarship that is based on such ethnic and cultural typologies—Edward Said calls it "orientalism"—has long informed the West's view of the Arab world more recently in treaties on "the clash of civilizations." See Samuel P. Huntington, "The Clash of Civilizations?," *Foreign Affairs* 72/3 (1993): 22–49; Bernard Lewis, "The Roots of Muslim Rage," *The Atlantic Monthly* 266 (1990); Dan Rabinowitz, "Oriental Othering and National Identity: A Review of Early Israeli Anthropological Studies of Palestinians," in *Across the Wall: Narratives*

of Israeli-Palestinian History, ed. Ilan Pappe and Jamil Hilal (London: I. B. Tauris): 45–73.

52. Falk, *Fratricide in the Holy Land*, 2004: 157; see also Ofer Grosbard, *Israel on the Couch: The Psychology of the Peace Process* (Albany, NY: State University of New York Press, 2003).
53. Interview B, 2008.
54. Falk, *Fratricide in the Holy Land*, 2004; see also Huntington, *Foreign Affairs*.
55. Interview G, 2008.
56. Falk, *Fratricide in the Holy Land*, 2004, 158.
57. Politically active psychologists are often associated with such NGOs as IMUT (Mental Health Professionals for Promotion of Peace), PsychoActive, and Physicians for Human Rights. See Nissim Avissar, "PsychoActivism—past, present and future: Examining the Israeli-Palestinian case," *paper presented at the Annual Meeting of the International Society of Political Psychology*, Classical Chinese Garden, Portland, Oregon, USA (July 4, 2007), accessed Sept. 26, 2009, http://www.allacademic.com/p204625_index.html.
58. According to international law, the Palestinian Territories are under Israeli occupation. However, the Israeli government maintains that its presence inside the West Bank has a unique legal character and does not constitute an occupying force (see Nizar Ayoub, "The Israeli High Court of Justice and the Palestinian Intifada" (Ramallah: Al-Haq—Law in the Service of Man, 2003); ICJ, "Legal Consequences of the Construction of a Wall"; Gisha: Legal Center for Freedom of Movement http://www.gisha.org, accessed June 11 2009; UN OCHA, 2007).
59. Interview R, 2008.
60. Interview B, 2008.
61. Interview R, 2008.
62. Interview A, 2008.
63. Palestinian Counseling Center (PCC) "The Psychological Implications of Israel's Separation Wall on Palestinians" (Jan. 13, 2004), accessed May 12, 2004, http://www.pcc-jer.org. For further information, see also Palestinian Counseling Center (PCC), accessed May 16, 2010, http://www.pcc-jer.org/english/ and the Gaza Community Mental Health Center, accessed May 16, 2010, http://www.gcmhp.net/.
64. Palestinian Counseling Center (PCC), "Israeli 'Security' Barriers and their Psychological Impact on the Individual and the Collective," (Jerusalem: Palestinian Counseling Center, 2002); Palestinian Counseling Center (PCC), "The Psychological and Mental effects of Systematic Humiliation by Israel against the Palestinians" (Jerusalem: Palestinian Counseling Center, 2003), accessed May 16, 2010, http://www.pcc-jer.org/english/.
65. Interview H, 2008.
66. David Cronin, "Israel's Psychological Siege," *The Electronic Intifada* (May 11, 2009), accessed Sept. 30, 2010, http://electronicintifada.net/v2/article10521.shtml; A. A. Thabet, Abu Tawahina, E. El Sarraj, and L. R. Punamaki, Gaza Community Mental Health Programme, "Coping with Stress and Siege in Palestinian Families in the Gaza Strip (Cohort

study III)," (2004), accessed May 16, 2010, http://www.gcmhp.net/; PCC 2002; 2004; 2005.

67. PCC, 2003, 6.
68. Nashashibi in PCC, 2003. See also Gaza Community Health Care Center, accessed May 16, 2010, http://www.gcmhp.net/; PCC, 2002.
69. PCC, 2003, 6.
70. PCC, 2002.
71. PLO Negotiations Affairs Department, "Barrier to Peace: The Impact of Israel's Wall Five Years after the ICJ Ruling" (July 2009), accessed Aug. 1, 2009, www.nad-plo.org.
72. Thomas P. Hughes, "The Seamless Web: Technology, Science, Etcetera, Etcetera," *Social Studies of Science* 16/2 (1986): 281–292. See also Greg Eghigian, Andreas Killan, and Christine Leuenberger, *The Self as Project: Politics and the Human Sciences, Osiris* 22 (Chicago: University of Chicago Press, 2007).
73. Sterling, 2009, 4.
74. Sterling, 2009, 315.
75. Davis in Rachel Pain, "Place, Social Relations and the Fear of Crime: A Review," *Progress in Human Geography* 24/3 (2000): 371.
76. See Peter Shirlow, "'Who Fears to Speak': Fear, Mobility, and Ethno-Sectarianism in the Two 'Ardoynes,'" *The Global Review of Ethnopolitics* 3/1 (2003): 76–91; Sterling, 2009; Haaretz, "Shin Bet: Separation fence fueling attacks by East Jerusalem Arabs" (Sept. 24, 2008), accessed Feb. 17, 2009, http://www.haaretz.com/hasen/spages/1024174.html.
77. Shirlow, "Who Fears to Speak," 2003, 81, 89.
78. Georges Canguilhem, *The Normal and the Pathological* (New York: Zone Books, 1991).
79. See Gerd Meyer, "Zwischen Autoritarismus und Demokratie. Persönlichkeitsstrukturen in postkommunistischen Gesellschaften," *Psychosozial: Geschichte ist ein Teil von uns* 67 (1997): 93–108.
80. Christiane Hartnack, "Visnu on Freud's Desk: Psychoanalysis in Colonial India," *Social Research* 57/4 (1990).
81. Alexandra Hildebrandt, *Die Mauer: Zahlen. Daten* (Berlin: Verlag Haus am Checkpoint Charlie, 2001).
82. Boeri, *Territories*, 53.
83. Interview S, 2008.

Bibliography

Ayoub, Nizar. *The Israeli High Court of Justice and the Palestinian Intifada.* Ramallah: Al-Haq—Law in the Service of Man, 2003.

Babineau, Raymond G. "The Compulsive Border Crosser." *Psychiatry* 35 (1972): 281–290.

Bar-On, Dan. "The Silence of Psychologists." *Political Psychology, Special Issue: Psychology as Politics* 22/2 (2001): 331–345.

Bar-Tal, Daniel. "Das Bild der Araber in der israelisch-jüdischen Gesellschaft." In *Zwischen Antisemitismus und Islamophobie: Vorurteile und Projektionen in Europa und Nahost*, edited by John Bunzl and Alexandra Senfft, 195–227. USA Verlag: Hamburg, 2008.

Bar-Tal, Daniel, and Dikia Antebi. "Siege Mentality in Israel." *Ongoing Production on Social Representations* 1/1 (1992): 49–67.

Bernhardt, Heike, and Regine Lockot (eds.). *Mit Ohne Freud: Zur Geschichte der Psychoanalyse in Ostdeutschland*. Giessen: Psychosozial-Verlag, 2000.

Berth, Hendrik, and Elmar Brähler (eds.). *Deutsch-deutsche Vergleiche: Psychologische Untersuchungen 10 Jahre nach dem Mauerfall*. Berlin: Verlag für Wissenschaft und Forschung, 1999.

Boeri, Stefano. "Border-Syndrome: Notes for a Research Program," in *Territories*, edited by Anselm Franke, Eyal Weizman, Stefano Boeri, and Rafi Segal, 52–64. Berlin: KW and Verlag der Buchhandlung Walter König, 2003.

Canguilhem, Georges. *The Normal and the Pathological*. New York: Zone Books, 1991.

Davis, Mike. "Beyond Blade Runner: Urban Control. The Ecology of Fear." *Criminal Perspectives: Essential Readings* 23. Open Magazine Pamphlet Series, 2003: 527–541.

Eghigian, Greg, Andreas Killan, and Christine Leuenberger. *The Self as Project: Politics and the Human Sciences, Osiris* 22. Chicago: University of Chicago Press, 2007.

Falk, Avner. "Border Symbolism." *The Psychoanalytic Quarterly* 4 Vol. XLIII (1974): 650–660.

———. "Border Symbolism Revisited." *Int. Rev. Psycho-Anal* 10 (1983): 215–220.

———. *Fratricide in the Holy Land: A Psychoanalytic View of the Arab-Israeli Conflict*. Wisconsin: The University of Wisconsin Press, 2004.

Grosbard, Ofer. *Israel on the Couch: The Psychology of the Peace Process*. Albany, NY: State University of New York Press, 2003.

Hacking, Ian. *Mad Travellers: Reflections on the Reality of Transient Mental Illness*. London: Free Association Books, 1998.

Hartnack, Christiane. "Visnu on Freud's Desk: Psychoanalysis in Colonial India." *Social Research* 57/4 (1990): 921–949.

Harrington, Ralph. "The Neuroses of the Railways." *History Today* 44/7 (1994): 15–21.

Hennig, Heinz. "Der Mensch im Spannungsfeld zwischen Mangel und Konsum." *Psychosozial* 18, 1/59 (1995): 59–70.

Hinrichs, Reimer. "Patient DDR." *Kursbuch 101*. Berlin: Rowohlt, 1990: 57–66.

Hobsbawm, Eric J. *Nations and Nationalism since 1780: Programme, Myth, Reality*. Cambridge: Cambridge University Press, 1992.

Holstein, James A. "Producing People: Descriptive Practice in Human Service Work." *Current Research on Occupations and Professions* 7 (1992): 23–39.

Hughes, Thomas P. "The Seamless Web: Technology, Science, Etcetera, Etcetera." *Social Studies of Science* 16 (1986): 281–292.

Huntington, Samuel P. "The Clash of Civilizations?" *Foreign Affairs* 72/3 (1993): 22–49.

Internationale Erich-Fromm Gesellschaft. *Die Charaktermauer: Zur Psychoanalyse der Gesellschafts-Charakters in Ost-und Westdeutschland*. Göttingen: Vandenhoeck and Ruprecht, 1995.

Jung, Carl G. *Man and His Symbols*. London: Aldus Books, 1964.

Kaplan, Markus J., and Moriah Kaplan. "Walls and Boundaries in Arab Relations with Israel: Interpersonal Distancing Model." *Journal of Conflict Resolution* 27/3 (1983): 457–472.

Kelman, Herbert C. "Israel in Transition from Zionism to Post-Zionism." *Annals of the American Academy of Political and Social Sciences* 555 (1998): 46–61.

Keshet, Yehudit Kirtein. *Checkpoint Watch: Testimonies from Occupied Palestine*. New York: Zed Books, 2006.

Kuhn, Thomas S. *The Structure of Scientific Revolutions*. Chicago: University of Chicago Press, 1962.

Leuenberger, Christine. "Constructions of the Berlin Wall: How Material Culture Is Used in Psychological Theory." *Social Problems* 53/1 (2006): 18–37.

———. "The End of Socialism and the Reinvention of the Self: A Study of the East German Psychotherapeutic Community in Transition." *Theory and Society* 31/2 (2002): 257–282.

———. "Socialist Psychotherapy and its Dissidents." *Journal of the History of the Behavioral Sciences* 37/3 (2001): 261–273.

Lewis, Bernard. "The Roots of Muslim Rage." *The Atlantic Monthly* 266 (1990).

Maaz, Hans-Joachim. *Gefühlsstau: Ein Psychogramm der DDR*. Berlin: Argon, 1990.

Meyer, Gerd. "Zwischen Autoritarismus und Demokratie. Persönlichkeitsstrukturen in postkommunistischen Gesellschaften." *Psychosozial: Geschichte ist ein Teil von uns* 67 (1997): 93–108.

Mizrachi, Nissim. "'From Badness to Sickness': The Role of Ethnopsychology in Shaping Ethnic Hierarchies in Israel." *Social Identities* 10/2 (2004): 219–243.

Moses, Rafael. "Some Sociopsychological and Political Perspectives of the Meaning of the Holocaust: A View from Israel." *Israel Journal of Psychiatry and related Sciences* 34/1 (1997): 55–68.

Moller, Michael L., and Hans-Joachim Maaz. *Die Einheit beginnt zu zweit: Ein deutsch-deutsches Zwiegespräch*. Berlin: Rowohlt, 1993.

Möller, Wolfgang. "Entfremdung. Eine Heilungsgeschichte." *Kursbuch 101: Abriss der DDR*. Berlin: Rowohlt, 1990: 67–73.

Müller-Hegemann, Dietfried. *Die Berliner Mauerkrankheit*. Bielefeld: Nicolaische Verlagsbuchhandlung, 1973.

Pain, Rachel. "Place, Social Relations and the Fear of Crime: A Review." *Progress in Human Geography* 24/3 (2000): 365–387.

Prime: Peace Research Institute in the Middle East. *Learning Each Other's Historical Narrative: Palestinians and Israelis*. Beit Jallah, PNA: A Prime Publication, 2003.

Rabinowitz, Dan. "Oriental Othering and National Identity: A review of Early Israeli Anthropological Studies of Palestinians," in *Across the Wall: Narratives of Israeli-Palestinian History*, edited by Ilan Pappe and Jamil Hilal, 45–73. London: I. B. Tauris, 2010.

Rose, Nikolas. "Individualizing Psychology," in *Texts of Identity*, edited by John Shotter and Kenneth J. Gergen. London: Sage, 1992: 119–132.

Rose, Nikolas. "Assembling the Modern Self," in *Rewriting the Self*, edited by Roy Porter. London: Routledge, 1997: 224–248.

Rosenberg, Charles. "Framing Disease: Illness, Society, and History," in *Framing Disease*, edited by Charles E. Rosenberg and J. Golden. New Brunswick: Rutgers University Press, 1992.

Sassen, Saskia. *Territory, Authority, Rights: From Medieval to Global Assemblages*. Princeton, NJ: Princeton University Press, 2006.

Schröder, Harry. "Identität, Individualität und psychische Befindlichkeit des DDR-Bürgers im Umbruch." *Zeitschrift für Sozialisationsforschung und Erziehungssoziologie* 1 (1990): 163–176.

Seidler, Christoph, and Michael Fröse. "Die Utopie von Individuation und Bezogenheit in Deutschland." *Psychologische Beiträge* 35 (1993): 307–314.

Shirlow, Peter. "'Who Fears to Speak': Fear, Mobility, and Ethno-Sectarianism in the Two 'Ardoynes.'" *The Global Review of Ethnopolitics* 3/1 (2003): 76–91.

Suleiman, Ramzi. "On Marginal People: The Case of the Palestinians in Israel," in *Psychoanalysis, Identity, and Ideology: Critical Essays on the Israel/Palestine Case*, edited by John Bunzl and Benjamin Beit-Hallahmi. Boston: Kluwer Academic Publishers, 2002.

Staritz, Dietrich. *Geschichte der DDR*. Frankfurt: Suhrkamp, 1996.

Sterling, Brent L. *Do Good Fences Make Good Neighbors? What History Teaches Us about Strategic Barriers and International Security*. Washington, D.C.: Georgetown University Press, 2009.

Turkle, Sherry. *Life on the Screen: Identity in the Age of the Internet*. New York: Simon and Schuster, 1995.

Wagner, Wolf. "'Deutscher, proletarischer und moralischer'—Unterschiede zwischen Ost-und Westdeutschland und ihre Erklärung," in *Deutsch-deutsche Vergleiche: Psychologische Untersuchungen 10 Jahre nach dem Mauerfall*, edited by H. Berth and E. Brähler. Berlin: Verlag für Wissenschaft und Forschung, 1999: 53–69.

Winnicott, Donald W. *Home Is Where We Start From: Essays by a Psychoanalyst*. New York: W. W. Norton and Company, 1986.

Zink, Valerie. "A Quiet Transfer: The Judaization of Jerusalem." *Contemporary Arab Affairs* 21 (2009): 122–133.

4

The Diminishing Relevance of *Ostalgie* 20 Years after Reunification

Paul Kubicek

The fall of the Berlin Wall and the reunification of Germany marked the end of the repressive, communist regime of East Germany (hereafter German Democratic Republic, GDR) and offered prospects for a more hopeful future for its former citizens. Former East German citizens could now take advantage of a variety of personal and civic freedoms. Integration into the larger, more dynamic West German economy and its substantial welfare state seemed likely to foster greater economic opportunity and raise living standards. Throughout the 1990s, the German government poured billions of marks into the former GDR to help transform and modernize its economy and promote social development.

Two decades later, it is apparent that not all the hopes engendered by the fall of the Wall have been realized. The eastern *Länder* remain poorer than those in the West. Unemployment in the East is twice as high as in the West.[1] West Germans did invest in the East, but Easterners did not always appreciate that Westerners' fatter wallets often came with a haughty attitude that either trivialized East German history or viewed the GDR exclusively as a *Stasi* state. Easterners, forced to conform to the West German system, complained that they felt like second-class citizens.[2] Some Westerners thought the Easterners were lazy and ungrateful,[3] and many believed Easterners lacked the same sense of shame and guilt about German history that had been hammered into the psyche of West Germans. Within a few years of reunification, observers began to speak of *die Mauer im Kopf* (the "wall in the mind"), a phenomenon also addressed by Hunter

Bivens in this volume.[4] One German politician suggested: "We might be the first country which has, by unifying, created two peoples."[5] Or, as one joke from 1990 had it: the East German says to the West German, "*Wir sind ein Volk*" (We are one people). The West German replies, "*Wir auch*" (We too).[6] Lest one think this problem would disappear over time, surveys conducted in 2010 by *Stern* for the twentieth anniversary of reunification found that under half (48 percent) of all Germans thought West and East Germans had grown together as a people and only 25 percent of former East Germans felt they were part of a united people.[7]

The problems—both real and perceived—faced by the Easterners have produced, at least in a certain segment of the population, *Ostalgie*: nostalgia for some elements from the GDR. This is not the same as legitimate grievances against contemporary economic or social problems since *Ostalgie* makes explicit comparisons with how life was (or how it was imagined to be) in the GDR and uses the GDR as a positive reference point. *Ostalgie* may or may not have real political importance. For example, some phenomena often classified as *Ostalgie*, such as participation in online "*Ossi*-Quizzes" or quests to find or reproduce East German products such as the traffic-light *Ampelmännchen* or the rattling two-cylinder Trabant, can be entirely nostalgic (if not kitschy) without making broader social or political commentary.[8] Some, such as a planned (but never built) theme park dedicated to East Germany or a *Stasi*-themed restaurant in East Berlin, are of more questionable taste. Others, such as voting for the Left (*Die Linke*) Party, the successor to the communist party of the GDR, may have more political import.

The impact of *Ostalgie*, however, remains an open question, and 20 years after reunification one might wonder if it remains a persistent and relevant phenomenon. This chapter does not examine the well-trod ground of cultural and literary depictions of *Ostalgie* in the 1990s and early 2000s—for example, Jana Hensel's memoir *Zonenkinder* (2002) or films such as *Sonnenallee* (1999) and *Goodbye Lenin!* (2003)[9]—but is instead focused on measuring the strength of *Ostalgie* over time and assessing its political relevance. While finding evidence that *Ostalgie* is still felt by many former East Germans, it appears to be less prevalent among younger people, and there is little evidence to suggest it has significant political importance.

Bases for *Ostalgie*

Before jumping ahead, it would be useful to explore briefly some of the reasons that *Ostalgie* might manifest itself in contemporary Germany. One reason might be that Easterners and Westerners were (and are) fundamentally different. In this view, the roughly 40-year division of Germany was long enough, thanks to differing educational systems, life experiences, government propaganda, et cetera, to create two distinct peoples with different values.[10] Both the West and East German states made efforts to define their identities in opposition to each other. Upon reunification, both sets of Germans initially found little in common. Even in the early 1980s, the author and essayist Peter Schneider remarked with considerable prescience, "It will take us longer to tear down the Wall in our heads than any wrecking company will need for the Wall we can see."[11]

Can this conjecture that there were, prior to reunification, significant differences in values between people living in the two Germanies be supported with solid evidence? The World Values Survey, conducted in the spring of 1990, provides us with some basis to answer this question. Findings from the survey on several types of questions are presented in Table 4.1. What is interesting is that, with some exceptions—on gender roles, value of equality, and speed of reform, all covered more extensively below—there are no marked differences. Many similarities, especially on core political and economic questions, stand out. Both sets of Germans were politically centrist, seemed to be pro-market and valued competition, and wanted a future where more emphasis would be placed on the individual. Surveys in 1991 and 1992 also found similarities between former East and West Germans on a wide battery of questions that probed attitudes toward democracy.[12] Henry Krisch argued that the protests of 1989, together with the attitudes found in post-reunification surveys, showed that key segments of East German society had fundamentally rejected the tenets and values of the GDR's socialist system.[13]

One should, of course, use such data with caution since attitudes of Easterners may not have been well established and were subject to change with different circumstances in the post-unification environment. Thus, rather than emphasizing alleged intrinsic differences that predate the fall of the Wall, some analysts have suggested it was the effects of reunification that led to both resentment toward the West and subsequent *Ostalgie*. Certainly, there were high expectations about how reunification would improve material conditions. In 1990, Chancellor Helmut Kohl famously promised East Germans "blossoming landscapes" within five years.[14] However, this vision was not realized, as economic restructuring and marketization in reunified Germany led to plant closings, extensive deindustrialization, and widespread unemployment. Furthermore, the speed of reunification and the fact that it meant the Western system was imposed on the East left Easterners with little familiar in the new political, economic, educational, and cultural institutions. This sparked resentment and, perhaps, a desire to revive some

Table 4.1 Differences in Values between Germans in 1990

Question	*West Germans*	*East Germans*
Do you favor more private (1) or state (10) ownership? (Mean)	3.7	3.1
Should individuals (1) or government (10) assume responsibility for people's lives? (Mean)	4.2	4.1
Is competition generally good (1) or harmful (10)? (Mean)	3.3	3.0
Where are you on a Left (1) to Right (10) political scale? (Mean)	5.3	5.0
Which is more important: freedom or equality?	Freedom 59.3% Equality 22.4%	Freedom 46.6% Equality 40.7%
In the future should more emphasis be on the individual? (% agreeing)	84.4	87.7
Is political reform moving too rapidly? (% agreeing)	38.4	68.5
Should husband and wife both contribute to income? (% agreeing)	55.0	83.0

Source: World Values Survey, online analysis at www.worldvaluessurvey.org. Questions are paraphrased from original.

of the symbols or memories of their past.[15] As noted above, in the spring of 1990, most in the East thought political reform was proceeding too rapidly. Some spoke of the colonization of the East by the West; reunification, whose prospect was initially widely celebrated, came to be seen by some as an imperialist project. Paul Betts noted, "No doubt this East German nostalgia is directly linked to the fact that the GDR has literally vanished from the political map. It was this speedy absorption—what East German detractors often call 'Kohl-onization'—that made the GDR story so unique."[16] Many East Germans were thrown into a situation where the values and social rights of their "mass utopia"—as explored by Bivens in this volume—were replaced by institutions, rules, and norms created by others. *Ostalgie* thus emerged as a response to "personal anguish and political confusion" created by the disappearance of the GDR.[17]

Following this line of reasoning, the emergence of nostalgia for the old system was not simply an abstract notion but was rooted in a belief that certain things were better in the GDR. This went beyond the *Spreewaldgurken* (East German pickles) procured by the protagonist Alex in the film *Goodbye Lenin!* so that his mother would continue to believe she was living in East Germany. Surveys as early as 1993, for instance, found that a majority of former East Germans believed that in many domains (job security, child care, crime prevention, gender equality, and social justice) the policies of the former GDR were superior to those in West Germany.[18] In the words of Harvey Greisman, *Ostalgie* is not the product of massive denial but "a painful accurate realization that life for many is tougher under freedom than it was in a dictatorship."[19]

Some studies singled out women as especially hard-hit, since many of the benefits they had under the old system, including generous maternity leave, funds for expectant mothers, and state-provided child care, were lost. The socialist order put great rhetorical emphasis on a woman's role in the workforce and guaranteed women pay equality: 98 percent of East German women worked outside the home.[20] In reunified Germany, many women in the eastern *Länder* found themselves out of work and experienced great difficulties getting new jobs as employers viewed women with children as a liability. In the first two years after reunification, women's unemployment increased to 23 percent.[21] In many other respects—gender-specific advertising for vacancies, discrimination in employment, exposure to sexual harassment, a gender gap in earnings, repeals of liberal divorce and abortion statutes—women fared poorly after 1990.[22]

Nostalgia for the old system also manifested itself politically in votes for the Party of Democratic Socialism (PDS, later *Die Linke* [The Left Party]), the successor to the GDR's Socialist Unity Party. This party, exploiting its status as the region's "home-grown" party and appealing to those with positive feelings for aspects of the GDR, regularly received over 20 percent of the vote in the eastern *Länder* and even won a near majority (47.6 percent) of the vote in regional elections in East Berlin in 2001.[23]

These considerations assume that *Ostalgie*, being rooted in the experience of the GDR, has a clear political-social intention as a sort of identity of defiance against the West (*Trotzidentität*[24]) and is primarily manifested among older East Germans and those who were "losers" in the postcommunist transition. However, *Ostalgie* is often linked in television,[25] film, and literature to cultural artifacts and sensory experiences (e.g., food), particularly those involving childhood and innocence.[26] In this sense, *Ostalgie* works to recall a simpler, more tranquil period, and is thus more about time and place, not ideology, politics, or economic circumstances.[27] In some of its forms, such as the reappearance of communist symbols on T-shirts and efforts to find or re-create GDR products, it also borders on *kitsch*—a sort of retro-cool movement more about style or the desire to shock than experiential links to the GDR or an ideological or political statement.

Measuring *Ostalgie*

Public opinion surveys in the post-reunification period capture, in a concrete and measurable way, aspects of nostalgia for the past among former East Germans who were disappointed with the results of reunification. For example, according to surveys commissioned by *Der Spiegel* and conducted among citizens of the former GDR in 1990 and 1995, there was growth in appreciation for certain aspects of life in the old system. In Table 4.2, one can see that whereas in 1990 the GDR was judged superior in three of the nine categories (predictably those of social security, gender equality, and maintenance of order), by 1995 the GDR was judged superior in seven of the nine categories, including, perhaps surprisingly, health and housing. These findings support the notion that *Ostalgie* arose because of post-reunification experiences, not because of innate differences. It is interesting to note, however, that whereas East Germans gave high marks for the GDR in specific categories such as schooling and housing, the overwhelming consensus was that the standard of living in the Federal Republic was better. Perhaps the difference can be explained in that former East Germans recognized a clear overall gap between the two systems but were unable to take advantage of this fact in tangible ways. Nonetheless, despite aspects of *Ostalgie* found in the 1995 survey, only 15 percent of those polled agreed that they "wished there had never been a reunification" of the two countries.[28]

Has this changed over time, as memories of the GDR recede and former East Germans become integrated into reunited Germany? Surveys in

Table 4.2 East German Assessment of Relative Merit of Aspects of East and West Germany, 1990 and 1995

Criterion	*1990*		*1995*	
	% West Superior	*% East Superior*	*% West Superior*	*% East Superior*
Standard of living	91	2	85	8
Protection against crime	13	62	4	88
Equality for women	10	67	3	87
Science and technology	87	2	63	6
Social security	16	65	3	92
Schools	36	28	11	64
Vocational training	36	33	12	70
Health system	65	18	23	57
Housing	34	27	21	53

Source: "Stolz aufs eigene Leben," *Der Spiegel* 27 (1995), cited in Jacoby, *Imitation and Politics*, 185.

the early 1990s among former East Germans, while unearthing evidence of *Ostalgie*, found optimism about the future and that the majority believed problems of misunderstanding between Germans would be overcome.[29] However, more recent evidence suggests that *Ostalgie* has remained relatively strong. For the eighteenth anniversary of the fall of the Wall, *Der Spiegel* commissioned a survey among older and younger Germans on both sides of the erstwhile divide. Table 4.3 presents some of the findings with respect to comparing the former GDR with today's Germany.[30] One finds many similarities to data presented previously: The GDR tends to be rated higher in terms of social security, education, prevention of crime, and gender equality, whereas reunified Germany gets higher marks for personal freedom, the political system, and overall standard of living. Interestingly, for many of the elements of *Ostalgie* related to social protections and gender issues, one sees a significant gap between older (35–50 years) and younger (14–24 years) respondents, the latter having very limited (at best) memories of the GDR. However, these younger respondents are more likely to rate the GDR as strong for personal freedoms and the political system, perhaps reflecting a naivety about realities of East Germany and/or their frustrations with their current situation. The survey also found that over 40 percent of those in the East believed communication problems between West and East Germans were increasing (compared with 35 percent of Westerners who felt this way), and over 60 percent believed it was bad that nothing remained of

Table 4.3 Attitudes of Former East Germans in 2007

East Germany Stronger:	*14–24 Years Old*	*35–50 Years Old*
Social welfare	47	92
Education	57	79
Prevention of crime	57	78
Social equality	39	73
Gender equality	37	73
Economy	26	19
Political system	22	11
Personal freedom	14	4
Today's Germany Stronger:		
Social welfare	51	26
Education	40	19
Prevention of crime	39	19
Social equality	45	22
Gender equality	67	36
Economy	62	75
Political system	51	60
Personal freedom	83	85

the things one could be proud of in East Germany. A significant percentage (37 percent of older respondents, 35 percent of younger ones) also indicated that if the Wall was still up they would prefer to live in East Germany.

Socio-Demographic Factors behind *Ostalgie*

What factors lie behind and may help account for feelings of *Ostalgie*? To this point, we have put forward several hypotheses (e.g., effects of age, gender, etc.) that might make an individual more susceptible to *Ostalgie*. These can be tested by analyzing existent survey data. The best set of surveys for this purpose is the ALLBUS (German General Social Survey), which is conducted every other year. The survey does not ask questions directly connected to *Ostalgie* (e.g., what aspects of the GDR do you most miss?), but it asks some general questions about the GDR and how reunification has been conducted. One general question, asked periodically since 1991, is to what extent respondents living in the former East Germany identify with the old GDR on a four-point scale.[31] General results are displayed in Table 4.4, which reveals that respondents in 2008 were *more* likely than in 1991 to identify with the GDR, despite the fact that by 2008 the GDR had not existed for nearly two decades.

Assuming this question can serve as a measure for *Ostalgie*, one can then look beyond the aggregate results and employ statistical analysis to assess what other variables are most related to this phenomenon. As suggested earlier, age should matter since older respondents with actual memories of the GDR should identify more strongly with it. Socioeconomics might also be important, since those who feel they are in a poor economic situation might consider themselves "losers" from

Table 4.4 Levels of Identification with the Former East Germany % of respondents

Level of Identification	*1991*	*2000*	*2008*
Strong	12.3	21.2	20.8
Fairly strong	30.9	47.9	44.3
A little	30.1	23.0	21.9
Not at all	26.6	7.9	13.0
Sample size	1494	730	626

Source: ALLBUS 2008, online data, available at http://www.gesis.org/en/services/data/survey-data/allbus.

Note: Responses of "do not know" or "cannot say" were dropped from the analysis. The sample size for all surveys is sufficient to conduct statistical analysis.

reunification and thus may have more positive feelings for the GDR. Because many women have lost status and benefits since reunification, gender might also play a role. Lastly, one could examine the effects of education (sometimes considered a proxy for social class or income) as this could color feelings about the GDR.

An ordinal logistical regression analysis was conducted with the data from the 1991, 2000, and 2008 surveys, when the question on identification with the GDR was asked. With such an analysis, one can look at the specific effects of one variable while others are held constant.[32] One can examine two issues with the data. First, what variables are most strongly related to identification with the GDR? Second, do these variables perform similarly across time or do they change, suggesting that "*Ostalgie*" itself captures different things at different points in time?

The results show that all but one of these factors matter, but their effects vary over time.[33] Table 4.5 presents a very basic picture, indicating which variables achieved statistical significance (at least $p < .05$) in the surveys. In the 1991 survey, the two variables with high statistical significance ($p < .01$) are gender and education.[34] The effect of gender was such that women were more likely to identify with the GDR, perhaps as a result of the immediate effects of reunification on job and socioeconomic status. Those with more education did identify more with the GDR, perhaps reflecting that these respondents were more likely to be part of the GDR elite and/or had a sense of tangible benefit of life in the GDR. Age did not appear as significant, which was not surprising: older respondents lived for 40 years in the GDR and younger ones knew nothing else but the GDR. There did not appear to be a socioeconomic effect. Responses to questions asking about the general economic situation in eastern Germany or about one's own personal economic condition did not significantly affect level of identification with the former GDR.

Results were different in 2000 and 2008. In 2000, there was still a gender effect, but a generational one also appeared: younger respondents

Table 4.5 Results of Regression Analysis on Identification with East Germany

Explanatory Variable	*1991*	*2000*	*2008*
Age		x	x
Gender	x	x	
Education	x		
Assessment of German economy			x
Assessment of one's economic situation			

Note: x shows that the variable has statistical significance.

were significantly less likely to identify with the GDR. The latter is not overly surprising, as by 2000 those under 30 had experienced a sizeable portion of their life in reunited Germany. Education, however, was no longer statistically significant, and socioeconomic assessments also showed little effect. In 2008, as one might have predicted, age mattered ($p < .001$) once again; education and gender, unlike in 1991, were not significant. As for socioeconomic assessments, one's assessment of one's own economic condition did not seem to matter, but one's assessment of the overall economic situation in Germany did have a modest effect; those thinking Germany was in a poor condition identified more strongly with the GDR. This finding appears to be counterintuitive, because one might expect one's personal condition to have more importance in shaping attitudes, but it appears that a general assessment about conditions in Germany is more important.

To go beyond discussion of statistical significance and illustrate the importance of various factors, data are presented in Figure 4.1, which shows how different groups of people identified with the GDR in 1991 and in 2008. This figure, in addition to showing more identification with the GDR in 2008 (e.g., the number of people "strongly" or "somewhat" identifying with the GDR in most categories moves up), one also sees how different factors or variables change over time. Moving from left to right, the first variable one sees is education. In 1991, university graduates were much more likely to identify with the GDR compared to those with a more basic education. This effect vanishes in 2008, as in that year those with less education claim more identification with the GDR than university graduates. Next is gender. One can see a modest gender effect in 1991—women identify more with the GDR—but this disappears in 2008. The age effect—here illustrating the youngest and oldest cohorts—is perhaps most striking, as there is no real difference between them in 1991 but a chasm between them in 2008, with the youngest cohort the only group in this figure to show less identification with the GDR in 2008. Lastly, with respect to economic assessments, one does see a modest effect by 2008, with those saying the economic situation in Germany is bad more likely to identify with the GDR. Overall, what comes across clearest is that demographic and socioeconomic conditions related to *Ostalgie* have changed over time, with the generational effect undergoing the largest transformation and becoming the most important explanatory variable by 2008.

One could employ other means to examine *Ostalgie* in these surveys. In some of the surveys, the ALLBUS asks respondents in general terms about the effects of reunification and whether people in western or eastern Germany should, respectively, make more sacrifices or exhibit more

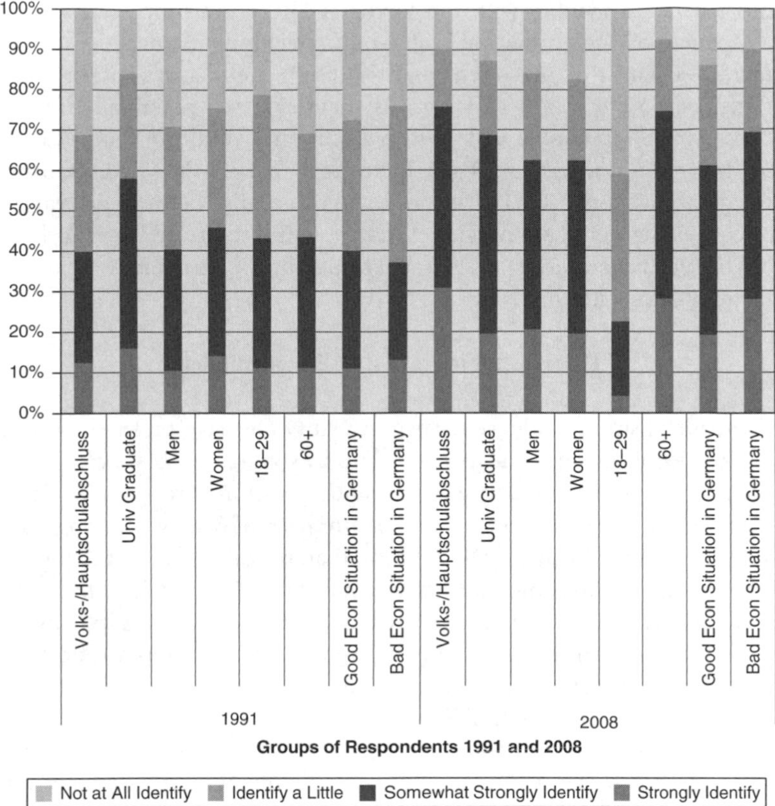

Figure 4.1 Effects of different variables on identification with the GDR

patience. These variables capture, more directly than anything yet presented, attitudes about the process and results of reunification, arguably factors that could foster *Ostalgie*. The only year in which these questions were asked in conjunction with the question about identification with the GDR was 2000. Not surprisingly, there is a statistically significant and positive correlation between identification with the GDR and the belief that reunification has been bad for East Germans and a significant negative correlation with the statement that people in the former GDR should show more patience. Moreover, assessments about and changes in one's economic condition correlate strongly with negative assessments about reunification.[35] In the latter case, those who thought things had gotten worse for them—the "losers," so to speak—were more likely to think poorly of reunification itself, but, interestingly, they were *not* significantly more likely to identify with the former GDR: correlation with a poor assessment of one's condition is .02 and correlation with negative assessment of changes in one's own condition is .06, neither of which obtains statistical significance.[36] This point is surprising and potentially important: being disappointed with personal economic results of reunification by itself does not seem to foster identification with the GDR. In other words, at least in the 2000 survey, one can distinguish between grievances or complaints about an individual's own predicament and larger feelings of *Ostalgie* that are, arguably, better captured by the variable asking about identification with the GDR.

Does *Ostalgie* Have a Political Impact?

There is still strong evidence to suggest that *Ostalgie* is a prevalent feeling among people living in the former GDR. By some measures, *Ostalgie* has even grown over time, and even though it is more strongly associated with the older generations, sizeable numbers of younger people also identify with the former GDR or think that, in some respect, the former GDR is superior to contemporary Germany. Whether and how this matters politically can be determined by looking at the relationship between identification with the GDR and phenomena such as support and trust in democratic institutions, voting, and overall identification with the contemporary German republic.

One possible concern about *Ostalgie* is that it translates into less trust and support for democratic institutions in contemporary Germany. Put differently, those who identify more with the former GDR, while not necessarily in favor of restoration of a nondemocratic political system, are nonetheless alienated from political life. Data from the most recent (2008) ALLBUS survey finds a modest amount of evidence for this proposition. For example, when one measures *Ostalgie* as identification with GDR, as we have throughout this chapter, one finds that "*Ostalgic*" individuals exhibit less trust in government institutions than do other Germans, whether they live in the East or West. Data are presented in Table 4.6. For these questions, respondents were asked to indicate their level of trust in various institutions on a seven-point scale, with seven being high degree of trust. However, only on the question of trust in the federal government does the difference obtain a modest degree ($p < .05$) of statistical significance. When an ordinal regression analysis is performed on data from respondents in eastern Germany, economic assessments are generally far more important factors in levels of trust than is identification with the GDR. As to a wider question of political alienation from democratic institutions, there is a correlation between

Table 4.6 Level of Trust in Political Institutions

Institution	*Trust Among All Surveyed*	*Trust Among All East Germans*	*Trust Among Those Who Identify with the GDR*
Federal Government	3.67	3.40	3.29
Bundestag	3.64	3.28	3.18
Constitutional Court	4.78	4.41	4.30
Political parties	3.10	2.94	2.84

Source: ALLBUS Survey, 2008. Table reports mean scores on a scale of 1-7, with 7 being a high degree of trust.

identification with the GDR and agreement with the idea that politicians don't care what people like me think. This relationship remains significant ($p < .02$) in a regression analysis once age, education, gender, and economic assessments are taken into account.

Might some of this distrust and alienation translate into an "*Ostalgic*" vote? As noted earlier, the Left Party, rooted in the former ruling party of the GDR, has established itself as a sort of protest party. Throughout much of the 1990s and 2000s, the Left Party and its predecessors found most of their voters in the former East Germany. However, in 2009 elections, thanks to the addition of Oskar Lafontaine, a long-time leader in the Social Democratic Party, it performed better in some regions of western Germany. While it still remains more of an "East German" party, is it true that this party finds more support among those who are more "*Ostalgic*"? The 2008 ALLBUS survey asked respondents about party identification and vote intention. One can examine whether those who identify more with the former GDR express different views and intentions than those who identify less with the GDR. Of those who identified strongly with the GDR, 22 percent said they intended to vote for the Left Party, as opposed to only 7 percent of those who did not identify with the GDR. Overall, 17 percent of East Germans stated they would vote for the Left Party. While these data do show a clear relationship and statistical correlation achieves a high degree ($p <. 001$) of statistical significance, it would be an exaggeration to assert that all or even most of those who strongly identify with the GDR support the Left Party. What lies behind the Left vote is harder to say. Whereas some would assert this is a "protest vote," there is no correlation between support of the Left Party and general distrust in political parties, and there is no significant correlation between support for the Left Party and assessments about one's own or the general German economic situation. There is, however, a strong correlation (.111, $p < .001$) between an intended vote for the Left Party and general distrust of the federal government. A binary logistic regression analysis on vote intention for the Left Party shows that identification with the GDR, distrust of the federal government, and, not surprisingly, age, are all statistically significant ($p < .001$). How significant in terms of consequences this is, however, is harder to say. Whereas the Left Party and its predecessors were anathema and almost assumed to be undemocratic a decade ago, today the Left Party has more respectability and has shown a willingness at the state (*Land*) level to cooperate with other political parties. To argue, as was done in the 1990s,[37] that support for the Left Party among those living in the former East Germany is a threat to German democracy seems like a bit of an exaggeration.

How far does this alienation extend? Specifically, how much less likely are those that identify with the GDR to identify with contemporary Germany and fellow Germans? Data from the 2008 ALLBUS are presented in figure 4.2. The results may be surprising, in that Germans who identify with the GDR are just as likely—if not slightly more so—to identify with the whole of Germany and all German citizens. Thus, it does not appear that *Ostalgie*, as measured in this analysis, is related to an existential crisis about German identity or, for that matter, poses a crisis of legitimacy for the state.

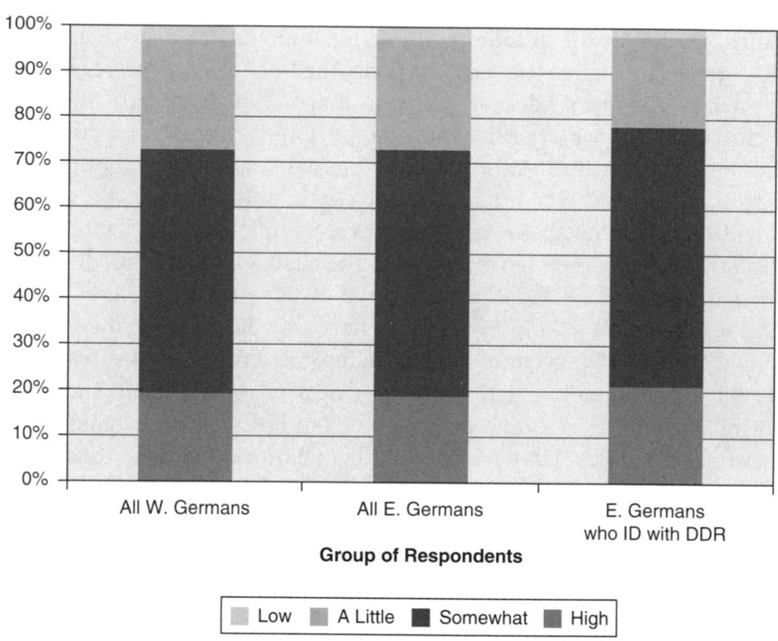

Figure 4.2 Level of identification with Germany as a whole

This is not to say that *Ostalgie* is wholly irrelevant; it may drive some to vote for the Left Party; it is a consequence (but likely not a cause) of bad feelings about reunification; and it continues to manifest itself in literary and popular culture as well as in general discussions about contemporary Germany. However, *Ostalgie*—be it through literary treatments, pop culture, Trabant clubs, or lingering feelings of identification with the GDR—is, in important ways, overwhelmingly backward looking. That is, it is designed to rehabilitate memory but is not attached to a broader forward-looking political or ideological program to transform Germany. *Ostalgie*, in this light, is relatively politically safe and harmless, wistful reflections perhaps on some aspects of life that were lost after 1989. These feelings have not been transformed into calls for action; there is no "*Ostalgic*" movement to reorder German society along the lines of that which existed in the GDR. This is hardly surprising; the GDR is not coming back and few would welcome imposition of its political system. *Ostalgie* in its various guises exists, therefore, at most as a critique, but it is incapable of imagining or advancing a pragmatic, positive vision of how society could be reshaped or of truly redressing problems engendered by reunification.[38]

The analysis presented in this chapter suggests that while *Ostalgie*—as measured chiefly by identification with the former GDR—is a real and surprisingly persistent phenomenon, one should be careful about exaggerating its political importance. Two decades after reunification, despite lingering resentment and the difficulties they encountered after 1990, most East Germans identify with today's Federal Republic, and their trust in political institutions, while not overwhelmingly high, is also not abysmally low. *Ostalgie*'s stronger presence among older East Germans should also mean that the phenomenon will recede over time with generational changes, and its saliency seems likely to decline also as memories of the GDR fade. This need not mean that former East Germans will be as content with institutions or their situation as those in the western German *Länder*, but even on this issue, there is a weak link between individual grievances and *Ostalgie*; and over time it will be harder for the GDR to be a touchstone as a point of reference or a place to imagine a better alternative.

Notes

1. The *New York Times*, "In East Germany, a Decline as Stark as a Wall," June 18, 2009.
2. One survey in 1991, for example, found that 84 percent of Eastern Germans felt like second-class citizens. See Michael Minkenburg, "The Wall after the

Wall: On the Continuing Division of Germany and Remaking of Political Culture," *Comparative Politics* 26, no. 1, (1993): 65.

3. A survey reported in *Spiegel Online International* found that 64 percent of 35–50-year-old West Germans did not think their efforts to develop the former East Germany were sufficiently appreciated. See *Spiegel OnLine International*, "Germany Still Divided 18 Years after the Fall of the Wall." November 9, 2007, available at: http://www.spiegel.de/international/germany/0,1518,516472,00.html. Accessed July 13, 2010.
4. See also Hans-Dieter Klingemann and Richard Hofferbert, "Germany: A New 'Wall in the Mind'?" *Journal of Democracy* 5, no. 1 (1994): 30–44 as well as Minkenburg, "The Wall after the Wall."
5. Wolfgang Nowak, a former minister in the government of Saxony, in "Getting Back Together Is So Hard." *The Economist*, September 18, 2004, 58.
6. Dominic Boyer, "*Ostalgie* and the Politics of the Future in Eastern Germany." *Public Culture* 18, no. 2 (2006): 371.
7. "Westdeutsche fühlen sich wiedervereinigter," *Stern*, September 29, 2010. A different survey reported, however, that 57 percent of East Germans were positive about reunification and only 19 percent were negative. See "East Germans Remain Positive on Unification," *Financial Times*, September 22, 2010.
8. For example, there is a Trabant car club in Berlin (www.trabigoerenberlin.de), and shops dedicated to the *Ampelmännchen* (http://www.ampelmann.de/html/shops.html). The online version of a store dedicated to a variety of East German products can be found at http://www.mondosarts.de. See also Daphne Berdahl, "'(N)Ostalgie' for the Present: Memory, Longing, and East German Things," *Ethnos* 2, no. 64 (1999): 192–211, and Martin Blum, "Remaking the East German Past: *Ostalgie*, Identity, and Material Culture," *Journal of Popular Culture* 3, no. 34 (2000): 229–253.
9. See Boyer, "*Ostalgie*"; Paul Cooke, *Representing East Germany since Unification: From Colonization to Nostalgia* (Oxford: Berg, 2005); and Anna Saunders, "'Normalizing' the Past: East German Culture and *Ostalgie*," in *German Culture, Politics, and Literature into the Twenty-First Century*, ed. Stuart Taberner and Paul Cooke (Rochester, NY: Camden House, 2006) 89–104.
10. Helga Welsh, "The Divided Past and the Difficulties of German Unification," *German Politics and Society* 30, no. 1 (1993): 75–86 and Martin Greiffenhagen and Sylvia Greiffenhagen, "Eine Nation. Zwei politische Kulturen," in *Deutschland: Eine Nation doppelte Geschichte*," ed. Werner Weidenfeld, (Köln: Verlag Wissenschaft und Politik, 1993), 29–45.
11. Peter Schneider, *The Wall Jumper* (New York: Pantheon, 1983), 119.
12. Russell Dalton, "Communists and Democrats: Democratic Attitudes in the Two Germanies," *British Journal of Political Science* 24 (1994): 469–493, and Klingemann and Hofferbert, "Germany: A New 'Wall in the Mind'?"
13. Henry Krisch, "German Unification and East German Political Culture: Interaction and Change," in *Germany after Unification: Coming to Terms with the Recent Past*, ed. Gert-Joachim Glaeßner (Amsterdam: Rodopi, 1996), 5–16.

14. Quoted in Harvey Greisman, "The German Democratic Republic in Nostalgia and Memory," *Humanity and Society* 25, no. 1 (2001): 46.
15. Boyer, "*Ostalgie*," 372–373.
16. Paul Betts, "The Twilight of the Idols: East German Memory and Material Culture," *The Journal of Modern History* 72, no. 3 (2000): 734.
17. Konrad Jarausch, "Reshaping German Identities: Reflections on the Post-Unification Debate," in *After Unity: Reconfiguring German Identities*, ed. Konrad Jarausch (Oxford: Berghahn, 1997), 9.
18. Reports from *Die Zeit*, October 1, 1993, cited in Klingemann and Hofferbert, "Germany: A New 'Wall in the Mind'?" 39.
19. Greisman, "The German Democratic Republic," 52.
20. Grace Marvin, "Two Steps Back and One Step Forward: East German Women since the Fall of the Wall," *Humanity and Society* 19, no. 2 (1995): 37–50.
21. Ibid., 38.
22. Helen Frink, *Women after Communism: The East German Experience* (Lanham, MD: University Press of America, 2001), 48.
23. Peter Barker, "The Party of Democratic Socialism as Political Voice of East Germany," in *United and Divided: Germany since 1990*, ed. Mike Dennis and Eva Kolinsky (New York: Berghahn, 2004).
24. Saunders, "'Normalizing' the Past," 90.
25. An example would be Katarina Witt, former champion figure skater and host of *The GDR Show* on RTL, appearing in a uniform of the young pioneers, the communist youth organization.
26. See Blum, "Remaking the East German Past," and Joseph Jozwiak, "The Wall in Our Minds? Colonization, Integration, and Nostalgia," *Journal of Popular Culture* 39, no. 5 (2006): 780–795.
27. This is well captured by Thomas Brussig, the screenwriter for *Sonnenallee*, who noted, "jeder Mensch erinnert sich gerne an die Kindheit oder Jugend." ("Everyone has fond memories of childhood and youth"). Quoted in Saunders, "'Normalizing' the Past," 101.
28. Reported in Wade Jacoby, *Imitation and Politics: Redesigning Modern Germany* (Ithaca, NY: Cornell University Press, 2000), 184.
29. Klingemann and Hofferbert, "Germany: A New 'Wall in the Mind'?" 40.
30. Data come from a sample 1,004 respondents, divided between younger (14–24 years) and older (35–50 years) respondents in both former Germanies ("East" Germans were those who resided in the East until 1989). Report is available at *Spiegel Online International*, "Germany still Divided."
31. One confounding factor is that one could be living in East Germany now but grew up in West Germany and is thus more of a "West German." According to the 2008 survey, however, only 2.8 percent of respondents in East Germany grew up in West Germany. An equal number grew up in former German territories (e.g., Silesia), and 3.7 percent were immigrants.
32. Because the dependent variable—level of identification with the GDR—is categorical rather than linear, this technique is preferred over the more familiar least-squares linear regression analysis. In this type of analysis, the independent effect of particular possible explanatory variables can be isolated and measured

by holding the other variables constant. Thus, one can assess the strength of relationship between each independent/explanatory variable (e.g., age, gender) and the dependent variable (identification with the GDR).

33. For simplicity's sake, I present a narrative and simple graphs rather than a more complex table with the statistical coefficients for each variable. When using the term "significant," I mean that the variable appears to be statistically significant ($p < .05$) in the regression analysis. The graphs are used to capture some of the magnitude of these effects.
34. The one scalar variable for education asked for the respondents' end of school certificate (*Arbitur*, *Mittlere Reife*, *Volksschulabschluss*, etc.). Dichotomous dummy variables (coded 0 if the individual lacked the attribute, 1 if they possessed it) allowed one to identify graduates of university, technical schools, et cetera.
35. For example, correlation coefficients with a negative assessment of reunification were .08 for identification with East Germany, .26 with poor assessment of one's own economic condition, and .17 with decline in one's economic situation.
36. This latter question was not, unfortunately, asked in the 1991 or 2008 surveys.
37. Barker, "The Party of Democratic Socialism."
38. This is similar to arguments made by Boyer, "*Ostalgie* and the Politics of the Future."

Bibliography

Barker, Peter. "The Party of Democratic Socialism as Political Voice of East Germany," in *United and Divided: Germany since 1990*, ed. Mike Dennis and Eva Kolinsky, 55–67. New York: Berghahn, 2004.

Berdahl, Daphne. "'(N)Ostalgie' for the Present: Memory, Longing, and East German Things." *Ethnos* 2, no. 64 (1999): 192–211.

Betts, Paul. "The Twilight of the Idols: East German Memory and Material Culture." *The Journal of Modern History* 72, no. 3 (2000): 731–765.

Blum, Martin. "Remaking the East German Past: *Ostalgie*, Identity, and Material Culture." *Journal of Popular Culture* 3, no. 34 (2000): 229–253.

Boyer, Dominic. "*Ostalgie* and the Politics of the Future in Eastern Germany." *Public Culture* 18, no. 2 (2006): 361–381.

Cooke, Paul. *Representing East Germany since Unification: From Colonization to Nostalgia*. Oxford: Berg, 2005.

Dalton, Russell. "Communists and Democrats: Democratic Attitudes in the Two Germanies." *British Journal of Political Science* 24 (1994): 469–493.

The Economist. "Getting Back Together Is So Hard." September 18, 2004.

Frink, Helen. *Women after Communism: The East German Experience*. Lanham MD: University Press of America, 2001.

Greiffenhagen, Martin, and Sylvia Greiffenhagen. "Eine Nation. Zwei politische Kulturen," in *Deutschland: Eine Nation doppelte Geschichte*, ed. Werner Weidenfeld, 29–45. Köln: Verlag Wissenschaft und Politik, 1993.

Greisman, Harvey. "The German Democratic Republic in Nostalgia and Memory." *Humanity and Society* 25, no. 1 (2001): 41–56.

Jacoby, Wade. *Imitation and Politics: Redesigning Modern Germany*. Ithaca, NY: Cornell University Press, 2000.

Jarausch, Konrad. "Reshaping German Identities: Reflections on the Post-Unification Debate," in *After Unity: Reconfiguring German Identities*, ed. Konrad Jarausch, 1–23. Oxford: Berghahn, 1997.

Jozwiak, Joseph. "The Wall in Our Minds? Colonization, Integration, and Nostalgia." *Journal of Popular Culture* 39, no. 5 (2006): 780–795.

Klingemann, Hans-Dieter, and Richard Hofferbert. "Germany: A New 'Wall in the Mind'?" *Journal of Democracy* 5, no. 1 (1994): 30–44.

Krisch, Henry. "German Unification and East German Political Culture: Interaction and Change," in *Germany after Unification: Coming to Terms with the Recent Past*, edited by Gert-Joachim Glaeßner, 5–16. Amsterdam: Rodopi, 1996.

Marvin, Grace. "Two Steps Back and One Step Forward: East German Women since the Fall of the Wall." *Humanity and Society* 19, no. 2 (1995): 37–50.

Minkenburg, Michael. "The Wall after the Wall: On the Continuing Division of Germany and Remaking of Political Culture." *Comparative Politics* 26, no, 1 (1993): 53–68.

Saunders, Anna. "'Normalizing' the Past: East German Culture and *Ostalgie*," in *German Culture, Politics, and Literature into the Twenty-First Century*, ed. Stuart Taberner and Paul Cooke, 89–104. Rochester, NY: Camden House, 2006.

Schneider, Peter. *The Wall Jumper*. New York: Pantheon, 1983.

Spiegel OnLine International. "Germany Still Divided 18 Years after the Fall of the Wall." November 9, 2007, available at: http://www.spiegel.de/international/germany/0,1518,516472,00.html. Accessed July 13, 2010.

Welsh, Helga. "The Divided Past and the Difficulties of German Unification." *German Politics and Society* 30, no. 1 (1993): 75–86.

5

Ending Cold War Divisions and Establishing New Partnerships: German Unification and the Transformation of German-Polish Relations

*Jonathan Murphy**

1989, An Overview

The Solidarity-led roundtable negotiations in Poland in June 1989 and subsequent peaceful transition to the first postcommunist government to be freely elected briefly caught the world's attention but was overshadowed by the tragic events at Tiananmen Square. The fall of the Berlin Wall in November that year came to epitomize the transformation and unification of Europe.[1] Much of the literature covering the transformations in Central and Eastern Europe during this period centers on the impact of Soviet foreign policy on the dramatic changes in the Eastern Bloc. Many historians and political scientists continue to overlook just how uncertain the early post–Cold War European continent was and how far the independently transitioning Central European states moved beyond Soviet Premier Mikhail Gorbachev's vision of reforming the bloc (as outlined in Robert Snyder and Timothy J. White's chapter) to move closer to the goal of European integration under the EU and ultimately NATO. Polish efforts to transform diplomatic relations with a rapidly unifying Germany are part of this unrecognized transformation. As Ilya Prizel argues, "only Poland seemed to understand from the start that

German unification was unstoppable and that Warsaw's interests would be best served by accepting the inevitable and using the unification process to normalize Polish-German relations."[2]

In 2009, at the twentieth anniversary celebrations to commemorate the fall of the Berlin Wall, German Chancellor Angela Merkel observed that the celebrations honored "that brave engagement of our neighbors to the East." She went on to assert, "the unity of [Germany] would have been unthinkable without our neighbors in Central and Eastern Europe. For that we are and will remain thankful from the bottom of our hearts."[3] German-Polish diplomatic relations steadily improved following the creation of a Solidarity-led government in Warsaw. The warming in relations was based on a perception that both countries shared common values and a congruence of interests. The West German (FRG) government supported Poland's democratic transition. In mid-1989 Helmut Kohl, leader of the Christian Democratic Union (CDU) and FRG Chancellor, declared, "the changes in Poland and Hungary were in the German national interest" and that the "Polish experiment" was directly connected with the prospect of unification.[4]

In order to move beyond the Cold War divide in Europe, Germany and Poland needed to end the post-1945 rift over their shared border along the Rivers Oder and Neisse. The Cold War had prevented any satisfactory resolution. Kohl pushed for rapid German unification, necessitating a final agreement with Warsaw regarding the two nations' shared border. In exchange, Bonn, advocating NATO and EU membership for her eastern neighbor, became Warsaw's new partner. For Poland there was a need to establish a new relationship with a unified Germany while not antagonizing her eastern neighbor, the Soviet Union, which was rapidly changing. The Polish Foreign Minister Krzysztof Skubiszewski worked to transform Poland's relations and form new relationships as the Cold War framework in Central-East Europe collapsed. He broadly led successive Warsaw governments in their understanding that the only way to guarantee normal relations with Germany and a final resolution of the Oder-Neisse border was by supporting German unification and full integration into the West. This remained a fundamental feature of postcommunist Polish foreign policy. German-Polish cultural relations following the fall of the Berlin Wall improved at a much slower rate than diplomatic relations between the two countries despite the official expressions of friendship and rapid transformation of diplomatic relations. Difficult issues such as German families expelled from Polish territory after 1945 complicated efforts at reconciliation and cooperation between the two nations.

The Oder-Neisse Legacy

At the end of March 1939, Britain signed a unilateral guarantee to come to Poland's aid in the event of a German threat to her independence. This was later hurriedly transformed into a Treaty of Mutual Assistance (1939), signed in London on August 25. Just two days earlier the Molotov-Ribbentrop Pact (1939) between Nazi Germany and the Soviet Union had secretly carved up Poland between the two dictatorships. The Soviet invasion of Poland on September 17 presented an awkward dilemma for the British.[5] In private, they pointed out to the beleaguered Poles that the Anglo-Polish agreement only extended to cover German aggression against Poland. Significantly, as British Prime Minister Winston Churchill was to remind the House of Commons after the Tehran Conference of November 1943, Britain had never guaranteed "any particular frontier line in Poland." Furthermore, Churchill declared he believed Soviet demands did not go "beyond the limits of what is reasonable and just."[6] During the Second World War, the Soviet dictator Joseph Stalin insisted Poland be shifted westward at Germany's expense. For Poland's eastern border with the Soviet Union, he sought to have the so-called Curzon Line imposed. This had been a demarcation line proposed by the British in 1919 following the Red Army's invasion of Poland. It approximated the same line established by the Molotov-Ribbentrop Pact (1939), had been tacitly agreed to at the Tehran Conference in November 1943, and was formally agreed to at Yalta in 1945. In contrast, Stalin's designs for the German-Polish border in the west caused friction within the Grand Alliance in the final years of the Second World War.

The first serious moves to draw the new German-Polish border were made at the Tehran Conference. Churchill made his first statements to the British Parliament that Poland could extend up to the River Oder.[7] At the end of the conference, Churchill and Stalin agreed to moving the Polish western frontier to the line of the Rivers Oder and Neisse. Churchill observed that the fact that there were two Neisse rivers, an eastern and western, with some two hundred kilometers between them, was not recognized at the time.[8] In 1939 there were some 2.7 million Germans living in the large part of Silesia between the two Neisse rivers.[9] This was to become a major stumbling block during the subsequent Yalta and Potsdam negotiations in February 1945 and into the Cold War.

At Yalta the Big Three agreed that Poland should receive substantial parts of German territory in the north from East Prussia and in the west, where the River Oder was accepted as one part of the new frontier. However, a disagreement concerning which River Neisse the border should follow soon emerged. Stalin advocated the western River Neisse, which would grant Poland a greater share of Germany, while American President Franklin Roosevelt and British Prime Minister Churchill both supported the eastern branch of the River Neisse. Churchill charged that Poland should not take more German territory than it could manage,[10] and Roosevelt supported him, agreeing that "there would appear to be little justification for extending [Polish territory] up to the Western Neisse."[11] By the end of the Yalta Conference there was still no agreement which of the River Neisses was to be followed.

With no firm agreement reached at Yalta, the issue of Poland's western frontiers was postponed further until the Potsdam Conference, by which time the situation had worsened. The newly installed communist government in Warsaw had formally advanced the Polish frontier up to the western River Neisse and was establishing their frontier with the support of Moscow. This posed huge problems for the West. First, this increased the number of ethnic Germans to be expelled to about 8 million, and second, much of Germany's grain came from the territories the Poles had seized. Thus, the Western Allies faced the problem of managing a ruined Germany whose wrecked industrial zones could not support a substantially increased and starving population.

Stalin argued that the western River Neisse had become the de facto frontier and should therefore be left where it was. He maintained that the Soviets had not been able to stop the Poles from taking the lands vacated by the Germans. He claimed not to be very worried about fixing the line, stating, "if the Conference cannot agree about one it can remain in suspense."[12] Though Churchill called for the return of Germans to their former territory, Stalin said this was impossible because what had occurred was not the result of a deliberate policy but "a spontaneous course of events."[13] The United States and Britain maintained that Poland had a very weak case for extending beyond the eastern Neisse to the western Neisse.

Churchill warned Stalin and the Poles at Potsdam that pushing the Polish border to the western River Neisse would stir up enmity between Germans and Poles for many years to come. The move was ominous in the eyes of Churchill: "For the future peace of Europe here was a wrong beside which Alsace-Lorraine and the Danzig Corridor were trifles. One day the Germans would want their territory back and the Poles would not be able to stop them."[14] Churchill's line of thinking was supported by British Foreign Secretary Anthony Eden. According to Eden, Polish claims were only making problems for the future, and "it suited the Kremlin both to deprive Germany of as much eastern territory as possible and to create as much bitterness as could be contrived between Poles and Germans, a useful secondary influence in support of Soviet authority in Warsaw."[15]

Eventually, the Potsdam Agreement placed the additional German territory seized beyond the eastern Neisse under Polish "administration" "pending the final determination of Poland's western frontier."[16] Germany's borders were to be finalized at a peace conference at an unspecified time in the future. However, the Agreement also sanctioned the expulsion of millions of Germans from that area, implying that Polish control of the land would be permanent. As the Cold War developed, the precise meaning of the Agreement became controversial; some argued it effectively meant Polish sovereignty over the territory while others argued it did not.

German-Polish Cross-Border Relations Prior to 1989

Relations between the GDR and Poland remained uneasy, even after the signing of the Treaty of Görlitz/Zgorzelec (1950) recognizing the Oder-Neisse border. The border was "hermetically sealed" with contacts limited to party delegations and semiofficial visits. Visa-free travel between the GDR and Poland was introduced in 1972, the first case of a border being opened within the socialist bloc. The opportunity to travel was taken up on a large scale and brought a modest improvement in relations. German expellees were able to visit their former homes for the first time. However, cultural relations remained problematic. In the face of growing economic difficulties in both countries, GDR customers found themselves unwelcome in Polish shops and vice versa.[17] The GDR-Polish border was sealed again in October 1980 due to the growing strength of the Solidarity movement in Poland, affecting both tourism and institutional cooperation. In order to balance the decision and explain it to his population, GDR leader Erich Honecker also introduced restrictions in traffic with the FRG. Though Polish workers were still allowed to commute on a daily basis due to the continuing labor shortage in the GDR, they were prohibited from purchasing consumer goods. Cross-border relations remained minimal throughout the 1980s.

Along with the exact location of the Oder-Neisse boundary issue, the existence and rights of the German minority in Poland was the subject of dispute between Poland and the FRG after the Second World War. All those persons of Polish origin who were nationals of the former German Reich within its frontiers of December 31, 1937, were treated as Germans under FRG municipal law. They were entitled to settle freely in the FRG, and many took advantage of this opportunity during hard economic times in Poland.[18] In the 1980s, this type of emigration became mass migration. Between 1981 and 1990, 740,000 registered ethnic Germans left Poland.[19] Poland objected, claiming this violated its sovereign rights. Bonn claimed it did not have the authority to change the legal status of ethnic Germans in Poland.[20] In 1970, Poland and the FRG had signed a treaty under which they agreed to confirm the inviolability of their existing frontiers and pledge absolute respect for each other's territorial integrity. They also declared that they had no territorial claims against each other and would not advance any in the future.[21] At the time, the Polish Prime Minister highlighted it was only on the basis of recognition for the Oder-Neisse frontier that the normalization of relations between the FRG and Poland could be agreed upon. In fact, the Poles had pushed for the question of the Oder-Neisse border to be dealt with in the first article of the agreement as the most important problem between the two countries.[22] Meanwhile, the FRG government played down this aspect. When it came to ratifying the Treaty in the FRG Parliament, however, there was much opposition. To secure its ratification, an all-party resolution was agreed upon under which the Treaty was described as an element of "the *modus vivendi* which the Federal Republic of Germany seeks to establish with its eastern neighbors."[23] As Ryszard Piotrowicz writes, "this was a reflection of the fundamental West German policy tenet that nothing was permanent pending German unification."[24] Despite some initial hopes, the Eastern treaties failed to provide a conclusive resolution of the Oder-Neisse border issue with Poland.

1989–90 German-Polish Relations

The FRG's position of 1970 helped ease Poland's fears but could not completely end Warsaw's anxiety. Poland continued to be heavily reliant on the Soviet Union as the only foreign power that was willing to defend the Oder-Neisse border against the possible threat of German revisionism. When the Berlin Wall fell and German unification became a near certainty, Polish fears concerning German irredentism returned. However, rather than opposing the German unification, which incidentally Skubiszewski and others in Solidarity viewed as plausible in early 1989,[25] Warsaw maintained a pragmatic position of support for German aspirations in return for agreement finalizing the Oder-Neisse border as the fixed border between the two states. Skubiszewski led the Warsaw government on this matter through consultations with Bonn and participation in the Two-Plus-Four negotiations on German unification. Final agreement was made possible with the support of Washington, Moscow, London, and Paris.

Within 24 hours of Kohl's long-scheduled and historic visit to Poland on November 9, 1989, events took an even more dramatic turn when the Berlin Wall fell. Although he immediately interrupted his visit to fly back to Germany and address the rapid changes in both the GDR and FRG, Kohl returned the following day. During the talks, he stressed that the Polish successes toward democracy were shared successes for all of Europe. Both Kohl and his Polish counterpart, Tadeusz Mazowiecki, recognized the "burden of history"[26] on their relations, and looked to better interactions based on the post-1945 Western European model of cooperation. The outstanding issue for both nations as Germany unified and Poland democratized remained the Oder-Neisse border. Kohl declared, "it is a task of European dimensions that is comparable with German-French reconciliation, without which the process leading to the unification of our part of Europe would not exist."[27] German unification had indeed become a real possibility after the fall of the Berlin Wall. The German government anticipated different degrees of difficulty in establishing good relations with neighboring states. Reconciliation with her largest eastern neighbor, Poland, was assumed to be the most challenging and lengthy.[28] Warsaw linked progress on German unification with a final settlement of the border issue.

Polish and German Perspectives

Poland rapidly went through four noncommunist-led governments following the elections in June 1989. Crucially for Polish-German relations, Poland enjoyed stability in foreign affairs, keeping the same foreign minister throughout this period. Skubiszewski brought much of the "new thinking" needed to resolve problems that had opened a gulf between Germany and Poland in the decades following the end of the Second World War. An acclaimed international lawyer and formidable academic in the field of Polish-German relations, he strove to end the uncertainty surrounding the Oder-Neisse border for the benefit of both nations. At his confirmation hearings in September 1989 he stated that he anticipated the likelihood of German unification.[29] Soon after, the Polish Foreign Minister told reporters that since the four powers still occupied Germany they needed to determine Germany's future as a unified state. This unification process would require all of Germany's neighbors, the two German states, and the four allied powers to conduct negotiations at the "all-European level."[30] Equal partnership, international law, and territorial inviolability were to be the new cornerstones of Polish foreign policy as it moved out of the Soviet sphere of influence. In February 1990, Skubiszewski made his first trip to Bonn where he set out the Polish position on German unity. He sought not only stronger commitments from the West German leadership regarding the Oder-Neisse border but also believed that the accelerating pace of German unification necessitated Warsaw's advocacy for Germany's stabilizing European role. He had become alarmed at calls from the GDR and Soviet leaderships for German neutrality after unification. He was the first senior European policymaker to publicly declare that a unified Germany belonged in Europe's current security system and specifically in NATO. He feared that German neutrality would leave Germany outside European security systems, resulting in a vacuum at the heart of Europe. While many in Warsaw grew concerned with Kohl's apparent posturing regarding the German-Polish border, Skubiszewski largely succeeded in reassuring his government colleagues and keeping relations on track.

Until events began to gather pace in 1989, Hans-Dietrich Genscher, leader of the small liberal Free Democratic Party (FDP) and Kohl's coalition partner in government, had been responsible for foreign policy while Kohl and his CDU party controlled defense policy. As events in 1989 suddenly merged foreign and domestic policy, Kohl increasingly moved into foreign policy. While the Chancellor had overall responsibility for the broad direction of policy, Genscher had operative responsibility. The two men were not close—their partnership resembled a marriage of convenience at times—yet they shared similar tactical skills and political instincts. Different political party concerns leading up to the March 18, 1990, elections to be exclusively held in the five GDR *Länder* (states) led Kohl to take an ambiguous line regarding the inviolability of the German-Polish border. The Chancellor was also keeping an eye on the first all-German elections scheduled for December 1990. Ultimately, his position was in line with the predominant thinking that the border should not be changed, but his maneuvering on the issue greatly tested his relationship with Genscher and vexed the key powers involved; further straining German-Polish diplomatic and cultural relations.

Kohl's Election Difficulties and his Ten-Point Plan

Despite conciliatory statements, the Polish government was greatly irritated by Kohl's handling of the Oder-Neisse border issue during the

March 1990 elections in the five GDR *Länder*. Both Kohl's Christian Democratic Union (CDU) and its sister party the Christian Social Union (CSU), headed by Theo Waigel, were concerned about the growing popularity of the right-wing *Republikaner* party, which sought to restore western Poland, the former Sudetenland in Czechoslovakia, and the former northern part of East Prussia in the Soviet Union to Germany.[31] For a brief time Kohl appeared to be facing a strong and unexpected challenge from the *Republikaner* party. With this and other issues in mind, Kohl took the initiative, beginning on November 28, 1989, with his bold Ten-Point Plan for a unified Germany. The Chancellor remained aware of the necessity to avoid alienating those Germans who were forcibly expelled from what had once been German territory in Poland. These groups were strong supporters of the CDU and its Bavarian-based sister party, the CSU, thus presenting him with a problem neither Genscher and his FDP, nor the German Social Democratic Party (SPD) faced. In addition, Kohl's Christian Democratic allies were thought by many to be trailing the SPD in the March 1990 elections. Therefore, as Stephen Szabo highlights, "he was sensitive to the strong anti-Polish sentiment of many East Germans and did not wish to alienate these new voters as well. Finally, he wished to keep the issue in reserve to offer the Soviets as part of the price he would pay for a final agreement."[32] The SPD response to Kohl's Ten-Point Plan was largely positive, though the party's foreign affairs spokesman, Karsten Voigt, argued that at least two other points needed to be added regarding nuclear weapons on German soil and the inviolability of Poland's western borders, which should be clearly and unequivocally supported.[33]

Skubiszewski responded to Kohl's political maneuverings by pressing harder for international acknowledgment of Poland's national interests. In a speech before the Polish Parliament in December 1989, he reiterated Poland's key concerns for relations with Bonn, particularly in the wake of Kohl's Ten-Point Plan for a unified Germany, which ignored the Oder-Neisse border question. He addressed Kohl's key point concerning the "unlimited respect for sovereignty and safety of each state," which referred to both German states but not to Poland. He declared that "sovereignty also means territorial sovereignty" and that Poland supported "the idea of a united Europe and the implementation of this idea through cooperation and integration of European states." As a result, he argued, "the changing relations between the German states should be part of the unification of Europe and achievements in this area on the scale of the entire continent." In order for German unification to succeed, "European unification should always be paramount."[34]

Inviolability of Frontiers

By Christmas 1989, American policy had swung round in support of German unification with two preconditions: that a unified Germany remains a member of NATO and that the security interests of its neighbors, principally Poland, are met. This built on President George H. Bush's earlier wishes that unification should occur with respect for the inviolability of borders as stated in the Helsinki Final Act.[35] In a conversation immediately after the Malta Summit, Bush effectively supported Kohl's program for unification, although neither politician expected it would occur within two years. Despite Bush's strong statement on the issue, however, Kohl appeared to cast doubt on his commitment to the inviolability of borders by pointing out that "the CSCE [Helsinki Final Act] says the borders can be changed by peaceful means."[36] At Camp David in February 1990, Bush and Kohl disagreed at a press conference on the Polish border issue. Bush declared Washington's support for the inviolability of the German-Polish border in line with the position taken in London, Paris, and Warsaw. Kohl sought to separate the questions of German unity and existing borders, claiming that only a freely elected all-German parliament could as a "legally competent sovereign" make a final decision on the matter. This was a return to the fundamental FRG Cold War policy tenet that nothing was permanent pending German unification.[37] Kohl's public position brought much disquiet in Europe and the United States, although in private he had moved to assure Bush that "the border question is not serious" and that the "vast majority [of West Germans] knows that this will be the border." He still maintained that the final decision must come from a treaty ratified by an all-German parliament.[38]

In a lecture to the German Foreign Policy Association in Bonn in early February 1990, Skubiszewski outlined Poland's position in light of the absence of any commitment to the Oder-Neisse border in Kohl's Ten-Point Plan:

> In the Europe that is growing into unity, this frontier belonged among the important factors of stability. Agreement is possible only in established frontiers and without territorial disputes. . . . We have been hearing for years that in the future united Europe, which will be a Europe of freedom, frontiers will lose importance. We do not dispute the correctness of that prophecy. Before then, however, there must be clarity about frontiers. Their importance will otherwise not become less, and reconciliation with neighbors will not come about.[39]

Spero argues that despite Skubiszewski's public pronouncements, which served to place the onus for progress on Bonn, the Polish Foreign Minister understood the German Chancellor's internal political difficulties and pressed his Ministry of Foreign Affairs and government colleagues to be patient as the German Chancellor dealt with fragile political alliances with far-right parties in upcoming elections. As a trained international lawyer, he also understood it would take time for Kohl to change FRG laws connected to the German 1937 frontiers. Alarmist voices were raised, however, in particular by the Polish Communists. These were led by the former Prime Minister Mieczyslaw Rakowski, who focused on the traditionally defined threat of German nationalism.[40] The British Prime Minister Margaret Thatcher and France's François Mitterrand also seized on the issue to cast doubts on Kohl's intended relations with Germany's neighbors.

Meanwhile, Mazowiecki and Skubiszewski hesitated to join Hungary and Czechoslovakia in calling for negotiations with Moscow on a withdrawal of Soviet forces from Poland. At one point the Polish Foreign Minister even suggested Warsaw Pact troops should remain in the territory of the GDR as a guarantee of Polish security.[41] The Polish government as a whole favored a guarantee on the Oder-Neisse border first before any withdrawal of Soviet forces from Poland. Though supportive of German unification, the Polish government remained uncertain of Bonn's commitment to territorial integrity. For a period, the government supported maintaining both the NATO and the Warsaw Pact alliances to ensure European stability until superseded by an all-European security system. In the end, however, Warsaw missed an early chance to remove Soviet troops from Polish soil due to its mistaken assumption that their presence might be needed as leverage to obtain united Germany's recognition of Poland's disputed Oder-Neisse border. The final negotiations with Moscow would prove long and arduous while the agreement with Germany passed off with little difficulty.[42] The episode does nevertheless demonstrate Warsaw's concern, which was shared by the Polish public. A public opinion poll carried out by the newspaper *Rzeczpospolita* on March 21, 1990, found that 69 percent of those responding expressed fear of a united Germany, while at the same time 48 percent supported German unification.[43] The Warsaw government remained anxious about possible consequences as the question of the Polish-German frontier was once again being raised as one of the "external aspects."[44]

Two-Plus-Four Talks on German Unity

The Two-Plus-Four Talks were established in early 1990 to place a united Germany in the new Europe. They included the two Germanies plus the

Four Powers. The key issues were those associated with creating what came to be called "the new European security architecture."[45] There was a desire to avoid another Treaty of Versailles, which set the stage for the Second World War. The talks aimed at meeting the legitimate national interests of both the new unified Germany and its neighbors, particularly regarding the stability of borders. In response to pressure from the other key players to help Poland protect its interests in the German unification process, the Bush administration took up the Polish case in Bonn. They also joined France, Britain, and the Soviet Union in agreeing to include Poland in the upcoming Two-Plus-Four discussions concerning the German-Polish border.

The Polish Prime Minister sought a full and final assurance that Poland's western territories were guaranteed to Poland by all the Allies and could not be simply viewed as "a gift from Stalin." Mazowiecki also assured Bush that while he fully trusted Kohl, many Poles still maintained concerns about the position a strong united Germany might take on the border issue.[46] There was agreement that Polish representatives should be present when issues affecting them were discussed. The Solidarity leader Lech Walesa, then a candidate in the upcoming Polish presidential elections, remained critical of Poland's exclusion from all aspects of the Two-Plus-Four Talks.

Before the talks began, Kohl and Genscher met Gorbachev in Moscow. Genscher assured the Soviet leader that the borders of the new Germany would comprise the territory of the FRG, GDR, and Berlin—"not less, but not more."[47] In contrast to Kohl's shifting position, Genscher had maintained a public commitment guaranteeing the frontiers of all Germany's neighbors through a series of newspaper interviews and a speech delivered to a conference on January 31.[48]

Following the dramatic victory of the East CDU in the GDR elections on March 18, 1990, Kohl had increasing opportunities to free himself from the Oder-Neisse issue. By June the parliaments of both German states had overwhelmingly passed resolutions recognizing Poland's western border as final and called for a treaty between Poland and Germany following unification. Kohl's accompanying declaration was deemed insufficient by the Polish government. In July, U.S. Secretary of State James Baker stated that the Four Powers might not dissolve their rights and responsibilities in Germany if the two German nations did not provide adequate assurances to Warsaw. This was done in Paris on July 17 following the successful conclusion of the Soviet-German talks where a Polish-German agreement was reached.[49]

The final round of talks on German unification took place in Moscow, concluding on September 12. The Moscow Treaty (1990) was signed by the six states involved, including Poland and Germany.[50] Article 1 states that the unified Germany's borders:

> [s]hall be the borders of the Federal Republic of Germany and the German Democratic Republic and shall be definitive from the date on which the present Treaty comes into force. The confirmation of the definitive nature of the borders of the united Germany is an essential element of the peaceful order in Europe.[51]

Article 2 declared the border was inviolable at all times and that Poland and Germany respect the other's sovereignty and territorial integrity. Article 3 stipulated that the two nations have no territorial claims against each other, nor would they assert any such claims in the future. "Thus the border issue may not be raised in the future, at least in the form of a claim."[52] The Treaty signified Germany's final acceptance that it must live within its current borders.

The Moscow Treaty also bound Bonn to make a separate agreement with Warsaw regarding the Oder-Neisse frontier. Following detailed negotiations and much delay, Skubiszewski and Genscher met in Warsaw on November 14 to sign a "Treaty on the Confirmation of the Polish-German Border (1990)." This Treaty represented the separate peace treaty envisaged in the Potsdam Agreement. The four external powers (France, Britain, the United States, and the Soviet Union) surrendered their say on the Polish-German border. With this Polish-German Treaty, German arguments that under the Potsdam Agreement it had been a "passive" subject of international law and that sovereignty could only be transferred to Poland by a unified Germany were finally overcome. In Article 1, the parties confirmed the existing Oder-Neisse boundary between them as defined in the Treaty of Görlitz/Zgorzelec (1950) with the GDR and in the Treaty of Warsaw (1970) with the FRG. From a Polish perspective the treaty was more declarative in nature as the boundary had been fixed by the previous treaties signed with the GDR and FRG, respectively.[53] Both Genscher and Kohl stated, "not only did the treaty play an important role in Germany's unification, but also it united instead of divided a border to reinforce Europe's unification."[54] The agreement also freed the Warsaw government to pursue a more determined line with Moscow regarding the Red Army forces stationed in the country.

Post-1989 Revolution in German-Polish Diplomatic Relations

Retrospectively, such an agreement was never in doubt. Few Germans seriously considered the prospect of revising the border. None of the

Second World War Allies would have tolerated such a move. For a while domestic political considerations made German intentions harder to fully judge, but Skubiszewski's patient work gave Kohl time to diffuse a potential wave of nationalist sentiment. With the border issue resolved, Germany moved swiftly to sign further treaties of friendship with her eastern neighbors. Poland was the first on June 17, 1991. This Treaty once again underlined the guarantee of territorial integrity, border inviolability, political independence, economic development, and equal minority rights for citizens living in each other's states. Article 20 defined the German minority in Poland and the Polish minority in Germany: "The Treaty adopts a subjective approach to minorities, stating that all persons have the right to declare themselves as belonging to a minority, and that those who make such a declaration cannot incur any negative consequences for having done so." However, the Treaty did set limits on minority rights. Members of minorities were required to be loyal to the state whose citizenship they held. Poland declined to recognize the dual nationality of members of the German minority in Poland despite FRG pressure for such a measure. Poland also rejected proposals for the use of bilingual local names.[55] Nevertheless, the Treaty marked an improvement in diplomatic relations between the two states. Skubiszewski declared, "there is not European unity and European order without a good accord and solid Polish-German cooperation and joint activity." In building that European unity and order, he explained, "the Germans support our strategic aim of entry into the European Community. . . . It points to relations of European dimensions, it stresses the direction of joint activities for a pan-European security system."[56]

German-Polish cooperation on NATO and EU membership continued to strengthen following the resolution of the Oder-Neisse border and unification of Germany. By October 1992, Polish Prime Minister Hanna Suchocka was able to declare that Germany "is today our liaison in contacts with the EC and NATO, at the same time the German road to the east leads through Poland."[57] By February 1993, the Polish government announced that the Polish navy would be participating in NATO's June maneuver exercise designated "Baltops 1993." This marked the first time a former Warsaw Pact state would be allowed to maneuver with NATO states and was an indicator of NATO's eagerness to cooperate with states such as Poland. In Poland, support to join NATO and particularly the EU can be largely attributed to the desire to attain Western living standards. This desire overcame any prejudices against western institutions, which, as in the case of NATO, had been specifically oriented against Poland and the Warsaw Pact.

Difficulties in German-Polish Cultural Relations

Cultural relations between Germany and Poland in the aftermath of the fall of the Berlin Wall did not keep pace with the rapid transformation of diplomatic relations. German expellee organizations became increasingly visible since 1989 under the umbrella organization *Bund der Vertriebenen* (*BdV*). The League of Expellees voted against the Border Treaty (1990) and against the Neighborhood Agreement with Poland (1991) because the latter did not commit the Poles to guaranteeing the rights of minorities.[58] For many Poles, the growing tendency to see Germans as victims, not solely perpetrators, of the Second World War raised widespread concern. In 2003, the *BdV* proposed "Center against Expulsions" in Berlin (commemorating victims of the postwar expulsions) sparked outrage in Poland and became an epicenter for tensions. The organizers arranged a temporary exhibition in 2006, which drew criticism for seeking, as Bill Niven describes, to "promote by implication a view of German expellees as in no way responsible for the fate which befell them."[59] Pawel Lutomski argues that Polish political and cultural elites were "not meeting the challenge posed by a cultural process in which important parts of German self-understanding are being redefined."[60] For the Polish public there were periodic fears that if Germans viewed themselves as victims this would raise the question of whether the roles of perpetrator and victim could be reversed.[61]

Conclusion

The resolution of the Oder-Neisse border dispute between Germany and Poland was an essential step in the unification of Germany and heralded the end of the Cold War division of Europe. Throughout, Skubiszewski broadly led successive Warsaw governments in their understanding that the only way to guarantee normal relations with Germany and a final resolution of the Oder-Neisse border was by supporting German unification and full integration into the West. This remained a fundamental feature of postcommunist Polish foreign policy. In fact, it can be argued that Warsaw's reaction to German unification was far more pragmatic than that of either France or Britain.

The discord over the Oder-Neisse border revived some of the deep Cold War–era divisions as the interests of both countries appeared irreconcilable. As Szabo writes, the episode "served as a disquieting portent of how things could go badly in the future of a united Germany."[62] Warsaw's initial hesitancy in negotiating a withdrawal of Soviet forces in a perceived effort to maintain leverage over Germany seemed to be a return to considering Germany a real danger to Poland's security. Kohl's actions arguably attributed more diplomatic importance to the border issue than existed in Germany. However, with the final agreed confirmation of the Oder-Neisse border and subsequent "Good Neighborly Relations and Friendly Co-operation" Treaty (1991), the relationship became marked by a growing congruence of strategic objectives. For Poland, the united Germany was a vocal advocate in the EU and NATO for eastern enlargement. For Germany, Polish membership in these organizations would bring economic benefits and greater stability on her eastern border.

It is important for all those researching the transition in German-Polish diplomatic relations to acknowledge the fresh thinking in the Polish response to German unification. This was essential to resolve the issues created at the end of the Second World War and frozen by the Cold War. Historically, Poland has found herself battling to survive between her two more powerful neighbors, Germany and Russia. In this precarious position, she has often resorted to attempts to play the two off each other, avoid them, or, at times, restrict their threat through subordination. This thinking was put aside in 1989 and replaced with a drive to work to support German unification as a part of overall European unification.

Throughout the process, any question of German "reunification," which implied the joining together of territories that made up prewar Germany, raised obvious concerns for Poland. Kohl's actions during the elections allowed this fear to take root in some sections of the Polish government despite Genscher's efforts throughout to allay Polish concerns. Often the terms "unification" and "reunification" are used interchangeably, frequently without any intention to make a distinction. By becoming more aware of Polish perspectives of the German unification process, researchers, lecturers, and students can become more mindful of the overtones the term "reunification" carried for Germany's neighbors. It is equally important to acknowledge that most members of the *BdV* did not advocate a hard-line revanchist approach to Poland but belonged to the League due to emotional and familial reasons. Despite the diplomatic agreements between the two nations, fears persisted in Poland that unresolved German restitution and compensation claims of former expellees would be revived. This continued to disturb German-Polish relations and made a shared German-Polish culture of memory difficult. However, guided by the example of the Franco-German post-1945 reconciliation, putting German-Polish diplomatic relations on equal footing created a new opportunity for cultural relations to steadily improve.

Notes

* The author wishes to thank Richard C. Barkley, U.S. Ambassador to the German Democratic Republic (GDR), 1988–90, for his review of the original draft and invaluable insights.

1. 1989 was a year marked by several turning points around the world. As Shannon Granville's chapter highlights, in Japan the death of Emperor Hirohito in January 1989 was "a watershed moment . . . a break in historical continuity as politically and symbolically charged as the fall of the Wall," 38.
2. Ilya Prizel, *National Identity and Foreign Policy Nationalism and Leadership in Poland, Russia, and Ukraine* (Cambridge: Cambridge University Press, 1998), 117.
3. "World Leaders Line Up to Mark Fall of Berlin Wall," http://www.rferl.org/content/World_Leaders_Line_Up_To_Mark_Fall_Of_Berlin_Wall/1872793.html, accessed November 9, 2009. Merkel grew up in the GDR and was among the huge crowds who crossed to West Berlin on November 9, 1989.
4. Marcin Zaborowski, *Germany, Poland and Europe* (Manchester: Manchester University Press, 2004), 81.
5. For an excellent overview of this dilemma see Keith Sword, "British Reactions to the Soviet Occupation of Eastern Poland in September 1939," *The Slavonic and East European Review* 69, no. 1, (Jan 1991), 81–101.
6. Jan Karski, *The Great Powers and Poland 1919–45* (Lanham, MD: University Press of America, 1985), 504.
7. Winston Churchill, *Closing the Ring*, Vol. V (London: Cassell, 1952), 285.
8. Ibid., 317, 319.
9. Timothy Garton Ash, *In Europe's Name* (London: Jonathan Cape, 1993), 221.
10. Churchill, *Triumph and Tragedy*, Vol. VI (London: Cassell, 1954), 327.
11. Ibid., 329.
12. Ibid., 567.
13. Ibid., 570.
14. Ibid., 561.
15. Anthony Eden, *The Reckoning; the Memoirs of Anthony Eden, Earl of Avon* (Boston: Houghton Mifflin Co., 1965), 545.
16. Protocol of the Potsdam Conference as cited by Ryszard W. Piotrowicz et al., *The Unification of Germany in International and Domestic Law* (Amsterdam: Rodopi, 1997), 48.
17. Ulrich Best, *Transgression as a Rule: German-Polish Cross-border Cooperation, Border Discourse and EU-enlargement* (Münster: LIT Verlag, 2007), 74.
18. Wladyslaw Czaplinski, "The New Polish-German Treaties and the Changing Political Structure of Europe," *The American Journal of International Law* 86, no. 1 (January 1992), 169.

19. Agata Gorny et al., "Selective Tolerance? Regulations, Practice and Discussions Regarding Dual Citizenship in Poland," in *Dual Citizenship in Europe: From Nationhood to Societal Integration,* ed. Thomas Faist (Aldershot, U.K.: Ashgate Publishing, Ltd., 2007), 152.
20. Czaplinski, "New Polish-German Treaties," 169.
21. Piotrowicz et al., *Unification of Germany in International and Domestic Law*, 55.
22. Claus Arndt, "Legal Problems of the German Eastern Treaties," *The American Journal of International Law* 74, no. 1 (January 1980), 128.
23. Krzysztof Skubiszewski, "Poland's Western Frontier and the 1970 Treaties," *The American Journal of International Law* 67, No. 1 (January 1973), 33.
24. Piotrowicz et al., *Unification of Germany in International and Domestic Law*, 55–56.
25. See Skubiszewski's statement at his September 1989 confirmation hearings, Joshua B. Spero, *Bridging the European Divide: Middle Power Politics and Regional Security Dilemmas* (Lanham, MD: Rowman and Littlefield Publishers, 2004), 60. Prior to the June 1989 Roundtable discussions in Poland, which brought Solidarity into a power-sharing arrangement, Artur Hajnicz, a leading expert on Germany in Solidarity and later advisor to Skubiszewski, wrote on the need for a new framework for Polish-German relations that recognized the potential for German unification. See ibid., 102.
26. Ibid., 63.
27. Ibid., 64.
28. Ibid., 63.
29. Spero, *Bridging the European Divide*, 60.
30. Ibid., 60.
31. The *Republikaner* party members maintain that "German unification is not yet complete until Germany has successfully unified within the borders of 1937." They assert that "eastern Germany" has been excluded from this "partial unification." See Christina Schori Liang, "Nationalism Ensures Peace," in *Europe for the Europeans,* ed. Christina Schori Liang (Aldershot, U.K.: Ashgate Publishing, Ltd., 2007), 148.
32. Stephen Szabo, *The Diplomacy of German Unification* (New York: St. Martin's Press, 1993), 73.
33. Ibid., 40.
34. Spero, *Bridging the European Divide*, 65–66.
35. Szabo, *Diplomacy of German Unification*, 42.
36. Document No. 4 "Memorandum of Conversation of George H. W. Bush, John Sununu, Brent Scowcroft, and Helmut Kohl December 3, 1989," part of Electronic Briefing Book No. 296 available at http://www.gwu.edu/~nsarchiv/NSAEBB/NSAEBB296/index.htm, accessed February 2, 2010. Although the Helsinki Acts contained solemn undertakings to "regard as inviolable . . . the frontiers of all States in Europe," all commitments were qualified by the declaration they could be changed "by peaceful means and by agreement" as Kohl outlined to Bush. See Ash, 223.

37. Piotrowicz et al., *The Unification of Germany in International and Domestic Law*, 55–56.
38. George H. W. Bush and Brent Scowcroft, *A World Transformed* (New York: Knopf, 1998), 251.
39. Renata Fritsch- Bournazel, *Europe and German Unification* (Oxford: Berg Publishers, 1992), 108–109.
40. Spero, *Bridging the European Divide*, 66.
41. Prizel, *National Identity and Foreign Policy*, 117.
42. Vojtech Mastny and Malcolm Byrne, eds., *A Cardboard Castle? An Inside History of the Warsaw Pact 1955–1991* (Budapest: Central Europe University Press, 2005), 70.
43. See Prizel, *National Identity and Foreign Policy*, 116.
44. Ryszard W. Piotrowicz, "The Arithmetic of German Unification: Three into One Does Go," *The International and Comparative Law Quarterly* 40, no. 3 (July 1991), 639.
45. Szabo, *Diplomacy of German Unification*, 53.
46. Debra J. Allen, *The Oder-Neisse Line: The United States, Poland, and Germany in the Cold War* (Westport, CT: Praeger, 2003), 287.
47. Szabo, *Diplomacy of German Unification*, 63.
48. Bush and Scowcroft, *A World Transformed*, 236.
49. Szabo, *Diplomacy of German Unification*, 75.
50. Piotrowicz, "Arithmetic of German Unification: Three into One Does Go," 642.
51. Ibid.
52. Piotrowicz et al., *Unification of Germany in International and Domestic Law*, 64.
53. Czaplinski, "New Polish-German Treaties," 166.
54. Spero, *Bridging the European Divide*, 74.
55. Czaplinski, "New Polish-German Treaties," 170–72.
56. Spero, *Bridging the European Divide*, 78.
57. Ibid., 85.
58. Bill Niven, "Implicit Equations in Constructions of German Suffering," in *Germans as Victims: Remembering the Past in Contemporary Germany*, ed. William John Niven (Basingstoke: Palgrave Macmillan, 2006), 109.
59. Ibid., 120.
60. Pawel Lutomski, "The Debate about a Center against Expulsions: An Unexpected Crisis in German-Polish Relations?" *German Studies Review* 27, no. 3 (October 2004): 449.
61. Ibid., 458.
62. Szabo, *Diplomacy of German Unification*, 76.

Bibliography

Allen, Debra J. *The Oder-Neisse Line: The United States, Poland, and Germany in the Cold War.* Westport, CT: Praeger, 2003.

Arndt, Claus. "Legal Problems of the German Eastern Treaties," *The American Journal of International Law* 74, no. 1 (January 1980): 122–33.

Ash, Timothy Garton. *In Europe's Name: Germany and the Divided Continent.* London: Jonathan Cape, 1993.

Best, Ulrich. *Transgression as a Rule: German-Polish Cross-Border Cooperation, Border Discourse and EU-Enlargement.* Münster: LIT Verlag, 2007.

Bush, George H. W., and Brent Scowcroft. *A World Transformed.* 1st ed. New York: Knopf, 1998.

Churchill, Winston. *Closing the Ring,* Vol. V. London: Cassell, 1952.

———. *Triumph and Tragedy,* Vol. VI. London: Cassell, 1954.

Czaplinski, Wladyslaw. "The New Polish-German Treaties and the Changing Political Structure of Europe," *The American Journal of International Law* 86, no. 1 (1992): 163–73.

Eden, Anthony. *The Reckoning the Memoirs of Anthony Eden, Earl of Avon.* Boston: Houghton Mifflin Co., 1965.

Faist, Thomas, ed., *Dual Citizenship in Europe: From Nationhood to Societal Integration.* Aldershot, U.K.: Ashgate Publishing, Ltd., 2007.

Fritsch-Bournazel, Renata. *Europe and German Unification.* Oxford: Berg Publishers, 1992.

Karski, Jan. *The Great Powers and Poland 1919–45: From Versailles to Yalta.* Lanham, MD: University Press of America, 1985.

Liang, Christina Schori. *Europe for the Europeans.* Aldershot, U.K.: Ashgate Publishing, Ltd., 2007.

Lutomski, Pawel. "The Debate about a Center against Expulsions: An Unexpected Crisis in German-Polish Relations?," *German Studies Review* 27, no. 3 (2004): 449–468.

Mastny, Vojtech, and Malcolm Byrne, eds. *A Cardboard Castle? An Inside History of the Warsaw Pact, 1955–1991.* National Security Archive Cold War readers. Budapest: Central European University Press, 2005.

Niven, William John. *Germans as Victims: Remembering the Past in Contemporary Germany.* Basingstoke: Palgrave Macmillan, 2006.

Piotrowicz, Ryszard W. "The Arithmetic of German Unification: Three into One Does Go," *The International and Comparative Law Quarterly* 40, no. 3 (1991): 635–648.

Piotrowicz, Ryszard W., Sam Blay, Gunnar Schuster, and Andreas Zimmermann. *The Unification of Germany in International and Domestic Law.* Amsterdam: Rodopi, 1997.

Prizel, Ilya. *National Identity and Foreign Policy Nationalism and Leadership in Poland, Russia, and Ukraine.* Cambridge: Cambridge University Press, 1998.

Rhode, Gotthold, and Wolfgang Wagner, eds. *The Genesis of the Oder-Neisse Line in the Diplomatic Negotiations during World War II: Sources and Documents.* Stuttgart: Brentano-Verlag, 1959.

Skubiszewski, Krzysztof. "Poland's Western Frontier and the 1970 Treaties," *The American Journal of International Law* 67, no. 1 (1973): 23–43.

Spero, Joshua B. *Bridging the European Divide: Middle Power Politics and Regional Security Dilemmas*. Lanham, MD: Rowman and Littlefield Publishers, 2004.

Sword, Keith. "British Reactions to the Soviet Occupation of Eastern Poland in September 1939," *The Slavonic and East European Review* 69, no. 1, (1991): 81–101.

Szabo, Stephen. *The Diplomacy of German Unification*. New York: St. Martin's Press, 1993.

The National Security Archive Electronic Briefing Book No. 296: http://www.gwu.edu/~nsarchiv/NSAEBB/NSAEBB296/index.htm, accessed February 2, 2010.

Zaborowski, Marcin. *Germany, Poland and Europe*. Manchester: Manchester University Press, 2004.

6

The Fall of the Berlin Wall: The Counterrevolution in Soviet Foreign Policy and the End of Communism

Robert Snyder and Timothy J. White

The fall of the Berlin Wall and the end of the Cold War sparked a debate in the study of world politics. Scholars scampered to offer explanations for these unforeseen events. Some argued that the end of the Cold War demonstrated the importance of agency and ideas—specifically Mikhail Gorbachev's New Thinking. Others responded that traditional theories of power politics could explain the changes in Soviet foreign policy that transformed Eastern Europe in the late 1980s. We contend that one cannot explain the fall of the Berlin Wall and the end of the Cold War without placing Soviet Union foreign policy in its unique revolutionary context. Soviet foreign policy had been based on the principle of externalization, going back to the period immediately after the revolution. Threats from abroad justified extreme centralization, repression, and monopolistic one-party rule. Gorbachev strove to revitalize the idea of the Soviet Union as a revolutionary state and acted as a "counterrevolutionary" in attempting to change the fundamental assumptions of Soviet foreign policy, promoting a friendly international environment that would help to decentralize the Soviet system, end repression, and advance a more pluralist order. This counterrevolution failed and led to the collapse of the Berlin Wall, the Soviet empire, and the Soviet state itself. Contrary to the popular "victory of capitalism" narrative that many came to believe at the end of the Cold War, we demonstrate that

Gorbachev transformed Soviet foreign policy to promote his domestic-reform agenda.

The Theoretical Debate

The fall of the Berlin Wall was not only a sudden and dramatic event in world history, but it was a critical moment that began a reevaluation of theories of international relations. In failing to predict the end of the Cold War, realism, the dominant paradigm of the post–World War II period, came under scrutiny and open to question.[1] Realism had emphasized the role of material factors as the basis for a state's power and foreign policy. States utilized power based on economic and military capabilities to maximize their influence in international relations. Throughout the Cold War realist scholars had assumed that the international system was characterized by a bipolar distribution of power and influence between the Soviet Union and the United States. Realists also had assumed that the massive conventional army and nuclear capability of the Soviet Union reflected their great power status in world politics. Nevertheless, one must question how effective realism was as a paradigm if it could not predict the sudden and dramatic collapse of the Soviet Union as a great power. After all, was not realism built to explain the logic of great power behavior, in this case Soviet foreign policy? Constructivists had emerged in the 1990s to challenge the assumptions of realism, placing primacy on the contingent nature of a state's foreign policy. Ideology, identity, and agency or the role of individuals were emphasized in explaining foreign policy, and the role of simple calculations of power and power relations were deemphasized in explaining foreign-policy behavior. In criticizing realism, constructivists have argued that agency and ideas, specifically Gorbachev's new policies of glasnost and perestroika, explain the sudden and surprising end of the Cold War. Glasnost or "openness" attempted to expose institutions or individuals who were performing poorly in the Soviet system while perestroika or "restructuring" called for new political institutions and mechanisms in the Soviet state that would be more innovative and effective.

Constructivists have gained credibility because of their ability to explain the end of the Cold War in ways that seem superior to realists' explanations. While realists have claimed that domestic economic problems and reduced capabilities explain the Soviet decline,[2] many have come to focus on the personal role and ideology of Gorbachev as being critical to understanding both the transformation of Soviet foreign policy as well as the end of the Cold War. Gorbachev's revolutionary thinking and policies were linked to the crisis of the Soviet Union in the 1980s. As a former or ossified revolutionary state, the Soviet Union had proclaimed foreign threats as justification for an aggressive foreign policy as well as centralized party rule. In acting as a counterrevolutionary, Gorbachev reversed this process. The outside world was now seen as friendly and benign in order to justify domestic reforms—promoting decentralization, liberalization, and the emergence of a new governing coalition.[3] Although Gorbachev hoped to transform Soviet foreign and domestic policy in order to save the Soviet Union, his reforms ironically and ultimately led to its demise. On the way, Soviet control over Eastern Europe collapsed, leading to the fall of the Berlin Wall.

Realists maintain that Soviet economic decline was "endogenous" to Gorbachev's ideas.[4] They argue that Moscow's economic problems gave rise to new thinking. From the 1920s through the mid-1960s, the Soviet economy grew at impressive rates. By the late 1960s, however, the economy began a steady decline until it hit zero growth by the early 1980s. Industrial production and labor productivity also began to drop sharply by the mid-1970s.[5] Given the long and seemingly irreversible decline of the Soviet economy, Gorbachev and other Soviet leaders had to know that their economy could not keep up with the impressive growth of the U.S. economy in the 1980s. Most of the other economically advanced states were also prospering and allied with their principal rival, the United States. For realists, the decline of the Soviet Union and the end of the Cold War were the result of the collapse of the Soviet economic system, not the policy choices of a new leader with a new approach to power and governance.

Material explanations offered by realists, however, cannot explain the magnitude of change Gorbachev made in Soviet foreign policy. Realists erroneously imply that Gorbachev's policies and the end of the Cold War were inevitable when, in fact, few among the Soviet elite favored Gorbachev's radical approach.[6] Moreover, realists exaggerate the importance of material factors in explaining Gorbachev's new foreign policy. The role of ideas and earlier conceptualizations of Soviet-American relations were critical for Gorbachev's reformulation of Soviet foreign policy. For example, it is difficult to imagine that Gorbachev would have made the overtures to the West he did if détente had not occurred. We know that many mid-level Soviet leaders learned during détente that cooperation with the West offered the Soviets many benefits. Moreover, Soviet conceptions of the importance of the Eastern Bloc to their own security had also evolved since the enunciation of the Brezhnev Doctrine in 1968.[7] This doctrine stated the Soviet Union reserved the right to intervene in any socialist state in order to prevent counterrevolutionary forces from dislodging friendly communist governments. It had been used to justify Soviet action in Czechoslovakia and appeared to justify Soviet intervention in Poland if the Solidarity movement threatened the communist government there.

Soviet learning did not just take place when the United States followed conciliatory policies toward the Soviets. Nevertheless, military might was the key to Soviet power in the Cold War era. If Moscow could have forced political concessions from the West, it might have been able to continue the Cold War despite its economic decline and challenges. Yuri Andropov believed he could intimidate and fragment the North Atlantic Treaty Organization (NATO) by targeting missiles at Western Europe. The U.S. decision to deploy Cruise and Pershing II missiles in Western Europe helped to foreclose this strategy since the Soviets had failed to divide and break the alliance.[8] Some credit the Reagan military buildup for forcing the Soviets to change their policy by overburdening their defenses, but this alone did not cause the transformation in Soviet foreign policy under Gorbachev.[9] The argument that the Soviets were forced to retreat because of their economic decline minimizes the choices Soviet leaders considered and neglects the obvious critique that if the economic demise of the Soviets was inevitably going to lead to their political demise, why did so few scholars predict the end of the Cold War?[10]

More importantly, the claim that retrenchment was Moscow's only option mischaracterizes Gorbachev's choices. Gorbachev went well beyond retrenchment, promoting instead a revolution in Soviet foreign policy. Gorbachev's advocacy of common security, universal human rights, and the renunciation of nuclear weapons was in no way seeking to reinforce earlier policy. His new foreign policy was more than rhetorical as he made asymmetrical cuts in nuclear and conventional arms, ended support for international communist movements, and promoted regional cooperation rather than seeking local allies in regional conflicts to counter states and groups allied to the United States. Significantly, Gorbachev's radical approach came before he was overtaken by events such as the fall of the Berlin Wall. He announced the principle of noninterference in Europe in 1988. After the fall of the Wall and in spite of a deteriorating domestic political situation, Gorbachev allowed a unified Germany to be a member of NATO. Thus, the retrenchment argument falsely assumes Gorbachev's domestic goals were based merely on reducing costs. Instead, we believe it is better to understand Gorbachev's policies as they were actually intended: to transform the Soviet system. This is because of the close relationship between foreign policy and the domestic goals of Gorbachev's policy agenda.

According to the leading constructivist Alexander Wendt, Gorbachev's abandonment of class struggle as the basis for Soviet foreign policy changed the "identity" of the Soviet state and how it defined its national interests.[11] Several scholars concur with this analysis and give primacy to ideational factors and agency, for they contend material factors alone do not explain Soviet foreign policy at the end of the Cold War.[12] Nations' and leaders' conceptions of identity are largely constructed through their interactions with other states. Gorbachev's renunciation of class struggle triggered a process of improved relations between the United States and the Soviet Union as each came to define its interests in less hostile terms. Rey Koslowski and Friedrich Kratochwil contend that Gorbachev transformed international politics by his renunciation of the Brezhnev Doctrine,[13] which had prevented the Eastern European states from choosing their own domestic systems. This transformation occurred not just because of changes in the international system or material conditions based on American policies during the Reagan administration, but because of revolutionary changes in the "norms" governing the Eastern Bloc.[14] These were changes instigated by Gorbachev as part of his new thinking in foreign policy, and Kratochwil argues that the changes in norms on how the Soviets perceived their interests in Eastern Europe should not be viewed in instrumental terms.[15]

Although constructivists successfully identify how the Cold War began to wind down due to changed Soviet interests and identity, they do not emphasize the domestic purposes of Gorbachev's revolution in foreign policy. Gorbachev was using this new foreign policy to reconfigure the ruling coalition in the Soviet system by weakening the military-industrial establishment as well as hard-line ideologues within the party who were reluctant to help implement his domestic-reform agenda. One of the key questions surrounding Gorbachev was the origin of his new ideas. Several scholars have argued that transnational actors were critical to the ideas and policies Gorbachev sought to implement.[16] However, Gorbachev first selected a path of conciliation toward the West and then later accepted the ideas of transnational actors. Deborah Welch Larson and Alexei Shevchenko find that Gorbachev's new policies and ideas were not based on negotiations with Western diplomats.[17] Instead, through a creative process, Gorbachev conceived of a path where the Soviets would gain status by leading the world in a peaceful transformation. However, this effort at what has been identified as social identity theory neglects the domestic politics of Gorbachev's reform agenda. As a revolutionary (or better, in this context, a counterrevolutionary), Gorbachev sought to transform the international political system to foster his domestic agenda of radical decentralization and liberalization of the Soviet domestic system.

The Counterrevolution in Soviet Foreign Policy

Gorbachev's counterrevolution in Soviet foreign policy intended to overturn the extant institutions and political coalition of the state and to create a new regime based on principles antithetical to its origins. Gorbachev's "elite-led revolution"[18] in foreign policy was not meant to be diversionary or externalize domestic conflict as much as it was an effort to transform domestic politics by ending a revolutionary foreign policy and shocking the domestic Soviet political system into supporting his efforts at reform—perestroika. Specifically, Gorbachev sought a dramatic reduction in the role of the military, a decentralization of the command economy, openness and empowerment of new groups historically marginalized in Soviet domestic politics (groups outside the party), and an effort for the Soviets to play a leading role in promoting global integration, thereby legitimating the Soviet regime and gaining it external support for his domestic-reform agenda. Instead of conceiving of the outside world as one of hostile capitalist encirclement, Gorbachev hoped to make the outside world friendly to Soviet interests. This would undermine those who opposed his efforts at reversing centralization, repression, and the party's monopoly of power.

As a counterrevolutionary, Gorbachev was changing foreign policy in order to support his domestic agenda.[19] Our analysis of the role foreign policy played in the Soviet State differs from realism's historical assumption that because states are functionally equivalent, domestic politics are not important in shaping a state's foreign policy.[20] Since the fall of the Berlin Wall, the end of the Cold War, and the opening of Soviet archives, many have come to recognize the distinctiveness of the Soviet Union as a state.[21] The most important revelation with respect to Soviet foreign policy is that ideology played a much greater role than earlier believed.[22] Drawing on these findings, Nigel Gould-Davies argues that Soviet foreign policy sought "geoideological" goals as opposed to the geopolitical and security goals of most other states.[23] As an "ideological state," the Soviet Union sought to accumulate power beyond its immediate security needs. It sought to influence the domestic politics and reproduce its own domestic system in other states. Even though some of the revolutionary zeal of Soviet foreign policy faded over time, Nikita Khrushchev, Leonid Brezhnev, and other party elites continued to call for class struggle and the achievement of ideological goals associated with the revolution.[24] Most importantly, Soviet foreign policy still believed the outside world was hostile and the state had overextended itself in defense of its ideological goals. Nichols contends, "Moscow never abandoned the idea that the great task facing the USSR was to weaken and eventually to eradicate competing systems."[25] Thus, by the mid-1980s, the Soviet Union had become an ossified revolutionary state. The failure of the Soviet communist system internally thus required rethinking of Soviet foreign policy and helps account for the end of the Cold War and the ultimate fall of the Berlin Wall.[26]

Jack Snyder demonstrates the importance of domestic factors in the formulation and execution of Soviet foreign policy as it emerged as a great power in the twentieth century.[27] The domestic context most important to our argument is that the Soviet Union was a revolutionary state. As such, its foreign policy emerged from the externalization of domestic conflicts.[28] The ruling elite, in this case the Politburo of the Communist Party and especially its General Secretary, employed external enemies or threats to mobilize the population in order to achieve national goals as well as justify repression of potential rivals. To secure their positions, the rulers typically concentrated power in their own hands through centralized decision making. Often to defeat internal rivals, those in power attempted to link their domestic rivals with foreign adversaries to disgrace them in the domestic political context and weaken their potential threat to the ruling regime. Finally, foreign-policy goals were formulated in a global context and tended to exaggerate the external threats to the regime. This caused the state to overextend itself in search of security. This excessively ambitious and costly foreign policy led to imperial overstretch where the Soviet Union's commitments could not be sustained and thus undermined its capacity to remain a great power.[29]

As Gorbachev came to power, he first concentrated on the domestic economic crisis at hand, and he recognized that Soviet defense commitments were too costly given the needs of the domestic economy.[30] This meant a subordination of historic foreign-policy goals to that of his domestic agenda.[31] Gorbachev sought to overcome the stifling effects of the command economy and revitalize it through the implementation of market mechanisms and the initiation of leases and cooperatives. In his first year in power, he did not attempt to overturn or revolutionize the system. Instead, he encouraged its "acceleration" (*uskorenie*).[32] Gorbachev's modest domestic agenda paralleled his foreign policy. Focusing primarily on reducing tensions with the West since the invasion of Afghanistan, he met European leaders and President Reagan in Geneva. Gorbachev acknowledged that Moscow's aggressive behavior and the Brezhnev-Andropov view that détente was attributable to a favorable change in the "correlation of forces" for the Soviets justifiably caused the West to scrap détente in the early 1980s. He expressed new thinking in suggesting that the two blocs extend cooperation beyond that of the 1970s and eliminate their roles as enemies. Still, he failed to make any significant changes in

Soviet security policy. Instead, as the new General Secretary, he promoted the same policies he had inherited. In fact, he actually increased military spending and reaffirmed existing Soviet interests around the world, including winning the war in Afghanistan.

Gorbachev began his revolution in February 1986 at the thirty-sixth Party Congress with his renunciation of class struggle as the basis for Soviet foreign policy. This transformation period culminated with the signing of the Intermediate Nuclear Force (INF) Agreement in December 1987. The reason for this change in foreign policy was the evolution of his domestic goals. The pace of reforms and perestroika had stalled, and Gorbachev developed his new foreign policy in response to his frustration with the lack of success in his domestic agenda.[33] Gorbachev was attempting to use changes in foreign policy to shock the governing system in the Soviet Union and promote perestroika.[34] The means Gorbachev used to shake the system were intended to scale back the role and power of the military while simultaneously overhauling the central-command economy. By reallocating resources away from the military, Gorbachev undermined the military mobilization that defines a revolutionary state. Beyond a more efficient allocation of decreasing resources, Gorbachev hoped that undermining the military's control of the economy would trigger what has been called the third industrial revolution.[35] Gorbachev recognized that the development of individualism and innovation needed to spur on the new economy was unlikely without a major shift away from hierarchical authority and undifferentiated masses.[36]

In renouncing class struggle and seeking dramatic cuts in nuclear arms, Gorbachev undermined the rationale for military dominance in society. In place of class struggle, Gorbachev advocated working to improve the human condition as the new goal of Soviet foreign policy. While less successful in his overall efforts at reforming the central-command economy, Gorbachev proved more successful in the foreign-policy realm. He was able to reduce the military's influence largely due to the hierarchical nature of the party system that allowed him to remove unsupportive Politburo members and move much of the foreign-policy decision making to the foreign ministry where he had a close ally in Eduard Shevardnadze. He was able to fire the Defense Minister, Marshal Sokolov, after a West German teenager flew his plane undetected into Red Square. Gorbachev chose Dimitrii Yazov as the new Defense Minister, and he proved far more docile to Gorbachev's dramatic foreign-policy moves, such as the INF treaty with the United States.[37]

Gorbachev's greatest challenge as a counterrevolutionary was to overhaul an ossified central-command economy that had grown increasingly inefficient and incapable of innovation. Because powerful interests in the ministries and state bodies had concentrated power in their own hands for so long, party and bureaucratic leaders were reluctant to allow any reforms. The only choice was "shock therapy," whereby the old institutions and controls would have to be destroyed and new ones put in their place.[38] Gorbachev recognized the unwillingness of those who had held such significant control of the economy to let go of their bureaucracies.[39] Gorbachev thus viewed disarmament and foreign-policy maneuvers—such as promoting joint ventures and granting multinationals operations within the Soviet Union—as a way of challenging and defeating those members of the bureaucracy and *nomenclatura* who opposed his domestic reforms. Thus, in autumn of 1986 Gorbachev proposed total nuclear disarmament of the two superpowers at the summit at Reykjavik, and throughout 1987, the Soviets were generally cooperative in regard to U.S. demands in the foreign-policy realm.[40]

Gorbachev promoted another even more dramatic change in Soviet foreign policy in 1988 by rescinding the Brezhnev Doctrine at the Nineteenth Party Congress. Western observers had already calculated the East Bloc was now more of a burden on the Soviet Union than a benefit.[41] Thus, the revocation of the Brezhnev Doctrine was not caused by pressure from the West as much as Gorbachev's domestic-reform agenda.[42] In a speech made at the UN in December of 1988, Gorbachev announced massive cuts in conventional arms and forces in Europe. This precluded the possibility that the Soviets would have the capability of a conventional military attack on the West or be able to continue to support weak, unpopular, or unsustainable regimes that had been part of the Eastern Bloc for decades. In 1989, the Soviets publicly endorsed the idea of an alternative party, Solidarity, competing in Polish elections.

It was change in East Germany, however, that accelerated the end of the Cold War and brought its symbol, the Berlin Wall, down. Gorbachev feared that, unless Eastern European states reformed, unrest would erupt and the Soviets would be forced to intervene. Soviet intervention would surely doom perestroika, as Gorbachev's opponents would use the failure of reforms elsewhere as justification for further retrenchment at home. Thus, Gorbachev encouraged reforms in East Germany and throughout the Eastern Bloc. East German leaders, however, feared a reform effort would spiral out of control and lead to the demise of their regime.[43]

Research on the domestic politics of the German Democratic Republic (GDR) has stressed the role of dissent in helping to undermine support for this regime.[44] Because of the oppressive nature of the regime, this opposition was not publicly visible or well organized. Instead, the latent opposition of the regime was primarily present in small informal or personal networks.[45] These groups and individuals had been intimidated but became less fearful as protest was increasingly tolerated. Throughout its history the government of the GDR had failed to develop strong and effective linkages between the citizen and the state.[46] This meant that despite the appearance of strong authoritarian control of society, the East German government had little domestic support. Moreover, the lack of a strong and distinct East German identity made leaders and some who opposed the regime reluctant to engage in reforms for fear of the loss of the state itself.[47] Though the East German state was attempting reforms by the end of 1989, it was already too late. The opening of borders and resultant emigration from East Germany signified dissent, the lack of loyalty of the East German population for the regime, and the regime's increased vulnerability.[48] The collapse of the Wall demonstrated not only the desire for many East Germans to live in the freedom that West Germany had to offer but also that the GDR had not enough legitimacy to continue as a functioning regime.

By 1989, the collapse of the external threat that the Soviet regime had posed to those opponents of the communist regime in East Germany meant the GDR needed to renegotiate its relationship to the public. Its intransigence and lack of support doomed any effort to redefine itself in a way palatable to East Germans. On the occasion of the celebration of the fiftieth anniversary of the East German State, a social movement blossomed calling for the Stalinist East German government to embrace Gorbachev's agenda. The growing groundswell of demonstrators encouraged Gorbachev in his visit to Berlin to demand the East German government remove its hard-line leader. While long-time leader Erich Honecker did resign, the efforts of his successor, Egon Krenz, at implementing a German version of perestroika came too late to gain legitimacy for the old regime. As was the case with Gorbachev's reforms, Krenz's policies only served to unleash opponents of the regime and led to its demise.[49] Thus, based on pressures from Moscow and from growing discontent in East Germany, the new and hapless government in East Berlin allowed the Wall to fall on November 9, 1989. By this time, Gorbachev was hoping the threat of a similar collapse of the Soviet system would finally trigger the kind of change he hoped for in the Soviet Union.[50] At the Nineteenth Party Congress Gorbachev called for democratization with elections to challenge recalcitrant party *apparatchiks* who refused to implement his domestic-reform agenda. As in East Germany, efforts at reforming the governing system of the Soviet Union failed.

In the summer of 1991, communist hard-liners attempted to reverse Gorbachev's policies and replace him in a putsch. This effort failed when

Boris Yeltsin and other reformers allied with many in Moscow, and some in the military defied the orders of the disgruntled hard-liners. By the fall of 1991, the Soviet Union disintegrated as its member republics declared their independence and the state formally ended on Christmas that year when Gorbachev left the Kremlin, a failed counterrevolutionary, but hailed internationally for his leadership that led to the end of the Cold War. In fact, his commitment to the tenets of what American leaders interpreted as liberal ideology convinced them the Cold War was over since there was no longer an ideological conflict between the United States and the Soviet Union.[51] Gorbachev's gamble of advocating a revolution in foreign policy to defeat his domestic rivals and formulate a new Soviet system had yielded not a renewed and reinvigorated Soviet Union but a fragmented set of states and a weakened Russia. It had allowed the disintegration of Soviet control over Eastern Europe and the collapse of the division of Europe, for so long symbolized by the Berlin Wall.

Conclusion

Part of the reason why the fall of the Berlin Wall is seen as such a historic event, one we commemorated in 2009 at an academic conference marking the twentieth anniversary of the fall, is that it surprised almost everyone. While the Wall had only been in existence since 1961, the Cold War had become such a defining part of international relations that it was difficult to imagine a world without it. This chapter has shown that both the economic challenges and ideological changes that came with a new generation of Soviet leadership transformed Soviet foreign policy and made the collapse of the Wall possible. Scholars of international relations failed to predict the collapse of the Soviet Union and communism because they neither understood the gravity of the economic problems the Soviets faced nor did they appreciate the domestic motivation of Soviet leaders struggling to reform a recalcitrant social system. Efforts to explain Gorbachev's policies that brought about the end of the Cold War focusing on international factors alone fail to appreciate the counterrevolutionary domestic context of Gorbachev's decisions.[52] As Gorbachev sought to transform Eastern European states to trigger a similar reform process in the Soviet Union, he unwittingly denied the support states like East Germany needed to maintain control in their society. Gorbachev's failure as a counterrevolutionary changed not only the history of the Soviet Union but the communist states in Eastern Europe that had come to rely on Soviet support for their existence.

Notes

1. See, for example, Richard Ned Lebow, "The Long Peace, the End of the Cold War, and the Failure of Realism," *International Organization* 48 (1994): 249–278.
2. Vinod Aggarwal and Pierre Allen, "Cold War Endgames," in *The End of the Cold War: Evaluating Theories of International Relations*, ed. Pierre Allen and Kjell Goldmann. (Norwell, MA: Kluwer Academic, 1992), 24–54; Stephen G. Brooks and William G. Wohlforth, "From Old Thinking to New Thinking: Qualitative Research," *International Security* 26, no. 4 (2002): 93–111; Stephen G. Brooks and William G. Wohlforth, "Power, Globalization, and the End of the Cold War: Reevaluating a Landmark Case for Ideas," *International Security* 25, no. 3 (2000/01): 5–53.
3. Note our explanation differs from those who argue the Soviet leaders confronted a changed world and this accounted for the change in Soviet foreign policy. For this perspective, see Daniel Deudney and G. John Ikenberry, "The International Sources of Soviet Change," *International Security* 16, no. 3 (1991): 74–118.
4. Brooks and Wohlforth, "From Old Thinking to New Thinking," 93–111; Brooks and Wohlforth, "Power, Globalization, and the End of the Cold War," 5–53.
5. Anders Aslund, *Gorbachev's Struggle for Economic Reform* (Ithaca, NY: Cornell University Press, 1989); Michael Ellman and Vladimir Kontorovich, *The Destruction of the Soviet Economic System: An Insider's Account* (Armonk, NY: M. E. Sharpe, 1998); Clifford G. Gaddy, *The Price of the Past* (Washington: Brookings, 1997); Marshall I. Goldman, *What Went Wrong with Perestroika* (New York: Norton, 1991).
6. Robert D. English, "Power, Ideas, and New Evidence on the Cold War's End: A Reply to Brooks and Wohlforth," *International Security* 26, no. 4 (2002): 70–92.
7. Matthew J. Ouimet, *The Rise and Fall of the Brezhnev Doctrine in Soviet Foreign Policy* (Chapel Hill: University of North Carolina Press, 2003).
8. John Lewis Gaddis, "Hanging Tough Paid Off," *Bulletin of Atomic Scientists* 45 (1989): 11–14; Robert G. Patman, "Reagan, Gorbachev and the Emergence of New Political Thinking," *Review of International Studies* 25 (1999): 577–601.
9. Mike Bowker, *Russian Foreign Policy and the End of the Cold War* (Aldershot: Dartmouth, 1997), 252; Fred Chernoff, "Ending the Cold War: The Soviet Retreat and the US Military Buildup," *International Affairs* 67 (1991): 111–126; Raymond L. Garthoff, "Why Did the Cold War Arise, and Why Did it End?" in *The End of the Cold War: Its Meanings and Implications*, ed. Michael J. Hogan. (New York: Cambridge University Press, 1992), 129.
10. Kjell Goldmann, "Introduction: Three Debates about the End of the Cold War," in *The End of the Cold War: Evaluating Theories of International Relations*, ed. Pierre Allen and Kjell Goldmann. (Norwell, MA: Kluwer Academic, 1992), 1–11.

11. Alexander Wendt, "Anarchy Is What States Make of It: The Social Construction of Power Politics," *International Organization* 46 (1992): 391–425.
12. See Gavan Duffy and Brian Frederking, "Changing the Rules: A Speech Act Analysis of the End of the Cold War," *International Studies Quarterly* 53 (2009): 325–347; Robert D. English, *Russia and the Idea of the West: Gorbachev, Intellectuals, and the End of the Cold War* (New York: Columbia University Press, 2000); Robert G. Herman, "Identity, Norms and National Security: The Soviet Foreign Policy Revolution and the End of the Cold War," in *The Culture of National Security: Norms and Identity in World Politics*, ed. Peter J. Katzenstein. (New York: Columbia University Press, 1996), 271–316; Akan Malici, "Reagan and Gorbachev: Altercasting at the End of the Cold War," in *Beliefs and Leadership in World Politics: Methods and Applications of Operational Code Analysis*, ed. Mark Schafer and Stephen G. Walker (New York: Palgrave Macmillan, 2006), 127–149; Wesley W. Widmaier, Mark Blyth, and Leonard Seabrooke, "Exogenous Shocks or Endogenous Constructions? The Meanings of War and Crises," *International Studies Quarterly* 51 (2009): 747–759.
13. Rey Koslowski and Friedrich V. Kratochwil, "Understanding Change in International Politics: The Soviet Empire's Demise and the International System," *International Organization* 48 (1994): 215–247.
14. Sheldon Anderson, *Condemned to Repeat It: "Lessons of History" and the Making of U. S. Cold War Containment Policy* (Lanham, MD: Lexington Books, 2008), 186–194; Fred Halliday, "The Cold War: Lessons and Legacies," *Government and Opposition* 45 (2010): 13–15.
15. Friedrich Kratochwil, "The Embarrassment of Changes: Neorealism as the Science of Real-politik without Politics," *Review of International Studies* 19 (1993): 65.
16. Jeffrey T. Checkel, *Ideas and International Political Change: Soviet/Russia Behavior and the End of the Cold War* (New Haven, CT: Yale University Press, 1997); Matthew Evangelista, *Unarmed Forces: The Transnational Movement to End the Cold War* (Ithaca, CT: Cornell University Press, 1999); Thomas Risse-Kappen, "Ideas Do Not Float Freely: Transnational Coalitions, Domestic Structures, and the End of the Cold War," *International Organization* 48 (1994): 185–214.
17. Deborah Welch Larson and Alexei Shevchenko, "Shortcut to Greatness: The New Thinking and the Revolution in Soviet Foreign Policy," *International Organization* 57 (2003): 86–87.
18. For the theory of elite-led revolutions, see Ellen Kay Trimberger, "A Theory of Elite Revolutions," *Studies in Comparative International Development* 7 (1972): 191–207. For the idea that Gorbachev led a revolution in Soviet foreign policy, see Robert Legvold, "The Revolution in Soviet Foreign Policy," in *The Soviet System: From Crisis to Collapse* (Revised Edition), ed. Alexander Dallin and Gail W. Lapidus (Boulder: Westview, 1995), 421–432.
19. This argument is also made in Nick Bisley, *The End of the Cold War and the Causes of the Soviet Collapse* (New York: Palgrave Macmillan, 2004), 2; Randall Collins, "Prediction in Macrosociology: The Case of the Soviet

Collapse," *American Journal of Sociology* 100 (1995): 1573; and Matthew Evangelista, "Norms, Heresthetics and the End of the Cold War," *Journal of Cold War Studies* 3, no. 1 (2001): 24. This approach emphasizing the role of international factors determining domestic politics is taken from Peter Gourevitch, "The Second Image Reversed: the International Sources of Domestic Politics," *International Organization* 32 (1978): 881–911.

20. Kenneth N. Waltz, *Theory of International Politics* (Reading, MA: Addison-Wesley, 1979).
21. William E. Odom, "Soviet Politics and After: Old and New Concepts," *World Politics* 45 (1992): 66–98; Philip G. Roeder, *Red Sunset: The Failure of Soviet Politics* (Princeton, NJ: Princeton University Press, 1993).
22. John Lewis Gaddis, *The Cold War: A New History* (New York: Penguin, 2005); Sergei N. Goncharov, John W. Lewis, and Xue Litai, *Uncertain Powers: Stalin, Mao and the Korean War* (Stanford: Stanford University Press, 1993); Halliday, "The Cold War," 5–7; Douglas J. MacDonald, "Communist Bloc Expansion in the Early Cold War: Challenging Realism, Refuting Revisionism," *International Security* 20, no. 3 (1995/96): 152–188; John Mueller, "What was the Cold War About? Evidence from Its Ending," *Political Science Quarterly* 119 (2004/05): 609–631; Ronald E. Powaski, *The Cold War: The United States and the Soviet Union, 1917–1991* (New York: Oxford University Press, 1998); Geoffrey Roberts, *Stalin's Wars: From World War to Cold War, 1939–1953* (New Haven, CT: Yale University Press, 1993); Odd Arne Westad, "Secrets of the Second World: The Russian Archives and the Reinterpretation of Cold War History," *Diplomatic History* 21 (1997): 259–271; Timothy J. White, "Cold War Historiography: New Evidence Beyond Traditional Typologies," *International Social Science Review* 75, no. 3/4 (2000): 35–44; Vladislav Zubok and Constantine Pleshakov, *Inside the Kremlin's Cold War: From Stalin to Khrushchev* (Cambridge, MA: Harvard University Press, 1996).
23. Nigel Gould-Davies, "Rethinking the Role of Ideology in International Politics during the Cold War," *Journal of Cold War Studies* 1, no. 1 (1999): 90–109.
24. Douglas W. Blum, "The Soviet Foreign Policy Belief System: Beliefs, Politics, and Foreign Policy Outcomes," *International Studies Quarterly* 37 (1993): 373–394.
25. Thomas M. Nichols, *Winning the World: Lessons for America's Future from the Cold War* (Westport, CT: Praeger, 2002), 9.
26. John Lewis Gaddis, *The United States and the End of the Cold War: Implications, Reconsiderations, Provocations* (New York: Oxford University Press, 1992), 160–162; David Remnick, *Lenin's Tomb: The Last Days of the Soviet Empire* (New York: Vintage Books, 1993).
27. Jack Snyder, *Myths of Empire: Domestic Politics and International Ambition* (Ithaca, NY: Cornell University Press, 1991).
28. Robert S. Snyder, "The U.S. and Third World Revolutionary States: Understanding the Breakdown of Relations," *International Studies Quarterly* 43 (1999): 265–290.

29. Paul Kennedy, *The Rise and Fall of the Great Powers: Economic Change and Military Conflict from 1500–2000* (New York: Random House: 1987).
30. Bowker, *Russian Foreign Policy and the End of the Cold War*, 2 and 28.
31. Jacques Lévesque, *The Enigma of 1989: The USSR and the Liberation of Eastern Europe*, trans. Keith Martin (Berkeley: University of California Press, 1997).
32. Melvyn P. Leffler, *For the Soul of Mankind: The United States, the Soviet Union, and the Cold War* (New York: Hill and Wang, 2007), 374–375.
33. William E. Odom, *The Collapse of the Soviet Military* (New Haven, CT: Yale University Press, 1998), 97.
34. Leffler, *For the Soul of Mankind*, 391.
35. Philip G. Cerny, "Globalization and the Changing Logic of Collective Action," *International Organization* 49 (1995): 495–625; Peter F. Drucker, *Post-Capitalist Society* (New York: Harper Business, 1981); Alvin Toffler, *The Third Wave* (New York: Bantam, 1981).
36. For a similar argument see Daniel Deudney and G. John Ikenberry, "Soviet Reform and the End of the Cold War: Explaining Large Scale Historical Change," *Review of International Studies* 17 (1991): 225–250. Robert W. Campbell chronicles the failure of the Soviet economic system in *The Failure of Soviet Economic Planning: System, Performance, Reform* (Bloomington: University of Indiana Press, 1992).
37. Anatoliy Dobrynin, *In Confidence: Moscow's Ambassador to America's Six Cold War Presidents (1962–1986)* (New York: Random House, 1995), 626.
38. Jerry F. Hough, *Democratization and Revolution in the USSR, 1985–1991* (Washington, D.C.: Brookings, 1997), 122. The architect of this policy was the American economist Jeffrey Sachs who served as an advisor to East Bloc economies seeking to transition to capitalist economies. See Jeffrey Sachs, "The Economic Transformation of Eastern Europe: The Case of Poland," *Economics of Planning* 25 (1992): 5–19.
39. Mikhail Gorbachev, *Memoirs* (New York: Doubleday, 1996), 227.
40. Philip Zelikow and Condoleeza Rice, *Germany Unified and Europe Transformed: A Study in Statecraft* (Cambridge, MA: Harvard University Press, 1995), 149–150.
41. Valerie Bunce, "The Empire Strikes Back: The Evolution of the Eastern Bloc from a Soviet Asset to a Soviet Liability," *International Organization* 39 (1985): 1–46.
42. Mike Bowker, "Explaining Soviet Foreign Policy in the 1980s," in *From Cold War to Collapse: Theory and World Politics in the 1980s*, ed. Mike Bowker and Robin Brown (Cambridge: Cambridge University Press, 1993), 106.
43. Judy Batt, "The End of Communist Rule in East European Politics," *Government and Opposition* 26 (1991): 368–390; Dirk W. W. Rumberg, "Glasnost in the GDR? The Impact of Gorbachev's Reform Policy on the German Democratic Republic," *International Relations* 9 (1988): 197–227; M. E. Sarotte, "Elite Intransigence and the End of the Berlin Wall," *German Politics* 2 (1993): 270–287.

44. Roland Bleiker, "Stroll Through the Wall: Everyday Poetics of Cold War Politics," *Alternatives* 25 (2000): 391–408; Gareth Dale, "'A Very Orderly Retreat': Democratic Transition in East Germany, 1989–90," *Debatte* 14 (2006): 7–35; Steven Pfaff, "The Politics of Peace in the GDR: The Independent Peace Movement, the Church, and the Origins of the East German Opposition," *Peace and Change* 26 (2001): 280–300; Detlef Pollack, "Mass Pressures, Elite Responses-Roots of Democratization: The Case of the GDR," *Communist and Post-Communist Studies* 35 (2002): 305–324; Damon A. Terrill, "Tolerance Lost: Disaffection, Dissent and Revolution in the German Democratic Republic," *East European Quarterly* 28 (1994): 349–379. Inga Markovits highlights the way the growing sense of legal rights undermined authoritarian rule in East Germany in "Transition to Constitutional Democracy: The German Democratic Republic," *Annals of the American Academy of Political and Social Science* 603 (2006): 140–154.
45. Timur Kuran, "Now Out of Never: The Element of Surprise in the East European Revolution of 1989," *World Politics* 44 (1991): 7–48; Charles S. Maier, *Dissolution: The Crisis of Communism and the End of East Germany* (Princeton, NJ: Princeton University Press, 1997); Karl-Dieter Opp and Christiane Gern, "Dissident Groups, Personal Networks and Spontaneous Cooperation: The East German Revolution of 1989," *American Sociological Review* 58 (1993): 659–680; Steven Pfaff, "Collective Identity and Informal Groups in Revolutionary Mobilization: East Germany in 1989," *Social Forces* 75 (1996): 91–118.
46. Beate Völker and Henk Flap, "Weak Ties as a Liability: The Case of East Germany," *Rationality and Society* 13 (2001): 397–428. Vladimir Tismaneanu in "Nascent Civil Society in the German Democratic Republic," *Problems of Communism* 38 (1989): 90–111 contends that opposition groups had begun to create the beginnings of a civil society by the mid-1980s. Some dispute the narrative that there was a dormant civil society waiting to emerge from the totalitarian control of the East German Government, see Sigrid Roßteutscher, "Competing Narratives and the Social Construction of Reality: The GDR in Transition," *German Politics* 9 (2000): 61–82.
47. Lukasz Galecki, "The German Democratic Republic: The Revolution that Wasn't," *East European Politics and Societies* 23 (2009): 509–517; Mark R. Thompson, "No Exit: 'Nation-stateness' and Democratization in the German Democratic Republic," *Political Studies* 44 (1996): 267–287.
48. Ulrich Albrecht, "The Role of Social Movements in the Collapse of the German Democratic Republic," *Global Society* 10 (1996): 145–165; Albert O. Hirschman, "Exit, Voice, and the Fate of the German Democratic Republic: An Essay in Conceptual History," *World Politics* 45 (1993): 173–202; Steven Pfaff, "Exit-Voice Dynamics in Collective Action: An Analysis of Emigration and Protest in the East German Revolution," *American Journal of Sociology* 109 (2003): 401–444.
49. Kurt-Henning Tvedt, "The East German Transition Game," *Journal of Communist Studies and Transition Politics* 20 (2004): 80–82.
50. Hough, *Democratization and Revolution in the USSR*, 197.

51. Mark L. Haas, "The United States and the End of the Cold War: Reactions to Shifts in Soviet Power, Policies, or Domestic Politics?" *International Organization* 61 (2007): 145–179.
52. See, for example, Akan Malici, *When Leaders Learn and When They Don't: Mikhail Gorbachev and Kim Il Sung at the End of the Cold War* (Albany, NY: State University of New York Press, 2008).

Bibliography

Aggarwal, Vinod, and Pierre Allan. "Cold War Endgames." In *The End of the Cold War: Evaluating Theories of International Relations.* Edited by Pierre Allen and Kjell Goldmann. Norwell, MA: Kluwer Academic, 1992.

Albrecht, Ulrich. "The Role of Social Movements in the Collapse of the German Democratic Republic." *Global Society* 10 (1996): 145–165.

Anderson, Sheldon. *Condemned to Repeat It: "Lessons of History" and the Making of U.S. Cold War Containment Policy.* Lanham, MD: Lexington Books, 2008.

Aslund, Anders. *Gorbachev's Struggle for Economic Reform.* Ithaca, NY: Cornell University Press, 1989.

Batt, Judy. "The End of Communist Rule in East European Politics." *Government and Opposition* 26 (1991): 368–390.

Bisley, Nick. *The End of the Cold War and the Causes of Soviet Collapse.* New York: Palgrave Macmillan, 2004.

Bleiker, Roland. "Stroll Through the Wall: Everyday Poetics of Cold War Politics." *Alternatives* 25 (2000): 391–408.

Blum, Douglas W. "The Soviet Foreign Policy Belief System: Beliefs, Politics, and Foreign Policy Outcomes." *International Studies Quarterly* 37 (1993): 373–394.

Bowker, Mike. "Explaining Soviet Foreign Policy in the 1980s." In *From Cold War to Collapse: Theory and World Politics in the 1980s.* Edited by Mike Bowker and Robin Brown. Cambridge: Cambridge University Press, 1993.

———. *Russian Foreign Policy and the End of the Cold War.* Aldershot: Dartmouth, 1997.

Brooks, Stephen G., and William G. Wohlforth. "From Old Thinking to New Thinking: Qualitative Research." *International Security* 26 (2002): 93–111.

———. "Power, Globalization, and the End of the Cold War: Reevaluating a Landmark Case for Ideas." *International Security* 25 (2000/2001): 5–53.

Bunce, Valerie. "The Empire Strikes Back: The Evolution of the Eastern Bloc from a Soviet Asset to a Soviet Liability." *International Organization* 39 (1985): 1–46.

Campbell, Robert W. *The Failure of Soviet Economic Planning: System, Performance, Reform.* Bloomington: Indiana University Press, 1992.

Cerny, Philip G. "Globalization and the Changing Logic of Collective Action." *International Organization* 49 (1995): 595–625.

Checkel, Jeffrey T. *Ideas and International Political Change: Soviet/Russia Behavior and the End of the Cold War.* New Haven, CT: Yale University Press, 1997.

Chernoff, Fred. "Ending the Cold War: The Soviet Retreat and the US Military Buildup." *International Affairs* 67 (1991): 111–126.

Collins, Randall. "Prediction in Macrosociology: The Case of the Soviet Collapse." *American Journal of Sociology* 100 (1995): 1552–1593.

Dale, Gareth. "'A Very Orderly Retreat': Democratic Transition in East Germany, 1989–90." *Debatte* 14 (2006): 7–35.

Deudney, Daniel G., and G. John Ikenberry. "The International Sources of Soviet Change." *International Security* 16 (1991): 74–118.

———. "Soviet Reform and the End of the Cold War: Explaining Large Scale Historical Change." *Review of International Studies* 17 (1991): 225–250.

Dobrynin, Anatoliy. *In Confidence: Moscow's Ambassador to America's Six Cold War Presidents (1962–1986)*. New York: Random House, 1995.

Drucker, Peter F. *Post-Capitalist Society*. New York: Harper Business, 1993.

Duffy, Gavan, and Brian Frederking. "Changing the Rules: A Speech Act Analysis of the End of the Cold War." *International Studies Quarterly* 53 (2009): 325–347.

Ellman, Michael, and Vladimir Kontorovich. *The Destruction of the Soviet Economic System: An Insider's Account*. Armonk, NY: M. E. Sharpe, 1998.

English, Richard. "Power, Ideas, and New Evidence on the Cold War's End: A Reply to Brooks and Wohlforth." *International Security* 26 (2002): 70–92.

———. *Russia and the Idea of the West: Gorbachev, Intellectuals, and the End of the Cold War*. New York: Columbia University Press, 2000.

Evangelista, Matthew. "Norms, Heresthetics and the End of the Cold War." *Journal of Cold War Studies* 3 (2001): 5–35.

———. *Unarmed Forces: The Transnational Movement to End the Cold War*. Ithaca, NY: Cornell University Press, 1999.

Gaddis, John Lewis. *The Cold War: A New History*. New York: Penguin, 2005.

———. "Hanging Tough Paid Off." *Bulletin of Atomic Scientists* 45 (1989): 11–14.

——— . *The United States and the End of the Cold War: Implications, Reconsiderations, Provocations*. New York: Brookings, 1992.

Gaddy, Clifford G. *The Price of the Past*. Washington, D.C.: Brookings, 1997.

Galecki, Lukasz. "The German Democratic Republic: The Revolution that Wasn't." *East European Politics and Societies* 23 (2009): 509–517.

Garthoff, Raymond L. "Why Did the Cold War Arise, and Why Did it End?" In *The End of the Cold War: Its Meanings and Implications*. Edited by Michael J. Hogan. Cambridge: Cambridge University Press, 1992.

Goldman, Marshall I. *What Went Wrong with Perestroika*. New York: Norton, 1991.

Goldmann, Kjell. "Introduction: Three Debates about the End of the Cold War." In *The End of the Cold War: Evaluating Theories of International Relations*. Edited by Pierre Allan and Kjell Goldmann. Norwell, MA: Kluwer Academic, 1992.

Goncharov, Sergei, John W. Lewis, and Xue Litai. *Uncertain Partners: Stalin, Mao and the Korean War*. Stanford: Stanford University Press, 1993.

Gorbachev, Mikhail. *Memoirs*. New York: Doubleday, 1996.

Gould-Davies, Nigel. "Rethinking the Role of Ideology in International Politics during the Cold War." *Journal of Cold War Studies* 1 (1999): 90–109.

Gourevitch, Peter. "The Second Image Reversed: The International Sources of Domestic Politics." *International Organization* 32 (1978): 881–911.

Haas, Mark L. "The United States and the End of the Cold War: Reactions to Shifts in Soviet Power, Policies, or Domestic Politics?" *International Organization* 61 (2007): 145–179.

Halliday, Fred. "The Cold War: Lessons and Legacies." *Government and Opposition* 45 (2010): 1–28.

Herman, Robert G. "Identity, Norms, and National Security: The Soviet Foreign Policy Revolution and the End of the Cold War." In *The Culture of National Security: Norms and Identity in World Politics*. Edited by Peter Katzenstein. New York: Columbia University Press, 1996.

Hirschman, Albert. "Exit, Voice, and the Fate of the German Democratic Republic: An Essay in Conceptual History." *World Politics* 45 (1993): 173–202.

Hough, Jerry F. *Democratization and Revolution in the USSR, 1985–1991*. Washington, D.C.: Brookings, 1997.

Kennedy, Paul. *The Rise and Fall of the Great Powers: Economic Change and Military Conflict from 1500–2000*. New York: Random House, 1987.

Koslowski, Rey, and Friedrich V. Kratochwil. "Understanding Change in International Politics: The Soviet Empire's Demise and the International System." *International Organization* 48 (1994): 215–248.

Kratochwil, Fred. "The Embarrassment of Changes: Neorealism as the Science of Real-Politik without Politics." *Review of International Studies* 19 (1993): 63–80.

Kuran, Timur. "Now Out of Never: The Element of Surprise in the East European Revolution of 1989." *World Politics* 44 (1991): 7–48.

Larson, Deborah Welch, and Alexei Shevchenko. "Shortcut to Greatness: The New Thinking and the Revolution in Soviet Foreign Policy." *International Organization* 57 (2003): 77–110.

Lebow, Richard Ned. "The Long Peace, the End of the Cold War, and the Failure of Realism." *International Organization* 48 (1994): 149–278.

Leffler, Melvyn P. *For the Soul of Mankind: The United States, the Soviet Union, and the Cold War*. New York: Hill and Wang, 2007.

Legvold, Robert. "The Revolution in Soviet Foreign Policy." In *The Soviet System: From Crisis to Collapse* (Revised Edition). Edited by Alexander Dallin and Gail W. Lapidus. Boulder, CO: Westview, 1995.

Lévesque, Jacques. *The Enigma of 1989: The USSR and the Liberation of Eastern Europe*. Berkeley: University of California Press, 1997.

Malici, Akan. "Reagan and Gorbachev: Altercasting at the End of the Cold War." In *Beliefs and Leadership in World Politics: Methods and Applications of Operational Code Analysis*. Edited by Mark Schafer and Stephen G. Walker. New York: Palgrave Macmillan, 2006.

———. *When Leaders Learn and When They Don't: Mikhail Gorbachev and Kim Il Sung at the End of the Cold War*. Albany: State University of New York, 2008.

MacDonald, Douglas J. "Communist Bloc Expansion in the Early Cold War: Challenging Realism, Refuting Revisionism." *International Security* 20 (1995/96): 152–188.

Maier, Charles S. *Dissolution: The Crisis of Communism and the End of East Germany*. Princeton, NJ: Princeton University Press, 1997.

Markovits, Inga. "Transition to Constitutional Democracy: The German Democratic Republic." *Annals of the American Academy of Political and Social Science* 603 (2006): 140–154.

Mueller, John. "What was the Cold War About? Evidence from Its Ending." *Political Science Quarterly* 119 (2004/05): 609–631.

Nichols, Thomas M. *Winning the World: Lessons for America's Future from the Cold War*. Westport, CT: Praeger, 2002.

Odom, William E. *The Collapse of the Soviet Military*. New Haven, CT: Yale University Press, 1998.

———. "Soviet Politics and After: Old and New Concepts." *World Politics* 45 (1992): 66–98.

Opp, Karl-Dieter, and Christiane Gern. "Dissident Groups, Personal Networks and Spontaneous Cooperation: The East German Revolution of 1989." *American Sociological Review* 58 (1993): 659–680.

Ouimet, Matthew J. *The Rise and Fall of the Brezhnev Doctrine in Soviet Foreign Policy*. Chapel Hill: University of North Carolina Press, 2003.

Patman, Robert G. "Reagan, Gorbachev and the Emergence of 'New Political Thinking.'" *Review of International Studies* 25 (1999): 577–601.

Pfaff, Steven. "Collective Identity and Informal Groups in Revolutionary Mobilization: East Germany in 1989." *Social Forces* 75 (1996): 91–118.

———. "Exit-Voice Dynamics in Collective Action: An Analysis of Emigration and Protest in the East German Revolution." *American Journal of Sociology* 109 (2003): 401–444.

———. "The Politics of Peace in the GDR: The Independent Peace Movement, the Church, and the Origins of the East German Opposition." *Peace and Change* 26 (2001): 280–300.

Pollack, Detlef. "Mass Pressures, Elite Responses-Roots of Democratization: The Case of the GDR." *Communist and Post-Communist Studies* 35 (2002): 305–324.

Powaski, Ronald. *The Cold War: The United States and the Soviet Union, 1917–1991*. New York: Oxford University Press, 1998.

Remnick, David. *Lenin's Tomb: The Last Days of the Soviet Empire*. New York: Vintage Books, 1993.

Risse-Kappen, Thomas. "Ideas Do Not Float Freely: Transnational Coalitions, Domestic Structures, and the End of the Cold War." *International Organization* 48 (1994): 185–214.

Roberts, Geoffrey. *Stalin's Wars: From World War to Cold War, 1939–1953*. New Haven, CT: Yale University Press, 2007.

Roßteutscher, Sigrid. "Competing Narratives and the Social Construction of Reality: The GDR in Transition." *German Politics* 9 (2000): 61–82.

Roeder, Philip G. *Red Sunset: The Failure of Soviet Politics.* Princeton, NJ: Princeton University Press, 1993.

Rumberg, Dirk W. W. "Glasnost in the GDR? The Impact of Gorbachev's Reform Policy on the German Democratic Republic." *International Relations* 9 (1988): 197–227.

Sachs, Jeffrey. "The Economic Transformation of Eastern Europe: The Case of Poland." *Economics of Planning* 25 (1992): 5–19.

Sarotte, M. E. "Elite Intransigence and the End of the Berlin Wall." *German Politics* 2 (1993): 270–287.

Snyder, Jack. *Myths of Empire: Domestic Politics and International Ambition.* Ithaca, NY: Cornell University Press, 1991.

Snyder, Robert S. "The U.S. and Third World Revolutionary States: Understanding the Breakdown of Relations." *International Studies Quarterly* 43 (1999): 265–290.

Terrill, Damon A. "Tolerance Lost: Disaffection, Dissent and Revolution in the German Democratic Republic." *East European Quarterly* 28 (1994): 349–379.

Thompson, Mark R. "No Exit: 'Nation-stateness' and Democratization in the German Democratic Republic." *Political Studies* 44 (1996): 267–287.

Tismaneanu, Vladimir. "Nascent Civil Society in the German Democratic Republic." *Problems of Communism* 38 (1989): 90–111.

Toffler, Alvin. *The Third Wave.* New York: Bantam, 1981.

Trimberger, Ellen Kay. "A Theory of Elite Revolutions." *Studies in Comparative International Development* 7 (1972): 191–207.

Tvedt, Kurt-Henning. "The East German Transition Game." *Journal of Communist Studies and Transition Politics* 20 (2004): 73–97.

Völker, Beate, and Henk Flap. "Weak Ties as a Liability: The Case of East Germany." *Rationality and Society* 13 (2001): 397–428.

Waltz, Kenneth N. *Theory of International Politics.* Reading, MA: Addison-Wesley, 1979.

Wendt, Alexander. "Anarchy Is What States Make of It: The Social Construction of Power Politics." *International Organization* 46 (1992): 391–425.

Westad, Odd Arne. "Secrets of the Second World: The Russian Archives and the Reinterpretation of Cold War History." *Diplomatic History* 21 (1997): 259–271.

White, Timothy J. "Cold War Historiography: New Evidence Beyond Traditional Typographies." *International Social Science Review* 75 (2000): 35–44.

Widmaier, Wesley W., Mark Blyth, and Leonard Seabrooke. "Exogenous Shocks or Endogenous Constructions? The Meanings of Wars and Crises." *International Studies Quarterly* 51 (2007): 747–759.

Zelikow, Philip, and Condoleeza Rice. *Germany Unified and Europe Transformed: A Study in Statecraft.* Cambridge, MA: Harvard University Press, 1995.

Zubok, Vladislav, and Constantine Pleshakov. *Inside the Kremlin's Cold War: From Stalin to Khrushchev.* Cambridge, MA: Harvard University Press, 1996.

7

"Seventh of November" from *Berliner Ensemble*

Douglas Cowie

"Seventh of November" is the central chapter—both in terms of plot and thematic content—of a novel-in-progress, Berliner Ensemble, *which is set approximately thirty years following the fall of the Berlin Wall. The novel follows Peter Kokemus, a young American who, shortly after moving to Berlin, is coerced into involvement with a small terrorist group in a Berlin teetering on the edge of social and economic collapse. The group, comprised of young Berliners both East and West, all of whom were infants or small children in 1989, blows up the Reichstag, as well as a series of post offices and historical monuments in Berlin. Peter spends much of the novel being coerced into various violent activities and tries throughout to convince himself he understands why he is involved—and that he wants to be involved—in the work of the group. Thematically, the novel investigates justifications for terrorism and understandings of history, in particular the social and historical legacy of the Cold War and the lived legacy of its collapse for different individuals. In the climactic scenes at the end of the novel, Peter will find himself kidnapped, drugged, and repeatedly threatened by the group.*

In the scene immediately preceding this chapter, Peter has been forced by Matthias, the intimidating and emotionally erratic leader of the terrorist group, to shoot in the knee a young man who they caught pickpocketing patrons at a bar. One tension running through the novel is whether the scene included here, as well as other incidents and encounters, actually happen, or whether Peter has hallucinated them. This tension links thematically to the historical events about which Peter reads, and the political events around him in the novel, most of which he only experiences through newspaper reports; Peter is a naïve and unreflective young man who finds himself at the center of a complex intersection of personal, social, historical, and geopolitical events, without understanding his own role in those events.

* * *

Peter called in sick for the entire next week and only left the apartment to go to the corner shop to buy his daily newspaper. He scoured the paper every day looking for a report about the shooting. He wasn't worried about being caught. No. There was little to go on, even if the musicians had been able to give a description. He wanted to see the story, though; he wanted to know how it would be described by someone else. Wanted it in print, a validation of what he'd done, as though it hadn't happened unless it appeared in the newspaper. But it went unreported. Instead the papers were filled with the numbers from the latest layoffs, with photographs of the metalworkers' union marching down Karl-Liebknecht-Strasse demanding job and pension guarantees and demanding Chancellor Detweiller either step in to help or resign. They were filled with commentary on the latest expert reports about Islamist motivations in Germany and with speculation on whether the government could convince NATO or the EU or the UN to let it bomb a variety of suspected terrorist camps in a range of Middle East and Asian countries, which is what the majority of the public, constitutional questions or not, wanted. Peter cut out the articles and added them to the stack on his windowsill, weighing them down with the scissors.

There were long hours when Peter realized he was back to the beginning, when he'd first arrived, alone, in Berlin. He would sit in the window and stare at the building across the street, the exposed bricks where the façade had crumbled away. Without the group he didn't have much to do, wasn't living much of a life. Even with the group he wasn't. He thought about going back to that bookshop, maybe to find another history or just to talk to somebody, but he didn't. One evening he decided to write a letter to his sister and took out a piece of paper. He sat at the kitchen table, yellow light splashed across the white page, but didn't write anything. Not even a date, a place. Not even "Dear April." What was he supposed to say? I'm a terrorist—but was he? I'm a criminal. I'm a thug. He sat for an hour and stared at the blank page, holding a capped ballpoint pen. He wrote nothing. After another hour he crumpled the empty sheet and tossed it onto the windowsill, opposite his stack of clippings.

Other days he looked at the dates on the newspaper mastheads and wondered how long before Matthias and Joachim returned and someone knocked on his door to tell him it was time to do something. And this was only the first few days. He might have to sit alone, he realized, for a month, for two or three months. He wanted to go to the apartment in Christinenstrasse. He wanted to see if Heike was there. But he knew he couldn't. He knew she'd be furious if he showed up. Or maybe she wouldn't. But Matthias would find out, and Matthias would be furious. And Matthias had the gun.

And so, Peter found himself taking to the sidewalks again, wandering the densely packed streets of Prenzlauer Berg and up into Pankow, to Wedding. He didn't take the history book with him any longer, he just walked, looking at the city as it was, not as it had been, or without trying to imagine how it had been. Every bench seemed occupied by someone in worn-out clothes, or wrapped in a ragged sleeping bag, young and old, faces gray with the Berlin air. Another day he might walk past the chipping paint of the East Side Gallery murals and over the bridge, the filthy river spread underneath, into Kreuzberg. On each of these walks he would pass at least one blown-out post office. Not on purpose—he didn't know where the others had placed their bombs, and sometimes it didn't occur to him that he was returning to his own bombsites. But he would turn a corner, and there was the crime-scene tape, the plywood hoardings, sometimes plastered with posters advertising concerts, clubs, or other events, as though these blank spaces were just billboards. Peter would step around the torn-up concrete and look at the black streaks that radiated across the stone buildings. People passed by and didn't even glance at it, or at him. Matthias had said their violence would crawl between people's memories, perceptions of their city, but these blackened post offices were no constant reminder of terror. They'd already melted into the background, part of the shifting landscape, too unimportant in comparison with the need to find a job, the need to feed the children, the need for another drink. Just another scar on the face of a city that already bore so many.

He went to Alexanderplatz, not to return to the scene of the crime, but to ride the carousel he'd seen there. It was something to do. He paid two euros and sat on a plastic, white horse with the handful of children scattered on the other horses, riding around and counting the number of times it made a complete revolution as he watched Alexanderplatz spin past, there the bank, there the row of shops and the hotel, the department store, train station and TV tower, the Peter Behrens blocks, the world clock, Henzelmann's Haus des Lehrers, and then back to the bank, 360 degrees, bank, shops, hotel, stores, station, tower, blocks, clock, Haus des Lehrers, bank, again and again and again, the horse rising and falling on its hydraulic pump, seven times around in the few minutes his two euros had purchased, mechanical organ music repeating its themes in hackneyed canon.

And sometime in the first week or two after the bank he arrived in Treptower Park and was standing beneath the stone archway that demanded, in Russian and German, ETERNAL GLORY TO THE HEROES WHO HAVE FALLEN FOR THE FREEDOM AND INDEPENDENCE OF THE SOCIALIST HOMELAND. He didn't have the book, but he'd read about this memorial. He knew it had been built in 1949—the same year as the founding of the GDR—by soldiers of the Red Army, building a memorial and cemetery for their own dead comrades. He wondered whether glory existed at all, let alone could last eternally, and whether eternal glory died with the temporary socialist homeland for which it had supposedly been earned. Whether Matthias was only fighting for a similar transient glory, to regain for his father a socialist homeland he had never known himself or to create—for whom?—a new utopia that would never exist. But maybe that didn't matter. Better to fight and recognize that what you were fighting for could only ever be approached, step-by-step, without the final step, the step of arrival, ever being made, than to give up even before the fight, or worse, to use it as an excuse to sit on your ass doing nothing, as long as prices remained low enough, as long as the sprinklers kept the grass green. He walked through the arch and down the cobbled pathway that led to a stone sculpture of a woman kneeling on a red marble plinth, mourning, he supposed, for those heroes, glorious, eternal, fallen. And that was the problem: at home nobody had room for heroes beyond home-run hitters and touchdown throwers, beyond people who smiled and praised God through diseases that ravaged them or drunk drivers who crippled them. None of whom were heroes any more than lottery winners or businessmen who paid for lakeside property and Cancun vacations with stock options, annual bonuses, and laundered money. They would apply the word hero to anything and everything until the word was empty, meaningless, and a president could demand he be called a hero because he staged photo ops on military bases and aircraft carriers, with firefighters, wearing a bomber jacket or a helmet to make himself look like one, while all he did was sign the papers that sent more young men and women to deserts to kill and die, neither glorious nor eternal nor heroic, merely courageous and wasted. And the collective apathy that fuels the engine, allows it to churn ever onward, but neither forward nor back, neither progression nor regression—that wasn't anything heroic, either. Peter looked down the memorial to the solider on the hill clutching a child in his arms, driving his sword through the shattered swastika. That was a hero. That was action. That wasn't sitting back. That was a real response to a real threat, not simple revenge against an innocent and manufactured enemy. Peter wandered the stone landscape, the stone depictions of people working, fighting, dying, and read the words of Stalin etched into the sixteen coffinlike sculptures. It told Peter a story he knew was propaganda but nonetheless held the echoes of something Matthias had said that night in the apartment. That people would only put up with so much clamping. Here was the story of people resisting the threat of Hitler's clamp, but of course—the part missing in this account—under another clamp. But hadn't they thrown that clamp off, too? It wasn't Gorbachev who tore down the Wall. And if history had shown that people will bear an unbelievable amount of pressure, then being the catalyst to more pressure, more restriction, was that not only speeding toward the day when the pressure released, exploded, like the Reichstag, like the post offices, like whatever they blew up next, exploded into a new fight, a new struggle—and if people got hurt along the way, they were the casualties on a road to heroism, like those carved into these stones and buried under this grass, soldiers, laborers, women with rifles, people who would be remembered, who would be part of a new story of eternal glory in the years long beyond this current struggle. It made sense to Peter. He wanted to go home, to write it down, to make himself a manifesto—make it for all of them, Heike, Matthias, Joachim, to show, when they returned, that he was no longer an addition to, but an integral part of the group, the mission, the war. Yes.

Sometime during his reverie the memorial had begun to fill, slowly at first, a trickle, then in larger groups and numbers, with old women, stooped, their heads covered, large dark shawls wrapped over their shoulders, some with canes, all carrying flowers. They set their bouquets around the base of the hill upon which the soldier stood. The women filled the vast flat area between the soldier and the steps that led to the monumental red marble flags towering halfway between the hill and the sculpture of the mourning woman. Hundreds. Peter couldn't be sure he remembered seeing any of them arrive, but now they surrounded him, he was a stone in the sea of old women chattering in Russian, incomprehensible to Peter, laying their flowers, pressing handkerchiefs into the corners of their eyes. It was cold and gray, but many had spread blankets and sat down, unpacking black breads, meats, vodka.

One of the women, sitting on a red blanket with a group of three others, beckoned to Peter. He watched her motioning, short sharp flicks of her wrist with a pointed finger. It took a moment before he realized she was gesturing to him. He walked over, stopping three times to avoid processions of women clutching flowers and heading toward the hill with the soldier.

She said something, smiling broadly, her arms spreading wide and then bringing them back together. It reminded Peter of Sunday School when he was a boy, singing, "He's Got the Whole World in His Hands," but he didn't understand what she'd said. She repeated her words, now nodding, and Peter understood he should sit.

She said something else—though all Peter could understand was that it was something else—while sweeping her arm across the red blanket, indicating the assortment of bread, meat, beets, and fish eggs.

"I—," Peter pressed his fingertips against his chest. "I don't speak Russian. Ich spreche Russisch nicht."

The women all laughed, open mouths, rocking back; one of them clapped, and another patted Peter's shoulder. The one who had called him over repeated whatever she'd said in Russian, pointed with both hands, palms up, at the food, indicated Peter again and mimed putting food in her mouth.

"Eat, American friend," she said in a thick accent.

Peter took a slice of the black bread and spread a small spoonful of the fish eggs onto it. The women watched Peter take the first bite, studying his expression as though waiting for the next bingo number. He nodded as he chewed and swallowed.

"It's good," he said.

"It's good!" they repeated as a broken chorus.

The woman to his right patted his shoulder again, and they all began eating, talking to each other between bites, gesturing to Peter to continue eating. There weren't any cups, but the women passed a bottle of vodka as though it were a joint, taking a swig, continuing the conversation, waving the bottle, taking another swig and passing it along to the next woman. The entire square between the marble flags and the soldier was littered with flowers and picnicking women, the seagull sounds of their chatter filtering up into the trees that ringed the memorial. It was like the Fourth of July, Peter thought, except it was the Seventh of November, a different celebration of nationhood, and a late autumn afternoon, so the sky was dark with clouds, the trees were mostly leafless, and the celebrants, rather than wearing shorts and T-shirts, were wrapped in the wool coats, shawls, and fur hats of autumn. No stars, no stripes, no hammers, no sickles. Old women who had laid flowers and were now sharing bread and meat and drink and conversation.

And although there were no fireworks, the chatter was loud, the conversations animated enough, that nobody heard the far-off shouts, and nobody heard them get louder; nobody paused to decode what was being said, until it was too late. The men appeared on the terrace above the square, the marble hammer and sickle flags as their backdrop they stood and waited. It was several minutes before Peter and the women noticed them, but when they did, the noise dissipated like a wave retreating from a beach, unrolling from one end to the other until the silence was cut only by an airplane passing high above.

It was hard to tell how many there were—only a few rows could be seen from the lower level. Most of them were shaven headed and wearing the regulation uniform of white T-shirt, blue jeans, red suspenders, white laces on black boots. But some were wearing suits, looked no different than a banker or lawyer on his way to work. And these were the more terrifying, as they descended the steps en masse, because they seemed the unknown quantity, the part that didn't fit in. The women knew what to expect from the skinheads, and since there was no time and no place to run, they prepared themselves for what would come, tensing their aging muscles, bringing their arms across their faces, enacting the movements like half-remembered drills of an ineffective martial art. The neo-Nazis marched in perfect formation, and their chant reemerged, "Ein Land, Ein Volk," a tired and meaningless statement, a timeless excuse responsible for more pain and death than a collection of words should be allowed. When they met the first group of picnickers it was with their fists and their feet; the formation broke, and they dispersed through the memorial, a blur of white and red and blue and black, a collage of fists and boots and shaven heads, punctuated by the occasional suit, kicking just as hard with their wing-tipped feet, hitting just as hard with their manicured hands. And the women received the blows uncomplaining, their old, liver-spotted arms no protection from the kicks, their red blankets not softening the falls, and no moan of pain, no cry for help, just the ugly thump as boots connected with skulls, as fists sunk into flesh, as the daughters of Russia suffered for their history without being given the chance to object that it might not belong to them.

In the middle sat Peter, unmoving, invisible, unnoticed and untouched, even as his dining companions fell bleeding. The action around him stuttered and jerked, moving now in real time, now slow motion, slamming into fast-forward. It was a pageant, a dance, violent choreography and noiseless soundtrack, a dumb show, shadow theater staged for his sole entertainment, no lesson, no history book, no statistics or dates or famous names, no cathartic release or tragic epiphany, no rescuing hero or deus ex machina, just a stupid, pointless exhibition for Peter's benefit, about which he would tell no one, and that would haunt him forever because he was the only one who would ever know, and he would try, but fail, to understand.

8

Specters of Work: Literature and Labor in Postsocialist Germany

Hunter Bivens

> *. . . the relationship between two people is good when there is a third thing available that applies to the interests of both.*[1]

The opening of the Berlin Wall in 1989 and the end of state socialism in Europe marked not only the exhaustion of a particular political project, but also, as Susan Buck-Morss has it, the passing of mass utopia that "was the driving ideological force of industrial modernization" in both its capitalist and socialist forms, with its "belief that the industrial reshaping of the world is capable of bringing about the good society by providing material happiness for the masses."[2] This mass utopia was based on the notion of full employment and a regime of social rights linked to the status of citizen as worker. This regime of social rights, although never properly universal or secure, finds itself today under erasure, and not only in formerly socialist countries. In his recent work *Bürger, ohne Arbeit* [Citizens, without Work], Wolfgang Engler argues that "the social question of the twenty-first century is the question of the fate of millions of people for whom contemporary capitalism apparently no longer has any use. What will happen with these surplus people?"[3] Complementing the chaotic nexus of informal labor and urbanization in the global south that Mike Davis describes in his *Planet of Slums*, the shrinking postindustrial cities of Europe and North America round out the picture of our contemporary conjuncture.[4] This is the conjuncture that Volker Braun's recent novel, *Machwerk oder Das Schichtbuch des Flick von Lauchhammer*

[Botched Job or, the Shift Log of Flick of Lauchhammer, 2008] maps through a densely metatextual montage referencing contemporary culture, film, art, theory, and political movements.

Machwerk, then, is an attempt to hold onto the connection between labor as social practice and our ability to respond creatively to, and think historically about, our current moment, where the unleashing of capitalist productivity paradoxically produces unemployment and postindustrial wastelands, and where the increasing consolidation of the world market seems to correspond to the loss of the very possibility of a collective social horizon.[5] Set largely in the postindustrial ruinscapes of the former GDR, Braun's novel asks how we are to conceive of the space left behind by that mass utopia Buck-Morss evokes, how to represent not only labor but also the subjects linked to it, in the context of the neoliberal global conjecture, which continues to be haunted by the expired promises of industrial modernity in the form of absences and ghostly after-images. Braun's text mobilizes these haunting effects of past labor, indeed of dead laborers themselves, as a way of localizing the former GDR within the complex flows of capital and culture that shape our present. The urgency of texts like those by Braun and Engler, I argue in this chapter, derive from a postsocialist awareness of the decline of wage labor as a *cultural* and even epistemological crisis, rather than a narrowly economic one. At the same time, Braun's interest in labor is not nostalgic. Rather, *Machwerk* assumes a critical yet faithful stance toward a Marxist-humanist notion of labor and human being that, recognizing the crippling social, ecological, and psychic consequences of human activity's imprisonment within the regime of labor, nevertheless gestured to a vision of human dignity based on an understanding of people as creative, productive, and social.[6] For both authors, labor remains the privileged figure of the social as such, the necessary third term that creates meaningful contexts between people. Rather than an object of nostalgic attachment, labor serves here as a metaphor for something yet to come—a placeholder for this third element that must now be renegotiated.

The Impasse

Toward the end of *Machwerk*, the eponymous Flick of Lauchhammer is lured into a movie theater by "a terrifying notice . . . WORKINGMAN'S DEATH."[7] Flick, from the brown coal fields of the eastern German Niederlausitz region, "had filled his whole life with labor, it was his highest human need and now became, since it had been withdrawn from him, a real compulsion and obsession."[8] Settling into his seat, Flick is transported into a misty, yellow landscape, where

> [w]iry bodies tightly drawn into poses that seemed familiar to the man from Lausitz and that were now here in Indonesia! demonstrated or staged. But of course these beings had nothing to do with the actual people that he knew and the adept imitation had something pathetic about it. Thus the tourists also paused and photographed this pack for a few Rupiahs as it stopped for a break, smoked cigarettes as thick as thumbs and devoured rice wrapped in banana leaves.[9]

What we are "seeing" here along with Flick is the third segment of Michael Glawogger's 2005 documentary, *Workingman's Death*, titled "Ghosts," and set in the sulfur mines of East Java.[10] Recognizing the physical *gestus* of labor, Flick nonetheless interprets it as staged, a spectacle for the tourists we see buying mementos and paying to be photographed with the workers in the film. As Margrid Birken has written, Glawogger's film mobilizes the representation of labor to show us "the inter-relatedness of our lives on various places across the globe."[11] But here the transnational commonality of labor is disavowed, briefly affirmed only to be suspended. What accounts for Flick's failure to be interpellated into this global context? One answer might be the lack of a historical dimension in Glawogger's handling of labor in East Java. In this sense, the Indonesian workers do in fact appear as ghosts, since Glawogger's nuanced attentiveness to the quotidian aspects of the workers' experiences leaves the historical dimension largely to the side. In contrast to segments filmed in the Ukraine or the People's Republic of China, we learn little of the political and social ligatures of their labor. The sulfur miners we see are rendered ghostly precisely through this lack. Nevertheless, Braun's text does not cease to present laboring bodies as ghosts.

Both *Workingman's Death* and Braun's novel start from more or less the same place, a fact Braun elides by having Flick miss "Heroes," the first segment of the film set in the Ukraine's Donbas, once heart of the soviet coal industry. Weaving a palimpsest of past and present, of the living and the dead, Glawogger contrasts the men on screen, essentially scavengers in these abandoned mineshafts, to the bygone Soviet Union's Heroes of Labor, who had supported a social imaginary linking labor, place, and political identification in the figuration of the Soviet Union as "a nation of Stakhanovite heroes." The men on screen explain they are no Stakhanovites. Acknowledging the propagandistic aspect of the Stakhanovite movement, they also recognize the "enthusiasm" conveyed by that spectacle. The illegal miners, however, are no longer motivated by enthusiasm. "We work to survive," one of them tells the camera. "If you don't work, you freeze to death and that's that." Their labor is no longer public; it no longer founds and sustains the life of the nation or its symbolic edifice. Rather, it is an activity of survival, occurring outside the sanction of the state and below the radar of the public sphere. Yet the Stalinist iconography of heroic labor still sutures collective life in the Donbas; Glawogger shows us a young wedding party venturing out in the snow to lay flowers before the statue of Stakhanov. This scene marks the spectral presence of modernity's utopian promises inside a different temporal mode, one that Lauren Berlant describes as "survival time, the time of struggling, drowning, holding on to the ledge, treading water, *not stopping*."[12]

Berlant develops the trope of "the impasse" in relation to the precarity of the post-Fordist subject, to whom the "normal life" of Fordist accumulation is foreclosed, but who still labors under the attachments and expectations that sustained the previous social formation. "The impasse," Berlant writes, is "a name for the transitional moment between a habituated life and all of its others . . . a rhythm people can enter into while they're dithering, tottering, bargaining, testing, or otherwise being worn out by the promises that they have attached to in this world."[13] It is this space of the impasse that we see in the first section of Glawogger's film and in Braun's description of the postindustrial landscape where his novel begins as follows:

> Today the Niederlausitz lies there smoldering and still, a landscape that labor has passed through, fabled region that *has its best days behind it* and has been abandoned by the work teams and machines and all that one sees are slag heaps, ghost towns, re-vegetated grounds, the final image of great times.[14]

Like the Soviet Donbas, the Niederlausitz served as a principle site of the mythology of collective labor that underpinned (at great environmental and social cost) a discourse and social imaginary of the GDR as a socialist nation. This was the site of the massive Schwarze Pumpe brown coal facility, one of the major loci of the GDR's myth of socialist construction as a sort of Wild West epic, and a flash point of the GDR's experiment in cultural revolution, the *Bitterfelder Weg*.[15] This landscape, its best days behind it, is released from human activity and given over to reclamation by nature, albeit in the form of artificial lakes for tourists.[16]

Braun's novel does not let the inhabitants of this postindustrial landscape rest, and neither does the German state, for as we learn in the opening pages, "they should, idle, nevertheless do something . . . specifically they must register themselves at the agency, which would contrive the work on its own this time,"[17] which is to say, they become subject to the punitive Hartz IV welfare reform with its One-Euro-Job provision.[18] Demobilized, stripped of the professional identities that sutured their receding "normal lives," those ejected from the contracting world of labor are exposed to an "undesired intimacy with the full pestilence of human activities,"[19] as the deadening idyll of unemployment is recast into a peculiar form of state-sponsored precarity. In Braun's novel, then, the state introduces and enforces survival time, allowing us to conceive of the new precarity as a result of mundane and quotidian exercises of power in a situation where the policies of the neoliberal state preserve wage labor as a cultural and economic norm through a tightened regime of social discipline aimed at the unemployed, rather than through a commitment to full employment. In this vein, Braun describes his own novel as itself a product of state interventionism, as a text "stipulated by the authorities."[20]

This is the impasse into which Braun introduces Flick, at once tragic and ridiculous, whose overdetermined name evokes both the German verb for patching up, mending, and so forth, and the Flick industrial dynasty, which helped bankroll the NSDAP and used slave labor from the Nazi camps to manufacture weapons for Hitler's war effort. Laid off from the Schwarze Pumpe, Flick was no ordinary worker, but a *Havariemeister*, loosely translatable as "master of disaster." Always already a professional improviser in the chaos of the East German planned economy, "he was summoned: in times of need, when the work stopped moving along."[21] Braun locates Flick's work ethic in a specifically East German *habitus*, based on improvisation, provisional solutions, and tinkering that renders Flick not only a privileged figure for discussing the exhaustion of industrial modernity as a cultural field but paradoxically also an ideal protagonist of the current moment.[22] In the post-Fordist regime of precarity, "an epoch of breakdown," Flick becomes "still/again an epoch-making figure."[23] Taking Hartz IV at its word, he shows up at the *Arbeitsagentur*, or employment agency, in "his uniform . . . his inevitable get-up, snap hooks on his belt, the red helmet,"[24] asking the incredulous case worker "so where's the fire?"[25] As Flick's labors become increasingly disembedded, leading him from the town of Lauchhammer across Germany and Europe, the novel becomes a picaresque by default, its form an implicit critique of the current global conjuncture, where "just as the sun wandered across the meridians, so did wage labor run across the earth."[26]

The Third Thing

Flick embodies a desperate attempt to hold together the dimensions of labor and social life. He is a man "of the old school,"[27] whose relationship to labor is shaped by that Stakhanovite legacy haunting Glawogger's Ukraine, of labor as a "matter of honor, glorious page."[28] Yet there is no possibility to patch up this gap, and Flick's efforts are rendered in a satirical rather than nostalgic vein. His compulsive "*zupacken*," or "knuckling down"—organizing a group of bystanders to fill in the holes dug by other One-Euro-Jobbers, or recruiting prostitutes to paint their brothel—inevitably results in disaster. Flick's first deployment by the *Arbeitsagentur*, to clear the grounds of an abandoned Red Army installation, provides occasion for a comic meditation on the socially constituting function of labor. Following the completion of their task, the group of One-Euro-Jobbers are inspired by Flick to clear out hiking paths through the surrounding forests, their enthusiasm provoking the throw-away comment from a laid-off economist from Karlshorst, who speaks of: "'The Role of Labor in the Transition from Ape to Man' etc.," evoking Friedrich Engels' insight that "labor itself created man," only to quickly dismiss this Marxist anthropology as "a rerun of the old economic bullshit."[29]

Despite this dismissal, *Machwerk* casts labor as a lack, a missing figure for the social as such, as well as the symbolic order that sustains this realm, precisely through this citational mode. In *Bürger, ohne Arbeit*, Engler describes "labor the spider": a social practice that "connects social, temporal, and spatial networks to a four-dimensional timespace, a terrestrial cosmos."[30] For Engler, the essence of a given labor is a mode of social relationality that allows not only for a "collective metabolism with nature," but also "forms about itself, much like a corona, a society in miniature."[31] Work in this conception becomes a material figure for a kind of *tertium datur*, a third term of comparison that establishes the basis of relationality between subjects. The status of the "terrestrial cosmos" Engler evokes is also at stake in *Machwerk*, the relational frame, or perhaps symbolic order, a framework that lends coherence and duration to relationality itself. Indeed, the crisis of labor becomes a crisis of meaning in Braun's novel:

> since the control center, the head office for truths, found itself in liquidation . . . and the old reason could hardly be recognized. How to think the relation, above all: how do our actions produce relation?[32]

This question of relationality is not only one of cultural identity, but, importantly, also one of narrative representation. As previously remarked,

Braun's novel is a loose structure of episodes, linked to one another in various ways—through character, locale, thematics—which nevertheless retain their relative independence over and against the whole. We are not, however, simply left with stories without plot. "The writ of history, carved by struggles, are the historical scars, yet we do not recognize their new features," Braun writes.[33] It is not the foreclosure of the historical that shatters plot in *Machwerk*, but rather its catastrophic opacity. History, like the letters of the law upon the body of the condemned in Kafka's penal colony, can only be deciphered by the wounds it inflicts.[34] The question animating *Machwerk*'s engagements with contemporary culture thus becomes one of the discourses or practices that could be mobilized to begin to limn the illegible script of the present moment, to begin to discern the relation of life and thought in late capitalism.

Implicitly countering Charity Scribner's suggestion that "in postindustrial, unifying Europe, it is not the factory as such but the cultural residues of collective labor that promise a new forum" for the politics of memory, representation, and social justice, Braun's text implies this openness is bounded by befuddlement and nostalgia—a memory of praxis no longer or not yet praxis itself.[35] In one episode, Flick is assigned by the *Arbeitsagentur* to guard what appears to be the "Friedrich Christian Flick Collection" at Berlin's Hamburger Bahnhof, a "Museum of the Present."[36] Here, Flick encounters Jason Rhoades's 1998 installation *Creation Myth*, a piece that confronts Flick as "a lot of machinery and tools in a jumble, serviceable, but not so that he had any desire to knuckle down." Flick can find no point of entrance into the work, "deadweight, dead labor at its zero degree (or ground zero)."[37] Following Flick's attempt to perform CPR on another installation, composed of a dead woman and a totaled motorcycle, Flick is sent to a different museum, properly a "Museum of the Past," where he comes face-to-face with *The Forge* [*Das Eisenwalzwerk*, 1872–1875] by Adolph von Menzel, a *Gründerzeit* painting combining a realist mode of representation with a Promethean pictorial *gestus*, so that "the workers, exerting the whole of their power and skill, seemed transformed into mythic giants, 'modern' cyclopses."[38] This work, which interpellates Flick in a sense that the more contemporary pieces at the Hamburger Bahnhof do not, suggests there is in fact something other than memory at stake in what Braun describes as Menzel's "great archaic utopian composition."[39] Yet neither work is presented by Braun as properly timely. Rhoades's work refuses a relation to practice, but Menzel's painting is itself presented as irreducibly in the past tense, as archaic precisely in its totalizing pictorial vocabulary. Neither of these works provides Flick with a frame of *productive* engagement.

In a chapter titled "Theater Work or: a Cheap Learning Play,"[40] Flick finds himself involved in a theatrical experiment at Berlin's *Volksbühne* that points toward the pathos of nonproductivity. For a Euro's wage, Berlin's unemployed are invited by the management to create their own theater, spontaneously. Predictably, nothing happens as the unemployed wait out their hour. "That was strain enough, though nothing came out of it, because they did not produce; nothing uplifting," Braun writes of this theater, which rather than combining performers and spectators has neither one nor the other.[41] Whereas Brecht's *Lehrstück* was to be a structure for organizing group experience, and was institutionally linked to working-class counter publics in the Weimar Republic,[42] what we see in Braun's *Volksbühne* is an aesthetic conceit, a nostalgic homage to the possibility of political art as such, which in turn becomes, if not culinary (since there is nothing here to savor), then at the very least inconsequential, the sine qua non of Brecht's critique of ideology.[43] "What a malfunction," Flick ponders, "here they were all together, it was up to them alone; and nothing."[44] Frustrated by the pointlessness of the exercise, but at the same time gripped by a longing "for this powerful instrument that sets everything in motion, transforms, unifies,"[45] Flick takes matters into his own hands and mounts the stage. The moment Flick reaches for the powerful instrument of the aesthetic, its own lack of autonomy is revealed. "What means would have to be brought to bear in order to forestall the calamity," Flick asks himself, "in this field in which he had never been active."[46]

For Brecht, the performance served a collective cultivation of skills and capacities rather than a clearly defined political project. Roswitha Mueller points out that if the *Lehrstück* was meant to bridge the binaries "[of] pleasure and productivity, of entertainment and information, of experience and knowledge," then "the audience must be *literalisiert*, that is, informed and trained especially for the theatrical event in order to be productive."[47] Both literary text and organizational context are lacking in the One-Euro-*Lehrstück*. There is no object or articulated situation, no third thing as Brecht might put it, upon which this instrument could be brought to bear. For Brecht, of course, this third thing was none other than social relations themselves, and epic theater can be taken as a complex apparatus for placing quotation marks around social reality, so that that very reality could be varied, played with, experimented upon, or as Brecht put it "the theater was required to deliver different representations of man's life together."[48] Without this mediating frame for the disparate experiences and capacities of the masses of unemployed, what we are given at the *Volksbühne* is less the Brechtian method of moving from multiplicity to contradiction, to paraphrase Fredric Jameson, but rather the dissolution of that framing of contradiction into multiplicity, further atomizing and alienating the audience, throwing them back into their own isolation.

Locality and the Dead

In the course of the novel, Flick takes part, as the cleaning staff, in an academic symposium under the motto "I LABOR, THEREFORE I AM,"[49] as well as a rally of *Die Glücklichen Arbeitslosen*, or the Happy Unemployed, a Berlin group that takes seriously Paul Lafargue's slogan of the right to laziness.[50] Like art, politics and theory are portrayed in *Machwerk* as partial enterprises that circle about the question of "*what work makes sense?* And: *How is it to be shared among us all*?"[51] What we are left with instead are images of blockage, collapse, and stasis, exemplified in Flick's oneiric vision of a "strange monument": "a human mass baked in solid, bloated in the refuse, more precisely: the equipment of a century and the packaging of a decade. USED UP was the taunting motto, a shithouse slogan that went through the rows."[52] And yet, Braun reminds us that the Swedish energy firm Vattenfall continues the GDR legacy of displacing Sorbian villages to get to the brown coal under the earth of the Niederlausitz, and Flick is sent to clear out the village of Horno.[53] Not only must the village be moved, but "following the extraction of the living, the dead would also have to be stashed away somewhere."[54] This is thus the logic of state and economy, logics of extraction and accumulation that cut through and continue to work upon the dead landscape of the Niederlausitz. "The task is thus to represent human error," Braun writes, "magnificent, actual, fantastic. Art belongs here, might and malfeasance, war and shady dealings."[55]

Braun's stance toward the dead counters the logic of this error (which, as Braun hints, is the inescapable consequence of "productivity" in the Brechtian sense). In Horno, Flick finds himself occupied with the labor of reassembly when the truck carrying the corpses stops short, scattering the desiccated body parts. This work, which Braun calls "work of the soul,"[56] can be read as a construction of a local history based on the employment of "dead" labor into the landscape of the Niederlausitz:

> because that was two or three generations of peasants and workers, to be screwed and imagined back together in their full magnanimity (of spirit). . . . They had worked more ground and served under more skies and spilled more sweat, these Germanized Sorbs and Wendish Germans, tillers and field-gray heroes of labor. . . . Their being, heavy as it is, was probably sunk deeply down, and on the other hand too fleeting not to

> rise up! This misery, the hopes would have to be dug out or in some other way looked after. . . . He would have to rummage through all of humanity to liberate the dead from their struggle and sorrow, their conniving and cowering, their wholly futile silence.[57]

Braun uses this passage to literalize Marx's economic metaphor of living and dead labor.[58] Following Raymond Williams's observation that "a working country is almost never a landscape," W. J. T. Mitchell argues if landscape, as a matrix of representation, corresponds to something like the symbolic order, place itself can be regarded "as the location of the Lacanian Real, the site of trauma or the historical event."[59] Against the empty vistas of abandoned strip mines and artificial lakes, Braun insists on the underground memory of the earth, dissolving the landscape into "the indissoluble merging of nature, industrial and human working over, and history"[60] of the "working country." No one in the novel is content to let the dead rest; rather the Niederlausitz becomes a locality defined by its very undeadness—to borrow Eric Santner's framing of this term—"its paradoxical mixture of deadness and excitation, of stuckness and agitation."[61] Rather than enacting Benjaminian mode of redemptive memorialization,[62] Braun's novel casts the Niederlausitz as a creaturely landscape given over to the invasions of capital even as it is relegated to the edges of the world system.

The mission to liberate the dead leads Flick into a series of Orphic journeys, which provide the reader with a not entirely redemptive archeology of labor. If the Niederlausitz is posited in the book as a territory constituted by superannuated labor of the dead, this is not to say that *Machwerk* is some sort of nostalgic exercise in local history or *Heimatkunde*. On the contrary, Braun's picaresques highlight the double character of industrial labor in modernity. The *nekyia*, or ritual invocation of the dead, at Horno is complemented with a historical *katabasis*, a journey to the land of the dead,[63] as Flick von Lauchhammer finds himself employed in the factory of his namesake, Friedrich Flick. Flick's productive *gestus* is projected back into National Socialism in this oneiric vision, where Flick denounces a female slave laborer for sabotaging hand grenades. Flick's denunciation is not motivated by political conviction but rather by his love for this "mechanical landscape, where he knows his way around, with cable trees and acid rivers."[64] This landscape of production stands under the sign of a fascist collective labor of destruction: "now he recognized, with a backward glance, above the gate a wholly ironic composition: ARBEIT MACHT FREI. Work had been provided for. Outside the howitzers fired, and bombs rained down."[65] In this account of "Auschwitz as workplace" to quote Werner Hamacher, Braun suspends the Marxist-humanist conceptions of labor, and work becomes an industrialized annihilation of otherness, the *völkisch* community's "form of liberation from all that is not itself" through the production of the bearers of perceived difference from "*das Volk*"—Jews, Communists, homosexuals—as corpses.[66] This exterminationist logic of instrumentality counters Engler's capacious evocation of labor the spider, patiently weaving the connections that make up our worlds. At this point, Braun reintroduces Menzel's *The Forge*, but now this "great archaic utopian composition" is figured quite differently, as the Nazi cannon are forged from the incandescent skein of molten steel that is the composition's axis. The narrator observes: "the highly excited groups in their striped clothing appeared as though transformed into lemurs. As one spoke in mining of the under-man, the talk here was of subhumans."[67] Here Braun's reading of *The Forge* echoes Peter Weiss's meditation on the same painting in his *The Aesthetics of Resistance*. Describing Menzel's work as "the apotheosis of labor," Weiss notes its depiction of a work that is nothing but work, toil for profit rather than "work as a system of self-realization." Menzel's "praise of labor," Weiss writes, is "a praise of subordination."[68] In this turn of Wenzel's painting, in the move from solidarity to hierarchy, the old East German humanist cliché about the road from "I to we"[69] joins with Adorno's insight that "genocide is the absolute integration,"[70] as hell opens itself to Flick—a catastrophic topography that is paradoxically his very element. "His heart set to barking," Braun writes, "his snout perked up. He knew to what purpose he was summoned; he stoked the fires of hell, he kept the pot boiling."[71]

Sunday's Children?

In Braun's account, the decoupling of life and labor is represented as what Seth Moglen calls a social injury, the mourning of which demands that "we invent or adopt cultural practices that enable us to name our continued yearnings for forms of social activity that have been denied by the social orders in which we live."[72] But if we push further to specify the injury, we see that, for Braun, the loss of work is itself a secondary process, to remain with the Freudian metaphor, and the primary trauma is none other than work itself, the alienated labor that Marx describes so vividly in his classic account of machinery and large-scale industry in the first volume of *Capital,* as well as the parallel destruction of traditional life worlds that is attendant on what Marx denotes as original accumulation.[73] If the capitalist regime of production arises from the separation of the laborer from the instruments of labor, what we now face is the prospect of a separation of the person qua labor power from labor itself. The task is perhaps less to remember "*was die Arbeit war*" (what labor was),[74] than to recall what labor has not been, to salvage those elements of human sociality and practice from the wreckage of the value form. In this sense, the East Germans of 1989 liberated themselves not only from the oppressive GDR state but also from the regime of industrial labor itself, their refusal of a labor-based socialism read here as an attempt to "extirpate wage labor."[75] Yet, as Wolfgang Engler points out, "rather than even so much as initiating the restoration of the 'whole person,' the loss of the intrinsically inane gymnastics, this accursed labor, leads directly to the confrontation with the diminished radius of one's own possibilities."[76]

Braun poses this question directly when Flick confronts the *Mittagsfrau*, a riddle-posing mythological demon. The riddle in this case revolves around the semantic play of metaphysical and physical ground in relation to labor, history, and the memory of the earth. "Only Sunday's children," says the woman, "can see to the bottom."[77] Flick responds by asking if she means to see the ground, or *Grund*—with its semantic play of metaphysical and physical ground—only to receive the reply, "they never reached the ground."[78] The Sunday's children in question, in other words, turn out not to be the former citizens of the GDR; "they had work, housing, bread," but they remained, according to the *Mittagsfrau*, "children of the working day . . . pious and content. They had everything to hand, earth, water, machinery,"[79] and yet, "they could not have cared less. They made nothing of it. They did not possess it," the *Mittagsfrau* says of the relation of the public to the public property of the old GDR.[80] This is a nonproductive relation, and the old Sorb seems to be saying the East Germans were never truly owners of their means of production for the same reason the One-Euro-Jobbers in the *Volksbühne* are unable to make anything of the *Lehrstück*; Braun suggests here that East Germans failed in some vital way to *take possession* of their instruments of production. Nevertheless, "the ground," the *Mittagsfrau* informs Flick "is labor."[81] But this answer tells us nothing, it only begs the following question in the sequence: "which labor?"[82] This is the question Braun's book seeks to pose, but cannot answer: What is the labor of Sunday's children?

The question of what human activity after, beyond, or outside of labor is perhaps the way we should understand the turn to the thematics of futurity and reproductive labor in the last section of the novel, "that apart from the work with machines there is that with people. . . . *That* work still existed."[83] Here we would also include Flick's pedagogical relationship with his never-do-well grandson, Luten, "a problem child," who "makes no effort to hire himself out, but rather loafed about his mother's house."[84] Flick drags Luten across Europe chasing work and its dignity, but, as the novel tells us, Luten belongs to a century that learns in its cradle that "there was no longer sufficient work, or peaceful work at any rate, to go around."[85] Luten's generation will be the material of what Braun describes as a "state-sponsored assault that will introduce a new regime into humanity."[86] Yet this is also the century and the generation, for Braun, that might possibly gather from these "untenable conditions,"[87] resources that might augur the emergence of the "childish countenance"[88] of a coming humanity emerging from the "antique groan" of "bread and games, shit and war."[89]

In closing, I would like to return to the opening scene of this chapter and the refusal of recognition with which Flick confronts Glawogger's images of work in the sulfur kitchen. Through this failed relay of the image as the signifier of the commonality of labor, Braun's novel evokes the necessity of a theory of culture that would articulate the ligatures of the division of labor in both a historical and a transnational framework, attending to the discrepancy between the global North and South as an articulation of ebbs and flows of capital as well as local strategies of adaptation and resistance. Obviously people are still working, but the recognition of that labor, legally and culturally, has become increasingly opaque.[90] The impasse Braun's *Machwerk* articulates then might be that with the collapse of the socialist project, we lose the very framework that allowed us to recognize work as universal. Michael Denning has argued there have been two global cultures, one of "commodity aesthetics, the culture of transnational corporations," and the other with "its social roots in the huge migration of the rural Third World to the trench towns of the planet," and "its aesthetic roots . . . in one of the first explicitly international cultural movements, the worldwide movement of plebeian artists and writers to create a proletarian culture, a socialist realism."[91] "Ghosts," in Braun's reading, at any rate, shows us the collapse of this distinction, as the significance of labor is rendered now not through the experience of the workers themselves but rather through the gaze of the tourists, the vehicles and operators of global capital and the commodity spectacle.

Notes

1. "dass das Verhältnis zwischen zwei Menschen gut sei, wenn da eine dritte Sache vorliege, der das Interesse beider gelte." Bertolt Brecht. *Gesammelte Werke 12: Prosa 2* (Frankfurt-Main: Suhrkamp Verlag 1967), 555. I thank Tyrus Miller, Jamie Trnka, and John Urang for their comments on previous drafts of this chapter.

2. Susan Buck-Morss. *Dreamworld and Catastrophe: The Passing of Mass Utopia in East and West* (Cambridge, MA and London: MIT Press, 2000), ix.
3. "Die soziale Frage des einundzwanzigsten Jahrhundert, ist die Frage nach dem Schicksal von Millionen von Menschen, für die der Gegenwartskapitalismus anscheinend keine Verwendung mehr hat. Was wird mit diesen Überflüssigen geschehen?" Wolfgang Engler. *Bürger, ohne Arbeit. Für eine radikale Neugestaltung der Gesellschaft* (Berlin: Aufbau Taschenbuch Verlag, 2005), 183. There is of course an extensive literature on the "end of work" and the decline of wage labor as a structuring principle of social and economic life, but see, beyond Engler, André Gorz. *Paths to Paradise. On the Liberation from Work*. Trans. Malcolm Imrie, (Boston: South End Press, 1985) and Robert Kurz. *Der Kollaps der Modernisierung: Vom Zusammenbruch des Kasernensozialismus zur Krise der Weltökonomie* (Leipzig: Reclam, 1994).
4. See *Shrinking Cities, v.1: International Research/v.2: Interventions,* ed. Philipp Oswalt (Ostfildern-Ruit: Hatje-Cantz, 2005/6) and Mike Davis, *Planet of Slums* (New York and London: Verso Press, 2006).
5. In a recent essay on *Valences of the Dialectic* by Fredric Jameson, Gopal Balakrishnan poses the question distinctly in regard to Jameson's work: "what are the political forms in which this post-historical situation might be experienced historically? . . . what is the genre in which the historical in this paradoxical post-historical sense by made to appear?" Gopal Balakrishnan. "The Coming Contradiction: On Jameson's *Valences of the Dialectic*." *New Left Review* 66 (November/December 2010) 52.
6. This chapter will not follow Hannah Arendt's celebrated but problematic distinction between labor and work, but obviously the question of the relationship between social forms and modes of labor is at the base of her critique of Marx and socialist thought. Whereas Marx sees the form of wage labor as a result of the development of capitalist relations of production and domination, Arendt seems to see contemporary forms of social domination arising from labor itself as a transhistorical expression of the weight of necessity on human life. See Hannah Arendt, *The Human Condition*. Second Edition (Chicago: University of Chicago Press, 1998). Marx classically articulates his theory of estranged labor in Karl Marx, *The Economic and Philosophical Manuscripts of 1844* (New York: International Publishers, 1964), 106–119.
7. "eine schreckliche Mitteilung . . . WORKINGMAN'S DEATH." Volker Braun, *Machwerk oder Das Schichtbuch des Flick von Lauchhammer* (Frankfurt am Main: Suhrkamp Verlag, 2008), 182.
8. "hatte sein ganzes Leben mit Arbeit zugebracht, sie war sein oberstes Lebensbedürfnis und wurde jetzt, da sie ihm entzogen war, eine wahre Sucht und Besessenheit." Ibid., 14.
9. "und die drahtigen Körper straffen sich zu Posen, die dem Mann aus der Lausitz bekannt vorkamen und die nun hier, in Indonesien! vorgeführt oder inszeniert wurden. Aber natürlich hatten diese Wesen nichts mit den wirklichen Menschen zu tun, die er kannte, und die geschickte Nachahmung hatte etwas Armseliges. Darum blieben auch die Touristen stehen und fotographierten das Pack für ein paar Rupien, wenn es rastete,

daumendicke Zigaretten rauchte und den in Bananenblätter gewickelten Reis verzehrte." Ibid., 184.

10. *Workingman's Death: Fünf Bilder zur Arbeit im 21. Jahrhundert*, Dir. Michael Glawogger. Lotus / Quinte /ARTE, 2005.
11. "den Zusammenhang unserer Leben an den verschiedenen Orten auf dem Globus." Margrid Birken. "Workingman's Death—Vorwort." *Argonautenschiff* 15 (2006), 10.
12. Lauren Berlant. "Nearly Utopian, Nearly Normal: Post-Fordist Affect in *La Promesse* and *Rosetta*." *Public Culture* 19, no. 2 (2007), 279.
13. Lauren Berlant. "Cruel Optimism." *Differences: A Journal of Feminist Cultural Studies* 17, no. 3 (2006), 23.
14. "Die Niederlausitz liegt heute ruhig rauchend da, eine Landschaft, durch die die Arbeit gegangen ist, berühmte Gegend, die *es hinter sich hat* und verlassen wurde von den Mannschaften und Maschinen, und nur Halden, Wüstungen, wiederbewachsene Böden sieht man, das Endbild großer Zeiten." Braun, *Machwerk*, 13.
15. On Braun, the Lausitz and the lignite mines, see Karin Bothe. "Der Text als geologische Formation. 'Archäologisches Schreiben' als poetologisches Programm im Werk Volker Brauns." *Volker Braun in Perspective. German Monitor*, no. 58. ed. Rolf Jucker (New York and Amsterdam: Rodopi, 2004), 1–36. There is a wide literature on Bitterfeld, but see most recently *Bitterfelder Nachlese. Ein Kulturpalast, seine Konferenzen und Wirkungen*, ed. Simone Barck and Stefanie Wahl (Berlin: Dietz Verlag, 2007).
16. On the postindustrial reshaping of the Lausitz, see Kerstin Barndt, "'Memory Traces of a Set of Abandoned Futures': Industrial Ruins in the Postindustrial Landscapes of Germany." *Ruins of Modernity*, ed. Julia Hell and Andreas Schönle (Durham and London: Duke University Press, 2010), 270–293.
17. "Sie sollten, untätig, doch was tun. . . sie hatten sich nämlich wieder auf dem Amt zu melden; das diesmal selber die Arbeit ersann." Braun, *Machwerk*, 15.
18. On the German state's attempts to introduce neoliberal regimes of labor and social welfare since 2003, see Perry Anderson, "A New Germany?" *New Left Review* 57 (May/June 2009), 5–40.
19. "ungewollte Bekanntschaft mit dem ganzen Aussatz von Tätigkeiten." Braun, *Machwerk*, 16.
20. "vorgeschrieben . . . von den Behörden." Ibid., 22.
21. "Man rief ihn: in der Not, wenn die Arbeit nicht weiterging." Ibid., 14.
22. On this point, see Wolfgang Engler. *Die Ostdeutschen als Avantgarde* (Berlin: Aufbau Taschenbuch Verlag, 2004), 72–97.
23. "eine *Epoche* des Unfalls...noch/wieder eine epochmachende Figur." Braun, *Machwerk*, 107–108.
24. "seiner Montour . . . seiner unvermeidlicher Kluft, Karabinerhaken am Koppel, roter Helm." Ibid., 15.
25. "Wo brennt's denn?" Ibid., 20.
26. "wie die Sonne wanderte über alle Meridiane, so lief die Lohnarbeit um die Erde." Ibid., 178.

27. "vom alten Schrott und Korn." Braun, *Machwerk*, 30.
28. "Sache der Ehre, Ruhmesblatt." Ibid., 29.
29. "'Die Rolle der Arbeit bei der Menschenwerdung des Affen' etc. . . . 'Wiederholung der alten ökonomischen Scheiße.'" Ibid., 26. See Frederick Engels. "The Part Played by Labor in the Transition of Ape to Man." *The Origin of the Family, Private Property, and the State* (New York: International Publishers, 1972), 251.
30. "die Spinne Arbeit . . . die verknüpft soziale, zeitliche, und räumliche Netze zu einem vierdimensionalen Zeit-Raum, zum irdischen Kosmos des Menschen." *Bürger, ohne Arbeit*, 51.
31. "um ihn herum, einer Korona gleich, formt sich oftmals eine Gesellschaft im kleinen." Ibid., 52.
32. "denn die Zentrale, eine Hauptverwaltung der Wahrheiten, befand sich in Auflösung...und die alte Vernunft war kaum wiederzuerkennen. Wie den Zusammenhang denken, vor allem: wie stellen ihn unsere Handlungen her?" Braun, *Machwerk*, 137.
33. "Die Schrift der Geschichte, von den Kämpfen eingeritzt, sind die historischen Narben, doch ihre neuen Züge kennen wir nicht." Ibid.
34. Franz Kafka. "In the Penal Colony." In *The Complete Stories,* ed. Nahum N. Glatzer (New York: Schocken, 1971), 148.
35. Charity Scribner. *Requiem for Communism* (Cambridge, MA and London: MIT Press, 2003), 9.
36. "ein Museum der Gegenwart." Braun, *Machwerk*, 47. Friedrich Christian Flick, the scion of the Flick dynasty, began collecting art in the 1980s. In 2004, after unsuccessful attempts to exhibit or donate his collection of contemporary avant-garde art in a number of cities, Flick arranged to loan the collection to Berlin's Hamburger Bahnhof for a period of seven years. Given the association of the Flick fortune with war crimes under the National Socialist regime, the exhibit has met with controversy and protest. See Reesa Greenberg, "Redressing History: Partners and the Friedrich Christian Flick Collection." *Kritische Berichte*, October 2005. Accessed on May 17, 2010, http://www.yorku.ca/reerden/ Publications/redressing_history.html.
37. "Viel Gerät und Werkzeug im Gerümpel, funktionsfähig, aber nicht, dass er Lust verspürte, zuzupacken . . . totes Zeug, tote Arbeit auf den Punkt (oder den Haufen) gebracht." Ibid., 47. For a reading of Rhoades's "slacker aesthetics," see Johanna Drucker. *Sweet Dreams: Contemporary Art and Complicity* (Chicago: University of Chicago Press, 2005), 93–103. For Drucker, Rhoades's art can be read as a purposeful, self-reflexive devaluation of labor and skill.
38. "ihre ganze Kraft und Geschicklichkeit einsetzenden Arbeiter scheinen in mythische Riesen, 'moderne Cyclopen' verwandelt." Braun, *Machwerk*, 49.
39. "große archaische utopische Komposition." Ibid., 50.
40. "Theaterarbeit oder: Ein billiges Lehrstück." Ibid.
41. "das war Anstrengung genug, bei der nur nichts herauskam, weil sie sich nicht produzierten; nichts Erhebendes." Ibid., 53.

42. On Brecht's *Lehrstück* as a form of pedagogy, see Roswitha Mueller, *Bertolt Brecht and the Theory of Media* (Lincoln and London: University of Nebraska Press, 1989), 23–43.
43. Fredric Jameson, *Brecht and Method* (London and New York: Verso Press, 1998), 25.
44. "Was für ein Defekt...jetzt waren sie alle zusammen, es lag nur an ihnen; und nichts." Braun, *Machwerk*, 53.
45. "nach diesem mächtigen Instrument, das alle in Bewegung setzt, verwandelt, vereint." Ibid.
46. "Welche Mittel mußten zum Einsatz kommen, um das Unglück aufzuhalten... in dem Bereich, in dem er nie tätig war." Ibid.
47. Mueller, *Bertolt Brecht,* 24–25.
48. Bertolt Brecht. "Short Organum for the Theater." In *Brecht on Theatre: the Development of an Aesthetic,* ed. John Willett (New York: Hill and Wang, 1964), 182.
49. "ICH ARBEITE. ALSO BIN ICH." See Braun, *Machwerk,* 139–142.
50. See ibid., 132–136.
51. "*Welche Arbeit hat Sinn?* Und: *Wie ist sie unter allen zu teilen?*" Ibid., 141.
52. "eine Menschenmasse festgebacken, gedunsen in dem Müll, genauer gesagt: der Gerätschaft eines Jahrhunderts und der Verpackung eines Jahrzehntes. AUSGEDIENT war die höhnische Losung, eine Scheißhausparole, die durch die Reihen lief." Ibid., 59.
53. See Peter Barker, "Dislocation and Reorientation in the Sorbian Community (1945–2008)." In *Dislocation and Reorientation: Exile, Division, and the End of Communism in German Culture and Politics. German Monitor,* no. 71, ed. Axel Goodbody, Pól Ó Dochartaigh, and Dennis Tate, (New York and Amsterdam: Rodopi, 2009), 179–196.
54. "nach dem Abzug der Lebenden mußten die Toten beiseite geschafft werden." Braun, *Machwerk*, 128.
55. "Es ist also *Menschheitsirrtum darzustellen*: herrlicher, realer, phantastischer. Kunst gehört dazu, Macht wie Mißbrauch, Krieg und Wirtschaftsschwindel." Ibid., 170.
56. "Seelenarbeit." Ibid., 130.
57. "denn das waren zwei oder drei Generationen von Bauern und Arbeitern, die zusammenzuschrauben und zu -glauben waren in ihrer ganzen (Seelen)größe.... Die hatten mehr Boden bearbeitet und unter mehr Himmeln gedient und Blut und Schweiß vergossen, diese eingedeutschten Sorben und gewendeten Deutschen, Ackerbürger und feldgrauen Aktivisten. . . . Diesem Elend, den Hoffnungen mußte nachgegraben werden oder anders nachgeblickt. . . . Er mußte die ganze Menschheit hervorwühlen, um die Toten zu befreien von ihrem Kampf und Kummer, ihrem Dulden und Ducken, ihrem ganz vergeblichen Schweigen." Braun, *Machwerk,* 130. On the exhuming of the dead and similar tropes of archeological writing common in Braun's oeuvre, see Bothe above and Axel Goodbody, "Political Dislocation and Poetic Reorientation in Volker Braun's *Bodenloser Satz*." *Dislocation and Reorientation,* 21–32.

58. See Karl Marx, *Capital. A Critique of Political Economy, Volume One*. Trans. Ben Fowkes (New York: Vintage Books, 1977), 289, 982.
59. W. J. T. Mitchell. "Preface to the Second Edition of *Landscape and Power*. Space, Place, and Landscape." *Landscape and Power*, 2nd ed. Ed. W. J. T. Mitchell (Chicago and London: University of Chicago Press, 2002), xi.
60. Bothe, Der Text als geologische Formation, 5.
61. Eric L. Santner. *On Creaturely Life: Rilke, Benjamin, Sebald* (Chicago and London: University of Chicago Press, 2006), 81.
62. See Walter Benjamin. "Theses on the Philosophy of History." *Illuminations: Essays and Reflections*, ed. Hannah Arendt, trans. Harry Zohn (New York: Schocken Books, 1969), especially 260: "Not man or men, but the struggling, oppressed class itself is the depository of historical knowledge. In Marx it appears as the last enslaved class, as the avenger that completes the task of liberation in the name of generations of the downtrodden."
63. The topos of the journey into hell links Braun's novel to German literature of the early postwar period as well. See Thomas Pekar, "Experiences of Delocalization and *Katabasis* in the Literature of the Early Postwar Period in Germany." *Exile and Otherness: New Approaches to the Experience of the Nazi Refugees*, ed. Alexander Stephan (Bern: Peter Lang, 2005), 49–63.
64. "Eine mechanische Landschaft, in der er sich auskannte, mit Kabelbäumen und Säureflüssen." Braun, *Machwerk*, 80.
65. "Er erkannte nun, rückwärts blickend, über dem Tor, die ganze ironische Dichtung: ARBEIT MACHT FREI. Es was für die Arbeit gesorgt. Drauβen schossen die Howitzer. Bomben schlugen nieder." Ibid., 81.
66. "die Form seiner [das Volk, HB] Befreiung von allem, was es nicht selbst ist." Werner Hamacher. "Arbeit Durcharbeiten." In *Archäologie der Arbeit*, ed. Dirk Baecker (Berlin: Kulturverlag Kadmos, 2002), 163.
67. "die stark bewegten Gruppen, in ihren gestreiften Kleidern, schienen in Lemuren verwandelt. Wie man im Bergbau vom Untermann sprach, wurde von Untermenschen geredet." Ibid., 81.
68. Peter Weiss. *The Aesthetics of Resistance*, Volume 1. Trans. Joachim Neugroschel (Durham and London: Duke University Press, 2005), 311.
69. "Ich zum Wir." Braun, *Machwerk*, 80.
70. Theodor W. Adorno. *Negative Dialectics*. Trans. E. B. Ashton (New York: Continuum, 1990), 362.
71. "Sein Herz bellte, er spitzte die Schnauze. Er wußte, wozu er gebeten war; er heizte die Hölle, er hielt sie in Gang." Braun, *Machwerk*, 81.
72. Seth Moglen. "On Mourning Social Injury." *Psychoanalysis, Culture and Society* 10, no. 2 (2005), 163.
73. Marx, *Capital*, 492–642, especially 517–542 and 873–940.
74. Braun, *Machwerk*, 29.
75. "die Lohnarbeit auszurotten." Ibid., 123.
76. "Statt die Wiederherstellung des 'ganzen Menschen' auch nur einzuleiten, führt der Verlust der an sich nichtigen Gymnastik, dieser verfluchten Arbeit, unmittelbar zur Konfrontation mit dem geschrumpften Radius der eigenen Möglichkeiten." *Bürger, ohne Arbeit*, 43.

77. "Nur Sonntagskinder können bis unten sehen." Braun, *Machwerk*, 114.
78. "den Grund haben sie nie erreicht." Ibid., 115.
79. "Sie hatten Arbeit, Wohnung, Brot," but they remained, according to the *Mittagsfrau*, "Werktagskinder… zufrieden und fromm." Ibid.
80. "Sie hatten von allem. Erde, Wasser, Gruben, Gerät…Es war ihnen *gleich*. Sie haben nichts daraus gemacht. Sie haben es nicht besessen." Ibid.
81. "Die Grund . . . ist die Arbeit." Ibid., 118.
82. "Welche Arbeit?" Ibid.
83. "dass es außer der Arbeit mit den Maschinen die mit den Menschen gab. . . . *Die* Arbeit gab es noch." Ibid., 163.
84. "Ein Sorgenkind" who "keine Anstalt machte, sich zu verdingen, sondern bei seiner Mutter lungerte." Ibid., 16.
85. "Die Arbeit, hieß es, lange nicht mehr hin, die friedliche jedenfalls." Braun, *Machwerk*, 11.
86. "staatliche Nötigung, die ein neues Regime in die Menschheit bringt." Ibid., 12.
87. "unhaltbare Zustände!" Ibid., 189.
88. "dies kindliche Antlitz." Ibid., 212.
89. "Ein antikisches Stöhnen. . . . Brot und Spiele, Scheiße und Krieg." Ibid., 215.
90. For a terse critique of the conception of immaterial labor, which ignores both the persistent commodification and deskilling of intellectual work and its relationship to material labor, see Keya Ganguly. "Introduction: After Resignation and Against Conformity." *The South Atlantic Quarterly: Special Issue on Intellectual Labor* 108, no. 2 (Spring 2009), 243–246.
91. Michael Denning, *Culture in the Age of Three Worlds* (New York and London: Verso Press, 2004), 32.

Bibliography

Adorno, Theodor W. *Negative Dialectics*. Translated by E. B. Ashton. New York: Continuum, 1990.

Anderson, Perry. "A New Germany?" *New Left Review* 57 (May/June 2009): 5–40.

Arendt, Hannah. *The Human Condition*. Second Edition. Chicago: University of Chicago Press, 1998.

Balakrishnan, Gopal. "The Coming Contradiction: On Jameson's *Valences of the Dialectic*." *New Left Review* 66 (November/December 2010): 31–53.

Barck, Simone, and Stefanie Wahl, eds. *Bitterfelder Nachlese. Ein Kulturpalast, seine Konferenzen und Wirkungen*. Berlin: Dietz Verlag, 2007.

Barker, Peter. "Dislocation and Reorientation in the Sorbian Community (1945–2008)." In *Dislocation and Reorientation: Exile, Division, and the End of Communism in German Culture and Politics. German Monitor* 71, edited by Axel Goodbody, Pól Ó Dochartaigh, and Dennis Tate, 179–196. New York and Amsterdam: Rodopi, 2009.

Barndt, Kerstin. "'Memory Traces of a Set of Abandoned Futures': Industrial Ruins in the Postindustrial Landscapes of Germany." In *Ruins of Modernity,* edited by Julia Hell and Andreas Schönle, 270–293. Durham and London: Duke University Press, 2010.

Benjamin, Walter. "Theses on the Philosophy of History." In *Illuminations: Essays and Reflections,* edited by Hannah Arendt, translated by Harry Zohn, 253–264. New York: Schocken Books 1969.

Berlant, Lauren. "Cruel Optimism." *Differences: A Journal of Feminist Cultural Studies* 17, no. 3 (2006): 20–36.

————. "Nearly Utopian, Nearly Normal: Post-Fordist Affect in *La Promesse* and *Rosetta.*" *Public Culture* 19, no. 2 (2007): 273–301.

Birken, Margrid. "Workingman's Death—Vorwort." *Argonautenschiff* 15 (2006): 7–11.

Bothe, Karin. "Der Text als geologische Formation. 'Archäologisches Schreiben' als poetologisches Programm im Werk Volker Brauns." In *Volker Braun in Perspective. German Monitor,* no. 58, edited by Rolf Jucker, 1–36. New York and Amsterdam: Rodopi, 2004.

Braun, Volker. *Machwerk oder Das Schichtbuch des Flick von Lauchhammer.* Frankfurt am Main: Suhrkamp Verlag, 2008.

Brecht, Bertolt. *Gesammelte Werke 12: Prosa 2.* Frankfurt-Main: Suhrkamp Verlag, 1967.

———. "Short Organum for the Theater." In *Brecht on Theatre: The Development of an Aesthetic,* edited and translated by John Willett, 179–208. New York: Hill and Wang, 1964.

Buck-Morss, Susan. *Dreamworld and Catastrophe: The Passing of Mass Utopia in East and West.* Cambridge, MA and London: MIT Press, 2000.

Davis, Mike. *Planet of Slums.* New York and London: Verso Press, 2006.

Denning, Michael. *Culture in the Age of Three Worlds.* New York and London: Verso Press, 2004.

Drucker, Johanna. *Sweet Dreams: Contemporary Art and Complicity.* Chicago: University of Chicago Press, 2005.

Engels, Frederick. "The Part Played by Labor in the Transition of Ape to Man." In *The Origin of the Family, Private Property, and the State,* 251–264. New York: International Publishers, 1972.

Engler, Wolfgang. *Bürger, ohne Arbeit. Für eine radikale Neugestaltung der Gesellschaft.* Berlin: Aufbau Taschenbuch Verlag, 2005.

———. *Die Ostdeutschen als Avantgarde.* Berlin: Aufbau Taschenbuch Verlag, 2004.

Ganguly, Keya. "Introduction: After Resignation and against Conformity." *The South Atlantic Quarterly: Special Issue on Intellectual Labor* 108, no. 2 (Spring 2009): 243–246.

Glawogger, Michael. *Workingman's Death: Fünf Bilder zur Arbeit im 21. Jahrhundert.* Lotus / Quinte /ARTE, 2005.

Goodbody, Axel. "Political Dislocation and Poetic Reorientation in Volker Braun's *Bodenloser Satz.*" *Dislocation and Reorientation: Exile, Division, and the End of Communism in German Culture and Politics. German Monitor*, no. 71, edited by Axel Goodbody, Pól Ó Dochartaigh, and Dennis Tate, 21–32. New York and Amsterdam: Rodopi, 2009.

Gorz, André. *Paths to Paradise: On the Liberation from Work.* Translated by Malcolm Imrie. Boston: South End Press, 1985.

Hamacher, Werner. "Arbeit Durcharbeiten." In *Archäologie der Arbeit*, edited by Dirk Baecker, 155–200. Berlin: Kulturverlag Kadmos, 2002.

Jameson, Fredric. *Brecht and Method.* London and New York: Verso Press, 1998.

Kafka, Franz. "In the Penal Colony." In *The Complete Stories*, edited by Nahum N. Glatzer, 140–167. New York: Schocken Books, 1971.

Kurz, Robert. *Der Kollaps der Modernisierung: Vom Zusammenbruch des Kasernensozialismus zur Krise der Weltökonomie.* Leipzig: Reclam, 1994.

Marx, Karl. *Capital. A Critique of Political Economy, Volume One*, translated by Ben Fowkes. New York: Vintage Books, 1977.

———. *The Economic and Philosophical Manuscripts of 1844.* New York: International Publishers, 1964.

Mitchell, W. J. T. "Preface to the Second Edition of *Landscape and Power.* Space, Place, and Landscape." In *Landscape and Power*, Second Edition, edited by W. J. T. Mitchell, vii–xiv. Chicago and London: University of Chicago Press.

Mueller, Roswitha. *Bertolt Brecht and the Theory of Media.* Lincoln and London: University of Nebraska Press, 1989.

Moglen, Seth. "On Mourning Social Injury." *Psychoanalysis, Culture and Society* 10, no. 2 (2005): 151–167.

Oswalt, Phillipp, ed. *Shrinking Cities, v.1: International Research/v.2: Interventions.* Ostfildern-Ruit: Hatje-Cantz, 2005/6.

Pekar, Thomas. "Experiences of Delocalization and *Katabasis* in the Literature of the Early Postwar Period in Germany." In *Exile and Otherness: New Approaches to the Experience of the Nazi Refugees*, edited by Alexander Stephan, 49–63. Bern: Peter Lang, 2005.

Santner, Eric L. *On Creaturely Life: Rilke, Benjamin, Sebald.* Chicago and London: University of Chicago Press, 2006.

Scribner, Charity. *Requiem for Communism.* Cambridge, MA and London: MIT Press, 2003.

Weiss, Peter. *The Aesthetics of Resistance, Volume 1*, translated by Joachim Neugroschel. Durham and London: Duke University Press, 2005.

9

The End of an Event

Benjamin Robinson

The Fall Minus the Jubilation

In Jürgen Böttcher's 1990 documentary, *The Wall*, filmed in late fall and early winter immediately after the Berlin Wall was opened, we see how little its dismantling wants to become an event. The chisels tapping away at the Wall, even the bursts of pneumatic hammers, make an intermittent clatter. Instead of harmonizing, the metallic raps erupt and fade solipsistically. To be sure, the camera records tourists converging from all over the world to touch the Wall's remains or to revel at the New Year's celebrations at the Brandenburg Gate. But Böttcher's lens documents something less sensational than the sensation produced out of the Wall's demise by, for example, the concert of Beethoven's Ninth conducted by Leonard Bernstein on December 25, 1989, or a roster of international rock stars performing Pink Floyd's *The Wall* the following July. Why the quiet, nearly solemn tone? Is there not something willful in the choice to focus on the Wall as an object since the resistant material quality of a reinforced concrete barrier influences the film's rhythm more than the galloping pace of the events that overtook east European socialism? Nowadays, it is taken for granted that events must come fast, furious, and fulsome in the programming rotation. In his anthology *Der Trend zum Event* Peter Kemper diagnoses an "event fad" at the outset of the new millennium, while Peter Schneider sees a "dictatorship of velocity" in the competition among media outlets to beat each other to the latest spectacle.[1]

Running counter to this rule, Böttcher's theme is not elation over the Wall's fall but its transformation from a totem charged with the power of good and evil into mere material to be chipped away. The pacing makes a viewer aware of the sort of effort, indifferent to media cycles, that may go into finding ways to represent a moment many experienced in quiet isolation but felt as a great simultaneity of exultation. Rather than prolonging that sense of subjective activation, the film depicts an anticlimax. Agency—or what felt like agency even in the confines of one's private routines—takes on the physical characteristics of an object whose history is as precarious as its newfound physical vulnerability. Once a villain, the Wall is Böttcher's sensitive—albeit inert—hero. At the film's conclusion, classical music has replaced the tapping, and we see trees quivering in the wind with sunlight filtered through their branches. Dismantled segments of the Wall are lined up in a construction yard. Instead of serving as a catalyst for violence, the narrow sections look like headstones no longer associated with the person for whom they were erected: they have become remnants in a country churchyard.

Is there something inappropriate about portraying the desacralizing of a potent historical site as a tedious, occasionally awkward routine, as though such a backstage depiction might be evading a duty (perhaps to freedom) that requires the site's profanation to be celebrated? What's wrong with this film that it doesn't want to party? By resisting the expected, often demanded, celebration of the Wall's end, Böttcher's film provokes reflection on just what an event actually is: Does the fall of the Wall even qualify as an event? Does an event ever really resemble its commemoration, which seeks to prolong a feeling of collective elation that is arguably an event's most short-lived feature? By reifying a social movement into the object that is its most famous symbol, Böttcher's film alienates viewers from the bustle of nonevents, suggesting that the real event lies elsewhere, hidden in a fraught relationship between subjective activation and passive objectification. Our intuition of an event, after all, hovers between passive and active verbs—we think of something happening more than of our doing something, of being surprised more than intending an outcome, of being seized by a crisis more than choosing an option. The film's disregard for the enthusiasm of the moment highlights how the will to replay jubilantly the Wall's demise is a desire to forget what really happened there: the Wall enacted the (failed) determination of real socialism to endure. For the sheer wishing that its fall be present for us as an act of "freedom," another presence is effaced, that of an event—organized socialism—whose truth, for all its brutality, lay in providing grounds for a worldwide, multigenerational commitment.

The term *event* serves here to designate an occasion whose significance lies in its invitation to conscious engagement. An event disrupts the flow of expectations and adaptations. Holding that the fall of the Wall, in a global historical view, opened no new perspectives on structuring human affairs, and indeed called for no persistent loyalty to its unique moment, this chapter finds in Uwe Tellkamp's 2008 epic of the GDR's decline and fall, *Der Turm* (*The Tower*), a consummate expression of how 1989 represents a moment of relief rather than challenge. To grasp the disquiet of the actual event whose end occasioned so much relief, one needs to contrast an epic in which the GDR still appears as an open proposition, as a speculation not settled by the teleology of reintegration that defines *Der Turm*'s post-Wall narrative arc. For this contrast, I consider Uwe Johnson's 1959 *Mutmaßungen über Jakob* (*Speculations about Jacob*), a work that still demands its readers *think* socialism.

Does Effervescence Constitute an Event?

Perhaps, though, Böttcher's film gets it exactly wrong in taking the metaphor of a falling wall too literally, whereas the essence of November 1989 in fact lies in its heady effervescence. Other GDR films from the same period as Böttcher's documentary—films such as *Latest from the Da Dae R* (dir. Jörg Foth, 1990), *The Land Beyond the Rainbow* (dir. Herwig Kipping, 1991), *The Mistake* (dir. Heiner Carow, 1991), and *November Days* (dir. Marcel Ophüls, 1990)—make highly theatrical use of carnival, cabaret, and burlesque elements to evoke the spirit of the times.[2] In *A Carnival of Revolution*, Padraic Kenney argues that the diverse social movements of late-eighties Eastern Europe were characterized by a stance motivated less by any vision than by the feeling that being on the street, acting out, and savoring a theatrical atmosphere of possibility could usher in a change. "Most had as their goal the end of communism," Kenney writes, "but often it was just as important to articulate a new style, and thus to change the social or natural environment. . . . This opposition never took itself, or the regime, too seriously."[3]

Other analysts use terms related to the carnival to characterize the period from the mid-1980s until the implosion of the Soviet Bloc. Drawing on the concept of "collective effervescence" coined by Émile Durkheim in *Elementary Forms of Religious Life* (1915), Edward A. Tiryakian interprets the "'velvet revolutions' of 1989 in various countries of Eastern Europe ... as manifestations of an historical moment of 'collective effervescence.'"[4] In the East German case, Jan Palmowski, drawing on Victor Turner's *Anthropology of Performance*, examines how small towns used "cultural performances" to renew a sense of local belonging but also to evade the large-scale centralized mandates of the state: "In the cultural setting of carnival, for instance, villagers were able to articulate publicly their controversy with the potash mines. . . . This not only provided encouragement for further political action it also helped integrate the dispute into the self-identifications of [villagers]."[5] The carnivals that secured provincial identification and loyalty during the reign of the SED turned their effervescent energy against the SED once its grip on power had loosened.

I highlight the carnivalesque aspects of the *Wende*—the German term for the fall of the Wall that denotes a turning point while demurring on attribution of agency—in order to point out how much our perception of the *Wende* depends on its affect of relief and reversal. Effervescence, with its diffuse agency—its intransitive (objectless) quality—seems to explain these European movements more accurately than alternate terms that attribute a special moral and political energy to them. Kenney's focus on punks, actors, writers, and artists seems more plausible than a focus on the achievements of the leaders of the citizen movements and nascent political parties of East Germany, the approach taken by historians such as Fritz Stern, Mary Fulbrook, and Konrad Jarausch.[6] The aesthetics of carnival help us see how the theatrical excesses of the moment distract and entertain us, letting us overlook the crucial question whether we are justified in considering 1989's "carnival of revolution" to be the great event it is often taken for.

In order to answer that question, we need a rigorous concept of an event. After all, for Durkheim, "collective effervescence" does not describe the singularity of a historical event but a recurrent feature of social integration responsible for resacralizing the profane routines of daily life and renewing a social order fallen into disenchantment. Such effervescence, moreover, results from "the influence of some great collective shock." In response to this jolt, "men look for each other and assemble together more than ever." The effervescence explains "many of the scenes, either sublime or savage, of the French Revolution."[7] While collective effervescence explains the theater of a historical caesura, it is not a criterion for deciding whether a historical occurrence has an outstanding singularity to it. The open question is thus: What constitutes the collective shock that occasions effervescence? What kind of occurrence gives rise to the charismatic passions that sustain its intellectual and material legacy across generations? Without doubting the depth or sincerity of the public elation, I believe a sharper definition of an event clarifies why 1989 was not an event, but *the end of an event*, the close parenthesis marking the outer boundary of the socialist event that began with the October Revolution.

An Event and Its End

After describing "a kind of people's assembly, soldiers without cockades, sailors with carbines hung around their necks, women, all with red ribbons, and between them the delegates," Harry Graf Kessler closes his diary entry for November 9, 1918, "so concludes this first day of revolution, which in only a few hours has seen the fall of the Hohenzollerns, the dissolution of the German army, the end of the hitherto existing social form in Germany. One of the most memorable, horrible days of German history."[8] Nearly a century later, Katja Lange-Müller finds herself, by contrast, struggling for the right word for November 9, 1989—"the mood was, how should I put it, maybe: carnivalesque."[9] Reinhard Jirgl recollects a "strange lassitude (one acknowledges it, secretly, with a wry grin): *Something* is at an end— . . . the diffuse state of alarm of the past days had found its event."[10] The elated outburst of that night follows a long ordeal and discharges an accumulated burden of anticipation. It is surely a memorable moment, but is there a fateful sense of generation or, instead, a great relief at being released from fate, freed to embrace normality? Is it about a scarcely conceivable task, or about the chance to escape capital-letter demands like Class, History, and New Social Form; the sudden solace of dropping out of a losing game?

If the *Wende* marks the end of an event, how does one characterize the difference between an event and its end? An event, I maintain, puts a common subjective burden on its participants to realize its historical singularity. Failing to achieve this, the event becomes another anthropological constant, falling back into the cyclical time of human affairs (and foibles) as natural history. The burden of realizing singularity implies persistence in tracing the consequences revealed by the event having taken place at all. For my conception of the event, I draw on the work of Alain Badiou, for whom events are rare occurrences that confront us with a singular occasion for re-axiomatizing our politics and establishing the authority of a new subjective commitment over future eras.[11] Badiou holds that an event is the "opening of an epoch, transformation of the relations between the possible and the impossible," and as such, demands from its protagonists that they "proceed from singularity to universality and vice versa."[12] A novel event—in our case the October Revolution—is both within its time and a singular exception to it, calling forth a subject who, "far from fleeing from the century . . . must live with it, but without letting oneself be shaped, conformed. It is the subject, rather than the century, who, under the injunction of his faith, must be transformed" (110).

Badiou's philosophy describes how an event is unproven at the moment of its appearance, so that acting upon it demands a sustained leap of faith. A true event, however, is not just a prophetic sign demanding faith, but must inaugurate a process addressed universally to all. The worst betrayal is to mistake an event for the private property of one prophet or an opportunity for momentary, particular advantage. The term *event* thus designates not only how a prophetic mentality arises from a unique conjuncture but also how it is constantly tested by a fidelity to its universal dimension. An example helps make this idea of an event more intuitive. When Pasteur first proposed that airborne microbes, not spontaneous generation, caused fermentation, he was vehemently opposed—his persistence in the face of supposedly contradicting facts allowed his hunches to become the basis for successful experiments demonstrating the presence of organisms in atmospheric dust.[13] Fidelity to an intangible *eureka* moment—to the event—is demanded if an insight is ever to become the transformative event that it only becomes due to its having inspired the very persistence that led to its later success.

If we suppose, however, that the communist revolutions of early last century are the actual event at stake in the *Wende*, then doesn't the failure of 1989 prove what liberal and conservative commentators had asserted all along: that communism is no transformative event, but a maladaptation of modernity, one more false premise foisted on people by effervescing ideologues? My counter claim is that the event that failed in 1989 did not *falsify* the communist hypothesis that underlay it (the hypothesis, simply put, that a social organization other than market society is possible, one that surpasses market society on measures of liberty, equality, and solidarity).[14] Rather, the *Wende* demonstrated that, after 70 years of trying to discover how to hold radical nonmarket power, the single-party state economies of the Soviet Bloc *failed to confirm* the hypothesis of such an alternate modernity.

For all its euphoria of relief, the *Wende* itself left us without any profound sense of truth emerging from the moment. On the one hand, it is obvious enough that personal freedoms triumphed over real socialism's stultifying collective constraints. On the other hand, our search for an enduring testament ends up, if not with pomp at the Brandenburg Gate, then with a decidedly mixed bag of heroes—Helmut Kohl? Mikhail Gorbachev? Ronald Reagan (whose 1987 Berlin Wall speech inspired the German Foreign Mission's rubric for the twentieth-anniversary commemorations in 2009)? But despite the anticlimax of 1989, we are bound to see it as something more than a provincial episode in European history, since its consequences—if not its profound meaning—have been felt worldwide, most clearly in the shift of global conflict from a military standoff between antagonistic socioeconomic systems to a rivalry between religious-social worldviews, and most deeply in the return to global bloc politics between Asia, Europe, and the United States around control of market share and capital flow. What, then, are we to do with this nonevent that has a global scale, but hardly a coherent thought behind it? What would be the alternative to seeing 1989 as an event?

One alternative would be to see it as a counterrevolution, a political turn back to reliable social forms (see, for example, Robert Snyder and Timothy White's case in this volume for seeing Gorbachev as a counterrevolutionary). Another alternative is to see it as announcing a failure of the communist experiment that, using Peter Sloterdijk's formulation, "was in the end subject to the rules of falsification and thus, however problematic, was still a part of the project of modernity."[15] If 1989 is less an unprecedented event than a failure on the grounds of trial and error, then it would seem to indicate a world where any global alternative has passed from the agenda. In *Requiem for Communism*, Charity Scribner observes, "state socialism's ruin signaled that industrial modernity had exhausted its utopian potential."[16] From being a global actuality, real socialism would now appear to be a refuted hypothesis. Once "risen from the ruins and turned to the future," as Johannes R. Becher's 1949 national anthem put it, the GDR now represents "a future that has become a past once again like so many futures before it" ("eine Zukunft, die schon wieder Vergangenheit ist wie die anderen vor ihr"),[17] as Heiner Müller describes the graveyard of ideals in *The Mission*, his 1979 play about the moment when a revolutionary task loses its task master.

A third alternative (the one I defend) to seeing 1989 as a counterrevolution or the foreclosure of change is intimated by taking a closer look at Müller's extraordinary play. In this view, the hypothetical imperative of communism, after the short, nasty twentieth century, appears not to be dead, but just the opposite, to be as open-ended as it had been before two world wars, at the outset of the past century. Müller's play depicts three characters deputized with spreading the French Revolution to the West Indies. When Napoleon liquidates the revolution in France, they are stranded in Jamaica without support. What becomes of their mission when the homeland of liberty, equality, and fraternity has disappeared? What, by extension, does socialism mean when there is no more really existing socialism? The slave Sasportas suggests that in this moment, "[t]he homeland of the slave is the uprising."[18] This, as Müller realizes, is a terrifying thought. An uprising, unlike really existing socialism, has no regularity, no boundaries, and no firm direction. It threatens all of our expectations, our norms, our normalcy, by its unpredictable omnipresence.

Returning to 1989, what we might save of the *Wende* in its global scope is how resolutely it has thrown us, after 70 years in which real socialism oscillated around its final collapse, into a situation where socialism holds no formal political power and capitalist development has before it the same inconceivable prospects for expansion it beheld a century earlier. It is, in some respects, as if the nineteenth century—the era of progressivism, positivism, and imperialism—has returned to the historical stage despite all our self-conscious examinations of postnational sovereignty, supranational demographic flows, and deterritorialized identities. Among the canonical statements of deterritorialized modernity, Ernst Jünger's 1930 essay "Total Mobilization" finds particular resonance today. Jünger characterizes the Anglo-American preparation and conduct of World War I as a postterritorial liquefaction of national identity in favor of complete devotion to the omnipresence of economy. Don't *think* economy, Jünger enjoins, but *be* it: existential legitimation comes through economic success. In Jünger's view, the global mobility of the victors of World War I is the apotheosis of nineteenth-century rationalism—it is economic liberation from the aristocratic constraints of land and loyalty. As Jünger explains, "in order to develop energies on such a scale, it is no longer enough to arm with the sword—one needs to militarize the inmost core . . . each individual life becomes ever more clearly a worker's life and the wars of knights, kings, and citizens are succeeded by wars of workers."[19]

Since the days when Jünger first envisioned the "New Man" flowing into the conveyor belt, our New Man has become only more mobile, leaving the Fordist production line to circulate in today's vast financial markets. Not production but marketing now legitimates today's global protagonist. It is Market Man who has been rediscovered in the recent populist explosion of libertarianism in the industrial world. Referring to the classical spiritedness that drives a person to seek recognition, Sloterdijk calls such fervor "thymotic outpourings." The rise in the United States of small-government populism against the established conservative party, and the renewed strength of the liberal FDP in Germany are just two examples of the contemporary libertarian thymos. These populists thrill to a human who is postterritorial and postproductive, whose ebb and flow is not solidarity or inner cultivation but purchasing power or credit. Sloterdijk himself has announced his astonishment at the lack of "fiscal civil war" in wealthy lands, since "the all too plausible liberal thesis of the exploitation of productive [i.e., creditor] classes by unproductive [i.e., debtor] is putting paid to the much less plausible leftist thesis of the exploitation of labor by capital."[20] The fiscal warrior that Sloterdijk calls up in 2009 is none other than the arising European he conjured under the spell of the *Wende* in his 1994 pamphlet *If Europe Should Awaken*.

Despite the open view through the Brandenburg Gate down Unter den Linden, two blockages stand in the way of the total mobilization of Credit-Worthy Man; two opacities cloud his prospects, just as they did in the nineteenth century. One is regional sovereignty. Claims of national, ethnic, and religious identities, often framed as the "clash of civilizations," have exploded in the post-1989 world in the form of market-impermeable opposition to Market Man's final liberation from territory. In light of today's reawakened religious sensitivities (what Habermas calls "post-secular society"[21]), the evangelical market zeal with which Reagan concluded his Berlin Wall speech is astonishing in its nonchalance:

> Years ago . . . [East Germans] erected a secular structure: the television tower at Alexander Platz. Virtually ever since, the authorities have been working to correct what they view as the tower's one major flaw, treating the glass sphere at the top with paints and chemicals of every kind. Yet even today when the sun strikes that sphere—that sphere that towers over all Berlin—the light makes the sign of the cross.[22]

Where Reagan's Christianity once blended blithely into the capitalist crusade against communism, acrimonious claims of religious and regional difference have returned to oppose the profane system prerogatives of the market.

A second blockage is internal limitations, as opposed to external rivalries, whereby a system undermines the very elements and relations that compose it. This is the immanent blockage foretold by Marx but hinted at in each evolutionary transformation of the market from the merchant economy to the global finance system. This second opacity, which clouds the prospects of a single market future, can be discussed in terms of the communist hypothesis that an alternative system is possible, superior with respect to the criteria of liberty, equality, and solidarity. In the Cold War, however, the second blockage to the nineteenth century's market apotheosis became the first. The internal system constraints of liberal capitalism (and state socialism) became externalized as a Cold War rivalry. Since the Russian Revolution, socialism's systemic threat (that of the poor against the rich) has become figured as a claim of state power against market autonomy. Socialism is the state leviathan that would deprive Market Man of transparent prepolitical liberty (Adam Smith's invisible hand).

But the real significance of 1989 has bypassed libertarian denunciations of socialism. When Napoleon seized control of Paris in 1799, just as when the Berlin Wall fell, socialism became detached from its specific mechanism for holding power. What socialism gained with the *Wende* was an open relationship to whatever sovereign form it might eventually assume. In the void of a relationship between an alternative to capitalism and the systemic form it might adopt, the *Wende* reinvigorates the hypothesis that some other relationship between economy and political will exists other than that tolerated by the North Atlantic consensus.

An Epic of a Nonevent and an Epic of an Event

I want to explore some implications of the *Wende* for the way we read contemporary culture dealing with the GDR 20 years after its demise. Over the past two decades cultural criticism has, by and large, been content to let socialism fall from its field of reference except as a geographical allusion on par with "the East." It is usually relegated to a hazy background against which potentially abiding GDR determinants like nation, region, race, gender, and generation are analyzed. In the political and historical sciences, too, socialism mostly amounts to a technology of authoritarianism—a welfare dictatorship (Konrad Jarausch), a surveillance state (Jens Gieseke), a niche society (Günter Gauss), or a functionally dedifferentiated system (Sigrid Meuschel)[23]—that does not point beyond its instrumentality to any tenable idea. Some commentators have explicitly deprived socialism of any pretension to reality. Richard Rorty suggested, "the time has come to drop the terms 'capitalism' and 'socialism' from the political vocabulary of the left."[24] And Anthony Giddens declared the "death of socialism," "at least as a system of economic management."[25]

The derealization of socialism makes the cultural product of historical socialism largely incoherent. What do the intense artistic engagements with the socialist distinction mean once the concept has been reduced to sheer ideology without any purchase on reality? Rereading critical socialist authors from Christa Wolf to Franz Fühmann with students today, it becomes nearly impossible to present their works as anything but rejections of socialism. What is hardest to extrapolate is why these texts, by criticizing socialism from within its constraints, conceive themselves as affirming it more deeply. Recently, Wolf conceded, "we never would have contested that we lived in a dictatorship, the dictatorship of the proletariat. A transition period, an incubation period for the new man, you understand?"[26] With no real socialism to refer to, one is challenged to explicate why such dictatorship was a tolerable, even welcome ordeal for Wolf. Jakob Norberg recently observed, "while we may retain a sense of socialism's own rhetoric, and also remember quite clearly, or perhaps still espouse, the major arguments against the socialist system developed in the West during the Cold War, the ideologically and politically *socialist* critique of the nations in the Eastern Bloc is now almost completely concealed from us."[27] Of course, many do just fine without the socialist element of GDR literature and, assimilating all worthwhile Eastern Bloc writing to the Western dismissal of socialism, draw perfectly coherent lessons about illiberalism from the remnants of East German culture. Yet beyond explicating a local European legacy, the reason for resisting the disappearance of the socialist referent of this culture is that the socialist hypothesis—so I hold—remains a practical imperative (indeed the imperative of progress), and we come closer to accomplishing it by acknowledging the unsettling force of socialist art.

A contrast between two epic novels about the GDR highlights this force: Uwe Tellkamp's 2008 novel *The Tower*, crowned with the German Book Prize, and celebrated as the long-awaited *Wenderoman*; and Uwe Johnson's 1959 novel *Speculations about Jakob*.[28] My claim is that *The Tower* enjoys its celebrity because it brilliantly—if contrary to its own apocalyptic panorama—gives us 1989 as a colossal *nonevent*. Over the course of 973 pages, the novel unwrites the ontological distinction of GDR socialism, rewriting it as an ideological and technological backwater and, at the same time, a sanctuary for the interior life of the German *Kulturnation*, sequestered from the fads of Western popular culture as much by the "sweet malady Yesterday" ("süße Krankheit Gestern")[29] as by the Iron Curtain. Tellkamp conveys GDR daily life with an intimacy of sensual (and breadth of technical) detail that brings the scrambling over birthday and wedding preparations, the resentful spatial negotiations of subdivided homes, and the field-lazaret solidarity of basement communal baths into the quasi-logical clarity of lived experience. He artfully renews German tropes—such as the tension in the national psyche between the craftsman-engineer and the beautiful soul—in the context of the GDR's informal barter-and-tinker economies and the private salons of the surviving *Bildungsbürgertum* (cultivated elite). Despite the novel's rich invocation of GDR daily life (or just because of it), it refuses to inhabit the extrapersonal, historical stakes of the situations it recounts. Its subjective experiences remain, proudly, those of individual personalities who might stand up with the personalities of the traditional German literary canon.

By contrast, Uwe Johnson's *Speculations about Jakob*, organized around the death of a protagonist whose inner life is left almost entirely opaque, remains urgent in its speculation over whether this death is accidental or somehow compelled. Its epic goal is to present the GDR as an invitation for belonging, such that accepting the invitation would (or would not) verify a socialist hypothesis. Johnson's novel not only tries to recover some trace of the coherent personality of its hero, the railroad dispatcher and presumptive suicide, Jakob Abs, but also, working back and forth from situated insights to situating overviews, effects the *mise-en-scène* of a personal pronoun into a railway schedule, placing "you" or "she" into the technical framework of Kantorovich's linear programming or Marx's historical *Gesetzmäßigkeiten* (regularities).

Returning, first, to Tellkamp's novel, we encounter a family saga organized around three protagonists from Dresden's elite. Christian Hoffmann is a student whose medical ambition is derailed when he is sentenced to extended service in the Nationale Volksarmee (NVA) for reading a banned Nazi-era novel; Richard Hoffman is his driven surgeon father; and Meno Rohde, his beloved uncle, is a literary editor and gentleman biologist, raised in Moscow exile as the son of Communists. Besides evoking the complementary sensibilities of doers and thinkers, engineers and poets, each protagonist gives the narrative an opportunity to sketch a distinct GDR milieu. Meno, an intellectual with access to both power and dissent, provides a perspective on the GDR intelligentsia. As Julia Hell has noted, Tellkamp "portrays these intellectuals—dissident and non-dissident Marxists—as belonging to an ossified elite, caught up in ritualized meaningless negotiations."[30] The competitive Richard shows us the rivalry, frustration, and duplicity among GDR professionals. Each group appears as one social caste among others, as it would in a sociological study of a national elite. With his narrative parceling, Tellkamp approaches the GDR with the same taxonomic spirit as the amateur biologist Meno, despite the rich, lived experiences he invokes. The narrative pathos lies decisively outside the socialist event bounded by the Wall and the Russian Revolution. The novel is indifferent to the effort to think socialism and, without feigning any narrative justification for its characters' pragmatic GDR ambitions, justifies them instead through their timeless cultivation: the cultivation of the clockmakers, not the opportunism of those whose time is marked by the striking clocks. Meno's thoughts never reach back to a logic of commitment that might once have gone beyond his social position but flower as melancholy caste traits, by turns pathetic, endearing, ennobling, and damning. In Johnson's novel, by contrast, even the Stasi agent Rohlfs—whose contemptible interference in Jakob's personal life likely drives him to suicide—is presented as a subjective gambit, as a speculative position and also a speculation about a position in socialist society.

Under Meno's narrative dominion, Tellkamp includes the perspectives of writers who fought in World War II and others who, like Meno and his family, were Moscow exiles who witnessed Stalin's purges. These are the old guard, the intellectual elite whose political instincts, shames, and traumas weigh ever more awkwardly, because irrelevantly, on the opportunities of a new generation. In the novel's final section, "The Maelstrom," the voices of those witnesses are edited into a montage juxtaposing scenes of the Wehrmacht's Eastern European anabasis with scenes of Stalinist self-betrayal among the German communists stranded in Moscow's Hotel Lux, who would go on to found the GDR. These brutal memories—focused around moments of patricidal and matricidal intensity—are in turn spliced with scenes of the *Wende*, alternating between Christian's NVA unit (called up to suppress unrest at the Dresden rail station in October 1989) and his family's activities among the civil protesters there. The effect is to bring together a series of German apocalypses—a cycle of self-immolating events—and to close off their Oresteian sequence with a maelstrom that in the end is *not* immolating. Although sexually and socially betrayed by his father, Christian—who as an NVA soldier, albeit a sapped and indifferent one, executes state power—refuses to raise a baton against his family. State power—and fidelity to the events of 1917 and 1949—dissipates in one last, helpless reiteration of the savage theatrics of European war and revolution.

In the novel's final paragraph, the accumulated papers of German postwar history—"*written upon and blank . . . jubilant, circumspect, shadowy, opaque, official, countermanding; paper for the TRUTH, the press mirror, NEUES DEUTSCHLAND, JUNGE WELT, PRAVDA*"[31]—are washed down the drain. "*Out of the downspout gushes pressed juice, fluid as precious as blood and sperm, out of the papers of the archives*— . . . but then all at once . . . the clocks struck, struck the 9th of November, 'Germany undivided fatherland,' struck at the Brandenburg Gate:"[32] Tellkamp's gesture of ending the book with a colon, however, falls short—a close parenthesis bracketing Germany's socialist event would have been more telling.

This apotheosis of paper and clocks recalls the key scene of Müller's *The Mission*, when the three revolutionaries in Jamaica receive a note from Paris informing them that their mission has been countermanded: on the eighteenth Brumaire—November 9, 1799—Napoleon deposes the revolutionary Directory. Debuisson announces the news to his coconspirator, the slave Sasportas, who is at first incredulous. Debuisson, infinitely relieved to be so unexpectedly freed of the revolution's burden, warns him:

> Think about it, Sasportas, before you risk your neck for the liberation of the slaves in an abyss that has become bottomless since this news arrived—which I'm now going to swallow, so no trace of our efforts remains. Do you also want a scrap? That was our mission, all that's left of it is the taste of paper.[33]

If Tellkamp's *Tower* is the novel of 1989, and I believe it is, then it is so because it so colorfully and polyphonically presents 1989 not as an event but as the end of an event, as the moment when a historical task, a leap, turns into a scrap of paper whose headline once proclaimed *Truth—Pravda*! In the place of socialism's tortured whole, the novel ends with environmentally correct paper recycling.

Returning to Johnson's *Speculations* highlights just how different Tellkamp's narrative of a nonevent is from an epic that struggles with an actual event, albeit one that has, since Johnson's novel, passed from the stage. In a crucial passage from *Speculations*, Johnson presents Jakob's railroad timetable as a very different sort of paper than the pulped archives of Tellkamp's story:

> [Jakob] had to exploit the minutes of his work thriftily and weigh each carefully; he knew each one individually. The paper on the sloping drafting table was divided into vertical and horizontal lines for the temporal and spatial sequence of planned and unplanned events, he noted with variously colored pencils the movement of the trains in his sector from block to block and from minute to minute . . . in the end the minutes didn't add up to a day, but a plan.[34]

The paper at stake for Jakob is precisely his mission—it does not represent an ideological point of view but itself organizes time and space, epochs and territories, which he cannot take in as an individual, only get back, as the movement of trains . . . eventually over his own body. Johnson gives us Jakob as both the object of an all-seeing gaze and as a subject casting just such a gaze. The challenge for Johnson is how to present the gaze in which one is oneself observed, the epochal gaze of the visible hand, as a gaze that also comes from within oneself? How, in other words, can one make a suprapersonal difference between systems into a personal intuition of time and space, into an affect? This question—the question of simultaneously judging objectively and producing subjectively the distinction that will have become the GDR—is the ultimate quarry of Johnson's speculations about Jakob.

Everything about Johnson's language seeks to bring the figurative resources of narrative prose back to a literal intuition. A latecomer in the wrong is really an actionable status, not a metaphor. "Each decision," Johnson continues:

> was a matter of state conscience, no answer achieved an equilibrium, thus subjecting to guilt whoever had been drawn into making a decision. . . . Each event drew mutually implicated dependencies behind

> it in a bristling tail, foresight in one's own sector became uncertainty, punctualities once achieved stood to be potentially spoiled again by irregularities.[35]

Johnson's language of intertwining gazes—where insight is called to correspond with oversight, spectacle to reconcile with foresight—is beautiful but not celebratory. In this epoch-making activity, the planning gaze and operating gaze never converge in a closed cosmos. "Superimposed and transparent," the passage concludes, "the plan and the actual track record wouldn't have matched, but would have appeared as mixed northern and southern star systems."[36] Even in this misalignment, what Johnson's novel holds open—and Tellkamp's forecloses—is the hypothesis that maybe Jakob's death was an accident after all and the deeper irregularity lay elsewhere, perhaps in today's bustling attempts to secure our present course.

To be sure, Tellkamp is writing 50 years after Johnson, and his epic chronicles just the demise of the GDR that unfolded during those intervening years. Who would expect Tellkamp to imagine the open prospect of socialism that Johnson could still envisage? The point, however, is not to praise Johnson for vainly holding open a future whose futility Tellkamp, informed by history, plainly sees. Rather, the point is that just as Johnson's novel responded to the unsettling event of real socialism, Tellkamp's novel responds with appropriate intuition to the nonevent of real socialism's failure. It captures a moment of relief and return that does not—and perhaps cannot—demand the sort of epochal reflection that Johnson's novel urges upon its readers. Tellkamp's story does not invite us to take an intellectual risk; instead, it offers us an intellectual rest. It welcomes back the century's prodigal sons, daughters, and states who have erred and suffered for 40 or 70 years, and now draw comfort from returning to the fold.

Epilogue: Waiting for a Surprise

Reflecting on the role of aesthetic experience in mediating the old and new, Hans Robert Jauss asked, "Is it possible to identify actual beginnings or the division of epochs? Can contemporaries really experience them or can they only be understood retrospectively?"[37] Jauss was taking up a line of questioning inaugurated by Georg Lukács concerning the relationship of a literary world to its historical caesurae. That relationship has been the concern of this chapter as well. What does the contrast between Tellkamp and Johnson tell us about our epoch? Jauss himself insisted that "the role of aesthetic experience" should be "creating expectations—creating them in order to reveal and test what is thinkable or desirable."[38] Contrary to Jauss, my suggestion here is that aesthetic experience has only an indexical relationship to the event of epochal change. It cannot depict the event, but only point to it beyond the happenings of plot. Aesthetic experience cannot return the whole of time—its leaps, its divergences—into its representations. Such would be, according to Lukács, who was clear-sighted in his critique of aesthetics, a "hypostasy of aesthetics into metaphysics—a violence done to the essence of everything that lies outside the sphere of art."[39] It is not so much a content or theme that links Johnson's novel to the *event* of socialism, but its mindset of speculative tension toward the event's open question. Tellkamp's novel shares a central theme with Johnson's (the fate of socialism), but no hint of a social project emerges in the aesthetic perceptions it fosters, whereas Johnson's novel (all historicizing questions of real socialism aside) investigates the very boundary of prudential/existential choice.

What does this comparison imply about reading literature after the GDR, reading both the socialist literary legacy and the new writing that aspires to inflect the discourse of European contemporaneity in the wake of socialism? Despite the relaxation of its intellectual tensions, our era is not a second Biedermeier, a chronic retreat from public concerns. On the contrary, Tellkamp's castle keep of high culture over the Elbe has been stormed and its contents liberated for the world of competition and public criticism. What my approach urges is not ideology critique, but a phenomenology of aesthetic experience such that we attend to the kind of projects—amorous, political, moral, revolutionary—that come to appear, not thematically or iconically, but by-the-by, in the fiber of the writing, its tension, its mindset. Or, equally, that we attend to the projects that do not appear because we encounter a moral discourse unable to discover meaning in its own concepts, or an amorous passion communicating too fluently with a calculative one, or a revolutionary commitment lacking anything to commit to. In this phenomenology we probably won't discover Jauss' conscious testing of imagined expectations (because we're looking for just that which is not depicted) but we might, just as likely in a musty text from the surpassed legacy as in a shiny text heralded on the front pages of the feuilletons, notice some indications of an actual event that, true to its nature, no one has been expecting.

Notes

1. Peter Kemper, ed., *Der Trend zum Event* (Frankfurt a. M.: Suhrkamp, 2001). Peter Schneider, "Die Diktatur der Geschwindigkeit," in Schneider, *Die*

Diktatur der Geschwindigkeit: Ausflüge, Zwischenrufe (Reinbeck: Rowohlt, 2000), 39–52, 41.

2. Nora Alter explores the camp aspects of Ophüls' documentary in Nora Alter, "Marcel Ophüls' *November Days*: German Reunification as 'Musical Comedy,'" *Film Quarterly* 51, no. 2 (Winter 1997–1998), 32–43.
3. Padraic Kenney, *A Carnival of Revolution: Central Europe 1989* (Princeton, NJ: Princeton UP, 2002), 4.
4. Edward A. Tiryakian, "Collective Effervescence, Social Change and Charisma: Durkheim, Weber and 1989," *International Sociology* 10, no. 3 (September 1995): 269–281, 269.
5. Jan Palmowski, *Inventing a Socialist Nation: Heimat and the Politics of Everyday Life in the GDR, 1945–1990* (Cambridge: Cambridge UP, 2009), 254.
6. Fritz Stern, *Five Germanys I Have Known* (New York: Farrar, Straus, and Giroux, 2006), esp. 454–465; Mary Fulbrook, *A History of Germany 1918–2008: The Divided Nation*, 3rd ed., (West Sussex: Wiley-Blackwell, 2009), esp. 265–285; Konrad Jarausch, "Germany 1989: A New Kind of Revolution." Accessed July 20, 2010, at: http://vimeo.com/9410601.
7. Émile Durkheim, *The Elementary Forms of Religious Life*, trans. Joseph Ward Swain (London: Allen and Unwin, 1976 [1915]), 210–211.
8. Harry Graf Kessler, *Tagebücher, 1918–1937*, ed. Wolfgang Pfeiffer-Belli (Frankfurt: Insel, 1961), 19, 20.
9. Katja Lange-Müller, "Bochum und Bohnsdorf," in *Die Nacht, in der die Mauer fiel: Schriftsteller erzählen vom 9. November 1989*, ed. Renatus Deckert (Frankfurt: Suhrkamp, 2009), 48–55, 54.
10. Reinhard Jirgl, "Theater ist Draußen," in *Die Nacht, in der die Mauer fiel*, 73–82, 75–78.
11. Alain Badiou, *Being and Event*, trans. Oliver Feltham (London: Continuum, 2005) esp. 173–183.
12. Badiou, *Saint Paul: The Foundation of Universalism*, trans. Ray Brassier (Stanford: Stanford UP, 2003), 45.
13. Louise Robbins, *Louis Pasteur and the Hidden World of Microbes* (New York: Oxford UP, 2001) 17.
14. Badiou, "The Communist Hypothesis," *New Left Review* 49 (Jan.-Feb. 2008): 29–42.
15. Peter Sloterdijk, *Falls Europa erwacht* (Frankfurt a. M.: Suhrkamp, 1994), 30.
16. Charity Scribner, *Requiem for Communism* (Cambridge: MIT Press, 2003), 3.
17. Heiner Müller, *Der Auftrag*, in *Der Auftrag und andere Revolutionsstücke* (Stuttgart: Reclam, 1988), 48–76, 72.
18. "Die Heimat der Sklaven ist der Aufstand." Müller, *Der Auftrag*, 74.
19. Ernst Jünger, "Die Totale Mobilmachung," *Sämtliche Werke, v. 7, Essays I* (Stuttgart: Klett-Cotta, 1980), 119–141, 127–128.
20. Sloterdijk, "Die Revolution der gebenden Hand," *Frankfurter Allgemeine Zeitung*, June 13, 2009.

21. Jürgen Habermas, "Die Dialektik der Säkularisierung," *Blätter für deutsche und internationale Politik* 4 (2008): 33–46.
22. Ronald Reagan, "Tear Down this Wall." Speech delivered in West Berlin, June 12, 1987. Accessed July 20, 2010, at: http://www.historyplace.com/speeches/reagan-tear-down.htm.
23. For an overview of terms of art in GDR studies, see *Dictatorship as Experience: Towards a Socio-Cultural History of the GDR*, ed. Konrad Jarausch (New York: Berghahn, 2001); especially Jarausch's contribution, "Care and Coercion: The GDR as Welfare Dictatorship," 47–69; Jens Gieseke, *Staatssicherheit und Gesellschaft: Studien zum Herrschaftsalltag in der DDR* (Göttingen: Vandenhoeck and Ruprecht, 2007); Günter Gaus, *Wo Deutschland Liegt* (Hamburg: Hoffmann und Campe, 1983); Sigrid Meuschel, *Legitimation und Parteiherrschaft in der DDR* (Frankfurt a. M.: Suhrkamp, 1992).
24. Richard Rorty, "The End of Leninism and History as Comic Frame," in *History and the Idea of Progress*, ed. Arthur M. Melzer, Jerry Weinberger, and M. Richard Zinman (Ithaca, NY: Cornell UP, 1995), 211–26, 212.
25. Anthony Giddens, *The Third Way: The Renewal of Social Democracy* (Cambridge: Polity, 1998), 2–3.
26. Cited by Lothar Müller in his review of Wolf's *Stadt der Engel*, "Ich habe Margarete vergessen," *Süddeutsche Zeitung*, June 19, 2010. Accessed July 21, 2010, online at: http://sz-shop.sueddeutsche.de/mediathek/shop/Produktdetails/Buch+Stadt_der_Engel+Christa_Wolf/5519787.do.
27. Jakob Norberg, "Disappearing Socialism: Volker Braun's *Unvollendete Geschichte*." *Monatshefte* 102, no. 2 (2010): 177–191, 177.
28. Uwe Tellkamp, *Der Turm* (Frankfurt a. M.: Suhrkamp, 2008); Uwe Johnson, *Mutmaßungen über Jakob* (Frankfurt a. M.; Suhrkamp, 1959).
29. Tellkamp, *Der Turm*, 11.
30. Julia Hell, "Dissolution/Revolution: Uwe Tellkamp's post-89 Novel *Der Turm* and the Peculiar Configuration of the Public Sphere in the Late GDR," *Transformations of the Public Sphere*. Accessed July 23, 2010, at: http://publicsphere.ssrc.org/hell-uwe-tellkamps-post-89-novel-der-turm-and-the-peculiar-configuration-of-the-public-sphere-in-the-late-gdr/.
31. "beschriebenes und weißes . . . jubelndes, vorsichtiges, schattiges, undurchsichtiges, amtliches, widerrufendes Papier; Papier für die WAHRHEIT, den gedruckten Spiegel, NEUES DEUTSCHLAND, JUNGE WELT, PRAWDA." Tellkamp, Der Turm, 972.
32. "*Aus den Traufen quillt der Preßsaft, Flüssigkeit kostbar wie Blut und Sperma, aus den Papieren der Archive*— . . . aber dann auf einmal . . . schlugen die Uhren, schlugen den 9. November, "Deutschland einig Vaterland," schlugen ans Brandenburger Tor:" Tellkamp, *Der Turm*, 973.
33. "Denk darüber nach, Sasportas, eh du deinen Hals riskierst für die Befreiung der Sklaven in einen Abgrund, der keinen Boden mehr hat seit dieser Nachricht, die ich mir jetzt einverleiben werde, damit von unserer Arbeit keine Spur bleibt. Wollt ihr auch einen Fetzen. Das war unser Auftrag, er schmeckt nur noch nach Papier." Müller, *Der Auftrag*, 72.

34. "Die Minuten seiner Arbeit musste [Jakob] sparsam ausnutzen und umsichtig bedenken, er kannte jede einzeln. Das Papier auf der schrägen Tischplatte vor ihm war eingeteilt nach senkrechten und waagerechten Linien für das zeitliche und räumliche Nacheinander der planmässigen und der unregelmässigen Vorkommnisse, er verzeichntete darin mit seinen verschiedenen Stiften die Bewegung der Eisenbahnzüge auf seiner Strecke von Blockstelle zu Blockstelle und von Minute zu Minute . . . am Ende machten die Minuten keinen Tag aus sondern einen Fahrplan." Johnson, *Mutmaßungen*, 20.
35. "Jede Entscheidung [war] eine Frage des staatlichen Gewissens, keine Antwort ergab ein Gleichgewicht, jede machte mit Notwendigkeit den schuldig, der sich hierauf hatte einlassen müssen. . . . Jedes Ereignis zog einen borstigen Schwanz wechselseitig bedingter Abhängigkeiten hinter sich, die Voraussicht war im eigenen Gebiet unsicher geworden, einmal erreichte Pünktlichkeit wurde vielleicht verdorben von den Unregelmässigkeiten." Johnson, *Mutmaßungen*, 23.
36. "übereinandergelegt und durchsichtig hätten Planblatt und Betriebsblatt ausgesehn nicht wie zwei ähliche sondern mehr wie ein nördliches und ein südliches Sternensystem ineinander." Johnson, *Mutmaßungen*, 24.
37. Hans Robert Jauss, "Tradition, Innovation, and Aesthetic Experience," in *The Journal of Aesthetics and Art Criticism* 46, no. 3 (Spring 1988): 375–388, 378.
38. Jauss, "Tradition, Innovation," 386–387.
39. Lukács, *Theory of the Novel*, trans. Anna Bostock (Cambridge: MIT Press, 1974), 38.

Bibliography

Alter, Nora. "Marcel Ophüls' *November Days*: German Reunification as 'Musical Comedy.'" *Film Quarterly* 51, no. 2 (Winter 1997–98): 32–43.

Badiou, Alain. *Being and Event*, trans. Oliver Feltham. London: Continuum, 2005.

———. "The Communist Hypothesis." *New Left Review* 49 (Jan.-Feb. 2008): 29–42.

———.*Saint Paul: The Foundation of Universalism*, trans. Ray Brassier. Stanford: Stanford UP, 2003.

Böttcher, Jürgen, dir. *Die Mauer* (1991).

Durkheim, Émile. *The Elementary Forms of Religious Life*, trans. Joseph Ward Swain. London: Allen and Unwin, 1976.

Fulbrook, Mary. *A History of Germany 1918–2008: The Divided Nation*, 3rd ed. West Sussex: Wiley-Blackwell, 2009.

Gaus, Günter. *Wo Deutschland liegt*. Hamburg: Hoffmann und Campe, 1983.

Giddens, Anthony. *The Third Way: The Renewal of Social Democracy*. Cambridge: Polity, 1998.

Gieseke, Jens. *Staatssicherheit und Gesellschaft: Studien zum Herrschaftsalltag in der DDR*. Göttingen: Vandenhoeck and Ruprecht, 2007.

Habermas, Jürgen. "Die Dialektik der Säkularisierung." *Blätter für deutsche und internationale Politik* 4 (2008): 33–46.

Hell, Julia. "Dissolution/Revolution: Uwe Tellkamp's post-89 Novel *Der Turm* and the Peculiar Configuration of the Public Sphere in the Late GDR," *Transformations of the Public Sphere*. Accessed July 23, 2010, at: http://publicsphere.ssrc.org/hell-uwe-tellkamps-post-89-novel-der-turm-and-the-peculiar-configuration-of-the-public-sphere-in-the-late-gdr/.

Jarausch, Konrad. "Care and Coercion: The GDR as Welfare Dictatorship." In *Dictatorship as Experience: Towards a Socio-Cultural History of the GDR*, ed. Konrad Jarausch. New York: Berghahn, 2001, 47–69.

———. "Germany 1989: A New Kind of Revolution." Accessed July 20, 2010, at: http://vimeo.com/9410601.

Jauss, Hans Robert. "Tradition, Innovation, and Aesthetic Experience." In *The Journal of Aesthetics and Art Criticism* 46, no. 3 (Spring 1988): 375–388.

Jirgl, Reinhard. "Theater ist Draußen." In *Die Nacht, in der die Mauer fiel: Schriftsteller erzählen vom 9. November 1989*, ed. Renatus Deckert. Frankfurt: Suhrkamp, 2009, 73–82.

Johnson, Uwe. *Mutmaßungen über Jakob*. Frankfurt a. M.; Suhrkamp, 1959.

Jünger, Ernst. "Die Totale Mobilmachung." *Sämtliche Werke, v. 7, Essays I*. Stuttgart: Klett-Cotta, 1980, 119–141.

Kemper, Peter, ed. *Der Trend zum Event*. Frankfurt a. M.: Suhrkamp, 2001.

Kenney, Padraic. *A Carnival of Revolution: Central Europe 1989*. Princeton, NJ: Princeton UP, 2002.

Kessler, Harry Graf. *Tagebücher, 1918–1937*, ed. Wolfgang Pfeiffer-Belli. Frankfurt: Insel, 1961.

Lange-Müller, Katja. "Bochum und Bohnsdorf." In *Die Nacht, in der die Mauer fiel: Schriftsteller erzählen vom 9. November 1989*, ed. Renatus Deckert. Frankfurt: Suhrkamp, 2009, 48–55.

Lukács, Georg. *Theory of the Novel*, trans. Anna Bostock. Cambridge: MIT Press, 1974.

Meuschel, Sigrid. *Legitimation und Parteiherrschaft in der DDR*. Frankfurt a. M.: Suhrkamp, 1992.

Müller, Heiner. *Der Auftrag*. In *Der Auftrag und andere Revolutionsstücke*, ed. Heiner Müller. Stuttgart: Reclam, 1988.

Norberg, Jakob. "Disappearing Socialism: Volker Braun's *Unvollendete Geschichte*." *Monatshefte* 102, no. 2 (2010): 177–191.

Palmowski, Jan. Inventing a Socialist Nation: Heimat and the Politics of Everyday Life in the GDR, 1945–1990. Cambridge: Cambridge UP, 2009.

Reagan, Ronald. "Tear Down this Wall." Speech delivered in West Berlin, June 12, 1987.

Robbins, Louise. *Louis Pasteur and the Hidden World of Microbes*. New York: Oxford UP, 2001.

Rorty, Richard. "The End of Leninism and History as Comic Frame." In *History and the Idea of Progress*, ed. Arthur M. Melzer, Jerry Weinberger, and M. Richard Zinman. Ithaca, NY: Cornell UP, 1995, 211–26.

Schneider, Peter. "Die Diktatur der Geschwindigkeit." In *Die Diktatur der Geschwindigkeit: Ausflüge, Zwischenrufe,* ed. Peter Schneider. Reinbeck: Rowohlt, 2000, 39–52.

Scribner, Charity. *Requiem for Communism*. Cambridge: MIT Press, 2003.

Sloterdijk, Peter. *Falls Europa erwacht*. Frankfurt a. M.: Suhrkamp, 1994.

———. "Die Revolution der gebenden Hand." *Frankfurter Allgemeine Zeitung*. June 13, 2009.

Stern, Fritz. *Five Germanys I Have Known*. New York: Farrar, Straus, and Giroux, 2006.

Tellkamp, Uwe. *Der Turm*. Frankfurt a. M.: Suhrkamp, 2008.

Tiryakian, Edward A. "Collective Effervescence, Social Change and Charisma: Durkheim, Weber and 1989," *International Sociology* 10, no. 3 (September 1995): 269–281.

10

Building Consensus: Painting and the Enlightenment Tradition in Post-Wall Germany

Anna M. Dempsey

No recent group of German painters has attracted as much global attention as East German born Neo Rauch (born 1960) and the younger generation of Western painters who studied with him at Academy of Visual Arts, Leipzig. According to Joachim Pissaro, chief curator of painting and sculpture at New York's Metropolitan Museum of Art, these artists have "taken the art world by storm."[1] Known as the New Leipzig School, they employ an illusionistic style that builds on the GDR's socialist-realist painting tradition, a convention that was once derided as propagandistic and derivative.[2] Rauch and his younger colleagues adapt this style by incorporating popular cultural references and modernist Western forms into their traditional illusionistic aesthetic. Like the previous generation of West German painters, such as Jörg Immendorf, Gerhard Richter, and Anselm Kiefer, the Leipzig artists reflect on Germany's complex past. As Stephanie D'Alessandro puts it, "For more than fifty years, German artists have struggled with such direct repercussions of the past, and . . . [with] the burden of the idea of history itself."[3] For these artists, however, this burden has largely been lifted. For post-Wall German painters, D'Alessandro concludes, "the war is no longer the limit and sole focus of historical consciousness—they are free to select from multiple pasts and use them to varying degrees in their work."[4]

Arthur Lubow, a *New York Times* art critic, asserts that the New Leipzig School employs a traditional painterly style in order to reflect "the disenchantment endemic to Germany, especially the former GDR."[5] Yet, as this chapter argues, their images are more than pessimistic reflections about post-Wall Germany. Rauch, Matthias Weischer, and Tim Eitel all participate in the contemporary cultural debates regarding the place of the individual and of Western Enlightenment tradition in a globalized world, where—as Jean Baudrillard provocatively concludes—"the [aesthetic] object is eviscerated of [its] substance and history."[6] The Leipzig painters employ an illusionistic Kantian-derived visual language in order to recuperate the painted object's history from its consignment to Baudrillard's hyperreal world of global commodity capitalism.[7] Enlightenment and classic German philosophy has often been caricatured as a systematic and rigid set of universal, rational rules applied by a transcendental subject to make sense of the phenomenal world. This assumption is misleading.[8] In the writings of Johann Wolfgang von Goethe and Friedrich von Schiller, reason operated as an organizing, interpretive framework for the disparate feelings, sensations, and impressions that confronted the individual.[9] Both writers, in turn, based their conclusions on Immanuel Kant's concept of practical reason.[10] For Kant, certain categories or *forms* of knowledge, including artistic language, enabled the individual to organize the multiple sense impressions that bombard the eye. During the early twentieth century, the German art historian Erwin Panofsky asserted that Renaissance linear perspective represented one of these organizing, Kantian forms. Indeed, Panofsky's conclusions influenced the development of modern art history.[11] As Keith Moxey articulates, ultimately perspectival construction became a "metaphor for knowledge" and an "epistemological guarantee for historical interpretation."[12] To the Western eye, it has allowed artists to create authentic windows into the past and the present.[13] During the twentieth century, this realist convention was appropriated and distorted by the National Socialists and then by the Communists to further each of their divergent ideological values. Despite their differences, officials in both political parties believed that artists should further the state's goals by creating idealized portraits of individuals—such as Stalin or Lenin—or nonspecific but heroic representations of ordinary workers who contribute to the government's aims.[14]

In the West, the realist style—and the universal humanist philosophy that underpinned it—was largely discarded because of its association with the fascist and nationalist upheavals of war. Poststructuralist critics rejected the notion of a transcendental, enlightened subject who was guided by a universal set of values to which all humankind could subscribe. Michel Foucault, in his seminal *Discipline and Punish*, argued that the human subject is formed by cultural discursive practices embedded in institutional power relations.[15] Undoubtedly, the socialist-realist art of the Communists and Fascists supported his claim. Thus, Foucault declared that there is no singular rational truth—whether visual, moral, historical, or ethical—that underpins knowledge and understanding. As anthropologist Donna Haraway states, our awareness and knowledge of the world is "situated" within the social circumstances through which we have acquired it.[16] For poststructuralist art historians and critics, such as Norman Bryson, all realist imagery cannot provide us with a window to the past or to the present because artworks are coded with the values of the particular social and cultural conditions under which they have been created.[17]

The German philosopher and sociologist Jürgen Habermas and American art historian Barbara Stafford have opposed many of the poststructuralists' positions. During the 1980s, Habermas famously argued that Foucault's rejection of universal consensus and his espousal of the contextual relativity of meaning was conservative and nihilistic.[18] While Habermas did not support Kant's belief in the transcendental subject, he did subscribe to Kant's notion of the unifying concept of reason. For Habermas, this meant that judgment must be a product of civic consensus.[19] Stafford essentially supports Habermas' conclusions in her analyses of textual and visual art. She contends that the "hardening" of the subjective/objective dualism that "began with the Jena romantics" has led to our contemporary "mosaic society in which arguing groups exclusively seek to promote their own separate interests."[20] She observes that Goethe dismissed the "romantics' glorification of the chaotic fragment" because the writer believed that the unification—rather than the separation—of disparate parts is far more efficacious for the production of genuine art.[21]

The Leipzig artists—especially Rauch—reflect on these cultural debates that animate contemporary cultural criticism, as I argue in this chapter. Given that all three studied traditional painting techniques at the Leipzig Academy, it is certainly not surprising that their work is informed by the aesthetic conventions associated with German classic culture and philosophy. Nevertheless, these painters do not simply ape the mimetic conventions of their artistic predecessors. In their works, they reference Greenbergian abstract aesthetics and contemporary popular culture in order to prompt the viewer to re-view the values associated with German philosophical and cultural traditions.[22] Borrowing from Angelika Rauch, we might regard their use of tradition as the "facilitation of remembrance."[23] In an extensive analysis of two of Rauch's works and a briefer engagement with the images of his younger colleagues, I argue that the Leipzig artists employ a representational aesthetic to prompt the viewer to reflect on how tradition continues to inform the present—and how and whether it might help us reframe the future.

Neo Rauch and German Classic Aesthetic and Cultural Tradition

During the past decade, Neo Rauch has emerged as an international painting superstar. By 2002, as Gregory Volk asserted, "Rauch very quickly became crucial for top collections" around the world.[24] This included Myra and Donald Rubell, who loaned some of Rauch's and other Leipzig artists' works for a 2004 traveling exhibition titled *Life after Death: New Leipzig Painting from the Rubell Family Collection*. In 2007, the Metropolitan Museum of Art in New York staged an exhibition of Rauch's work titled "Para," a show that helped cement his international reputation. By 2010, Stefan Nicola posited that Rauch was "the undisputed star of the German art scene."[25] Indeed, during the summer of 2010, he received the unusual honor of a dual-venue career retrospective at the Museum der Bildenden Künste in Leipzig and at the Alte Pinakothek in Munich.

Despite these accolades, some contemporary (and earlier) critics have been less than enthusiastic about his recent work. In 1993, Roberta Smith of the *New York Times* stated that Neo Rauch's "intriguing" paintings exhibited "extraordinary paint handling"[26] but had concluded by 2007 that Rauch's "figurative style ha[d] become as predictable as a coloring book's . . . He seems to have settled prematurely into a groove, and a middlebrow one at that."[27] Henry Lehmann, in the November 4, 2006, edition of the *Montreal Gazette*, stated that art world "fads" are responsible for Neo Rauch's star status while Karen Rosenberg of the *New York Times* argued that "Mr. Rauch's paintings [at the Metropolitan Museum of Art] looked static and hemmed in by history."[28]

Some of this criticism has occurred because of Rauch's visual aesthetic. Smith's conclusion that Rauch's style is "predictable" and Peter Schjeldahl's that it is "conservative"[29] reflect both Western critics' dismissals of illusionist, representational painting in favor of the avant-garde exploration of new visual form.[30] Given the influence of Panofsky's neo-Kantian aesthetic philosophy on the practice of modern art history, not surprisingly some critics also assume that an educated viewer should be able to uncover the meaning of Rauch's illusionistic artwork.[31] Schjeldahl, for example, states that Rauch displays a great "technical mastery" of his medium but that his paintings are "inscrutable." Yet, paradoxically, he finds a shadow of meaning in the artist's work. Schejeldahl suggests that there is something apocalyptic about these images:

> Rauch's redolences of Socialist Realism are like a dead-virus vaccine: a virulence deprived of its power to sicken and, thereby, offending sickness. Violence and danger there may be. People are prone to madness . . . I would like to despise the artist for this, but his visual poetry is too persuasive. Present day reality is a lot more like one of his pictures than I wish it were.[32]

Are his images, as this critic suggests, vague pessimistic reflections on contemporary culture? Or are they, as Smith has concluded, displays of color and form that are easily digested by a "middlebrow" audience? Although Schejeldahl correctly states that we cannot decipher one singular meaning, on closer inspection we will see that Rauch's work is a collage of multiple, minivisual narratives and that his images do comment on contemporary German culture.

In *Vorführung* (Fig. 10.1), the title of which could be interpreted as a display or theater performance, Rauch depicts an assortment of contemporary and historical figures gathered together in a traditional German landscape setting. Like the Baroque and Neoclassical painters of the seventeenth and eighteenth centuries, he arranges them on a narrow stage and employs a falling telephone pole/tree log to open the theater curtain. On the stage, we first see a non-Western woman crowned with a garland of bright yellow flowers followed by an open-mouthed gentleman wearing a ruffled shirt, a top-hatted Biedermeier dandy/circus impresario, two European women in cold war GDR garb, and a crouched horned figure that could be from Shakespeare's *A Midsummer Night's Dream*. The artist flanks these individuals with a playful yellow "seal" balancing a block on its nose and a pair of swooning yellow ducks. Like Brueghel's image of *Children's Games* (1560) or Bosch's *The Garden of Earthly Delights* (1504), Rauch depicts a carnivalesque world in which conventional rules are broken and the comic and the tragic are conjoined. Are the buttery yellow sunflowers on the woman's wrists an adornment or manacles? Are they both? Similarly, why do two figures wield threatening weapons that morph into a pencil or a paintbrush? Just as it is unclear as to what damage these implements might do, it is difficult to determine what narrative Rauch is illustrating or in what time period it might occur.

As Hans-Werner Schmidt, director of the Museum der Bildenden Künste in Leipzig, writes, "In Rauch, the site of the canvas becomes a crystallization point for all those images that circulate in the pictorial memory without boundary or restraint and that form ever new

Figure 10.1 Neo Rauch, *Vorführung*, 2006

Note: © 2011 Artists Rights Society (ARS), New York / VG Bild-Kunst, Bonn.
Source: Courtesy Galerie EIGEN + ART Leipzig/Berlin and David Zwirner, New York.

constellations as they await dramaturgical rendering."[33] The image functions as a kind of repository onto which cultural memories, dreams, and individual imaginings are suspended in a theatrical pastiche. Which minidrama comes to life depends upon the viewer.

Rauch has drawn his inspiration from many sources and has, to some extent, created a personal art-historical memory collage. His flattening, dynamic treatment of space is reminiscent of the works of Paul Cezanne, Max Beckmann, and Pablo Picasso, while his delicate color treatment reflects his knowledge of Renaissance masters such as Lucas Cranach.[34] At the same time, the cartoonish figures, speech bubbles, and garish pop-like colors illuminate his debt to American pop artists Roy Lichtenstein and to comic-book graphic designers. That is, Rauch amalgamates avant-garde modernist spatial configurations, traditional realist forms, and childhood popular characters into a dynamic theatrical world. Petra Lewey and Klaus Fischer suggest he "translates this mixture of subjective codes and familiar clichés of our past and present into expressive painterly color harmonies in a manner as commanding as it is vexing."[35]

Lewey and Fischer correctly state that the lime and magenta "color harmonies" command the viewer's attention. Moreover, color functions as a visual lure. The artist leads the eye diagonally from the nineteenth-century gabled structures in the upper left down to the prostrate ducks on the lower right. We stop here, poised between the representational figures and the swirling magenta field of abstract color. He does so, I would argue, to highlight his aesthetic balancing of the traditional realism of the Leipzig School and the abstract modernism of the pre-Wende West. His work, in fact, functions as a metaphorical bridge between these traditions. This type of balance between aesthetic form and illusionary content reflects what Michael Ann Holly refers to as a "settlement (*Auseinandersetzung*) between opposing values"—and is, moreover, a visual encapsulation of traditional art-historical interpretation.[36] At the same time, we could also regard this image as an ironic comment on the efficacy of this legacy. To determine which might be a more persuasive interpretation, we have to look more closely at the image and the German traditions that animate it.

In the early twentieth century, German-Jewish art historians Aby Warburg and Erwin Panofsky argued that the balance between form and content, between the rational known and irrational unknown is fraught with tension. Multiple artistic meanings (*Sinne*) erupt from this tense balancing.[37] While these early art historians believed that it was possible for educated viewers to rationally agree on a generally accepted meaning behind a work of art,[38] postmodernist critics such as Foucault regarded this view as illustrative of the institutionalized Western discourses of the time.[39] In Rauch's work, we see a shifting balance between forms and between form and narrative content as though he is illuminating the tensions between traditional and poststructuralist interpretations of the work of art. His collage of abstract and illusionistic forms—and traditional and contemporary content—suggests that the artist refuses to become trapped into choosing between the aesthetic he learned at the Academy of Visual Arts, Leipzig, or one that disavows conventional mimetic illusionism. This refusal, I contend, is manifest in the painting itself.

Formally, the representational stability of the nineteenth-century "Lübeck" façade seems to function as a spatial anchor for the image.[40] On the other hand, as next in line, it too may suffer the fate of the towers that are about to fall over into the magenta abyss. Yet the left-leaning overturned roof offsets the instability of these toppling towers. Nevertheless, to ensure that we do not simply see this as a balanced image, Rauch adds a rather odd rooftop "hook" that appears to "lift" up one of the central figures. The hook and the dynamic spatial planes, like the smoke seal and prostrate ducks, suggest that our traditional view of the real is precariously balanced and easily upended.

As with his construction of space, the artist's painted figures are not limited by conventional illusionistic aesthetics or by assumed biological definitions of what it means to be human. Like Salvador Dali's and Francis Bacon's surreal paintings or Haraway's theoretical cyborgs, Rauch's figures melt into other human and nonhuman forms.[41] One man's arm, for example, morphs into a coiling reptile, while the fuschia-clad central individual who thrusts a red-tipped paintbrush into the seated violet-robed character is about to disappear into a puff of yellow. That is, these illusionistic figures occupy an intangible, unfixed body/world that is about to dissolve into a seductive purple abyss.

Lewey and Fischer maintain that Germany's classic Weimar tradition is also about to disappear into the abstract, mauve impressionistic haze. They argue that "Assembled tableau-vivant-like on this painted stage are all those who participated in fulfilling the young Schiller's hope for wisdom and moral education through art. Yet, they fail to notice that these ideals are on the verge—much like the German monuments—of plunging into the abyss."[42] Clearly, the artist's visual allusions to classic German cultural tradition buttress this interpretation. Moreover, the skull-capped figure who appears to be sewing the "Schillerian" figure's mouth shut, points to the possibility that this influential writer's words no longer have a receptive audience.[43] The woman in modern dress, who holds up a book as she faces the nineteenth-century German edifice and mountainscape, appears to be making a last ditch effort to reclaim the place of tradition for the global present. Her position near the abstracted purple space suggests she and the book could soon disappear into the void as Lewey and Fischer suggest. In this regard, *Vorführung* visualizes our contemporary post-Wall, post-9/11 world where borders are permeable and the subject's sense of reality is lost to the spectacularly colored image or screen.

This interpretation could support Peter Schejeldahl's conclusion that Rauch is essentially a conservative painter with a pessimistic view of our contemporary world: "Conservatism takes grim, or not so grim, satisfaction in demonstrations of human folly. It has a major pictorial philosopher in Rauch, who calmly implicates himself, and art, in a vision of futility as destiny."[44] Is Rauch, as Schejeldahl suggests, a conservative painter who espouses a traditional view of image-making as a last cultural gasp in a post-Wall depersonalized present?

This hypothesis brings us back to the skull-capped gentleman who is pulling a string through or sewing the "Schillerian" figure's mouth shut. Although it is unclear exactly who this individual might be, the head-covering and noncontemporary dress indicate he might be a metaphor for nineteenth-century Jewish culture and its connection to German

Enlightenment tradition—specifically the notion of *Bildung*, the belief in the rational individual's ability to overcome superstition through cultural education.[45] For Johann Gottfried von Herder, a philosopher and writer who influenced Goethe's classic aesthetic theory, this concept was also associated with the political development of a people and eventually of the German nation.[46] According to historian George L. Mosse, political *Bildung* "transcended all differences of nationality and religion" and was a cornerstone for not only German unification but for German-Jewish assimilation and emancipation.[47] Is Rauch's Jewish figure then a metaphor for the interconnection between German-Jewish culture and German classic traditions? At the same time, do the skull-capped figure and the prostrate "Schiller" also reference the perversion of universal cosmopolitan ideals first by the National Socialists and later by the GDR Communists? At the very least, it would seem Rauch espouses a post-structuralist position that idealist certainty is no longer applicable in a world that commits genocidal atrocities.

Obviously, skepticism about universal values is not unique to post-World War II cultural critics. During the late nineteenth and early twentieth centuries, while philosophers Hermann Cohen and Ernst Cassirer and art historians Aby Warburg and Erwin Panofsky believed in the potential of art to uplift and to contain the "Dionysian" forces that could potentially destroy civilizations,[48] others from Friedrich Nietzsche[49] to Walter Benjamin[50] warned of its destructive power. Similar debates have preoccupied the late twentieth and early twenty-first centuries. According to Foucault, "criticism is no longer going to be practiced in the search for formal structures with universal value . . . [because the Kantian] foundation in utopian rationale had totalitarian implications."[51] Habermas famously questioned Foucault's assumptions. Like the German-Jewish philosophers before him, he believed that Kantian universal constructs could be adapted to promote civic consensus and that fear of the nationalist or anti-Semitic past should not stand in the way of the formation of a democratic collective.[52]

Peter Uwe Hohendahl has suggested that "Habermas' theory . . . [which] contained a superior understanding of the problematic of the welfare state and its impact on the public sphere . . . was predicated on a questionable normative notion of a pure and unified bourgeois public sphere."[53] Habermas insists, however, that civic consensus is not the same as assimilation and that cultural particularity can be part of a collective civic society. In a 2010 editorial for the *New York Times*, he stated that post-Wall Europeans should display "a resoluteness and cooperative spirit. Democracy depends on the belief of the people that there is some scope left for collectively shaping a challenging future."[54] Other contemporary critics, like Habermas, also disagree with the poststructuralist view of our post-Wall culture. Stafford, who appears to share his position, suggests we could equate Enlightenment consensus with the analogic. She states that human creativity "permits the mind to connect disparate things in analogic form . . . to jump through space and time to discover continuities."[55] She argues that, given "the current fragmentation of social discourse the inability to reach out and build a consensus on anything that matters, analogy's double avoidance of self-sameness and total estrangement again seems pertinent."[56] Public art may be one way to shape this consensus.

In *Vorführung*, Rauch's cast of characters includes multiple historical figures, a pop seal, speech balloons, and a non-Western woman who towers above the display like a praying Madonna. They suggest an imaginative arrangement of the disparate forms that characterize Stafford's analogies and Habermas' public collective. Moreover, Rauch has created a visual tableau, in which he metaphorically materializes Germany's pasts and places them beside its present. By staging them together, we are forced to think about their possible connections as well as find a balance between the traditional past and the post-Wall present.

Rauch asserts, "I don't really want to celebrate breakdown, the total emptying of meaning, the maximum extreme inside the square of the canvas; rather, I want to find a formula that enables us to have complete control over the incomprehensible, the horrible, without it being our undoing. Painting is a grand, controlling gesture. I'm trying to establish control over the uncontrollable things of this world."[57] His statement recalls the theories of the neo-Kantian German art historians and philosophers who developed the study of art history in the West and the contemporary critics who still believe in the applicability of this classic tradition for the present. That is, by assembling forms that reference colonialism, GDR communism, and contemporary terror onto the painted stage, the artist forces us to reconcile the past with all its tragedies and possibilities. In the public gallery, he engages viewers in a dialogue with the image and with each other about what the past—both its failures and its promises—can offer for the future.

What artist Michaël Borremann describes as Rauch's traditional or "detached universality" is also evident in *Ordnungshüter* (Keepers of Order) (Fig. 10.2).[58] As in *Vorführung*, the spectator sits before a set of staged events as though he or she were watching multiple plays at a dinner theater with windows that reflect the night sky and a waiter to take a drink order. Yet our separation from the events unfolding before us is not absolute. Rauch's kaleidoscopic spaces should be seen, as Werner Hofmann notes, as an "intricate interlocking of segmented spaces" that

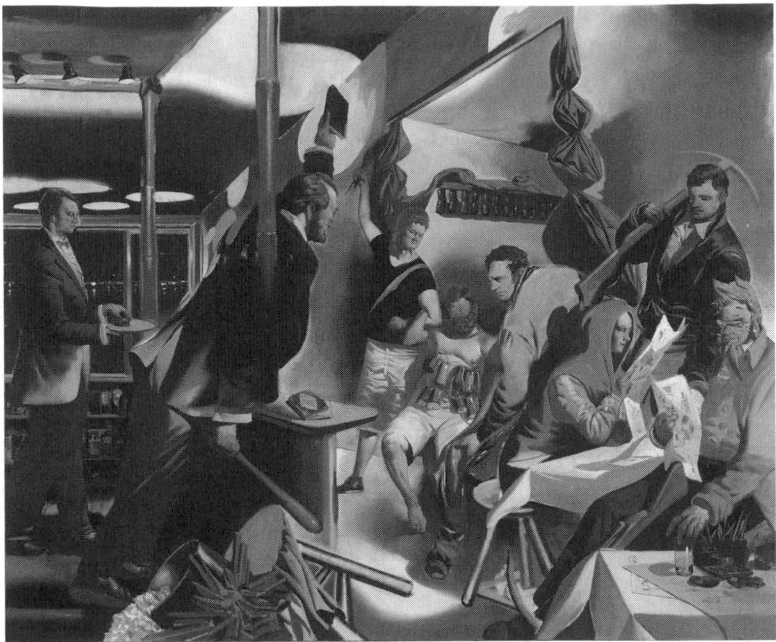

Figure 10.2 Neo Rauch, *Ordnungshüter*, 2008

Note: © 2011 Artists Rights Society (ARS), New York / VG Bild-Kunst, Bonn.
Source: Courtesy Galerie EIGEN + ART Leipzig/Berlin and David Zwirner, New York.

suggest multiple "plots."[59] In these "plots," the artist visually encodes imagined selections from the human history of terror and violence.

While this painting references the German past, it does so obliquely. Rauch's figures could be German, or indeed from any other European country. Though the artist's oddly clad, weapon-wielding individuals recall the idealized workers of GDR painters Werner Tübke and Walter Womacha and Jean Francois Millet's early-nineteenth-century noble farmers, Rauch's figures parody these earlier artists' heroic representations. The nineteenth-century muscular worker, who carries an implement that could be a pickax with a rifle handle or possibly a fourteenth-century crossbow without its strings, appears to emerge from a cinematiclike haze. Yet no one, including the spectacled Biedermeier figure, notices as he marches by. On another "stage," a woman in pink sneakers raises a victory banner—an allusion to the GDR's public parades—as she clutches the arm of the explosive-laden figure. This is no victory, however. With faces whose features and color seem to be fading, the woman and the bound man may soon disappear and with them the threat, the unfulfilled promises, and the material memories associated with the GDR. We should regard this scene, and indeed all the vignettes in this image, as memory fragments strewn together as if in a dream.

By placing these individuals in a tableau with other historical figures, such as the "medieval" newspaper-reading monk, Rauch also tangibly locates GDR history as one moment in the other moments of German and of European histories. The artist presents us with a collective historical narrative, one in which the horrific and the comic unfold before our eyes. In other words, Rauch connects our "nightmarish" present to other histories that are both frightening and banal.

How these disparate narratives interconnect is difficult to decipher. For example, a man with a book and a club approaches the restrained seated figure as if to force him to accept a written text—although what that might be is unclear. "In *Ordnungshüter*," Rudij Bergmann writes, "Neo Rauch has assembled his painting's figures in a wicked burlesque of terrorism and fanaticism. It is a central work of political painting whose coded subject is the catastrophic world with its civilizing disruptions."[60] Clearly, with its stage within a stage setting, the image is a rather sly representation of human attempts to civilize with blunt force—a kind of perverse legacy of universal Enlightenment values. It would seem the artist hints an impending catastrophe will occur because these values are about to be jettisoned.

Nevertheless, I would argue that the image is more than a "wicked" conflation of the past with the contemporary dehumanizing post-Wall present. Rauch's visual language contradicts such a singular reading of *Ordnungshüter*. Although the centrally seated character with dynamite ringed around his waist appears ready to blow up himself and all those around him, on closer inspection we see this is not possible. Both he and his companions occupy distinct spatial segments. The figures, either by themselves or in small groups, inhabit a stage within a stage. Thus, the club-carrying figure can hardly do any damage. Similarly, the brushes in the red-sandaled figure's hand are also not a weapon but a reminder that art can inspire enlightenment as well as terror. Like Kant, Cassirer, and Panofsky before him, Rauch reminds us that artworks help us make sense of the world. They can also, as Benjamin and later Foucault warned, anaesthetize us to the dangerous power struggles that limit human freedom. By employing traditional forms and content, Rauch also claims we might look to the past to help us reshape our isolated, often terrifying, post-Wall present. Indeed, the non-Western contemplative Madonna of *Vorführung*, though metaphorically chained to her colonial-gendered past, transcends it and the potential destruction all around her. Like the geometrically incised cube in the foreground—a cube whose shape and tree-framed garden placement suggests the *Altar to Agathe Tyche* (1777) at Goethe's home in Weimar—the female figure anchors the image and may even halt its possible implosion. The playful darts that Rauch "throws" at the foregrounded cube suggest, however, this may be a wistful, nostalgic illusion.

Matthias Weischer: Tradition and Memories of Home

Like his teacher at the Academy of Visual Arts, Leipzig, Matthias Weischer (born 1973) employs traditional GDR painting conventions. In contrast to Rauch, he paints depopulated architectural landscapes and interiors that are punctuated with material remnants and dreams of their former residents. In *Madonna* (Fig. 10.3), we see a cozy, bourgeois interior replete with the photographs, images, and heavy drapes that demarcate this space as a "living" room or parlor. On closer inspection, however, this painting seems to be a compilation of numerous memory corners. Rather than a single interior, the artist composes a collage of distinct and faded objects pulled together from numerous historical periods. Some chairs, which retain only their bare outlines, seem to be literally disappearing before our eyes. Others are covered with old-fashioned upholstery that locks them into another era. Like the Schillerian and bent-over horned figures from Rauch's *Vorführung*, these are objects that seem to have lingered past their historical time periods.

Weischer arranges this collection as though it were an array of paraphernalia in a fading photograph. On the one hand, the brown-ochre walls and the sculptural busts suggest a nineteenth-century interior aesthetic. On the other, the image is somewhat reminiscent of Wolfgang Becker's bedroom mise-en-scène in *Goodbye Lenin!* (2003). Weischer's painting appears at first to be a visual metaphor for home, particularly for many of the residents of the former GDR. Paul Betts rightfully notes that it may seem ironic that East German "material culture" has assumed a singular import in the "memory production" of GDR history.[61] GDR consumer objects are, according to Betts, metaphors for a dream deferred. He argues that "[t]hese formerly disdained articles suddenly became material reminders of a vanished world, newly idealized 'fragments of a crumbled identity.'"[62] Though Weischer has preserved representations of the faded remnants of GDR identity, the image is not just a nostalgic paean to this vanishing culture.

Like Rauch, the artist also references other German and Western art-historical traditions. In particular, realist nineteenth-century painting

Figure 10.3 Matthias Weischer, *Madonna*, 2005

Note: © 2011 Artists Rights Society (ARS), New York / VG Bild-Kunst, Bonn.
Source: Courtesy Galerie EIGEN + ART Leipzig/Berlin.

conventions and modern photographic allusions animate this image. Weischer claims this and his other "brown" paintings "are scenes of nineteenth-century studios, based on photographs of painter's studios."[63] Certainly, the inclusion of illusionistic sculptures, browned photographic portraits, and Arcadian landscape paintings suggest this could be just such an artist's atelier. Even the rather odd Madonna-like figure in the center could be a comic reference to an artist's model or to a canvas still in progress. Yet Weischer's insertion of the "sculpted" pillow and star arrangement points to the modernist, playful interiors that Ray and Charles Eames created in the United States in the 1950s.[64] Weischer, like Rauch, stages memory but uses objects rather than people. He incorporates visual allusions to the GDR alongside those from the pre-Wende and the postmodern German present as though he refuses to allow his work to be placed in any conventional critical category.

Weischer, moreover, conjoins realist and abstract spatial forms through his use of a visual grid. The artist's imposition of gridlike lines are a reference to the rationalization of pictorial space—to the notion that artists organize visual forms according to an intellectual rational construct that mediates between the outside world and our subjective experience of it. Renaissance and later realist and socialist-realist artists employed a similar grid to create illusionistic representations. Weischer's depiction of this art-historical trope, along with his inclusion of nineteenth-century objects and paintings, could be construed as a conservative effort to reclaim a German and Western aesthetic tradition that has played a significant role in German visual culture for the past five hundred years. His situation of the grid within a spatially ambiguous setting reminds us that *Madonna* may also be a postmodern ironic reflection on this traditional art-making process. This doubling of meaning is encapsulated by the simple child's alphabet block that lies in the foreground. While the alphabetic incisions recall the signature of the celebrated German Renaissance painter Albrecht Dürer, the cube is also a reference to the modernist aesthetic—to the belief that a gallery space or "white cube"[65] can neutrally frame a work of art. In other words, like Rauch, Weischer dissolves the boundary between the modern and the traditional. Though this picture is a postmodern pastiche, its resemblance to an early sepia photograph may prompt a contemporary viewer to think about the significance of tradition. Indeed, like Roland Barthes's photograph of his mother, this painting represents an arrested, brittle image of memories and traditions that may soon fade away.[66]

Memling (Fig. 10.4) would seem to be an entirely different work. Rather than a faded photograph-like interior, we see a bright, cheerful room in which disparate objects and partially painted canvasses are scattered about as though they are part of a theatrical stage set that is in the process of being torn down. According to Weischer, "Usually I start with the space; the structure of the space. I do it the way one would build a house. I often start with the walls, then the interior objects, and finally the images on the walls."[67] While this image appears to be a simple depiction of one stage of the artistic process, the artist's jarring spatial arrangement negates this obvious conclusion.

In *Memling*, Weischer focuses on the painting as a framed reality by including several partially painted "canvasses." Given that he situates these framed canvasses within a picture plane that dynamically shifts between the two and three dimensional—as though the actual frame is about to be torn asunder—the artist may be questioning the mimetic tradition that he

Figure 10.4 Matthias Weischer, *Memling*, 2006

Note: © 2011 Artists Rights Society (ARS), New York / VG Bild-Kunst, Bonn.
Source: Courtesy Galerie EIGEN + ART Leipzig/Berlin.

learned at the Academy of Visual Arts, Leipzig. At the very least, Weischer's framing of numerous frames, asks us to think about painted illusionary realities. Jacques Derrida defines this purposeful framing or screening of reality as a *parergon*, a "framing of the frame."[68] Film theorist Patrick Fuery states, "One of the driving forces in Derrida's study is the idea that the space of the *parergon* has a particular relation to meaning/truth, one which operates outside of it and is also part of it."[69] Weischer's repeated use of a frame underlines Derrida's conclusion that truth/reality is only partially perceptible and never fixed. Nevertheless, by "naming" this painting after the Northern Renaissance artist Hans Memling, Weischer also reminds us that humanist and classic cultural traditions have long helped us to rationally make sense of the world.[70] Moreover, the outline of a barely visible copy of an actual Madonna by Hans Memling (in *Memling*) and the faded outlines of bourgeois GDR chairs (in *Madonna*) suggest these traditions are disappearing. But by materializing them, or as Stafford puts it, by "putting the visible into [an analogic] relationship with the invisible [or disappearing]," he may ensure their survival.[71]

Tim Eitel: The Contemporary and the Evisceration of Tradition

Of the three artists discussed in this chapter, Tim Eitel (born 1971) might be regarded as the one who has pushed the Leipzig illusionist aesthetic to its photorealistic extreme. As with the twentieth-century English painter Francis Bacon, who influenced and inspired him, Eitel takes the old master painterly style and iconography as his point of departure.[72] In contrast to Bacon who produced skeletal, Gothic-like transformations of Velázquez's *Pope Innocent III*, Eitel's illusionistic canvasses appear to be reflections on a postmodern isolation with roots in the Romantic rather than the classic tradition. His figures, which are frozen in space and time, are reminiscent of Caspar David Friedrich's helpless individuals who stand awestruck before an overpowering nature.

Stafford, in her analysis of the theory of resemblance, stated that Romantics such as Friedrich produced images that undercut the analogizing of the painters of the Enlightenment—what Habermas might refer to as rupture with a collectivist ethic. For example, she argues it was "Friedrich's coldly crystalline *Shipwreck* [1823] that best instantiated the disanalogical 'laminated' style . . . [as demonstrated by] the bleak scene, dominated by a fractured sheet of ice, [which] mimicked upheaved geological strata that 'lie alongside each other' without ever merging."[73] We see similar cold, hard geometric spaces in Eitel's *Boot (Boat,* Fig. 10.5*)*. Though painted in a variety of muted blues, the river/floor's and sky/walls' sharply delineated edges fragment the enigmatic landscape into distinct, nonintersecting spatial planes—clearly reminiscent of Friedrich's iceberg shards.[74] Eitel inserts his figures into this denatured architectural landscape and locks them into a crystalline volume as though to protect them from falling over the edge. With their backs to us, they pause before an unknown void. Given that the figures in this anonymous spatial setting wear nondescript contemporary dress, we could assume we might be viewing a single scene from a science-fictional film or a hyperreal video game whose end we do not yet know. The isolated figures could be anywhere in his melancholic, hyperreal representation of post-Wall contemporary culture.

Because their backs are to us, we identify with the isolated figures who gaze out at this abstracted, unfathomable world.[75] In this image, Eitel has created a space in which memory and tradition have been eviscerated. He employs a traditional realist style to depict a world without borders—a self-contained individualized space in which the communal public sphere has vanished. In a sense, this image is an exemplification of Kant's sublime, which Stafford argues "prepared the ground for th[e] insurmountable division" between the abstract and the mimetic and thus "the pessimistic breakdown of the Enlightenment's progressive belief in the force of intelligence."[76]

Borrowing from Stafford, this and Eitel's other images could be regarded as "disanalogic," melancholic, and sublime reflections on the

Figure 10.5 Tim Eitel, *Boot*, 2004

Note: © 2011 Artists Rights Society (ARS), New York / VG Bild-Kunst, Bonn.

Source: Courtesy Galerie EIGEN + ART Leipzig/Berlin.

isolated individual. In contrast to Rauch's and Weischer's work, *Boot* largely rejects tradition and its "facilitation of remembrance."[77] That is, Eitel is not a "latent" romantic who produces awe-inspiring landscapes.[78] Like Rauch and Weischer, he prompts us to ask questions. Do the geometric sky-walls in *Boot* force us to think about our transformation of nature into an ordered, rationalized space? Indeed, are we looking at a window onto our sanitized, global-capitalized order? David Clark cogently argues that "capitalism has a tendency to turn all places into [an] 'abstract space,'" which is "simultaneously homogenized and functionalized."[79] Yet Eitel's homogenized, abstracted space is exactly what Bauhaus architects Walter Gropius and Mies van der Rohe had envisioned for the modern city—a vision that GDR planners ultimately realized with their *Plattenbau* construction during the 1960s and 1970s. In other words, Eitel's hyperreal works obliquely reference modernist German and GDR utopian traditions. In contrast to Rauch and Weischer,

Eitel empties these realist forms of any clear content. His exquisitely painted canvasses cannibalize traditional meaning and compel us to think about why it is absent.

Conclusion

Rauch and Weischer attempt, as the former notes about his own art, to "recuperate Germany's distant pasts."[80] Eitel, on the other hand, eviscerates the past in favor of a sublime present—one that lures the viewer into a beautiful abyss. Certainly, visual art can anaesthetize as well as politically engage the viewer. Cultural representations can reify rather than reconfigure or subvert dominant norms and cultural traditions. Rauch and Weischer are aware of this fact and confront German and Western viewers with both possibilities. If the disparate traditional works of all three artists are viewed together in a public space—what Stafford might refer to as an affirming collective gesture—a useful debate about German culture and memory would inevitably ensue. As Carol Duncan suggests, the museum "as a form of public space," can represent a place "in which a community may test, examine, and imaginatively live both older truths and possibilities for new ones."[81] In other words, whether Rauch's, Eitel's, or Weischer's works can reframe the public debate about German culture and memory depends on how these canvasses engage viewers with the images and with each other in what Habermas would regard as a genuine public discussion.

Notes

1. Quoted in Arthur Lubow, "The Leipzig School," in the *New York Times* (January 8, 2008), http://www.nytimes.com/2006/01/08/magazine/08leipzig.html?scp=8&sq=neo%20rauch&st=cse. Accessed March 10, 2010.
2. Realistic art, the category under which socialist realism falls, represents as Linda Nochlin states "a highly problematic concept of reality" despite the fact that its "aim was to give a truthful, objective and impartial representation of the real world." See Linda Nochlin, *Realism* (Harmondsworth and Baltimore: Penguin Books, 1971), 9. While realistic art is generally associated with the illusionistic, naturalistic images of everyday life in the middle of the nineteenth century, this artistic movement had its roots in Renaissance perspectival painting techniques. Socialist-realist artists, in turn, adapted the illusionistic forms of their nineteenth century and Renaissance predecessors in their efforts to create works that represented their versions of reality.

   Socialist realism is also not the same as social realism—although both are associated with illusionism. The latter depicts the supposedly actual, everyday world of "ordinary" people. In the early twentieth century, social-realist artists, such as the American painter John Sloan, represented the gritty streets of the New York streetwalker while avant-garde painters like Picasso explored the formal constructed nature of artistic space. In Germany, the social realist or new objectivity (*Neue Sachlichkeit*) painter Otto Dix depicted the horrors associated with war. By contrast, socialist-realist art is associated with the idealized, illusionistic art of the Soviet Union and its satellites. Though the Soviet Union initially encouraged the formalist explorations of avant-garde artists, in 1932 Stalin's government issued "On the Reconstruction of Literary and Art," which decreed that art should celebrate the workers and the state. The conjoining of recognizable visual forms with socialist political ideology eventually became what we now term socialist realism—the artistic expression that was encouraged in the Soviet Union, the GDR, and other Communist/socialist countries. Nevertheless, it is important to note that GDR "socialist-realist" painters also built upon the social-realist tradition of artists such as Otto Dix and the Expressionist painter Max Beckmann. See Matthew Bown's *Art under Stalin* (New York: Holmes and Meier, 1991) and *Bildende Kunst in Ost Europa im 20 Jahrhundert: Art in Eastern Europe in the 20th Century*, ed. Hans-Jürgen Drengenberg (Berlin: Berlin Verlag, Arno Spitz, 1991).

3. Stephanie D'Alessandro, "History by Degrees: The Place of the Past in Contemporary German Art," *Art Institute of Chicago Museum Studies* 28, no. 1 (2002): 66.
4. D'Alessandro, "History by Degrees," 66.
5. Lubow, "The Leipzig School."
6. Jean Baudrillard, *For a Critique of the Political Economy of the Sign*, trans. Charles Levin (St. Louis: Telos Press, 1981), 93.
7. For an insightful analysis of the left-leaning poststructuralist critics'—including Baudrillard's—evaluations of cinematic images in contemporary culture, see Anne Kibbey, *Theory of the Image: Capitalism, Contemporary Film, and Women* (Bloomington and Indianapolis: Indiana University Press, 2005).
8. Frederick C. Beiser in his *Diotima's Children* attempts to recuperate enlightenment rationalism from this oversimplification. Beiser, *Diotima's Children: German Aesthetic Rationalism from Leibniz to Lessing* (Cambridge: Oxford University Press, 2009).
9. See Friedrich Schiller, *On the Aesthetic Education of Man in a Series of Letters*, trans. Reginald Snell (New Haven, CT: Yale University Press, 1954). See Johann Wolfgang von Goethe, *Elective Affinities: A Novel*, trans. Elizabeth Mayer and Louise Bogan (Chicago: Henry Regnery, 1963).
10. Immanuel Kant, *The Critique of Judgment*, trans. J. H. Bernard (New York: Hafner, 1951). For a good introduction to Kant and the role of reason in his moral philosophy, see Garrath Williams, "Kant's Account of Reason," in *The Stanford Encyclopedia of Philosophy, ed.* Edward N. Zalta (Summer 2009); available online at the following URL address: http://plato.stanford.edu/archives/sum2009/entries/kant-reason.

11. For an excellent review of the impact of Panofsky's neo-Kantian philosophy of Art History, see Michael Ann Holly, *Panofsky and the Foundations of Art History,* (Ithaca, NY, and London: Cornell University Press, 1984).
12. Keith Moxey, "Perspective, Panofsky, and the Philosophy of History," *New Literary History* 26, no. 4 (Autumn 1995): 776.
13. Holly, in *Panofsky* states that "perspective developed during the Renaissance, has in fact, taught us how to see," 131. The association of perspectival construction with the "real" is even evident today in video games and digitally enhanced films. See Lev Manovich, *The Language of New Media* (Cambridge, MA: MIT Press, 2000).
14. On Soviet Art, see note 2. On art of the National Socialist period, see Peter Adam, *Art of the Third Reich* (New York: Harry N. Abrams, 1992). For a lucid analysis of National Socialist Art and the "Degenerate Art" exhibit of 1937, see Stephanie Barron, *Degenerate Art: The Fate of the Avant-Garde in Nazi Germany,* (New York: Harry N. Abrams, 1991).
15. Michel Foucault, *Discipline and Punish: The Birth of the Prison,* trans. Alan Sheridan (London: Allen Lane, 1987).
16. See Haraway's discussion of power structures in Donna Haraway, "Situated Knowledges: The Science Question in Feminism and the Privilege of Partial Perspective," *Feminist Studies* 14, 3 (Fall 1988): 575–599.
17. Norman Bryson, *Vision and Painting: The Logic of the Gaze* (New Haven, CT: Yale University Press, 1983); and Moxey, "Perspective, Panofsky," 782.
18. While the debates between Habermas and Foucault never actually took place, their philosophical disagreements have become legendary. See, for example, *Critique and Power: Recasting the Foucault/Habermas Debate,* ed. Michael Kelly (Cambridge, MA: MIT Press, 1994), especially Habermas, "Taking Aim at the Heart of the Present: On Foucault's Lecture on Kant's 'What is Enlightenment,'" 149, 156.
19. Jürgen Habermas, *The Philosophical Discourse of Modernity* (Cambridge, MA: MIT Press, 1987).
20. Barbara Maria Stafford, *Visual Analogy: Consciousness as an Art of Connecting* (Cambridge, MA: MIT Press, 1999), 2, 3.
21. Stafford, *Visual Analogy,* 19.
22. Clement Greenberg was an important American art critic who strongly influenced the practice of art-history and criticism during the middle of the twentieth century. In his 1939 essay "The Avant Garde and Kitsch," he famously warned against the contamination of art with mass culture. He believed the artist should focus "in upon the medium of his own craft" and purify his art from any extraneous influences from both other media and popular culture. That is, Greenberg valorized formalist over narrative art. He privileged abstract formal experimentation over "realist" politically shaped content. See Clement Greenberg, "Avant-Garde and Kitsch," in *Clement Greenberg: The Collected Essays and Criticism,* ed. John O'Brian (Chicago and London: University of Chicago Press, 1986), 9.

    For Greenberg, as Leah Dickerman notes, socialist realism should not be part of "the canon of Western modernism." See Dickerman's "Camera

Obscura: Socialist Realism in the Shadow of Photography," *October* 2000, 93 (Summer 2000): 139.

23. Angelika Rauch, "The Broken Vessel of Tradition," *Representations* 53 (Winter 1996): 84.
24. Gregory Volk "Neo Rauch: Time Straddler," *Art in America* (June/July 2010): 140.
25. Stefan Nicola, UPI.com (May 4, 2010); available online at the following URL address: http://www.upi.com/Top_News/Special/2010/05/04/Neo-Rauch-paints-Leipzig-back-on-top/UPI-83651272985108. Accessed November 15, 2010.
26. Cited in Volk, "Neo Rauch," 138.
27. Roberta Smith, the *New York Times* (June 15, 2007). Available online at this address: http://www.nytimes.com/2007/06/15/arts/design/15rauc.html?scp=2&sq=neo%20rauch&st=cse. Accessed March 10, 2010.
28. Karen Rosenberg, "Art in Review," the *New York Times* (May 23, 2008). Available online at the *New York Times* website at the following URL address: http://www.nytimes.com/2008/05/23/arts/design/23gall.html?pagewanted=2&sq=neorauch&st=cse&scp=16. Accessed August 1, 2010.
29. Peter Schejeldahl, "Paintings for Now: Neo Rauch at the Met," *The New Yorker* (June 4, 2007). Available online at the following URL address on *The New Yorker* website: http://www.newyorker.com/arts/critics/artworld/2007/06/04/070604craw_artworld_schjeldahl?currentPage=all. Accessed September 15, 2010.
30. Bryson notes that "a certain formalism in art history certainly exists. . . its main tendency is to examine the image in dissociation from the structure of its meaning," *Vision and Painting*, 55.
31. Peter Schejeldahl, "Neo Rauch at the Met."
32. Ibid.
33. Hans-Werner Schmidt, "Forward," in *Neo Rauch: Paintings Malerei*, ed. Hans-Werner Schmidt and Klaus Schrenk (Munich and Leipzig: Hatje Cantz, 2010), 9.
34. See Arthur Lubow's January 8, 2006, article in the *New York Times* as cited in note 1. In it he quotes Arno Rink, a painter and former teacher at the Leipzig Academy of Fine Arts, who states that the city of Leipzig "prided itself on being the birthplace of Max Beckmann and (if you looked back a few centuries and across Saxony to Wittenberg) on a painterly lineage begat by Lucas Cranach. 'The disadvantages of the wall are well known,' says Arno Rink, a 65-year-old recently retired professor of painting who served as director of the academy in Leipzig both before and after the wall came down. 'If you want to talk of an advantage, you can say it allowed us to continue in the tradition of Cranach and Beckmann. It protected the art against the influence of Joseph Beuys.'"
35. Petra Lewey and Klaus Fischer, "Vorführung: 2006," in *Neo Rauch Paintings*, 104.
36. Holly, *Panofsky*, 147.

37. As Holly articulates it, "In the essay on perspective, the concept of *Sinn* is stretched to span the traditional distinction between form and content. In the system of Renaissance perspective, the bridge that results is as broad as the geometry on which it is based. Sinn refers not simply to subject matter, but to content—the 'revelation' achieved when idea and form approach a 'state of equilibrium' [but one that is dynamic, not static]. The 'specific creative principle' anchored by the poles of necessity . . . which gives a painting in perspective its actual material existence, reflects a traditional neo-Kantian dialectic involving the opposition of the mind and the world, of subject and object, or, perhaps we could argue, of Fülle and Form." Holly, *Panofsky*, 148–149. For the original essay, see Erwin Panofsky, "Die Perspektive als 'symbolische Form,'" *Vorträge der Bibliothek Warburg* 1924–1925 (Leipzig and Berlin: Bibliothek Warburg, 1927).
38. Their conclusions are deeply imbedded in the German-Jewish cultural traditions of the nineteenth and early twentieth centuries. See Moxey, "Panofsky, Perspective," and George L. Mosse, *German Jews beyond Judaism* (Indianapolis: Indiana University Press, 1980).
39. See Foucault's first chapter in *The Order of Things: An Archaeology of the Human Sciences* (London: Tavistock, 1970) for an insightful "reading" of the operative "episteme" in Diego Velázquez' *Las Meninas* of 1656. In his reading, he focuses on how a viewer could interact with the image and thus bypasses the standard art-historical "tropes" for reading art.
40. By Lübeck architecture, I am referencing the postcard architectural views often associated with the town of Thomas Mann's birth and residence. Mann seems to be a noteworthy reference because his writing could be considered as a modern interpretation of Enlightenment/classic German tradition. See my Columbia University 1998 dissertation, "Erwin Panofsky and Walter Benjamin: German-Jewish Cultural Traditions and the Writing of History in Weimar Germany," PhD diss., Columbia University, 1998.
41. Donna Haraway, "A Cyborg Manifesto: Science, Technology, and Socialist-Feminism in the Late Twentieth Century," in *Simians, Cyborgs, and Women: The Reinvention of Nature* (New York: Routledge, 1991), 149–181.
42. Lewey and Fischer, "Vorführung: 2006," 104.
43. This could also be a visual allusion to Goethe's poem *Bei Betrachtung von Schillers Schädel.*" I thank the editors for pointing this out to me.
44. Peter Schjeldahl, "Neo Rauch at the Met," June 4, 2007.
45. See Sander Gilman's comments (in this volume) on the selling out of *Bildung* in contemporary German culture.
46. See F. M. Barnard, *Herder on Nationality, Humanity and History* (Montreal and Kingston: McGill-Queen's University Press, 2003).
47. George L. Mosse, *German Jews Beyond Judaism*, 3–4. See also Anson Rabinbach, who states that "[f]or German Jews of that earlier generation the 'Bildungsideal' of Kant, Goethe and Schiller assured them of an indissoluble bond between Enlightenment, universal ethics, autonomous art, and monotheism (stripped of any particularist 'Jewish' characteristics). The mission of the Jews could be

interpreted, as Leo Baeck did in his 1905 *Essence of Judaism*, as the exemplary embodiment of the religion of morality for all humanity." From Rabinbach, "Between Enlightenment and Apocalypse: Benjamin, Bloch and Modern German Jewish Messianism," *New German Critique* 34 (Winter 1985), 79.

48. Ernst Cassirer based his influential *Theory of Symbolic Forms* on neo-Kantian philosophy and Goethe's aesthetic theories. In it, he argued that humans have an innate propensity to create rational constructs (symbolic forms) that help us cognitively shape our experience of the world. Erwin Panofsky, his colleague at the University of Hamburg, adapted Cassirer's symbolic form for his theory of Iconology, a "scientific" rational framework for uncovering the "intrinsic" meaning of a work of art. This was possible, notes Keith Moxey, because "human nature affords human beings an adequate epistemological foundation on which to understand the world." Moxey, "Perspective," 772. Also see Ernst Cassirer, *The Philosophy of Symbolic Forms,* five volumes, trans. Ralph Mannheim, intro Charles Hendel (New Haven, CT: Yale University Press, 1955). For perspectives on Hermann Cohen, Cassirer, and Aby Warburg, see Mosse, *German Jews beyond Judaism* and Rabinbach, "Between Enlightenment and Apocalypse."
49. See Friedrich Nietzsche, *The Origin of German Tragic Drama,* trans. Walter Kaufmann, (New York: Vintage Books, 1967).
50. Though many of Benjamin's writings comment on the relationship of the political to the aesthetic, the most well-known of these is "The Work of Art in the Age of Mechanical Reproduction," in *Illuminations,* ed. and intro by Hannah Arendt, trans. Harry Zohn, (New York: Harcourt Brace Jovanovich, 1968), 217–252.
51. Quoted in Bent Flyvbjerg, "Habermas and Foucault: Thinkers for a Civil Society," *British Journal of Sociology* 49, no. 2 (June 1998).
52. See Bent Flyvbjerg, "Habermas and Foucault: Thinkers for a Civil Society" as well as Jürgen Habermas and Martha Calhoun, "Right and Violence: A German Trauma," *Cultural Critique* 1 (Autumn 1985): 139. In the latter, Habermas writes; "We now need another evolutionary thrust in order to approach that international law and order which Kant [and other Enlightenment thinkers] had in mind."
53. Peter Uwe Hohendahl, "Recasting the Public Sphere," *October* 73 (Summer 1995), 54.
54. Habermas, "Leadership and Leitkultur," *The New York Times* (October 29, 2010). Available online at the *New York Times* website at the following URL address: http://query.nytimes.com/gst/fullpage.html?res=9904E5DD153CF93AA15753C1A9669D8B63&ref=discrimination. Accessed October 14, 2010.
55. Stafford, *Visual Analogy,* 9.
56. Ibid., 10.
57. Neo Rauch, quoted in Jordan Mejias, "Neo Rauch: Malerei ist eine herrschaftliche Geste," *Frankfurter Allgemeine Zeitung,* May 22, 2007. Cited in Hans-Werner Schmidt, "'I don't fit in your system but you don't fit in mine,'" in *Neo Rauch: Paintings Malerei,* ed. Hans-Werner Schmidt and Klaus Schrenk (Munich and Leipzig: Hatje Cantz, 2010), 15.

58. Michaël Borremann, "On Warten auf die Barbaren," in *Neo Rauch Painting,* 46.
59. Werner Hofmann, "New Roles for Space," in *Neo Rauch Painting,* 39.
60. Rudij Bergman, "Ordnungshüter, 2008," in *Neo Rauch Painting,* 38.
61. Paul Betts, "The Twilight of the Idols: East German Memory and Material Culture," *The Journal of Modern History* 72, no. 3 (September 2000): 739.
62. Paul Betts, "Twilight of the Idols," 754.
63. Jean-Christophe Ammann, "It's a Search That Takes Place in the Mind, A Conversation with Matthias Weischer," in *Matthias Weischer: Malerei, Painting* (Ostfildern: Hatje Cantz Verlag, 2007), 94.
64. See Pat Kirkham, "Humanizing Modernism: The Crafts, 'Functioning Decoration' and the Eameses," *Journal of Design History* 11, no. 1 (1998): 15–29.
65. Please see Brian O'Doherty, *Inside the White Cube: The Ideology of the Gallery Space,* intro. Thomas McEvilley (Berkeley and Los Angeles: University of California Press, 1999).
66. See Roland Barthes, *Camera Lucida,* trans. R. Howard (London: Flamingo, 1984).
67. Ammann, "A Conversation with Matthias Weischer," 92.
68. Jacques Derrida, *The Truth in Painting,* trans. Geoff Bennington and Ian McLeod (Chicago: University of Chicago Press, 1987).
69. Patrick Fuery, *New Developments in Film Theory* (New York: St. Martin's Press, 2000), 153.
70. Weischer notes that his fellow students at the Academy viewed his art as "boring" and conservative. See Maura Egan, "Neue School," the *New York Times* (September 4, 2004); available online at the *New York Times* website at the following URL address: http://www.nytimes.com/2004/09/19/style/tmagazine/MAN40.html?sq=neorauch&st=cse&adxnnl=1&scp=10&adxnnlx=1291398242-tsqWVlX2wSPk8ZO3Zj0+eA.
71. Stafford, *Visual Analogy,* 23.
72. Hilarie M. Sheets, "Optical Delusions," in *Art News* 105, no. 10 (November 2006); available online at the *Art News* website at the following URL address: http://www.artnews.com/issues/issue.asp?id=10423. Accessed March 2, 2010.
73. Stafford, *Visual Analogy,* 68.
74. See Christoph Tannert, "Tim Eitel 'Aussichten,'" in *Tim Eitel Aussicht/Outlook* with text by Christoph Tannert (Berlin: Künstlerhaus Bethanien, 2002), 4–6.
75. See Sheets, "Optical Delusions," where Eitel discusses this.
76. Stafford, *Visual Analogy,* 81–82.
77. Rauch, "Broken Vessels," 140.
78. Dörte Zbikowski, "Ausnahmezustände/States of Emergency," in *Die Bewohner,* ed. Martin Hellmold and Dirk Luckow (Ostfildern, Germany: Hatje Cantz Verlag, 2008), 83.
79. Henry Lefebvre, *The Production of Space,* trans. Donald Nicholson Smith (Oxford: Blackwell, 1992), 355. Quoted in David Clarke, "In Search of

Home: Filming Post-Unification Berlin," in *German Cinema Since Unification*, ed. David Clarke (London and New York: Continuum, 2006) 161.
80. Lubow, "The Leipzig School."
81. Carol Duncan, *Civilizing Rituals: Inside Public Art Museums* (London and New York: Routledge, 1995), 133.

Bibliography

Adam, Peter. *Art of the Third Reich.* New York: Harry N. Abrams, 1992.

Ammann, Jean-Christophe. "It's a Search That Takes Place in the Mind, A Conversation with Matthias Weischer." *Weischer: Malerei Painting.* Ostfildern, Germany: Hatje Cantz Verlag, 2007.

Barnard, F. M. *Herder on Nationality, Humanity and History.* Montreal and Kingston: McGill-Queen's University Press, 2003.

Barron, Stephanie. *Degenerate Art: The Fate of the Avant-Garde in Nazi Germany.* New York: Harry N. Abrams, 1991.

Barthes, Roland. *Camera Lucida.* Translated by Richard Howard. London: Flamingo, 1984.

Baudrillard, Jean. *For a Critique of the Political Economy of the Sign.* Translated by Charles Levin. St. Louis: Telos Press, 1981.

Beiser, Frederick C. *Diotima's Children: German Aesthetic Rationalism from Leibniz to Lessing.* Cambridge: Oxford University Press, 2009.

Benjamin, Walter. "The Work of Art in the Age of Mechanical Reproduction." In *Illuminations.* Edited and with an Introduction by Hannah Arendt. Translated by Harry Zohn. New York: Harcourt Brace Jovanovich, 1968, 217–252.

Bergmann, Rudij. "Ordungshüter, 2008," In *Neo Rauch Painting.* Edited by Hans-Werner Schmidt and Klaus Schrenk, 38. Ostfildern, Germany: Hatje Catz Verlag, 2010.

Betts, Paul. "The Twilight of the Idols: East German Memory and Material Culture," *The Journal of Modern History* 72, no. 3 (September 2000), 731–765.

Borremann, Michaël. "Warten auf die Barbaren." In *Neo Rauch Painting.* Edited by Hans-Werner Schmidt and Klaus Schrenk, 46. Ostfildern, Germany: Hatje Cantz Verlag, 2010.

Bown, Matthew. *Art Under Stalin.* New York: Holmes and Meier, 1991.

Bryson, Norman. *Vision and Painting: The Logic of the Gaze.* New Haven, CT: Yale University Press, 1983.

Cassirer, Ernst. *The Philosophy of Symbolic Forms.* Five Volumes. Translated by Ralph Mannheim. Introduction by Charles Hendel. New Haven, CT: Yale University Press, 1955.

Clark, David. "In Search of Home: Filming Post-Unification Berlin." In *German Cinema since Unification.* Edited by David Clarke, 151–180. London and New York: Continuum, 2006.

D'Alessandro, Stephanie. "History by Degrees: The Place of the Past in Contemporary German Art," *Art Institute of Chicago Museum Studies* 28, no. 1 (2002).

Dempsey, Anna. "Erwin Panofsky and Walter Benjamin: German Jewish Cultural Traditions and the Writing of History in Weimar Germany." Ph.D. diss. Columbia University, 1998.

Drengenberg, Hans-Jürgen, ed., *Bildende Kunst in Osteuropa im 20 Jahrhundert: Art in Eastern Europe in the 20th Century* (Berlin: Berlin Verlag, Arno Spitz, 1991).

Derrida, Jacques. *The Truth in Painting.* Translated by Geoff Bennington and Ian McLeod. Chicago: University of Chicago Press, 1987.

Dickerman, Leah. "Camera Obscura: Socialist Realism in the Shadow of Photography." *October* 2000, 93 (Summer 2000): 138–153.

Duncan, Carol. *Civilizing Rituals: Inside Public Art Museums.* London and New York: Routledge, 1995.

Egan, Maura. "Neue School." The *New York Times* (September 4, 2004). http://www.nytimes.com/2004/09/19/style/tmagazine/MAN40.html?sq=neorauch&st=cse&adxnnl=1&scp=10&adxnnlx=1291398242-tsqWVlX2wSPk8ZO3Zj0+eA. Accessed August 15, 2010.

Fuery, Patrick. *New Developments in Film Theory.* New York: St. Martin's Press, 2000.

Foucault, Michel. *Discipline and Punish: The Birth of the Prison.* Translated by Alan Sheridan. London: Allen Lane, 1987.

———. *The Order of Things: An Archaeology of the Human Sciences.* London: Tavistock, 1970.

Flyvbjerg, Bent. "Habermas and Foucault: Thinkers for a Civil Society." *British Journal of Sociology* 49, no. 2 (June 1998).

Goethe, Johann Wolfgang von. *Elective Affinities.* Translated by Elizabeth Mayer and Louise Bogan. Chicago: Henry Regnery, 1963.

Greenberg, Clement. "Avant-Garde and Kitsch." In *Clement Greenberg: The Collected Essays and Criticism.* Edited by John O'Brian, 1, 5–22. Chicago and London: University of Chicago Press, 1986.

Habermas, Jürgen. *The Philosophical Discourse of Modernity.* Cambridge, MA: MIT Press, 1987.

———. "Taking Aim at the Heart of the Present: On Foucault's Lecture on Kant's 'What is Enlightenment.'" In *Critique and Power: Recasting the Foucault/Habermas Debate.* Edited by Michael Kelly. 149–156. Cambridge, MA: MIT Press, 1994.

———. "Leadership and Leitkultur." The *New York Times,* October 29, 2010. http://query.nytimes.com/gst/fullpage.html?res=9904E5DD153CF93AA1575 3C1A9669D8B63&ref=discrimination. Accessed October 14, 2010.

Habermas, Jürgen, and Martha Calhoun. "Right and Violence: A German Trauma." In *Cultural Critique* 1 (Autumn 1985): 125–139.

Haraway, Donna. "Situated Knowledges: The Science Question in Feminism and the Privilege of Partial Perspectives." In *Feminist Studies* 14, 3 (Fall 1988): 575–599.

———. "A Cyborg Manifesto: Science, Technology, and Socialist-Feminism in the Late Twentieth Century." In *Simians, Cyborgs and Women: The Reinvention of Nature,* 149–181. New York: Routledge, 1991.

Hohendahl, Peter Uwe. "Recasting the Public Sphere." *October* 73 (Summer 1995): 27–54.

Hofmann, Werner. "New Roles for Space." In *Neo Rauch Painting.* Edited by Hans-Werner Schmidt and Klaus Schrenk, 39. Ostfildern, Germany: Hatje Catz Verlag, 2010.

Holly, Michael Ann. *Panofsky and the Foundations of Art History*. Ithaca, NY: Cornell University Press, 1984.

Kant, Immanuel. *The Critique of Judgment.* Translated by J. H. Bernard. New York: Hafner, 1951.

Kibbey, Anne. *Theory of the Image: Capitalism, Contemporary Film, and Women.* Bloomington and Indianapolis: Indiana University Press, 2005.

Kirkham, Pat. "Humanizing Modernism: The Crafts, 'Functioning Decoration' and the Eameses." *Journal of Design History* 11, no. 1 (1998): 15–29.

Lang, Karen. "The Dialectics of Decay: Reframing the Kantian Subject." *Art Bulletin* 79, no. 3 (September 1997).

Lefebvre, Henry. *The Production of Space.* Translated by Donald Nicholson Smith. Oxford: Blackwell, 1992.

Lubow, Arthur. "The Leipzig School," *The New York Times,* January 8, 2008, http://www.nytimes.com/2006/01/08/magazine/08leipzig.html?scp=8&sq=neo%20rauch&st=cse. Accessed March 10, 2010.

Lewey, Petra, and Klaus Fischer. "Vorführung: 2006." In *Neo Rauch Painting.* Edited by Hans-Werner Schmidt and Klaus Schrenk, 104. Ostfildern, Germany: Hatje Catz Verlag, 2010.

Manovich, Lev. *The Language of New Media.* Cambridge, MA: MIT Press, 2000.

Mosse, George L. *German Jews Beyond Judaism.* Indianapolis: Indiana University Press, 1980.

Moxey, Keith. "Perspective, Panofsky, and the Philosophy of History." *New Literary History* 26, no. 4 (Autumn 1995): 775–786.

Nietzsche, Friedrich. *The Birth of Tragedy.* Translated by Walter Kaufmann. New York: Vintage Books, 1967.

Nochlin, Linda. *Realism.* Harmondsworth and Baltimore: Penguin Books, 1971.

O'Doherty, Brian. *Inside the White Cube: The Ideology of the Gallery Space.* Introduction by Thomas McEvilley. Los Angeles and Berkeley: University of California Press, 1999.

Panofsky, Erwin. "Die Perspektive als 'symbolische Form'." In *Vorträge der Bibliothek Warburg* 1924–1925. Leipzig and Berlin: Bibliothek Warburg, 1927.

Rabinbach, Anson. "Between Enlightenment and Apocalypse: Benjamin, Bloch and Modern German Jewish Messianism." *New German Critique* 34 (Winter 1985): 78–124.

Rauch, Angelika. "The Broken Vessel of Tradition." *Representations* 53 (Winter 1996): 84.

Rosenberg, Karen. "Art in Review." *The New York Times,* May 23, 2008. http://www.nytimes.com/2008/05/23/arts/design/23gall.html?pagewanted=2&sq=neorauch&st=cse&scp=16. Accessed August 1, 2010.

Schjehldahl, Peter. "Paintings for Now: Neo Rauch at the Met." *The New Yorker,* June 4, 2007. http://www.newyorker.com/arts/critics/artworld/2007/06/04/070604craw_artworld_schjeldahl?currentPage=all. Accessed September 15, 2010.

Schiller, Friedrich. *On the Aesthetic Education of Man in a Series of Letters.* (*Über die ästhetische Erziehung des Menschen in einer Reihe von Briefen,* first published 1794.) Translated by Reginald Snell. New Haven, CT: Yale University Press, 1954.

Schmidt, Hans-Werner. "Forward." In *Neo Rauch: Painting,* 7–17. Edited by Hans-Werner Schmidt and Klaus Schrenk. Munich and Leipzig: Hatje Cantz, 2010.

———. "'I Don't Fit in Your System but You Don't Fit in Mine.'" In *Neo Rauch: Paintings.* Edited by Hans-Werner Schmidt and Klaus Schrenk. Munich and Leipzig: Hatje Cantz, 2010.

Sheets, Hilarie M. "Optical Delusions." *Art News* 105, no. 10 (November 2006). http://www.artnews.com/issues/issue.asp?id=10423. Accessed March 2, 2010.

Smith, Roberta. *The New York Times,* June 15, 2007, http://www.nytimes.com/2007/06/15/arts/design/15rauc.html?scp=2&sq=neo%20rauch&st=cse. Accessed March 10, 2010.

Stafford, Barbara Maria. *Visual Analogy: Consciousness as an Art of Connecting.* Cambridge, MA: MIT Press, 1999.

Stefan, Nicola. "Neo Rauch Paints Leipzig Back on Top." UPI.com, May 4, 2010. http://www.upi.com/Top_News/Special/2010/05/04/Neo-Rauch-paints-Leipzig-back-on-top/UPI-83651272985108/. Accessed November 15, 2010.

Tannert, Christoph. "Tim Eitel 'Aussichten'." In *Tim Eitel Aussicht/Outlook* with text by Christoph Tannert, 4–6. Berlin: Kunstlerhaus Bethanian, 2002.

Volk, Gregory. "Neo Rauch: Time Straddler." *Art in America* (June/July 2010): 138–145.

Williams, Garrath. "Kant's Account of Reason." In *The Stanford Encyclopedia of Philosophy.* Edited by Edward N. Zalta. Summer 2009. http://plato.stanford.edu/archives/sum2009/entries/kant-reason. Accessed October 14, 2010.

Zbikowski, Dörte. "Ausnahmezustände/States of Emergency." In *Die Bewohner.* Edited by Martin Hellmold and Dirk Luckow, 83–89. Ostfildern, Germany: Hatje Cantz Verlag, 2008.

11

Berlin's History in Context: The Foreign Ministry and the *Spreebogen* Complex in the Context of the Architectural Debates*

Carol Anne Costabile-Heming

As the capital of united Germany, Berlin has sought to navigate a multitude of pasts in its quest to define its image in the twenty-first century. The city's topography provides ample examples of the multiple remnants of the past, which are visible equally in its architectural heritage as well as in its barren spaces. We can read Berlin's topography as a microcosm of twentieth-century German history: countless buildings, street corners, and squares remind residents and visitors alike of the layers of history embedded in the very fabric of the city. Finding ways to acknowledge such remnants from the past were at the forefront of debates about the rebuilding of Berlin following the reunification of East and West Germany and the redesignation of Berlin as the capital of united Germany. The construction of the "New Berlin" attracted considerable attention, not only from architects and urban planners but also from cultural historians and literary scholars.

A survey of the extant scholarship on the topic reveals there is no singular interpretation of Berlin's cityscape but rather a range of opinions about what is the appropriate architectural framework for the capital city. In his oft-cited work *The Ghosts of Berlin*, Brian Ladd, for instance, labels Berlin a "haunted city," one whose architecture and structures function as "repositories of memory."[1] Refining this perception, Peter Fritzsche suggests that the city serves as the geographic locus of German memory.[2] In his seminal essay, "The Voids of Berlin," Andreas Huyssen not only reads the city of Berlin as a historical text, but he argues convincingly that "absences" mark Berlin. Whereas Ladd focuses on existing architectural structures as embodiments of particular periods of German history, Huyssen views Berlin as a site of "discontinuous" and "ruptured history."[3]

The unexpected fall of the ubiquitous wall more than 20 years ago afforded Berlin the opportunity not only to rethink its role in Germany, but, even more significantly, to re-create itself and redefine the way the rest of the world sees it. In June 1991, the Bundestag narrowly approved a resolution to move the German capital from Bonn to Berlin, a decision that was met with skepticism by the German people as well as by the media. In the ensuing years, contentious debates raged about which image and which definition would exemplify the "New Berlin." Yet, the rush to unify the nation and to move the capital forced Berlin onto a fast track; decisions about destruction, construction, renovation, and reconstruction were made rapidly, often with little forethought, and frequently without much public input. Two Bundestag commissions were solely responsible for orchestrating the move of the government to Berlin: a newly founded Conceptual Commission advised on all financial, conceptual, and functional matters, while the Building Commission (in existence since 1949) was responsible for planning and construction. In this way, the public was removed from the decision-making process. Indeed, the public was never asked which image the city should project or even how best to project it. Rather, national and international design competitions played a primary role in determining the architectural character of the New Berlin. Thus, it should come as no surprise that debates surrounding the issues of image have thrust questions about Berlin's checkered history into the limelight. Because of publicity and the city's popularity, this image also must appeal to an increasingly international audience. Indeed, the very essence of Berlin seems to emerge from the remnants of the past that surreptitiously come into view from various corners.

Both in Berlin's historic center and in the areas immediately adjacent to it, architectural plans have been careful to account for the city's architectural history, making architectural citations an integral part of the newly emerging cityscape. Scholars and critics alike have focused their attention on the ways in which architects and city planners have either incorporated or ignored the past in their designs. Huyssen remarks, "architecture . . . has become ever more interested in site-memory and in inscribing temporal dimensions in spatial structures."[4] Whereas

Ladd focuses his analysis on the historical context of Berlin's architectural reconstruction, Michael Wise concentrates his investigation on the democratic symbolism of new structures.[5] More recently, Jennifer Jordan examines memorialization in Berlin in her 2006 monograph *Structures of Memory*. She situates public sites into not only a historical context but also examines them within their economic, cultural, artistic, bureaucratic, and legal frameworks. By broadening her locus of analysis beyond the historical context and functional aspects, she expands her study to include discussions about authenticity and collective memory. She focuses not only on memory but also on forgetting. By examining "forgotten" spaces, she expands the discussion: "The memorial landscape is not determined solely by the traces left in the built environment or in memory, official or otherwise, even as memorials come to seem self-evident and unmarked places seem to become ordinary."[6] For the purposes of this chapter, I investigate the role historical remnants of Berlin's past play in the conceptualization, design, and construction of postunification building projects. Several questions are central to this understanding: Which past or pasts are incorporated into building projects, and which are left out? How are decisions made? What implications for the future understanding of the city does this have? This chapter focuses specifically on two locations in Berlin: the *Spreebogen* area and the *Bundeskanzleramt* designed by Axel Schultes and Charlotte Frank,[7] and the *Haus am Werderschen Markt*, home to the Foreign Ministry and renovated by Hans Kollhoff. The juxtaposition of these two sites provides a fruitful line of inquiry into the larger context of the architectural debates, for it allows me to contrast the rebuilding of a barren space (*Spreebogen* and *Bundeskanzleramt*) with the renovation of an existing, historically weighted structure (*Haus am Werderschen Markt*). For both sites, memories and evidence of the Nazi and GDR architectural pasts remained, forcing the architects to confront these pasts as their revisioning of these spaces contributed to Berlin's attempts to renegotiate its identity.

Before examining these structures more closely, it is instructive to review some of the theories that informed the discussion about Berlin's reconstruction. Berlin's historic city center, in particular, presented itself as a canvas with multiple layers of history reflecting elements of the Wilhelminian, Nazi, and GDR eras. The extent to which newly constructed or reconstructed spaces attempted to dialog with this history was fodder for debate. The incorporation of a building or a site's past becomes a type of architectural citation, a practice that Rolf Goebel has defined as designs that "inscribe contemporary architectural style with allusive reinventions of previous cultural manifestations and discourses, incorporate actual remnants of older edifices, or use partial reconstruction for new purposes."[8] Rather than representing a return to an earlier age, such citation demonstrates the tension between past and present, and a desire to engage with the past. For the historical center of Berlin, this has significant ramifications. As the renowned architect Aldo Rossi wrote, "With time, the city grows upon itself; it acquires a consciousness and memory. In the course of its construction, its original themes persist, but at the same time it modifies and renders these themes of its own development more specific."[9] Drawing heavily on Rossi's memory principle, Berlin's city planners created a restrictive code for development within the historic city center. Thus, critical reconstructionists wanted to cite the city's historic façade, while at the same time creating spaces that were usable in a highly modern and technological society.

The question of accommodating the requests of diverse constituents formed the core of the debates about rebuilding Berlin. For Philipp Meuser, these debates devolved into a polemic of good versus evil, with architects using only "fascist stone or democratic glass, with the result being either a replication of the 19th-century city or an interpretation of the 21st-century metropolis."[10] This all-consuming engagement with history was at the heart of the German federal government's approach to crafting the image of unified Germany in Berlin. In an effort to demonstrate extreme sensitivity to history, the government has attempted to occupy old buildings while simultaneously avoiding any duplicating of past functions, with the exception of the parliament's return to the Reichstag and the Department of Defense's return to the Bendlerblock. This deference toward the past almost can be viewed as a fear, for the new Germany has vowed not to be associated with the pre-1945 governmental era. Such thinking poses considerable problems for architects and urban planners alike, whose buildings had to reflect the tension of the past in their renegotiated identities.

In his nearly 15 years as municipal building director for Berlin (1991–2006), Hans Stimmann began a critical reconstruction that met with considerable opposition from architects and others. Stimmann's perspective draws from his belief that the architectural footprint of the city is also its memory.[11] Moreover, Stimmann viewed the city as a collage, "in which architectural attitudes, social concerns, and a preoccupation with history manifest themselves structurally."[12] Throughout the 1990s, Stimmann's insistence on retaining Berlin's particular texture or character was a forceful factor at the center point of the architectural debates. In particular, his insistence on the need to depict the city's history throughout the reconstruction process informs my way of reading the Berlin landscape. As Stimmann looked to the future, he proposed, "At the beginning of a new millennium, [urban] planning cautions that it is architecture's job not only to promote continued creative development, but also to take into consideration cultural achievements, the retention of the memory of the city . . . as the basis for architecture in the European city."[13]

Stimmann draws much of his philosophy from Rossi's *The Architecture of the City* (1966). In this work, Rossi pleads for permanency in both the city outline and in memorial structures, in order to make the past remain present. The unnatural division of Berlin, however, precluded any such unified attempts, especially in the 1960s and 1970s. It was only during the *Internationale Bauausstellung* (IBA) in 1984, Stimmann argues, that this perspective began to gain acceptance. This is important for the debates that took place in united Berlin, for Stimmann wanted to avoid repeating the mistakes of the past.

Despite the political clout that Stimmann wielded through his office, his views have not been accepted so readily in the Berlin architectural world. Schultes, for instance, has been highly critical of his plans. Whereas Stimmann proposed a specific image of Berlin's historic center, namely, a tribute to Prussian neoclassicism, Schultes consistently pleads for a broader, more focused approach to the actual use of space. In particular as the debate raged about the redesign of the *Schlossplatz*, Schultes was adamant that a replica palace would not solve the city's woes.[14] Stimmann's approach proposes to fill the area with singular structures, a programmatic approach that Schultes claims leads to solitary buildings that do not welcome the public to spend time there. Architect and critic Bruno Flierl, who served on the international committee of experts for the design of the historical center of Berlin from 2001 to 2004, took a slightly different approach, criticizing what he views as a systematic attempt to overhaul the old city center, "which should be categorically reformulated until the GDR is no longer recognizable."[15] Yet, Svetlana Boym, in analyzing topography for its potential as nostalgic form, has argued, "Places are *contexts* for remembrances and debates about the future, not *symbols* of memory or nostalgia. Thus places in the city are not merely architectural metaphors; they are also screen memories for urban dwellers, projections of contested remembrances. Of interest here are not only architectural projects but lived environments, everyday ways of inhabiting the city."[16] Underlying these viewpoints are questions about historical authenticity. There are multiple layers of history present in Berlin's historic center, layers that also are fraught with contested legacies. Whereas Flierl suggests that city planners were attempting to erase remnants of the GDR from the landscape, Boym points out that Berlin's inhabitants will retain memories of the architectural landscape as they experienced it. Thus, there is an inherent tension between the official image city planners wish to project and the lived experiences residents want preserved.

In his article "Forget Berlin," in which he critiques Berlin's self-portrayal, Lutz Koepnick argues that architecture has assumed the role of "recalling the past and marking the nation's place after the Cold War."[17] For Koepnick, post-Wall Berlin has become a site where "democratic politics and impressive architecture" can unite.[18] In their attempts to rebuild and renovate older structures such as the Reichstag or the Federal Foreign Office, or the design of completely new spaces like the Federal Chancellery, both politicians and urban planners approach the redevelopment of the city as an overt expression of the German nation's democratic vision. As such, these buildings can be viewed as self-reflective. Meaning becomes obscured, however, when we look beyond the present-day façades to investigate the historical significances of these sites. It is this aspect that Koepnick critiques so strongly, for as he writes:

> Berlin's chief designers have chosen to provide highly choreographed environments enhancing local prestige and gratifying desires for historical continuity, livability and territorialization. They have fragmented urban space into a series of carefully developed, albeit isolated, zones of comfort and historical reference that undercut any attempt at seeing the city as an integrated space.[19]

Goebel, on the other hand, proposes that "buildings and streets . . . are preeminently hermeneutic objects because like narratives, they may reflect history (or conceal them), open up imaginary worlds (or are simply too boring for this sort of creativity), and stimulate public critique (or detract from it)."[20] Both Koepnick and Goebel frame their criticisms within the contemporary debates, neglecting to consider what effect the passage of time will have as memories of past regimes fade. Will these architectural citations continue to have meaning for future generations? Are the citations readable without extensive commentary and context?

More in-depth examination of the *Spreebogen* and the *Haus am Werderschen Markt* presents us with the opportunity to compare two different approaches to space utilization. Common to the two spaces is the historical association with both Nazi architecture and GDR oppression. While the *Spreebogen* site was barren and therefore offered city planners and architects the opportunity to create a new image for that site, the site that the *Haus am Werderschen Markt* now occupies was an already existing structure. It is instructive to compare how these sites were treated and whether or not the proposed goals have been achieved.

Schultes and Frank's prizewinning submission for the development of the *Spreebogen* envisioned an East-West "Spur des Bundes,"[21] a thread of buildings and spaces stretching from the *Moabiter Werder* to the

Friedrichstraße train station. Schultes and Frank envisioned a central forum that would be open to the public. Despite winning the design competition for the concept plan, the city did not award Schultes and Frank a contract to complete the entire parcel. Instead, city planners opted to create independent competitions for individual sites. Thus, from Schultes' perspective, the resulting project consists of solitary structures. Rather than engaging the totality of twentieth-century German history, as Schultes had intended for the *Spreebogen*, Schultes and Frank designed only the Federal Chancellery, which stands as a fragment without context.

The renovation of the *Haus am Werderschen Markt*, a building that has played a role in multiple periods of Berlin's history, stands in stark contrast to the barren space that the Federal Chancellery occupies. Kollhoff began the building's renovation in 1995, with the specific aim to remain true to its architectural history, leaving various phases of construction from the 1930s, 1950s, and 1970s visible. As a complement to this older structure, Berlin architects Thomas Müller and Ivan Reimann designed a new facility that adjoins the street and serves today as the main entrance to the Foreign Ministry. With its café and open atrium, this addition is one of the few federal buildings in the world that opens itself to the public, providing a public space in the way that Schultes and Frank had envisioned.

Spreebogen and Federal Chancellory

The design of the government quarters was a particular sticking point for politicians, for they had to navigate the court of public opinion carefully. The decision to move the federal capital from Bonn to Berlin was not entirely popular with voters, particularly because of the enormous costs associated with the move.[22] Moreover, construction just recently had been completed on new Bundestag facilities in Bonn, adding to the West German public's impression of waste. Furthermore, there was considerable debate within the Bundestag about the move and the appropriate quarters to house the parliament. The 150-acre site between Tiergarten and Spree had considerable empty space (due to the division and border) that easily could accommodate all necessary governmental functions. From the very outset, it was determined that the Reichstag and the *Spreebogen* would be the ideal location for the united German federal government. The centrality of this location would permit, as Nino Galetti argues, "the expression of a certain stately symbolism."[23] Yet it was precisely the question of symbolism that formed the very core of the debate.

As Ladd has argued, the glass and steel structures of the federal government in Bonn were thought to be "antiauthoritarian, unhierarchical, and democratic."[24] There were fears that the move to Berlin would signal a return to "centralization" and authoritarianism.[25]

Complicating matters were the differing perspectives that the federal government and the city of Berlin brought to the table. While the Berlin Senate desired an urban quarter akin to that under construction at Potsdamer Platz, the federal government preferred a parliamentary quarter, more analogous to that in Bonn. In Bonn, the federal offices and the heart of the city were side by side but had little to do with each other. Moreover, the city planners were advised that it was also their job "to reunite the formerly divided areas on this spot and to grant the Federal Republic an appropriate architectural representation in the new capital."[26]

The history of the site was particularly troublesome, for it was here that Hitler's architect Albert Speer had planned the North-South axis, which was to be framed by a gigantic domed *Volkshalle* at one end and an equally large victory arch at the other.[27] Because of this historical burden, Wise suggests that only East-West designs were considered seriously by German

Figure 11.1 Chancellery

Note: © Carol Anne Costabile-Heming.

members of the prize-evaluation commission.[28] Schultes and Frank's prizewinning submission to the 1992 competition for the development of the *Spreebogen* envisioned an East-West "Band des Bundes" or thread of the federation.[29] This ribbon was to stretch from the *Moabiter Werder* to the *Friedrichstraße* train station. Both the orientation and size of the ribbon reinforce the desire to engage with multiple layers of history that infuse the site. The East-West orientation cuts directly across Speer's grand axis, thus making the construction of a North-South corridor impossible in the future. In addition, the design consciously traverses the former death strip, signifying additionally a conscious effort to move beyond Germany's past division and at least visually unite the two halves of the city. Wise described the plan "as a gigantic girder or truss repairing the fissures of a metropolis torn asunder by decades of East-West conflict."[30] Sensitive to the accusations of monumentality that such a grand plan could evoke, Schultes and Frank broke up the ribbon by inserting a central forum, an area designed to be open to the citizenry. Thus, the initial design would house all manner of government buildings while simultaneously allowing the people access. The monumentality of the site aroused some criticism. Michael Mönninger points out, however, that the actual size was comparable to the space the government occupied in Bonn. The unity of government that Schultes and Frank created is similar, albeit smaller in scale, to the Mall in Washington, D.C.[31] The prize-selection committee viewed their submission as "a singularly strong structure whose courageous self-representation is appropriate for a democratic state."[32]

The hallmark of Schultes and Frank's design was "spatial integration."[33] Schultes emphasizes:

> Giving preference to a spatial, rather than an object-focused development of this place, and thereby avoiding the banality of a grand project, would not only be a tremendous political boost for the culture of the building, the culture of the country; the intimacy of the monument, which becomes a tangible possibility if a seat of government can evolve this way, would be able to unfold its power to integrate, its conciliatory effect, notably at a time when the country is in crisis.[34]

Reaction to the design was mixed. Peter Conradi, for instance, accused Schultes and Frank of monumentalist tendencies and categorically dismissed their proposal as "Speer quer."[35] The *Berliner Morgenpost* was particularly critical likening the *Spur des Bundes* to a new *Mauer* or wall that would once again cut through the cityscape.[36] The *Frankfurter Allgemeine Zeitung*, on the other hand, viewed the *Spur des Bundes* positively, with the East-West thread symbolically erasing the Nazi *Nord-Süd Achse*.[37]

While Schultes and Frank won the competition for the master plan for the *Spreebogen*, the designs for specific individual structures were determined again by competitions. Schultes and Frank won the competition to build the Federal Chancellery[38] but not the remaining portions of the original ribbon. Because Schultes and Frank were unable to realize their true plan for the thread of the federation, the resultant cityscape that has been created is, in Schultes' view, a mere fragment.[39] In the broader scheme of things, Schultes and Frank's vision was:

> to create "city" where it would spread even without planning: into the wasteland between the raised railway and the river; to define the *Tiergarten* landscape as generously as razing the *Alsen* district[40] had made it possible to conceive: the heart of the river bow would be a park enclave against the solid mass of development on the north bank; and to let the chain of federal buildings benefit from the meander in this town landscape. A place for the sovereign at the centre of the bow, a Civic Forum, to bind the executive and legislative institutions of our democracy and create architectural solidarity between the sites of our constitution.[41]

Schultes attributes the failure of his grand vision for the ribbon to a lack of understanding on the part of Berlin's city planners:

> the city itself does not understand that this idea has a scale all of its own, that the federal presence in Berlin is special, that the institutions marking their way from east to west cut across the grand axis of state carved by Speer, creating the city's most powerful icon of Germany's regained state unity.[42]

The Civic Forum will not be built, and the extension of the *Band des Bundes* to *Friedrichstrasse* also has been curtailed. To this day, Schultes expresses disappointment that he was unable to realize his vision for the *Band des Bundes*, and Wise maintains this decision "undermined Schultes's symbolic intent of inscribing unification into the Berlin urban landscape."[43] The eastern end of the ribbon extends across the Spree and incorporates parliamentary offices housed in two buildings, the *Paul-Löbe-Haus* and the *Marie-Elisabeth-Lüders Haus*, both of which were designed by Stephan Braunfels. Though these structures fit visually with Schultes' Federal Chancellery, they do not serve to complete the ribbon. The two elements of Schultes' design that had been most highly praised, the public forum and the complete ribbon, now are represented in the overall design as mere fragments. While financial constraints clearly played a role, the failure to complete the *Spreebogen* complex in its entirety casts a shadow over the city's desire to showcase itself as having overcome its past.

Federal Foreign Office

The *Haus am Werderschen Markt* became home to the Federal Foreign Office in 1999.[44] Though considered by many to be "doubly burdened"[45] through its association with both the Nazi and the Communist dictatorships, the building played witness to several important historical milestones. Constructed between 1934 and 1940 as an extension to the Reichsbank, important meetings regarding Nazi economic policy including the financing of World War II and the exploitation of victims of Nazi race laws were conducted within its walls. Following the end of World War II, the SED Central Committee took over the space and ruled the GDR from this location for 30 years. Following the collapse of the East German regime, the first freely elected *Volkskammer* met there and again within its walls approved the Treaty on the Establishment of German Unity.

Historically, the *Werderscher Markt* was once the center of the larger *Friedrichswerder* area west of the River Spree and home to court and government authorities as well as support facilities and housing. In the late seventeenth century, the construction of the Elector's *Jägerhof*

Figure 11.2 Foreign Ministry

Note: © Carol Anne Costabile-Heming.

occurred. Eventually, this building was used as the Hausvogt's residence. In 1765, King Frederick the Great (1740–1786) established the *Königliche Giro- und Lehnbank* there. The *Werderscher Markt* remained a center of finance, becoming the seat of the *Preussische Bank* in 1846 and then the *Reichsbank* in 1876. The *Reichsbank* quickly outgrew its original space, and by the end of 1932, planning for its expansion began. An open architecture competition took place in 1933; this was the "first large-scale building project under the direct influence of the Nazi regime."[46] The cornerstone was laid in May 1934 to great fanfare and ceremony, characteristic of National Socialist architecture. For the Nazis, this building "served as a towering symbol in the very centre of the city of the reconstruction which had been given such emphasis in National Socialist propaganda."[47] Unlike later architectural structures, the Reichsbank did not embrace the Nazi ideals of monumentality, following instead the conservative modernism of the 1920s.

The building sustained considerable damage during World War II, but it was structurally sound enough for the Berlin *Stadtkontor* to move in as early as June 1945. In 1949, the GDR Finance Ministry occupied the space until the SED Central Committee took over in 1959. From this point until 1989, the building housed the locus of power in the GDR; it was here that domestic and foreign policy decisions were made and regulations impacting everyday life of the GDR citizenry were passed. In 1990, the building was renamed "Haus der Parlamentarier" following the election of the first freely elected *Volkskammer* in March 1990. In 1995, the German federal government decided once and for all to locate the Federal Foreign Office in the building.

Before the Foreign Office could occupy the space, however, considerable renovation needed to occur. The Berlin architect Kollhoff won the European-wide competition for the renovation contract. Kollhoff was committed to respecting the historical substance of the building and to accomplish this he used a three-layer approach. To the greatest extent possible, the construction layers from the 1930s and the postwar period were to be retained, with the addition of a third layer where necessary. While the preservation of both the building's structural integrity and its heritage were essential to the success of the project, so too was the need to disentangle the building from its past history. Kollhoff sought to make the building's history an integral part of his design; at all costs, he wanted to avoid suppressing the history. To accomplish this, Kollhoff followed three main premises:

1. The new extension would reproduce modern features in order to keep it in line with the preservation of the old building;

2. Rooms used by the Foreign Office were kept as they had been during the SED period, including the Central Committee meeting room; and
3. A distinct color palette was devised to underscore the building's new function.

Kollhoff's approach garnered hefty criticism, for many considered him to be a fan of Nazi architecture. The selection of two additional Berlin architects, Müller and Reimann, to design the east-façade extension, served to mitigate these critiques to some extent. The competition guidelines stipulated "that the façade of the old building 'will be hidden from the public eye.'"[48] Thus, the desire to engage with history was coupled equally with the desire that this engagement not be too obvious. Despite overt attempts to incorporate the Nazi architectural past into the fabric of the New Berlin, the *Haus am Werderschen Markt* demonstrates that this could not be accomplished openly. When seen from the front, the extension blocks the view of the original Nazi structure. In this instance, Germany clearly has not yet mastered its anxieties about the image it projects to the world.

In an effort to connect the new extension to the old building, Müller and Reimann built a courtyard, creating an open space for welcoming foreign dignitaries. The extension also includes an open atrium, housing a Visitors' Center and a café. Though the need for security measures makes the entrance less inviting than originally intended, the atrium remains open to the public at large. In addition, the transparency effect that the open atrium affords plays well with the German government's chosen modus operandi, namely, that diplomacy is open, not secretive. Meuser proposes that the Foreign Ministry is an excellent example of reconfiguring a politically and historically charged site for new use.[49] Thus, this structure is a prominent example of how a building's new function can engage past history while also making that history public.

In the case of both the *Spreebogen* and the *Haus am Werderschen Markt*, the architects involved engaged openly and critically with the architectural citations that weighted their sites. Schultes and Frank's design for the *Spreebogen* clearly was intended to dialogue both with the history of the Nazi's North-South axis and the GDR's divisive wall by twisting the axis and traversing the former death strip. Nonetheless, the decision not to complete the entire thread of the federation renders this architectural citation incomplete. While economic factors precluded the completion of development from the *Moabiter Werder* to the *Friedrichstrasse* station, the solitary structures that make up the government quarter are unable to tell the story of unification and the mastery of Berlin's architectural past as Schultes and Frank had intended. Kollhoff was more successful in confronting Berlin's architectural history directly in the *Haus am Werderschen Markt* by making it possible for visitors to discover the remnants both of the former *Reichsbank* and the GDR *Volkskammer* within its walls. Yet even here, care was taken to block the Nazi architecture from immediate view. In both instances, the complexity of the architectural citations merits context and their relevance may not be obvious to the casual tourist. The Foreign Ministry has published a book that illuminates the building history and provides this context for visitors.

In 1910, Karl Scheffler described Berlin as a city that is never destined to arrive somewhere, but rather is damned to a state of "becoming."[50] Though Scheffler's statement was a direct response to the historical circumstances brought about by the first unification of Germany, it remains prescient as a description of Berlin throughout the twentieth and now into the twenty-first century. Since unification in 1990, Berlin has sought not only to conquer the ghosts of its beleaguered past but also to put on a face worthy of its stature. Both the Federal Chancellery and the Foreign Ministry attempt to contextualize historical remnants of the Nazi and GDR eras. As debates throughout the 1990s demonstrated, however, mastering Berlin's architectural past proves to be elusive. Much of the construction and renovation in the city center has been completed, with the *Schlossplatz* and *Alexanderplatz* as two notable exceptions, but Berlin's image remains a work in progress, one that continues to face the challenges of engaging with the city's past history while simultaneously creating usable and sustainable space for a modern, twenty-first-century metropolis.

Notes

* Research for this project was supported by a Richard M. Hunt Fellowship from the American Council on Germany. I am indebted to Dr. Rachel Halverson and Dr. Caryn Connelly for their insightful reading of this manuscript, as well as to the editors and editorial assistant for their suggestions for improvement.

1. Brian Ladd, *The Ghosts of Berlin: Confronting German History in the Urban Landscape* (Chicago: University of Chicago Press, 1997), 1, 4.
2. Peter Fritzsche, "History as Trash: Reading Berlin 2000," *Studies in Twentieth- and Twenty-First Century Literature*, Special Issue: *Writing and Reading Berlin*, ed. Stephen Brockmann 28, no. 1 (2004): 81.
3. Andreas Huyssen, "The Voids of Berlin," *Critical Inquiry* 24 (Autumn 1997): 58.
4. Andreas Huyssen, *Twilight Memories: Marking Time in a Culture of Amnesia* (New York: Routledge, 1995), 3–4.

5. Michael Z. Wise, *Capital Dilemma: Germany's Search for a New Architecture of Democracy* (New York: Princeton Architectural Press, 1998).
6. Jennifer A. Jordan, *Structures of Memory: Understanding Urban Change in Berlin and Beyond* (Stanford: Stanford University Press, 2006), 9.
7. Schultes and Frank are partners and submitted the design for the Spreebogen as a team. Subsequent mention may only refer to Schultes because I base my analysis on conversations conducted with Schultes in summer 2005, as well as on Schultes' writings.
8. Rolf J. Goebel, "Berlin's Architectural Citations: Reconstruction, Simulation, and the Problem of Historical Authenticity," *PMLA* 118, no. 5 (2003): 1268.
9. Aldo Rossi, *The Architecture of the City*, Introduction by Peter Eisenman. Trans. Diane Ghirardo and Joan Ockman, rev. ed. (Cambridge, MA: MIT Press, 1982), 21.
10. Philipp Meuser, "Die Suche nach Form," in *Von der Architektur- zur Stadtdebatte. Die Diskussion um das Planwerk Innenstadt*, ed. Hans Stimmann (Berlin: Verlagshaus Braun, 2001), 141. My translation.
11. Hans Stimmann, "Das Gedächtnis der europäischen Stadt," in *Von der Architektur- zur Stadtdebatte. Die Diskussion um das Planwerk Innenstadt*, ed. Hans Stimmann (Berlin: Verlagshaus Braun, 2001), 11.
12. Stimmann, "Das Gedächtnis der europäischen Stadt," 13. My translation.
13. Ibid., 27. My translation.
14. Conversation with the author. June 2005.
15. Bruno Flierl, "Zwischen DDR-Moderne und Planwerk-Inszenierungen in Berlin-Mitte," in *Von der Architektur- zur Stadtdebatte. Die Diskussion um das Planwerk Innenstadt*, ed. Hans Stimmann (Berlin: Verlagshaus Braun, 2001), 76. My translation.
16. Svetlana Boym, *The Future of Nostalgia* (New York: Basic Books, 2001), 77–78. Emphasis in original. Boym refers to Frances Yates *The Art of Memory* (Chicago: University of Chicago Press, 1966) and Michel de Certeau *The Practice of Everyday Life*, vol. 1, 117.
17. Lutz Koepnick, "Forget Berlin," *The German Quarterly* 74, no. 4 (Fall 2001): 344.
18. Koepnick, "Forget Berlin," 347.
19. Ibid.
20. Rolf Goebel, "Forget Hermeneutics? A Response to Lutz Koepnick," *The German Quarterly* 75, no. 2 (Spring 2002): 198.
21. This was later termed "Band des Bundes."
22. Indeed, the June 20, 1991, vote resulted in a 337 to 320 vote in favor of relocation.
23. Nino Galetti, *Der Bundestag als Bauherr in Berlin. Ideen, Konzepte, Entscheidungen zur politischen Architektur (1991–1998)* (Berlin: Droste Verlag, 2008), 208. My translation.
24. Ladd, *The Ghosts of Berlin*, 225.
25. Ibid.
26. Galetti, *Der Bundestag als Bauherr*, 220. My translation.

27. An earlier proposal for a North-South boulevard was proposed in 1917 by Martin Mächler, a fact mostly overshadowed by the later plan by Speer.
28. Wise, *Capital Dilemma*, 61.
29. I am using Mönniger's translation here. Michael Mönninger, "Yearning for the Lightness of Stone," in *Kanzleramt Berlin. Chancellery Berlin*, ed. Axel Schultes and Charlotte Frank (Stuttgart: Edition Axel Menges, 2002), 42.
30. Wise, *Capital Dilemma*, 62.
31. Mönninger, "Yearning for the Lightness of Stone," 42–43.
32. Quoted in Galetti, *Der Bundestag als Bauherr*, 225. My translation.
33. Axel Schultes, "The Chancellery in Competition," in *Kanzleramt Berlin. Chancellery Berlin*, ed. Axel Schultes and Charlotte Frank (Stuttgart: Edition Axel Menges, 2002), 67.
34. Schultes, "The Chancellery in Competition," 67.
35. Quoted in Galetti, *Der Bundestag als Bauherr*, 225–226.
36. Ibid., 226.
37. Ibid.
38. This site, too, was fraught with historical land mines. It occupied the site of Hitler's Reich Chancellery, which the Soviet army destroyed during its conquest of Berlin. Because the selection jury was unable to make a decision, it forwarded two designs to then Chancellor Helmut Kohl for the final award. See Wise, *Capital Dilemma*, 67–72 for details.
39. I draw on Schultes' own description, whereby a fragment is a free-standing element. See Schultes, "The Intimacy of the Monument," in *Kanzleramt Berlin. Chancellery Berlin*, ed. Axel Schultes and Charlotte Frank (Stuttgart: Edition Axel Menges, 2002), 75.
40. The Swiss embassy is located in the former Alsen district (which is not far from the Federal Chancellery). From what I can tell, the area around the Spreebogen previously was known as the Alsen district. It seems from Schultes' remarks that buildings in this area were raised to create the green space of the Tiergarten.
41. Schultes, "The Intimacy of the Monument," 75.
42. Ibid.
43. Wise. *Capital Dilemma*, 79.
44. Originally, Klaus Kinkel, foreign minister at the time insisted that his ministry be housed in a new structure on the site occupied by the *Palast der Republik*.
45. Wise, *Capital Dilemma*, 92.
46. *Das Haus am Werderschen Markt. Von der Reichsbank zum Auswärtigen Amt*" (Berlin: Jovis, 2002), 17.
47. Ibid., 20. Indeed, the building was to provide employment for 5,000 people and thus could serve as a testament to the National Socialist pledge to combat unemployment.
48. Quoted in Wise, *Capital Dilemma*, 97.
49. Meuser, "Die Suche nach Form," 148.
50. Karl Scheffler, *Berlin. Ein Stadtschicksal*, 2nd ed. (Berlin: Erich Reiss Verlag, 1910), 267.

Bibliography

Boym, Svetlana. *The Future of Nostalgia*. New York: Basic Books, 2001.

Flierl, Bruno. "Zwischen DDR-Moderne und Planwerk-Inszenierungen in Berlin-Mitte." In *Von der Architektur- zur Stadtdebatte. Die Diskussion um das Planwerk Innenstadt*, ed. Hans Stimmann, 75–81. Berlin: Verlagshaus Braun, 2001.

Fritzsche, Peter. "History as Trash: Reading Berlin 2000." *Studies in Twentieth- and Twenty-first Century Literature*. Special Issue: *Writing and Reading Berlin*, ed. Stephen Brockmann 28, no. 1 (2004): 76–95.

Galetti, Nino. *Der Bundestag als Bauherr in Berlin. Ideen, Konzepte, Entscheidungen zur politischen Architektur (1991–1998)*. Berlin: Droste Verlag, 2008.

Goebel, Rolf. "Berlin's Architectural Citations: Reconstruction, Simulation, and the Problem of Historical Authenticity," *PMLA* 118, no. 5 (2003): 1268–1289.

———. "Forget Hermeneutics? A Response to Lutz Koepnick.," *The German Quarterly* 75, no. 2 (Spring 2002): 197–200.

Das Haus am Werderschen Markt. Von der Reichsbank zum Auswärtigen Amt. Berlin: Jovis, 2002.

Huyssen, Andreas. *Twilight Memories: Marking Time in a Culture of Amnesia*. New York: Routledge, 1995.

———. "The Voids of Berlin." *Critical Inquiry* 24 (Autumn 1997): 57–81.

Jordan, Jennifer A. *Structures of Memory: Understanding Urban Change in Berlin and Beyond*. Stanford: Stanford University Press, 2006.

Koepnick, Lutz. "Forget Berlin," *The German Quarterly* 74, no. 4 (Fall 2001): 343–354.

Ladd, Brian. *The Ghosts of Berlin: Confronting German History in the Urban Landscape*. Chicago: University of Chicago Press, 1997.

Meuser, Philipp. "Die Suche nach Form." In *Von der Architektur- zur Stadtdebatte. Die Diskussion um das Planwerk Innenstadt*, ed. Hans Stimmann, 137–149. Berlin: Verlagshaus Braun, 2001.

Mönninger, Michael. "Yearning for the Lightness of Stone." In *Kanzleramt Berlin. Chancellery Berlin*, ed. Axel Schultes and Charlotte Frank, 27–47. Stuttgart: Edition Axel Menges, 2002.

Rossi, Aldo. *The Architecture of the City*. Introduction by Peter Eisenman. Trans. Diane Ghirardo and Joan Ockman, rev. ed. Cambridge, MA: MIT Press, 1982.

Scheffler, Karl. *Berlin. Ein Stadtschicksal*. 2nd ed. Berlin: Erich Reiss Verlag, 1910.

Schultes, Axel. "The Chancellery in Competition." In *Kanzleramt Berlin. Chancellery Berlin*, ed. Axel Schultes and Charlotte Frank, 67–73. Stuttgart: Edition Axel Menges, 2002.

———. "The Intimacy of the Monument." In *Kanzleramt Berlin. Chancellery Berlin*, ed. Axel Schultes and Charlotte Frank, 75–82. Stuttgart: Edition Axel Menges, 2002.

Stimmann, Hans. "Das Gedächtnis der europäischen Stadt.," In *Von der Architektur- zur Stadtdebatte. Die Diskussion um das Planwerk Innenstadt*, ed. Hans Stimmann, 11–27. Berlin: Verlagshaus Braun, 2001.

Wise, Michael Z. *Capital Dilemma: Germany's Search for a New Architecture of Democracy*. New York: Princeton Architectural Press, 1998.

12

Berlin *Mitte* and the Anxious Disavowal of Beijing Modernism: Architectural Polemics within Globalization

Daniel Purdy

Berlin and Beijing, at first glance you could joke that they both have walls in common, each their own historic defensive barrier that ultimately failed to stop the invasion from abroad, but what really has united them is that over the past 20 years both have undergone radical transformations brought on by the end of communism. The two cities can be compared as having two distinct architectural responses to the new urban spaces created by this nonviolent transformation. Ackbar Abbas hints at the spatial possibilities in both cities when he compares the disorientation created by the Chinese building boom with Gilles Deleuze's description of the flat, bombed out spaces of postwar Europe.[1] The broad empty lots that dotted German, French, Dutch, and Italian cities have also appeared in China, though there the open expanses were created without war. If we look at images of Chinese cities under construction, the similarities with Berlin *Mitte* after the Wall become quite striking. Sze tsung Leong's recent photographs of Shanghai reveal the emptiness akin to Potsdamer Platz before reconstruction.[2] We could readily argue that post-Wall Berlin's empty spaces, the unbuilt zone of the *Todesstreifen*, also presented city dwellers with a dizzying array of possibilities, wide-open voids that quickly elicited a multitude of architectural recommendations on how to fill in the emptiness.[3] (See Carol Anne Costabile-Heming's contribution for a discussion of the major commentaries on Berlin's empty spaces.) The new opportunities to build, which the end of communism created, brought a sense of vertigo in both Berlin and Beijing, yet policy makers in both cities responded quite differently to the opportunities that opened up before them. Their construction and zoning regulations point in opposite directions: Berlin imposed a uniform design code, while Beijing allowed a pluralism of styles. China has turned to high-rise construction to house the millions of new residents in its major cities, whereas Berlin resisted all plans for tall buildings in *Mitte*, making one symbolic exception in the reconstruction of Potsdamer Platz.

The Berlin Wall served as a metonym for the global conflicts of the Cold War and, to a lesser but nevertheless important extent, the reconstruction of Berlin (with its attendant controversies) has come to represent larger debates about urban culture in Europe. In the 1990s, both countries were faced with the possibility of introducing global architectural styles into their city centers, yet Hans Stimmann, the *Baudirektor* for the Berlin Senate, expressly rejected what he presented as the earlier forms of architectural internationalism.[4] China had had its own twentieth-century history of importing foreign designs, whether as colonial European styles on the coastal trading cities or Soviet Communist planning and construction. In Berlin, the Senate expressed a clear desire to end the process of what was characterized as the imposition of foreign Modernisms, whereas Chinese planners expressly encouraged the incorporation of imported (Post-) Modernisms.

Just as the Cold War ended in Berlin with the demise of dictatorship, the (West) Berlin Senate drew sharp regulations constraining individualized expression through architecture. The liberties allowed for persons were denied buildings, it seems, unless of course the Prussian building codes were an implicit reintroduction of a new conformity in response to the threatening potential of unchecked capitalism. Curiously, the Berlin Senate insisted on the need to constrain market forces just as the West had triumphed over communism. In the eyes of German planners today, 20 years later, Chinese architecture and city planning has much the same status that American big-city architecture once had. The fascination and fear induced by Manhattan and Chicago have now been transferred to Beijing and Shanghai. If Berlin planners presented their critical reconstruction of traditional Prussian architecture as a local defense against globalization, Beijing is described as the place where individual expression, long repressed, has now been unleashed. Whereas Berlin is seen as having held off the passing styles of contemporary architecture, the Beijing building boom is treated in the German press as an excess, nay almost an overabundance of architectural fashion. Robert

Kaltenbrunner warned, for example, against Beijing's "new libertinism in city planning and architecture."[5]

One building type stands at the center of these German anxieties: the skyscraper. Reluctance to construct very tall buildings in Berlin has been long standing. In the 1960s, while advocating for higher buildings in Germany, Walter Gropius felt obliged to defend skyscrapers against the negative example of American cities. "That the skyscraper districts of New York and Chicago are a planless chaos is no argument *per se* against the expediency of multi-storied office buildings."[6] Already in 1912, the *New York Times* reported that German engineers were concerned that in the event of a fire on the upper floors "elevator shafts would easily become chimneys and emergency staircases [would be] insufficient."[7] The post-Wall zoning restrictions reflect a larger discourse about "the European city" that juxtaposes a humanist tradition originating in the Renaissance that values the vantage point of the ordinary person walking the street, with the large-scale industrial modernization of American, and now, increasingly, Chinese centers.[8]

Although the number of German architectural firms in China is relatively small, about 20, the German media generates regular articles on the trend, as if the topic were an extension or an echo on the tremendous public debate over rebuilding Berlin in the 1990s. When Südwestrundfunk sent a young reporter to Beijing in January 2008 in order to understand "China's Construction Madness" ("China's Bauwut"), he characterized the city as a vast construction zone wherein no single style dominates. The Chinese are depicted as having given themselves over to the whims of fashion: "Construction fences are stretched around entire neighborhoods. Next to them the sheds of the migrant workers. Behind them new buildings: apartment blocks, office towers, shopping centers, thirty, sixty stories high. Some come to a point at the top, others are flat, some are strictly modern, others bear monstrous pagoda roofs. The city seems not to want to be tied down architectonically, it tries building styles out like someone shopping for clothes in a department store."[9] The description alludes to Berlin in the 1990s, which was also one giant construction site, but with the key difference that the architectural designs were strictly regulated. A common feature of German portrayals of Beijing is the complaint that zoning ordinances are lacking, the very feature for which Berlin's city planning was notorious. A German lawyer writing about the troubles German architects face in China complains, "German architects and city planners bemoan the lack of transparency in the pertinent Chinese legal code. As far as they can tell from the regulations, they often appear to be unclear, self-contradictory and full of gaps."[10] In general, the German representations of Beijing development tend to focus on the most visible aspects, such as the transformation of farmland into development zones or the demolition of traditional neighborhoods, without considering the larger institutional decision-making process.[11]The rationale behind zoning decisions are presented as arbitrary and hidden, known only to insiders, an accusation that frustrated architects might have leveled at the Berlin Senate as well, but which in all likelihood reflects German journalists' unfamiliarity with Chinese government's decision-making practices.

If New York was once the negative metropolis that fascinated Germans so long as it did not arise in their own country, now Beijing has assumed that standardized position of modernization's *Schreckbild* (horror image), the city that embodies everything German planners seek to avoid. If German planners consciously invoke Renaissance humanist analogies between architecture and the human body to explain their understanding of the city as a living organism, then the following description of Beijing's modernization, taken from *Die Zeit* January 2009, gives a drastically updated version of the Classical building-body analogy: "Nowhere are there as many spectacular buildings rising as in Beijing. The city is transforming itself at high speed—and destroying its history. If the city were a body, then Beijing is now lying in intensive care. The old body is slipping away, the tissue is decaying, even the breath is diminishing, everywhere there is only smog. Still the pulse is high, the heart hammers away relentlessly. Master surgeons are working everywhere, transplanting new organs, new limbs, giving Beijing a new face. Never has there been such a city operation. No other megalopolis has transformed itself as quickly, as radically as this one."[12] Just how much China's modernization reminded Germans of their own brutal history with modernization was made evident by the article's headline, "Betonrausch und Stahlgewitter" ("Cement Hallucinations and Storms of Steel") a direct allusion to Ernst Jünger's protofascist celebration of machine-gun warfare. China is the depository of all that Germans, or at least a few powerful conservative Berlin planners, do not want to build, whether it is the many instant cities built in the interior over the past decade to house the 400 million uprooted peasants or the spectacular experiments of global star architecture.

In all fairness, any comparison between the two cities must acknowledge also that Beijing differs dramatically from Berlin—first and foremost because the city is faced with an immense housing shortage given even greater magnitude in the past decades through the migration of rural peasants to the city. Housing was never a serious priority in rebuilding the center of Berlin, whereas Beijing has been faced with the pressing need to modernize and rehabilitate its living space. Many poor families live in overcrowded traditional courtyard buildings, where the inner open space has been filled in with self-built extensions. Basic urban services, such as water, sanitation, and solid waste collection and disposal, were inadequate.

Another crucial distinction between Berlin and Beijing is the question of whom to hold responsible for the demolition that has created the empty spaces. In the case of Berlin, the wide-open strip running through *Mitte* was ascribed to a discredited regime no longer in power, thus the issue of how and what to build there did not include accusations against the builders over the emptying out of the space in the first place. In the inner ring of Beijing, however, any construction also brings with it the question of how to treat the often ancient buildings that are being demolished in the process of raising new structures. The process of demolition and construction is directly intertwined, so that the one follows upon the other, leaving little time to contemplate and debate the process. The same agencies that raise new housing are held accountable for demolishing the preexisting building. Likewise, the political responses in the two countries have differed significantly. Whereas the debates over Berlin's reconstruction were bitterly polemical and thoroughly public, in Beijing, the speed of modernization has been but one of many (political) constraints on any debate about architecture and city planning. Rather than staging heated exchanges in the press, Chinese critics have turned, in a more restrained manner, to photography and film to represent the transformation of their city.

The media representation of Beijing today says much more about the ambivalences Germans seek to avoid in their own cities than those they desire from China. In the years leading up to the Beijing Olympics, the German architectural press hotly debated the political and moral status of new construction in China. This German debate over whether to build in China centered on at least two questions: whether architects should build for totalitarian regimes, and to what extent were Western, specifically German, architects participating in the destruction of traditional buildings and city centers in China. Both questions are reiterations of the debates played out in the 1990s over how to rebuild Berlin *Mitte* after reunification. Current debates over architecture in China revive the very heated polemics over how to reconfigure *Mitte* with the full realization that the Chinese government is pursuing a policy exactly opposite to that imposed on Berlin. Whereas the Berlin Senate did not allow star architects to build their signature designs in Berlin but instead imposed strict codes to preserve the supposed tradition of Berlin construction, Chinese urban policy is accused of demolishing ancient neighborhoods in the pursuit of grandiose projects that rival the most sweeping proposals of mid-twentieth-century Modernism. The current criticism of architects who build in China amounts to a global exportation of the earlier, specifically local, Berlin debate. Questions of how to preserve a city center's historic identity, coupled with the obligation to memorialize state oppression are now transferred from Berlin to Beijing. One might ask to what extent the current reiterations of the 1990s debate reflect concerns specific to German history and to what extent they constitute a critique of Modernist design principles as they spread globally.

A historical consciousness has long shaped German depictions of China. The first German portrayals emphasized the antiquity of Chinese society, whether in Leibniz's admiration for Confucianism as a natural theology that predated Greek thought or Hegel's characterization of China as a culture without history, a society eternally the same.[13] With the adoption of industrial modernization in the twentieth century, the cliché has swung to the opposite position; China is now portrayed as the culture with too much movement, all modernity and no time for preserving the past. The contemporary China of newspaper and Internet accounts is presented as having abandoned its ancient principles in favor of Western modernization, so that in the flutter of stereotypes it appears as both the oldest and the newest empire.[14] These two extremes are readily assumed within the Hegelian model, for as China was long described as outside history, it now suddenly embodies its internal movement. Yet, as we will note later, this tendency to describe Beijing as an ancient city engaged in modernization has itself reoccurred throughout the twentieth century.

Added to this temporal sensibility in any discussion of Beijing, there is also a distinct spatial awareness. Debates about globalization do not happen all "around the globe," they are inevitably situated in a well-defined place, hence we can readily argue that the German debates about China are not grounded outside the country; they are a thoroughly domestic creation. China is not experienced by German readers as a lived everyday space but rather as an imaginary construction. The newspaper articles about China create a filtered, secondhand account of Beijing that is augmented by website images and television documentaries. A recent interview in the *Neue Züricher Zeitung* with a Freiburg-trained Sinologist acknowledged that much of what Western readers know about Beijing has little relation to the experience of the ordinary Chinese. Strikingly this separation between Western discourse and Chinese streets is projected onto the Chinese, so rather than conceding that German and English-language media have contributed to the bifurcation between representations of Beijing intended to reinforce Western identities and more hermeneutic attempts to understand the Chinese differences, the newspaper suggests that the Chinese have deviously constructed a discourse in English to regulate and control foreigners.[15] So if we accept that Western media accounts do not mimetically represent the concerns of Chinese city dwellers, we are left with the suspicion that German cities are themselves the concrete space against which Beijing and other Chinese cities are juxtaposed. So when the German architectural press describes new Chinese cities as either tacky imitations of the traditional European city or, more often—and certainly in the case of Beijing—as abstract monoliths that erase all historical specificity through their monumental scale and indefinite Modernist style, they are addressing German concerns about their own cities. These press reports seek to emphasize the differences between modest, low-scale Berlin and booming Beijing; yet one cannot help suspecting that the German discourse about unhappy globalization of Beijing reflects the terms it seeks to disparage. By circulating representations of buildings that are themselves accused of erasing lived, historical space, the anxious German discussions about Beijing are already part of the very globalization processes they criticize. Worrying about Beijing while sitting in Berlin is itself another indication that architectural debates are no longer grounded just in the specific time and place of an individual historical city. By distinguishing itself from Beijing, Berlin traditionalists are not just invoking a distant threat to their own sense of local style, they are acknowledging the possibility that their Prussian Classicism is itself not merely a humble local tradition, but that it too is a style asserted as a political agenda within a global conjunction, that it too is a response to the postcommunist ideological vacuum.

To draw out the connections between utopian possibilities and the urban perceptions embedded in the German discussion of Chinese architecture, we might start with a comparison of two pictures, the first famous, the second quite recent. The well-known image depicts one of the many unrealized projects for Berlin: Mies van der Rohe's 1921 proposal for a glass skyscraper on Friedrichstrasse. Though Mies did not win the competition, and ultimately the financial chaos of the period prevented any building from being raised, the image's frequent reproduction in museum catalogues, as well as Mies's success building in the United States, meant that the montage of a glass-wedge skyscraper rising above Berlin's older five-story stone structure became an icon of an architectural future that might have been Berlin. The picture has come to represent the radical possibilities of Berlin's architecture avant-garde, its repression under Hitler and eventual reemergence as an international corporate style after World War II. As many critics like to point out, the Modernism of the early twentieth century now seems to find its greatest manifestation in China's high-speed industrialization.

Beijing and Berlin have historically been low-rise cities. Most traditional buildings in Beijing were no more than one story high. As the density within these older buildings has risen, planners and developers have advocated the kind of high-rise housing set apart from each to allow all apartments adequate access to light and air, a mode of urban planning directly descendent from the 1928 Third International Conference on Modern Architecture.[16] Precisely the type of architectural principles post-Wall Berlin sought to avoid—embodied in the high-rise housing of Märkisches Viertel and Marzahn—appear in Chinese cities.[17]

Architectural historians writing about Mies's image focus much of their attention on the glass-walled skyscraper; however, the nineteenth-century buildings that frame the glass tower are just as important in conveying the image's futurist utopian message. The picture presents

Figure 12.1 Luwig Mies van der Rohe (1886–1969)

Note: © ARS, NY. Friedrichstrasse Skyscraper Project, entry in the Friedrichstasse skyscraper competition. 1921. Photograph of lost photo-collage.

Source: The Museum of Modern Art, New York. Mies van der Rohe Archive, Gift of the Architect.

a struggle between nineteenth-century stone low-rise buildings and a technologically driven high-rise. In Berlin this conflict was ultimately resolved in favor of preserving the Wilhelmine buildings in the center of the old city. Large-scale Modernist high-rises were raised after World War II to meet desperate housing shortages, but the political and popular response since the 1960s has been to favor the older, lower building forms. In China, the tension seems to be resolving in the other direction, with the large-scale construction of high-rise housing for the millions of rural workers moving to the cities. Mies uses this contrast between technological high-rises and traditional middle-class housing to showcase his tower, and it is this very same conflict that defines the German discussion of contemporary Chinese construction.

If we compare the montage of the Friedrichstrasse skyscraper with another picture by Sze Tsung Leong we can elaborate on the relationship between Berlin debates about skyscrapers over the past century and China's building boom. Leong's photograph is one of a series of photographs recording the transformation of Chinese cities. His photos are often shot far above street level with a wide angle. Titled "History Images," they record present-day transformations that will become invisible once construction on these sites is completed. Mies noted in the essay accompanying his montage that certain aspects of a building are visible only during construction.[18] Understanding the historical significance of this process, Leong's photos depict urban spaces as they exist between their elimination and subsequent reconfiguration. One important difference between Mies's proposed skyscraper and Leong's photos is of course the media.[19] The Friedrichstrasse skyscrapers became famous in two forms, first as a photomontage wherein the proposed skyscraper is set in the center of a Berlin street photograph, then later as Mies edited the image, as a pencil and charcoal drawing on tracing paper. The image appeared in Bruno Taut's expressionist architecture journal *Frühlicht*, and was included in subsequent exhibitions of Modernist architecture. Leong's photograph has also been exhibited in galleries, yet it is most accessible through the artist's website. Mies's mixture of photography and architectural drawing heightens the sense that the skyscraper represents a nonexistent utopia, the pencil drawing hovers against a realism implied by the photograph of Berlin.[20] The five-story stone buildings, the blurry, dark pedestrians, the cobblestone streets, and the just-legible hotel signs situate the image in a historical moment, whereas the honeycombed skyscraper with a glass-curtain wall posited an ideal associated with several avant-garde movements.[21] The play of light and darkness that Mies found so fascinating in the glass high-rise is itself replicated in Leong's juxtaposition of historic stone buildings set in darkness against the luminous tower.[22] Leong's image also contrasts light and darkness to represent contemporary demolition and construction. As with the Mies montage, historic buildings in the foreground frame a gleaming, white honeycombed skyscraper. The red and gray buildings are slated for demolition; they represent an urban structure that is about to disappear, whereas Berlin today is still dominated by the gray five-story buildings that frame Mies's image. Leong names the district and the city, along with a year in a documentary manner.[23] His photograph is organized much like Mies's photomontage, with the key difference that the white skyscraper is actually standing and the framing buildings are about to be demolished. What Mies proposed has become actual in Xiamen. Leong's photograph shows the continuity between early twentieth-century skyscraper design and contemporary Chinese building. While the Xiamen high-rise does not have a glass-curtain wall, its balconies replicate the ribbing of the Berlin model. The kind of building that could not be raised on Friedrichstrasse in the 1920s exists now in many Chinese cities. Already a ghostly image in the original photomontage, the Friedrichstrasse skyscraper hovers in the architectural unconsciousness of modern city planning, in Leong's photograph, but also in post-Wall Berlin.

In order to see the differences between Berlin and Beijing skyscrapers, we need to consider the one site in the German capital where deliberately iconic high-rises were allowed in order to understand the specific intentions of this one exception. The construction of *Hochhäuser* on Potsdamer Platz has a double function: to provide a triumphal *Tor* (gate) marking the success of capitalism right at the boundary where the wall once stood and, second, to revive memories of Berlin as a cosmopolitan center prior to the rise of Hitler and collapse of World War II. The analogies between Potsdamer Platz and lower Manhattan serve both agendas—the narrow density of the streets, the stylistic allusions to American-style skyscrapers—for they transfer the capitalist internationalism of New York/Chicago onto Berlin, so that Berlin can present itself as a site of immigration and democratic openness and as a representation of Western capitalism. The distinct Berlin element in this symbolic mix is provided by Renzo Piano's glass-wedge skyscraper, which so clearly replicates the cutting edge of Mies van der Rohe's Friedrichstrasse proposal. There is no clearer demonstration of the lasting influence Mies's photomontage had than its reemergence in Potsdamer Platz. Yet, for all its celebration of Modernist architecture, Potsdamer Platz remains a well-defined, sharply delineated symbol. In a sense, it is framed by the strict application of zoning laws to neighboring Leipziger Platz, thus, by being confined to a single, well-defined location, the sharp juxtaposition of Mies's photomontage takes on a museal quality. As Leong's photograph

Figure 12.2 Sze Tsung Leong, *Beizhuanzi II, Siming District, Xiamen,* 2004

suggests, the Modernist agenda Mies proposed in 1928 pervades Chinese cities, while it remains quarantined within Berlin itself.

The skyscrapers in Potsdamer Platz are thus the exception that demonstrates how rigorously the Berlin Senate reigned in high-rise construction. As Carol Anne Costabile-Heming notes in her contribution to this volume, the1990s debate over how to rebuild Berlin *Mitte* centered on the building codes instituted by the Berlin Senate. These guidelines set strict limits on the height, shape, and materials used in the facades of any new buildings with the intention of creating a uniform street-level experience. In most areas, new buildings were required to follow the existing block structure with largely stone façades that rose no more than 22 meters above the sidewalk—in other words, no skyscrapers please. In Hans Stimmann's words, the new buildings should appear "disciplined, Prussian, reserved in their color, stony, more straight than curved."[24]

Among architectural critics and the general public, the Berlin debate circled around an article published in *Der Spiegel* by Vittorio Magnagni Lampugnani, the erstwhile director of the Deutsches Architektur Museum in Frankfurt and later professor at Eidgenössische Technische

Hochschule Zürich.[25] Lampugnani defended the new Berlin regulations by comparing post-Wall with postwar Berlin. The rapid construction of Modernist housing projects in the 1950s and 1960s had created a strong resentment against radical revisions of the traditional urban fabric, and Lampugnani warned that if internationally renowned architects were allowed free rein to raise their signature styles in the historic center of Berlin, the capital would face a similar defacement. Without much reference to the conditions created by aerial bombing, Lampugnani's argument focused on the style and quality of postwar Modernism in both East and West. The sudden availability of new spaces after the demise of the GDR and the dismantling of the Wall seemed to promise a second attempt at reconstructing the German capital, though this time with a wealthy and triumphant German Republic freed from foreign occupational powers. Lampugnani's article had the effect of directing the tumultuous and triumphant feelings brought on by the Soviet Bloc's collapse and German reunification into a critique of Cold War planning and construction. Modernist architecture became the mute and immovable scapegoat for the long-simmering resentment against the division of Berlin, the frustrating inability to hold GDR leaders accountable for their policies, the euphoria of having a second chance to rebuild Berlin, and the unspoken desire to punish someone or something for the Cold War. All these feelings were directed against the Modernist buildings raised hastily, urgently, and under strong Soviet or American pressure following the demolition of Berlin at the end of World War II. Of course, the resentment against the reconstruction of old neighborhoods through high-rise housing projects was hardly a German issue, it appeared in all of the Western, industrial world. England, France, and the United States have each undergone a popular movement against the construction of large-scale office and housing towers within historic city centers. From the eyes of those city activists who fought urban renewal in the West, the current building practices in China recapitulate the GDR's attitude to historic city centers, to build large-scale Modernist apartment buildings at the expense of older housing.

Defenders of High Modernist architecture were scarce in the 1990s. Despite the ferocious arguments coming from all directions, certain key terms were not to be heard. Abandoned were all references to the utopian transformation of society through the functional organization of space. Arguing in defense of critical reconstruction, Fritz Neumeyer, an architectural theorist at the Technical University Berlin, mocked the "fairy tale belief in the magical power of architecture to revolutionize the hearts and souls of people, indeed of the entire society."[26] The second Modernist lineage that Berlin traditionalists attacked was technological experimentation. Arguing for a return to the tectonics derived from Greek and Roman building, Hans Kollhoff revived an Idealist phenomenology of space, wherein the subject has a strictly corporeal relationship to his or her surroundings. "A person requires an environment that he can understand, so that his bodily perceptions can enter into the space." Kollhoff builds on the Classical Vitruvian analogy between body and building, updating it anatomically so it sounds more like Alberti by arguing that just as the body is made up of a skeleton and flesh, so too a house: "a person insists that he not encounter a house as a pile of constructed elements or a bundle of wires and pipes."[27] As critics quickly pointed out, Kollhoff seeks an architecture grounded on bodily perceptions that have not been altered by the speed of modern transportation or the perceptions of cinematic images. In other words, the new architectural turn to the nineteenth century depended upon a sensual experience of subjectivity that preceded industrialization.

Most books about Berlin architecture focus on the question of memory, an omnipresent concern in the German capital, but one which only tangentially explains the vicious polemics in the 1990s on how to rebuild *Mitte*. By and large the objections to avant-garde architecture were not targeted at Libeskind's Jewish Museum and the Holocaust Mahnmal that were eventually designed by Peter Eisenman. If postmodern architecture was ridiculed, it was the deconstruction of some other city, not Berlin's particular adoption of avant-garde experimentation as a means to recollect the Holocaust. It was almost as if the specifically Jewish reference of the two memorials exempted them from, indeed allowed and encouraged them to deconstruct, the very Classicist presumptions Critical Reconstruction was trying to impose on the rest of Berlin. Libeskind and Eisenman operated on a separate plane from those who worried about the façades of Pariser Platz and Friedrichstrasse. Eisenman's memorial to the murdered Jews has the appearance of a cemetery as well as a vast urban grid. This necropolis was designed well after the city codes were enacted; it conforms too perfectly to the insistence on buildings having a stone façade. Each stele can be read as a structure without windows or entrances, drawing the analogy between gravestone and building. The memorial houses the dead, even as it mimics the rigid Prussian rules for Berlin architecture. The standardization of the steles repeats the traditionalists' defense of such repetition. Lampugnani among other traditionalists affirmed the repetition that the code enforced. Eisenman mirrors this regularity back as death. The variations in the height of the steles flow across the grid as slopes in a natural field, as opposed to the jumble of elevations one sees in a dense city such as Manhattan. The memorial takes on the qualities of a landscape, bringing out the garden quality in a cemetery, the rising and falling topography. When the architectural polemics about the rest of *Mitte* did invoke the memory of Fascism, and they did so often, it was without the melancholy reverence reserved for the Holocaust. When one German architect accused another of designing Nazi architecture, genocide was not the central concern; instead, these angry architects were fighting over the role architecture had in transforming society. The conservatives were most eager to prevent large-scale avant-garde experimentation; their critique was aimed much more at Modernist high-rises for their refusal to integrate with the local traditions of "place," but to present themselves instead as links in a global network of interchangeable economic production units.

The accusation of fascism revived the critical question of postwar Modernism regarding architecture's relationship to state power. To what extent did glass and steel structures deny fascist values? To what extent did modernist office buildings and housing projects operate as a capitalist technology of control and regulation? Lampugnani opened his call for a new simplicity by defending himself against the obvious insinuation that this new, restrained, neoclassical design would remind one all too clearly of Nazi buildings, several of which were still standing meters away from the new construction sites.[28] Initially, the invocation of fascism in the architecture debate concerned questions about the discipline's right to aesthetic innovation and autonomy, more than any concern to recall or avoid the political past. When Libeskind responded to Lampugnani that the atmosphere in Berlin circles reminded him of the campaign against *Entartete Kunst*, he was arguing primarily against the restrictive building codes and the ideology that justified them because they did not recognize the architect as an independent artist.[29] However, in the Berlin debates, Libeskind also first began to formulate a moral proposition that he would later reiterate in his opposition to building in China, namely, that the design of a building required a series of ethical judgments. In Berlin the question was a formal one, whether a building's appearance and internal organization revived a totalitarian agenda. In China, where formal experimentation was actively encouraged, Libeskind has called on Western architects not to build in support of the regime at all because to build in China was tantamount to supporting totalitarianism.[30]

In general, however, Western criticisms of Chinese building policy do not directly follow Libeskind's reasoning, and they only occasionally focus on human rights violations or the oppression of Tibet; instead they stress the importance of preserving traditional city centers. In general, human rights appear only indirectly in the architectural discourse about China. Rather than discussing civil liberties and rights in China, the German, indeed Western, press focuses on the preservation of historic buildings. It quickly becomes clear that the debate over preserving historic cities is implicitly analogous with human rights. The argument claiming that German architects ought not to work for a state that does not protect individual freedoms finds its acceptable professional form within the architectural discourse in a discussion about historical preservation. The trope comparing buildings to people operates in the Chinese without any of the Renaissance humanist references to architectural style re-creating the human body. The analogies today are deliberately more abstract, less tied to particular forms of individualization, whether of people or buildings. The old neighborhoods of Beijing, as well as their residents, are taken up in the German press in the familiar terms of the helpless victims of a totalitarian modernization.[31] The failure to preserve architecture is represented in much the same manner as arguments about China's disregard for political rights.

Historical preservationists' arguments in China are more careful to balance the pressing needs for housing with historical survival of older buildings, whereas Western critics give memory priority over the immediate political demands. These arguments extend from Berlin and other Western cities to China. Berlin continues to be reconstructed as a memory city, both in terms of Mahnmal to the Holocaust and Nazi dictatorship as well as to its reinvention of bourgeois culture. In architectural criticism, the preservation of sites that recall past historical traumas and pleasures is often presented as more profound than the radical organization of these forces in the present. The concentration on memory presumes a relatively stable social structure, one that considers it vital that reflection on past conflict be incorporated within the power structure that regulates present-day tensions. German critics are not alone in faulting China for not recognizing the importance of preservation. Mario Gandelsonas, a Princeton architecture professor, uses an overtly spatial metaphor to express the priority memory has over economic necessity: "Underneath the considerations 'Where do we invest?' or 'How do we rule?' lies an even deeper question: 'What will we remember?' In Shanghai memories are selective, rendered incomplete through a particularly persistent kind of cultural amnesia."[32] Chinese responses to this critique are sometimes politely subdued. A recent survey of current Chinese architecture responded to the memory criticism by pointing out that: "[i]n English, there are many books about delicate Chinese gardens, splendid ancient cities, and buildings, the practice of *feng shui* and so forth, but precious little touching the essence of contemporary China and its architecture."[33]

German and English-language portrayals of Beijing's building boom focus particular attention on the preservation of narrow *hutongs*, the alleys that run between the traditional courtyard residences, *siheyuan*. The four structures of the *siheyuan* are oriented along north-south and east-west axes, with the main building positioned on the northern side and the entranceway in the southeastern corner of the courtyard formed by the four buildings. The *hutongs* usually ran east-west between the closely connected *siheyuan* residences. The neighborhoods around Beijing's Forbidden City were laid out in concentric *hutongs*. The further away from the imperial center, the smaller and narrower the *hutong*. From 1957 onward, the communist regime began the policy of replacing these small streets with large boulevards. The financial limits of redesigning Beijing that the Communists faced have been overcome in the past 20 years; the Konrad Adenauer Stiftung estimates that of the approximately 6,000 original *hutongs* in Beijing only 600 remain today.[34] German reports state that up to 165,000 people were forcibly removed from their living quarters to be resettled in modern housing complexes as the capital prepared for the Olympic Games in 2008. The regime in preparing for the Games also spent 12 million Euros to rehabilitate 44 *hutongs* along with almost 1,500 residences. These basic facts are repeated in many German press accounts, from *Die Zeit* to local newspapers. "With a mixture of fascination and horror we observe the gargantuan urbanization process in the Middle Kingdom. With amazement we learn about armies of millions of rural migrant workers, about giant cities in a fog of smog and sand storms, about the erased web of historic residences and at the same time the spectacular and tacky emerging commercial centers."[35]

The debate over preserving or reconstructing Chinese cities has a history of its own, and the current discovery of traditional housing needs to be understood in a longer context. When Communist forces took over Beijing, the imperial capital was a wholly intact medieval city, complete with its four rings of defensive walls. The mid-century efforts of Liang Sicheng, a professor at Tsinghua University in Beijing, to maintain Beijing's urban fabric met with strong opposition by the Communist Party, leading to his eventual disgrace during the Cultural Revolution.[36] Only after his death in 1972 was his image rehabilitated. Liang Sicheng had advocated the preservation of Beijing's traditional housing by recommending that the new government administrative center be developed in suburbs to the west of the historic center. Financial limits and the political preference to establish the new government in the traditional seat of power overruled the earliest recommendations to place new government construction at a distance from the traditional neighborhoods.[37] Already in the 1950s, large housing blocks were raised in place of traditional courtyards. Subsequent waves of construction established clusters of housing alterations to the inner city, particularly after the Cultural Revolution.[38] Most Western press accounts of *hutong* neighborhoods cite older residents as regretting the demise of Beijing's traditional housing, both because of the lost historical experiences that demolition brings and the uneasy feeling that this phase of modernization recapitulates the sweeping changes of the Cultural Revolution, though with wholly different social aims. Today a handful of academically motivated reform projects seek to build three- and four-story structures in a courtyard arrangement that restores the *hutong* alleyways that defined neighborhood movement and commerce. The debate over *hutongs* in Beijing shares some characteristics with the Berlin canonization of Wilhelmine neoclassicism as the distinctive style of Berlin. Even outside the radicalism of the Cultural Revolution, an old accusation hovers over discussions about traditional urban architecture: namely, that preserving traditional *hutongs* represents a preindustrial, elite intellectual interest that ignores Beijing's pressing housing needs.[39] Nevertheless, a few new developments have been designed that re-create the *hutong's* spatial form with modern materials.[40] This attempt to design modern housing according to traditional designs captures the spirit of West Berlin's attempt before 1989 to build new, innovative residences on the scale of the older nineteenth-century block construction.

After the outcry against urban renewal in the 1960s, it is admittedly difficult for American and German audiences to understand why Chinese cities are not moved to preserve *hutongs*. Chinese cinema provides one possible means of understanding Chinese urbanization in something other than either official monumental state ideology that celebrates massive construction projects or in the romantic terms of Western preservationism. If some of the new official buildings in Beijing have an "iconic" quality of being ready-made for photographs, postcards, backdrops for movies, then we might consider cinematic images that deliberately eschew the monumental in order to develop an understanding of the places depicted in Leong's photographs. The Beijing director Ning Ying caught critical attention for her film *I Love Beijing*, which follows a roving taxi driver's fares and affairs through the modernized capital. Yingjin Zhang has written compellingly about Ning Ying's *I Love Beijing* as a representation of class tensions in neoliberal Beijing,[41] but in order to find an (ambivalent) cinematic image of the older *hutongs*, one would have to turn to her equally nuanced 1995 film *On the Beat*. The film opens with a police captain reading the government guidelines on police procedure to his men but then quickly shifts to the street-level perception of urban space in the form of two officers talking as they ride through the streets of their precinct. While *On the Beat* has many ironic references to American cop movies, the street conversation in the early scenes makes clear that the big-city education of the protagonist follows a familiar pattern: older cop mentors rookie. In Beijing, this amounts to the senior officer explaining the layout of the city and the techniques used in the old days to spot criminal activity. Before all the recent changes, a policeman could spot every thief in his territory, now the streets have become too confused, he complains. *On the Beat* makes clear that Beijing's spatial reconfiguration has been accompanied by tremendous social upheavals, yet there is no nostalgia for the complex *hutong* arrangements. The film presents *hutongs* as abandoned sites, filled with refuse and, in one long sequence, a rabid dog. In the distant background, just outside the patrol area, stand the new white apartment buildings everyone knows will soon fill the precinct. The young protagonist lives in just such an apartment tower, and the film makes clear that this is the preferred environment for the younger generation. He cannot wait until everyone is in an apartment. If the arrival of migrants from the countryside has confused the old street codes, eventually, when everyone has moved into an apartment building, order will be more easily maintained. This juridical attitude is hardly as sinister as it would seem in Berlin or some other Western city. Beijing police have nothing more serious than domestic disputes, stray dogs, and drunken peddlers on their hands, thus the shift from *hutongs* to apartments does not represent a dramatic heightening of surveillance so much as a shift from one spatial system to another. The film's real subject matter is the social confusion created by the transition. The characters are oriented toward a point in the future when the move from *hutong* to high-rise has been completed.

If so much of Berlin's relation to architecture entails remembering a conscious, painstaking excavation of the spaces wherein historical events occurred as if the concrete shell could bear witness thereby preserving knowledge of the past, then Beijing is accused of erasing a past about which Westerners can only speculate. Europeans and Americans who bemoan the razing of old wood frame blocks do not have any direct connection to the historical past of these buildings. Indeed, they presume a mournful attitude toward that Chinese past they cannot save, making a universal principle out of what was in its initial Romantic conception two hundred years ago, a highly personal insistence on the particular importance of singular places. What was once a Romantic fascination with reconstructing the past from fragmentary ruins has become a universal standard to be applied to all cultures, even those whose pasts we hardly understand and are certainly not able to reconstruct. The obligation to remember, the value of preservation and of recalling traumatic histories, was acknowledged and shared by all parties in the Berlin debates, it motivated conservative city planners, avant-garde architects, and all who sought to set an architectural standard against fascism, yet this very same principle becomes a cultural presumption as Germans and other Westerners chide China with the paternalist warning that someday they too will regret their wholesale renovation of historic cities. The old "Zeitraum" (time-space) assumptions of world history have given the tension between urbanization and preservation a melancholic turn. The early modern belief that the further you traveled away from Europe the further back you went in the development of civilization reappears now as a weary warning against the dangers of modernization. "Do not build as we once did." Berlin presumes to have learned the lessons that Beijing has not yet begun to consider. Yet we must distinguish between the historical preservation of old cities generally and Berlin's particular memorials to past traumas in order to recognize which form of memory is specific to a given place. If as Berlin traditionalists argue, every city has its own distinct architectural history, Beijing's may well entail a degree of dynastic upheaval and reconstruction unimaginable within Berlin. Furthermore, if we universalize the moral obligation to recall the past, then we distract from Berlin's very local conjunction of history and architecture. For if we hold on to the Romantic notion of place, then Berlin's need to memorialize cannot be transferable to Beijing, nor can Chinese modernization justify amnesia in Germany. Ultimately, one might ask whether the German universalization of memory culture seeks to make a virtue of Berlin's traumatic past, as if to say the Chinese should remember as "Good Germans" rather than build as industrial Modernists.

Notes

1. Ackbar Abbas, "Faking Globalization," *Other Cities, Other Worlds: Urban Imaginaries in a Globalizing Age*, ed. Andreas Huyssen (Durham: Duke University Press, 2008), 244.
2. http://www.szetsungleong.com/h_suzhou.htm. Accessed July 12, 2011.
3. From voids to nonlieux, a number of theorizations arose in the 1990s to characterize the open spaces in modern metropoles, with Berlin as a particularly potent example, Andreas Huyssen, "The Voids of Berlin," *Critical Inquiry* 24, no. 1 (1997): 57–81; and Emer O'Beirne, "Mapping the *non-lieu* in Marc Augé's Writing," *Forum for Modern Language Studies* 42, no. 1 (2006): 38–50.
4. "In den fünfziger Jahren haben sich die Berliner aufgemacht, ihre Identität zu suchen: die einen in Amerika, die anderen in der Sowjetunion, später in Richtung Was-weiß-ich-wohin. Auf jeden Fall mußte es furchtbar international sein. Das war ein falscher Weg. Die Berliner müssen ihre eigenen Themen wieder Ernst nehmen." "Ich bin ein mächtiger Mann, Gespräche mit Senatsbaudirektor Hans Stimmann," *Der Baumeister* 90, no. 7 (1993), 51.
5. Robert Kaltenbrunner, "Werte und Umwertungen: Die Vitalität 'klassischer' Raumkonzepte in Peking, Neu-Delhi und Berlin," *Die alte Stadt* 2 (2003): 146.

6. Walter Gropius, *The New Architecture and the Bauhaus*, trans. P. Morton Shand (Cambridge: MIT Press, 1965), 108.
7. "Finds Skyscraper Unsuited to Berlin," the *New York Times*, December 29, 1912, 27.
8. For a recent, thorough summary of the Berlin debates and their invocation of a "European city," see Virag Molnar, "The Cultural Production of Locality: Reclaiming the 'European City' in Post-Wall Berlin," *International Journal of Urban and Regional Research* 34, no. 2 (June 2010): 281–309. Regarding the outspoken conservative defender of the European city, *Der Spiegel* noted rather ironically: "Perhaps it is a relief when the Italian Vittorio Lampugnani . . . states that he doubts that cities such as Shanghai will remain attractive in the long run; on the other hand, European metropoles with their historical layering offer a quality of life that will in future be in high demand . . . Lampugnani concedes that the next generation of architects that find their way to Asia can build skyscrapers almost right away, whereas graduates who stay in Europe can build a little house for their parents as their first project." *Der Spiegel* June 2, 2008, 162.
9. Südwestrundfunk SWR2 Leben—Manuskriptdienst "Vom Hofhaus zum Hochhaus," Wohnen in China Mittwoch 02.01.2008 10.05 Uhr, SWR 2.
10. Klaus Jakubowski, "Rechtliche Rahmenbedingungen für deutsch-chinesische Kooperationen von Architekten und Stadtplanern in China" *Nachhaltige Stadtentwicklung in Dalian, China* (Dokumente des 6. Deutsch-Chinesischen Symposiums zu Architektur und Stadtentwicklung in Dalian, Juni 2002) online publication 2004, http://www.stadtkultur-international.de/pubdalian/12Dalian_Jakubowski.pdf, 75. Accessed July 12, 2011.
11. For an analysis of the local zoning processes that seeks to go beyond media accusations of land speculation, see F. Frederic Deng and Youqin Huang, "Uneven Land Reform and Urban Sprawl in the Case of Beijing," *Progress in Planning* 61 (2004): 211–236, here 218.
12. Hanno Rauterberg, "Betonrausch und Stahlgewitter," *Die Zeit*, July 19, 2007, no. 30.
13. D. E. Mungello presents a concise history of Chinese cultural relations with Europe in the early modern period, *The Great Encounter of China and the West, 1500–1800*, 3rd ed. (Lanham, MD: Rowman and Littlefield, 2009). For a philosophical view of Leibniz's interest in Confucianism, see Franklin Perkins, *Leibniz and China: A Commerce in Light* (Cambridge: Cambridge University Press, 2004). Critical accounts of German representations of China often commence with an analysis of Hegel's lectures on the philosophy of history. See, for example, Birgit Tautz, *Reading and Seeing Ethnic Differences in the Enlightenment from China to Africa* (New York: Palgrave Macmillan, 2007) 20–30.
14. Georg Wilhelm Friedrich Hegel, *The Philosophy of History*, trans. J. Sibree (New York: Dover, 1956), 116.
15. Interview with Christopher Detweiler, "Gefahr des Platzens der Blase ist sehr gross," *NZZ*, October 29, 2010, http://www.nzz.ch/finanzen/nachrichten/autx_die_gefahr_des_platzens_der_chinesischen_immobilienblase_ist_sehr_gross_1.8176351.html. Accessed July 12, 2011.

16. Gropius, *New Architecture and the Bauhaus*, 103–109.
17. Dieter Hassenpflug, *Der urbane Code Chinas* (Berlin: Birkhäuser, 2009), 10.
18. Mies van der Rohe, "Hochhäuser," *Frühlicht* (1922), reprinted in Bruno Taut, *Frühlicht 1920–1922: Eine Folge für die Verwirklichung des neuen Baugedankens* (Berlin: Ullstein, 1963), 212.
19. Andres Lepik, "Mies and Photomontage," *Mies in Berlin*, ed. Terrence Riley and Barry Bergdoll (New York: Museum of Modern Art, 2001), 325–326.
20. The combination of photography and sketches was not unusual in architectural proposals. The earliest proposals for an elevated subway in Berlin also included photomontages, Sabine Bohle-Heintzenberg, *Architektur der Berliner Hoch- und Untergrundbahn—Planungen—Entwürfe—Bauten bis 1930* (Berlin: Willmuth Arenhövel, 1980), 19.
21. Detlef Mertins acknowledges that many critics associate the skyscraper with Bruno Taut's expressionist journal *Frühlicht*, but he points out that it was readily adapted to Neue Sachlichkeit as well. See his "Architectures of Becoming: Mies van der Rohe and the Avant-garde." In *Mies in Berlin*, 117–120.
22. Mies van der Rohe, "Hochhäuser," 212. See also Fritz Neumeyer, *Mies van der Rohe: Das kunstlose Wort* (Berlin: Siedler, 1986), 26–36.
23. http://www.szetsungleong.com/h_beizhuanzi.htm. Accessed July 26, 2010.
24. Jochen Becker, "Versteinertes Berlin, 'ARCH+, die Zeitschrift für Architektur und Städtebau,' beschreibt eine fatale Stadtentwicklung," *taz*, 23. July 1994, 15.
25. Vittorio Lampugnani, "Die Neue Einfachheit, Mutmassungen über die Architektur der Jahrtausendwende," reprinted in *Einfach schwierig: Eine deutsche Architekturdebatte, Ausgewählte Beiträge, 1993–1995*, ed. Gert Kähler (Braunschweig: Vieweg, 1995) 20–28.
26. Fritz Neumeyer, "Die Architekturkontroverse in Berlin: Rückfall in den kalten Krieg." In *Einfach Schwierig*, 67.
27. Hans Kollhoff, "Der Mythos der Konstruktion und das Architektonische," in *Über Tektonik in der Baukunst*, ed. Hans Kollhoff (Braunschweig: Vieweg, 1993), 11.
28. Vittorio Lampugnani, "Die Neue Einfachheit, Mutmaßungen über die Architektur des Jahrtausendwende," *Einfach schwierig: Eine deutsche Architekturdebatte*, ed. Gert Kähler (Braunschweig: Vieweg, 1995), 26.
29. Daniel Libeskind, "Die Banaliät der Ordnung," *Einfach schwierig*, 40.
30. Gerhard Matzig, "Die Form folgt der Macht," *Süddeutsche Zeitung*, March 3, 2008.
31. A popular American account is Michael Meyer, *The Last Days of Old Beijing: Life in the Vanishing Backstreets of a City Transformed* (New York: Walker, 2008).
32. Mario Gandelsonas, *Shanghai Reflections: Architecture, Urbanism and the Search for an Alternative Modernity* (Princeton: Princeton Architectural Press, 2002), 32.
33. Charlie Q. L. Xue, *Building a Revolution: Chinese Architecture since 1980* (Hong Kong: Hong Kong University Press, 2006), xii.
34. Konrad Adenauer Stiftung, http://www.kas.de/wf/de/71.6372/. Accessed July 12, 2011.

35. Dieter Hassenpflug, "Der Körper des Drachen," *Frankfurter Rundschau*, March 23, 2009, http://www.fr-online.de/kultur/debatte/der-koerper-des-drachen/-/1473340/2874366/-/index.html. Accessed July 12, 2011.
36. Nancy Shatzman Steinhardt, "China: Designing the Future, Venerating the Past," *Journal of the Society of Architectural Historians* 61, no. 4 (December 2002): 541–542.
37. Wu Liangyong, *Rehabilitating the Old City of Beijing* (Vancouver: University of British Columbia Press, 1999), 17–23.
38. Ibid., 49–51.
39. Nancy Shatzman Steinhardt, "The Tang Architectural Icon and the Politics of Chinese Architectural History," *The Art Bulletin* 86, no. 2 (June 2004): 248; Charlie Xue points out that "Liang's summary of 'national form' is the orthodox form of the Han nationality" and that his principles of Chinese national architecture overlook the "fifty-three minorities located in the periphery of the country." Charlie Xue, *Building a Revolution: Chinese Architecture since 1980* (Hong Kong: Hong Kong University Press, 2006), 14.
40. Wang Mingxian, "Notes on Architecture and Postmodernism in China," trans. Zhang Xudong, *boundary 2*, vol. 24, no. 3 (1997): 174
41. Yingjin Zhang, "Remapping Beijing: Polylocality, Globalization, Cinema," *Other Cities, Other Worlds*, 229–232.

Bibliography

Abbas, Ackbar. "Faking Globalization." *Other Cities, Other Worlds.* Edited by Andreas Huysssen. Durham: Duke University Press, 2008. 243–264.

Becker, Jochen. "Versteinertes Berlin." 'ARCH+, die Zeitschrift für Architektur und Städtebau,' beschreibt eine fatale Stadtentwicklung." *taz*, 23. July 1994.

Bohle-Heintzenberg, Sabine. *Architektur der Berliner Hoch- und Untergrundbahn—Planungen—Entwürfe—Bauten bis 1930.* Berlin: Willmuth Arenhövel, 1980.

Deng, F. Frederic, and Youqin Huang. "Uneven Land Reform and Urban Sprawl in the Case of Beijing." *Progress in Planning* 61 (2004): 211–236.

Detweiler, Christopher. "Gefahr des Platzens der Blase ist sehr gross." *NZZ*, October 29, 2010.

Gandelsonas, Mario. *Shanghai Reflections: Architecture, Urbanism and the Search for an Alternative Modernity.* Princeton: Princeton Architectural Press, 2002.

Hassenpflug, Dieter. *Der urbane Code Chinas.* Berlin: Birkhäuser, 2009.

———. "Der Körper des Drachen." *Frankfurter Rundschau*, March 23, 2009 http://www.fr-online.de/kultur/debatte/der-koerper-des-drachen/-/1473340/2874366/-/index.html. Accessed November 17, 2010.

Hegel, Georg Wilhelm Friedrich. *The Philosophy of History*, Trans. J. Sibree. New York: Dover, 1956.

Huyssen, Andreas. "The Voids of Berlin." *Critical Inquiry* 24, no. 1 (1997): 57–81.

———, ed. *Other Cities, Other Worlds: Urban Imaginaries in a Globalizing Age*. Durham: Duke University Press, 2008.

Jakubowski, Klaus. "Rechtliche Rahmenbedingungen für deutsch-chinesische Kooperationen von Architekten und Stadtplanern in China." *Nachhaltige Stadtentwicklung in Dalian, China* (Dokumente des 6. Deutsch-Chinesischen Symposiums zu Architektur und Stadtentwicklung in Dalian, Juni 2002) online publication 2004, http://www.stadtkultur-international.de/pubdalian/12Dalian_Jakubowski.pdf. Accessed November 17, 2010.

Kähler, Gert, ed. *Einfach schwierig: Eine deutsche Architekturdebatte, Ausgewählte Beiträge, 1993–1995*. Braunschweig: Vieweg, 1995.

Kaltenbrunner, Robert. "Werte und Umwertungen: Die Vitalität 'klassischer' Raumkonzepte in Peking, Neu-Delhi und Berlin." *Die alte Stadt* 2 (2003).

Lampugnani, Vittorio. "Die Neue Einfachheit, Mutmassungen über die Architektur der Jahrtausendwende." *Einfach schwierig: Eine deutsche Architekturdebatte, Ausgewählte Beiträge, 1993–1995*. Edited by Gert Kähler. Braunschweig: Vieweg, 1995. 20–27.

Lepik, Andres. "Mies and Photomontage." *Mies in Berlin*. Edited by Terrence Riley and Barry Bergdoll. New York: Museum of Modern Art, 2001.

Liangyong, Wu. *Rehabilitating the Old City of Beijing*. Vancouver: University of British Columbia Press, 1999. 325–326.

Libeskind, Daniel. "Die Banaliät der Ordnung." In *Einfach schwierig: Eine deutsche Architekturdebatte, Ausgewählte Beiträge, 1993–1995*. Edited by Gert Kähler. Braunschweig: Vieweg, 1995. 35–42.

Matzig, Gerhard. "Die Form folgt der Macht." *Süddeutsche Zeitung*, March 3, 2008.

Mertins, Detlef. "Architectures of Becoming: Mies van der Rohe and the Avant-garde." *Mies in Berlin*. Edited by Terrence Riley and Barry Bergdoll. New York: Museum of Modern Art, 2001. 106–133.

Mies van der Rohe, Ludwig. "Hochhäuser." *Frühlicht 1920–1922: Eine Folge für die Verwirklichung des neuen Baugedankens*. Edited by Bruno Taut. Berlin, Ullstein, 1963, 213.

Mingxian, Wang. "Notes on Architecture and Postmodernism in China," trans. Zhang Xudong. *boundary 2*, vol. 24, no. 3 (1997).

Molnar, Virag. "The Cultural Production of Locality: Reclaiming the 'European City' in Post-Wall Berlin." *International Journal of Urban and Regional Research* 34, no. 2 (June 2010): 281–309.

Mungello, D. E. *The Great Encounter of China and the West, 1500–1800*. 3rd ed. Lanham, MD: Rowman and Littlefield, 2009.

Neumeyer, Fritz. "Die Architekturkontroverse in Berlin: Rückfall in den kalten Krieg." In *Einfach schwierig: Eine deutsche Architekturdebatte, Ausgewählte Beiträge, 1993–1995*. Edited by Gert Kähler. Braunschweig: Vieweg, 1995. 60–68.

O'Beirne, Emer. "Mapping the *non-lieu* in Marc Augé's Writing." *Forum for Modern Language Studies* 42, no. 1 (2006): 38–50.

Perkins, Franklin. *Leibniz and China: A Commerce in Light*. Cambridge: Cambridge University Press, 2004.

Rauterberg, Hanno. "Betonrausch und Stahlgewitter." *Die Zeit*, July 19, 2007, no. 30. http://www.zeit.de/2007/30/Peking-Stadtplanung. Accessed December 8, 2010.

Steinhardt, Nancy Shatzman. "China: Designing the Future, Venerating the Past." *Journal of the Society of Architetural Historians* 61, no. 4 (December 2002): 537–548.

Stimmann, Hans. "Ich bin ein mächtiger Mann, Gespräche mit Senatsbaudirektor Hans Stimmann." *Der Baumeister* 90, no. 7 (1993), 48–51.

Südwestrundfunk SWR2 Leben—Manuskriptdienst "Vom Hofhaus zum Hochhaus" Wohnen in China Mittwoch 02.01.2008 10.05 Uhr, SWR 2.

Tautz, Birgit. *Reading and Seeing Ethnic Differences in the Enlightenment from China to Africa*. New York: Palgrave Macmillan, 2007.

Xue, Charlie Q. L. *Building a Revolution: Chinese Architecture since 1980*. Hong Kong: Hong Kong University Press, 2006.

Zhang, Yingjin. "Remapping Beijing: Polylocality, Globalization, Cinema." *Other Cities, Other Worlds*. Edited by Andreas Huyssen. Durham: Duke University Press, 2008. 219–241.

Notes on Contributors

Hunter Bivens is assistant professor of Literature and German Studies at the University of California, Santa Cruz. He received his PhD from the University of Chicago. He has presented and published on postwar German literature, film, and culture, including essays on the work of Anna Seghers and Brigitte Reimann. His current project, "Expropriated: Placing East German Literature," analyzes representations of space and affect in East German and post-GDR cultural productions, elucidating the conflicting legacies of both socialist and capitalist models of industrial modernity.

Jana Evans Braziel is professor of English and Comparative Literature and affiliate faculty in Africana Studies and Women, Gender, and Sexuality Studies at the University of Cincinnati. Braziel's scholarly and pedagogical interests are in American hemispheric literatures and cultures; Caribbean studies; Haitian studies; and the intersections of diaspora, transnational activism, and globalization. Braziel is the author of four monographs: *Duvalier's Ghosts: Race, Diaspora, and U.S. Imperialism in Haitian Literatures* (2010); *Caribbean Genesis: Jamaica Kincaid and the Writing of New Worlds* (2009); *Artists, Performers, and Black Masculinity in the Haitian Diaspora* (2008); and *Diaspora: An Introduction* (2008).

Carol Anne Costabile-Heming is professor of German and chair of World Languages and Literatures at Northern Kentucky University. An internationally recognized scholar, her research focuses on representations of Berlin in postunification literature and film and literary responses to the *Wende*. She has published on diverse authors including Ingeborg Bachmann, Volker Braun, F. C. Delius, Günter Grass, Günter Kunert, Peter Schneider, and Christa Wolf.

Douglas Cowie is the author of short stories, essays, and a novel, *Owen Noone and the Marauder*. He teaches in the Department of English at Royal Holloway, University of London.

Anna Dempsey, associate professor of Art History at the University of Massachusetts Dartmouth, teaches contemporary art, new media, and the history of design. She has published articles on public sculpture and urban architecture in Berlin, museum architecture and exhibitions in Germany, new media and the public sphere, and numerous articles on contemporary film and gender. She is currently working on a book titled *Working Women Artists: Images of Domesticity and the Construction of American Modernism*.

Katharina Gerstenberger is a professor of German and department head at the University of Cincinnati. She is the author of *Truth to Tell: German Women's Autobiographies and Turn-of-the-Century Culture* (2000) and *Writing the New Berlin: The German Capital in Post-Wall Literature* (2008). Her work has appeared in *Monatshefte*, *German Quarterly*, and *Gegenwartsliteratur*, and in several anthologies, including *German Literature in the Age of Globalization* (2004), *Spatial Turns: Space, Place, and Mobility in German Literary and Visual Culture* (2010), and *Generational Shifts in Contemporary German Culture* (2010). She coedited *German Literature in a New Century: Trends, Traditions, Transformations, Transitions* (2008) as well as *Women in German Yearbook* (2007–2010).

Sander L. Gilman is a distinguished professor of the Liberal Arts and Sciences as well as professor of Psychiatry at Emory University. A cultural and literary historian, he is the author or editor of over 80 books. His *Obesity: The Biography* appeared with Oxford University Press in 2010; his most recent edited volume, *Wagner and Cinema* (with Jeongwon Joe) was published in the same year. He is the author of the basic study of the visual stereotyping of the mentally ill, *Seeing the Insane*, published by John Wiley and Sons in 1982 (reprinted: 1996) as well as the standard study of *Jewish Self-Hatred*, the title of his Johns Hopkins University Press monograph of 1986. For 25 years, he was a member of the humanities and medical faculties at Cornell University where he held the Goldwin Smith Professorship of Humane Studies. For six years he held the Henry R. Luce Distinguished Service Professorship of the Liberal Arts in Human Biology at the University of Chicago and for four years was a distinguished professor of the Liberal Arts and Medicine and creator of the Humanities Laboratory at the University of Illinois at Chicago. During 1990–1991 he served as the visiting historical scholar at the National Library of Medicine, Bethesda, MD; 1996–1997 as a fellow of the Center for Advanced Study in the Behavioral Sciences, Stanford, CA; 2000–2001 as a Berlin prize fellow at the American Academy in Berlin; 2004–2005 as the Weidenfeld visiting professor of European Comparative Literature at Oxford University; 2007 to the present as professor at the Institute in the Humanities, Birkbeck College; 2010 to 2013 as a visiting research professor at The University of Hong Kong. He has been a visiting professor at numerous universities in North America, South Africa, The United Kingdom, Germany, Israel, China, and New Zealand. He was president of the Modern Language Association in 1995. He has been awarded a Doctor of Laws (*honoris causa*) at the University of Toronto in 1997, elected an honorary professor of the Free University in Berlin (2000), and an honorary member of the American Psychoanalytic Association (2007).

Shannon Granville is a graduate of the College of William and Mary in Williamsburg, Virginia, and the London School of Economics, where she studied twentieth-century international relations and European political history. She has published on late Cold War history and contemporary British political satire, and is working on additional papers that examine Japanese manga and animated series from historical and cross-cultural perspectives. Her current long-term research project involves controversies surrounding the publication of British political diaries and memoirs in the postwar period.

Paul Kubicek is professor of Political Science and director for the Center for International Programs at Oakland University in Rochester, Michigan. He has also been a Fulbright scholar in Ljubljana, Slovenia. His research is focused on postcommunist politics, Turkish politics, and European Union expansion. He has published his work in journals such as *Comparative Politics*, *Political Studies*, *Democratization*, *Review of International Studies*, and *Communist and Post-Communist Studies*, and he is the author of *European Politics: A Comparative Introduction* (Pearson, 2011).

Christine Leuenberger is senior lecturer in the Department of Science and Technology Studies at Cornell University. Her work has been published in various books, edited collections and in sociological, philosophical, and historical journals, including: *Osiris: Journal of the History of Science Society*; *Social Studies of Science; Social Problems; Theory & Society; Journal of the History of the Behavioral Sciences; Journal of Management Inquiry; Human Studies: A Journal for Philosophy and the Social Sciences*. She is currently working on the social impact of the West Bank Barrier and on the history and sociology of the human sciences in the Middle East.

Jonathan Murphy is a doctoral scholar in modern European history at University College Cork. His current research is focused on Britain's diplomatic relations with the Polish Government-in-Exile, 1939–1945. His research interests include British diplomacy, Anglo-Polish relations, Central and Eastern Europe, and Northern Ireland. His publications include studies of the Oder-Neisse border as an issue during World War II, and its ultimate resolution at the end of the Cold War; the border question in twentieth-century Polish and Irish history; and a comparative study of British policy toward Germany in the 1930s, and its handling of the republican dissident threat in contemporary Northern Ireland.

Daniel Leonhard Purdy is associate professor for German at the Pennsylvania State University. His study of German philosophical engagements with architecture will appeared in 2011 with Cornell University Press, *On the Ruins of Babel: Architectural Metaphors in German Thought*. His earlier books include: *The Tyranny of Elegance: Consumer Cosmopolitanism in the Era of Goethe* and *The Rise of Fashion*.

Benjamin Robinson is associate professor of German at Indiana University. He has published *The Skin of the System: On Germany's Socialist Modernity* (Stanford, 2009), which takes the work of Franz Fühmann as its touchstone to ask what it means to speak of socialism really existing. Recent and forthcoming publications include "One Iota of Difference: What is Socialist Literature Twenty Years after the Wall?" and essays on Alain Badiou, Bertolt Brecht, and the semiotics of existential reference. Robinson's current book project, a history and theory of indexicality, is *Out of All Scale: Indexicality and the Magnitude of the Present.*

Robert Snyder is a professor of Political Science at Southwestern University, where he teaches courses on International Politics. He has published journal articles on the Cold War, revolutions, terrorism, U.S. foreign policy, and the Middle East.

Timothy J. White is professor of Political Science at Xavier University in Cincinnati, Ohio. His previous research has focused on the origins and evolution of the Cold War among other interests. His research has appeared in the *Review of Politics*, *International Studies Perspectives*, the *European Legacy*, *Commonwealth and Comparative Politics*, and the *International Social Science Review*. He regularly teaches courses on International Relations, Comparative Politics, and U.S. Foreign Policy.

Index